WEB OF DECEIT

W.K.L. is a Research Fellow at the Royal Institute of International Affairs (Chatham House) and has written extensively on British and US foreign policies. His books include *The Management of Power*, *British Foreign Policy since 1945* (2nd ed, London, 1993), *The Great Depression*, *Anglo-American Power*, *Media Giants* (Pluto, London, 1991), and *People for the... Making Trade Work for Poor People* (Christian Aid, London, 2001). He has worked in the field of international development for the past ten years. His website address is www.mail.edu.htm

Mark Curtis

WEB OF DECEIT

BRITAIN'S REAL ROLE IN THE WORLD

With a Foreword by John Pilger

VINTAGE

Published by Vintage 2003

4 6 8 10 9 7 5

Copyright © Mark Curtis 2003
Foreword copyright © John Pilger 2003

First published in Great Britain by
Vintage, 2003

Vintage
Random House, 20 Vauxhall Bridge Road, London SW1V 2SA

Random House Australia (Pty) Limited
20 Alfred Street, Milsons Point, Sydney,
New South Wales 2061, Australia

Random House New Zealand Limited
18 Poland Road, Glenfield,
Auckland 10, New Zealand

Random House South Africa (Pty) Limited
Endulini, 5A Jubilee Road, Parktown 2193, South Africa

Random House UK Limited Reg. No. 954009
www.randomhouse.co.uk

A CIP catalogue record for this book
is available from the British Library

ISBN 0099448394

Papers used by Random House UK Ltd are natural, recyclable
products made from wood grown in sustainable forests. The
manufacturing processes conform to the environmental
regulations of the country of origin

Set in Scala by SX Composing DTP, Rayleigh, Essex
Printed and bound in Great Britain by
Bookmarque Ltd, Croydon, Surrey

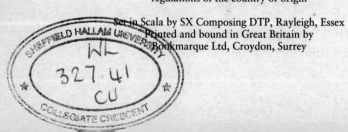

CONTENTS

LIST OF
ABBREVIATIONS

AIOC	Anglo-Iranian Oil Company (later BP)
ANC	African National Congress
BIOT	British Indian Ocean Territory
DFID	Department for International Development
DTI	Department of Trade and Industry
FAC	Foreign Affairs Committee (House of Commons)
GATS	General Agreement on Trade in Services
HRW	Human Rights Watch
IMF	International Monetary Fund
MAI	Multilateral Agreement on Investment
NATO	North Atlantic Treaty Organisation
NGO	Non Governmental Organisation
PKI	Indonesian Communist Party
TNC	Transnational Corporation
TRIPS	Trade-related intellectual property rights
UNCTAD	United Nations Conference on Trade and Development
UNDP	United Nations Development Programme
UNHCR	United Nations High Commissioner for Refugees
WTO	World Trade Organisation

FOREWORD
BY JOHN PILGER

Mark Higson was the Iraq Desk Officer at the British Foreign Office in 1989. In a setting the great satirist Dennis Potter might have conjured, Higson sat behind a little Iraqi flag and directly opposite the Iran Desk man, who sat behind the Ayatollah's flag. When I met him several years later, Higson described to me how ministers and officials systematically lied to parliament about illegal shipments of arms to Iraq. 'The draft letters I wrote for various ministers,' he said, 'were saying that nothing had changed, the embargo on the sale of British arms to Iraq was the same.'

'Was that true?' I asked.

'No, it wasn't true.'

'And your superiors knew it wasn't true?'

'Yes. If I was writing a draft reply to a letter from an MP for Mr Mellor or Mr Waldegrave (then Foreign Office ministers) I wrote the agreed line. But they knew things had changed. I also wrote replies to go to members of the public who were concerned about the gassing of the Kurds at Halabja by Saddam Hussein and wanted to know what the government was doing about it. A lot of MPs and members of the public thought the £340 million trade credits we gave to Iraq [following the Halabja atrocity] was absolutely disgusting.'

I said, 'You and your colleagues at the Foreign Office knew that British weapons were going illegally to Iraq. Is that correct?'

'Oh yes, yes. We were quite well aware that Jordan was being used [as the way into Iraq] . . . you see, Iraq was regarded as the big prize.'

'So how much truth did the public get?'

'The public got as much truth as we could squeeze out, given that we told downright lies.'[1]

At the 1994 public inquiry into the scandal of illegal arms sales to Iraq, Higson's honesty was commended by Lord Justice Scott, the chairman, a rare accolade. Britain's foreign policy establishment, Higson told the tribunal, 'is a culture of lying'.

Tim Laxton, an auditor assisting the Scott Inquiry and one of the few to hear almost all the evidence, believes that had Scott's terms of reference allowed him to conduct a truly open and wide-ranging investigation, 'hundreds' would have faced criminal investigation. 'They would include', he said, 'top political figures, very senior civil servants from the Foreign Office, the Ministry of Defence, the Department of Trade and Industry . . . the top echelon of the British government.'

The glimpse that Scott and Higson gave us of the ruthless and mendacious nature of great power was unprecedented. British imperialism has been second to none in projecting itself as benign, wise and essentially truthful, even a gift to humanity. With every generation, it seems, come new mythologists. That the opposite is true may shock some people. 'A truth's initial commotion', wrote the American sage Dresden James, 'is directly proportional to how deeply the lie was believed. It wasn't the world being round that agitated people, but that the world wasn't flat. When a well-packaged web of lies has been sold to the masses over generations, the truth will seem utterly preposterous and its speaker a raving lunatic.'

Mark Curtis' brilliant, exciting and deeply disturbing book unwraps the whole package, layer by layer, piece by piece. Not since Noam Chomsky's *Deterring Democracy* has there been such a disclosure, whose publication could not be more timely. In the aftermath of September 11th, 2001, the truths told in the following pages will seem far from preposterous to a great many people, now made aware of the rapaciousness and cynicism of power politics by current events. They see clearly the exploitation of September 11th by George W. Bush's gang and by Tony Blair and the unprovoked aggression against Iraq. At the time of writing these words, the claim of Blair and Bush of links between Iraq and Al Qaida, as justification for an attack on Iraq, is openly derided, having been contradicted by their own intelligence agencies. This was superceded by Blair's 'moral argument' for the attack, which is scorned by a significant section of the public, aware of the hundreds of thousands of deaths caused by the Anglo–American driven embargo of Iraq. Moreover, Blair's messianic promise to 're-order the world' is increasingly referred to as imperialism: until recently, a word virtually struck from the dictionary and declared unspeakable by conservatives and liberals alike.

Those who have long sought to reclaim noble words, like democracy and freedom, peace and security, from their corrupt service to imperial propaganda, can take heart from these pages. Here, the truth is told largely from official records, whose private revelations and true intentions Curtis has assembled; I know of no other historian who has mined British foreign policy files as devastatingly. Most of these files have long been in the public domain; and it shames journalism, where history's first draft ought to be written, that most of the facts are published for the first time.

Web of Deceit follows Mark Curtis' other works, *The Ambiguities of Power* and *The Great Deception*. These, too, were landmark books, but through no fault of the author's, were not widely noticed, making his arrival in the mainstream all the more welcome. I am personally grateful to Mark Curtis for the fruits of his research, especially on Indonesia. It was he who first revealed British government complicity in the bloodbath that brought General Suharto to power in 1965–6 (see chapter

20). He coined a term of exquisite, black irony, 'unpeople', which I adopted as a description of the victims of Western state terrorism: for example, the 20,000 unpeople who died during the British-supported American attack on Afghanistan in October 2001, whose deaths are seldom, if ever compared with the deaths of the 3,000 victims of September 11th. The American dead are worthy of our grief; the Afghan dead are not, for they are unpeople, like the Iraqis, whose deaths Madeleine Albright said were 'worth it'.

Near the top of his long list of unpeople, victims of British foreign policy, Curtis places the 1,500 Illois who were, to use the official term, 'removed' from their homeland in the Chagos island group in the Indian Ocean in 1966 by the government of Harold Wilson. This ruthless dispossession, secretly executed so that the largest island, Diego Garcia, could be handed to the American military, was 'the subject of systematic lying by seven British governments over nearly four decades,' writes Curtis. The Ministry of Defence even denied that the island had been populated at all. Today, Diego Garcia is controlled by the American air force as a staging point for its bombers that patrol and bomb the Middle East. Little is known about the fate of its people; BBC news readers routinely refer to Diego Garcia as 'uninhabited'.

In chapter 3, 'Explaining the "war against terrorism"', Curtis writes: 'The idea that Britain is a supporter of terrorism is an oxymoron in the mainstream political culture, as ridiculous as suggesting that Tony Blair should be indicted for war crimes. Yet state-sponsored terrorism is by far the most serious category of terrorism in the world today, responsible for far more deaths in many more countries than the "private" terrorism of groups like Al Qaida. Many of the worst offenders are key British allies. Indeed, by any rational consideration, Britain is one of the leading supporters of terrorism in the world today. But this simple fact is never mentioned in the mainstream political culture.'

Indeed, it makes a mockery of the Blair government's own

'war on terrorism' as any appendage of George W. Bush's gunslinging. For the Anglo–American intelligentsia, if not for the public, it is as if there is a grand illusion, morally and intellectually, about all of this. Richard Falk, Professor of International Relations at Princeton, once described how Western foreign policy was propagated in the media 'through a self-righteous, one-way moral/legal screen [with] positive images of western values and innocence portrayed as threatened, validating a campaign of unrestricted violence.' As Curtis points out, in Britain and the United States, the media's relentless channelling and echoing of a veiled, violent agenda can make the difference between war and peace and, for countless unpeople, life and death. My own view is that had the great broadcasting institutions and newspapers on both sides of the Atlantic not merely channelled and echoed the agendas and lies of government, but instead exposed and challenged them, the Bush/Blair attack on Iraq would have been made untenable.

Curtis illuminates this insidious media power in the final section, 'The Mass Production of Ignorance', in which he describes a virulent censorship by omission that 'promotes one key concept . . . the idea of Britain's *basic benevolence*. Mainstream reporting and analysis usually actively promotes, or at least does not challenge, the idea that Britain promotes high principles – democracy, peace, human rights and development – in its foreign policy.' The truth is simply left out.

Apart from the current aggression against Iraq, the only British military intervention in the past fifty years to be condemned or even questioned in the mainstream was the invasion of Egypt in 1956; and the reason was that the British elite was divided about what it called the 'Suez crisis'. In striking contrast, there was silence in 1965 when the Labour government supplied warships, logistics and intelligence in support of General Suharto's bloody seizure of power in Indonesia. The slaughter of perhaps a million people was simply ignored; the headlines said that communism had been defeated and 'stability' restored. Many years later, the BBC correspondent in Southeast Asia, Roland Challis, told me: 'There were bodies being washed up on the lawns of the British consulate in Surabaya, and British warships escorted a ship full of Indonesian troops down the Malacca Straits so that they could take part in this terrible holocaust . . . There was a deal, you see. In establishing the Suharto regime, the involvement of the IMF and the World Bank was part of it. Sukarno had kicked them out; now Suharto would bring them back. That was the deal.' None of this was reported at the time. 'It was a triumph for western propaganda,' said Challis. 'My British sources purported not to know what was going on, but they knew . . .'.

At the Labour party conference in 2001, Tony Blair declared his 'moral commitment' to the world. 'I tell you,' he said, 'if Rwanda happened again today as it did in 1994, when a million people were slaughtered in cold blood, we would have a moral duty to act.' The following day, this statement was reported without a single journalist reminding the British people that their government had *contributed* to the slaughter in Rwanda. Curtis describes how the British government 'used its diplomatic weight to reduce severely a UN force that, according to military officers on the ground, could have prevented the killings. It then helped ensure the delay of other plans for intervention, which sent a direct green light to the murderers in Rwanda to continue. Britain also refused to provide the capability for other states to intervene, while blaming the lack of such capability on the UN. Throughout, Britain helped ensure that the United Nations did not use the word 'genocide' so the UN would not act, using diplomatic pressure on others to ensure this did not happen.' Not a word about this appeared in the media at the time.

British support for the apartheid gang in South Africa and death squad regimes in Central America, British abandonment of the Chechens in Russia and the Kurds in Turkey and Britain's long history of terrorism in the Middle East, from the use of poison gas to cluster bombs and depleted uranium, have all been consigned to what George Orwell famously called the memory hole. Curtis describes one of the major terrorist acts of the 1980s, the car bombing in Beirut in 1985 outside a mosque which killed eighty men, women and children and left more than two hundred injured. The aim of the bombers was to kill Sheikh Fadlallah, the Shia leader. He escaped. Those responsible – the CIA, Saudi intelligence and Britain's MI6 – have never been exposed in the mainstream media.

The lessons are all too urgent in 2003. At the time of writing, the British Defence Secretary, Geoffrey Hoon, has crossed a threshold by threatening, almost as a boast, to use nuclear weapons against non-nuclear states. This, and the Blair government's extraordinary military interventionism, writes Mark Curtis, 'are sending a clear signal to others: any regime wanting to take on the West – or perhaps even any nation serious about pursuing an independent course of development – should now acquire nuclear weapons. If a country does not have these weapons, it may be threatened with destruction and pulverised, as in Afghanistan, Yugoslavia and Iraq . . . This lesson is surely being drawn by every repressive regime around the world, not to mention terrorist groups and perhaps some more benign governments too.'

For the rest of us, the immediate lesson to be drawn from this superb history is that a previously unidentified enemy of sanity and peace in international affairs is close to home, and that only we can do something about that.

AUTHOR'S
INTRODUCTION

Since achieving power in 1997, New Labour government ministers have ceaselessly made extraordinary claims about the morality of their foreign policies and wanting to be a 'force for good in the world'. Never in British history has there been such a gap between government claims and the reality of policy.

The reality is that Britain under New Labour is a systematic violator of international law and ethical standards in its foreign policy – in effect, an outlaw state. It is a key ally of some of the world's most repressive regimes that is consistently condoning, and sometimes actively aiding, human rights abuses. During a so-called 'war against terrorism', Britain is in fact one of the world's leading apologists for, and supporters of, state terrorism by allies responsible for far more serious crimes than Al Qaida or other official threats. And, in the era of globalisation, Britain under Labour is championing a fundamentalist economic ideology that is promoting the increasing takeover of the global economy by big business.

A web of deceit is obscuring this picture. People in Britain are largely unaware of what has been done in their name, even as government policies undermine our own interests. The public's understanding of Britain's real role in the world is being obscured by an ideological system – principally, the mainstream media – that is largely accepting at face value New Labour's rhetoric on its moral purpose.

Current British foreign policies are generally not only immoral, but also dangerous, for the British public as well as others. These policies are helping to make the world more insecure, unequal and abusive of human rights. In the post-September 11th world, the threat of terrorism by organisations like Bin Laden's Al Qaida is certainly real, but it is the policies of our own government, and our principal ally, the US, that are in reality the greatest threat to the public. It is in our self-interest, therefore, to press for fundamental changes to Britain's role in the world.

Blair government claims are often extraordinary. Labour's first Foreign Secretary, Robin Cook, spoke of 'putting human rights at the centre of foreign policy' and outlined an 'ethical dimension' to foreign policy one month after taking office. Tony Blair promises to help heal the 'scar on the conscience of the world', referring to poverty and conflict in Africa, and to 'fight for justice' globally. He ceaselessly stresses the concept of global interdependence and has outlined 'a new doctrine of international community', saying that national interest is 'to a significant extent governed by international collaboration'. 'We are all internationalists now', he declared in a speech in Chicago in April 1999.[1]

Former Foreign Office minister Peter Hain has written of 'our mission to conquer world poverty and build international peace and a world based upon justice, equality and human rights'. The International Development Secretary, Clare Short, says that British aims are to 'systematically reduce poverty and promote sustainable development in the poorest countries'. Even the Trade Secretary, Patricia Hewitt, says at every available opportunity that Britain is promoting 'fair trade' globally and is on the side of developing countries in the international trade negotiations that are reshaping the global economy. Officially, Britain is on the side of the angels.[2]

Never before has the public of a democratic country been

subject to such an extraordinary ongoing tirade of propaganda. For the government is, quite generally, promoting actual policies that are directly opposite to this rhetoric.

The reality of Britain's current and past role in the world can be shown by taking an independent look at current policy using a variety of sources beyond the mainstream and by revealing the formerly secret, now declassified government planning files. This book argues that we need to extricate ourselves from the web of reporting and analysis that obscures this reality and from the deceit promoted by the elite – and that behind the diplomatic language and presentation of policy-makers lies a peculiar British viciousness, evident all around the world, past and present. It is not that British elites are evil or that everything they do is immoral and dangerous. There are some exceptions to promoting generally unethical foreign policies – but they are few and pale in comparison with the broader picture.

Britain's real role in the world is a great betrayal of people in this country. I believe they expect the government to uphold the moral values abroad that most people uphold in their daily lives. This is partly why, as I argue in this book, the public is in reality seen by elites as the great threat to pursuing their priorities.

In the chapters that follow, I look at some of the major foreign policies of the Blair government: its illegal wars; its support for a 'war against terrorism' that is acting as a pretext for a new phase of global intervention and US imperial power; its support for repressive elites and state terrorism; its arms exports that help sustain repressive governments; its aim to reshape the global economy; and its extraordinary new role as recognised international expert on state propaganda (mis-labelled 'spin').

I also tell the story of several long-forgotten past British interventions revealed in now declassified documents – in Iran, Malaya, British Guiana and Kenya. These interventions were much more brutal than usually believed and make exceedingly worrying reading – in Kenya alone, 150,000 Africans died as a result of British policy in the 1950s. These interventions reveal a contempt for grand ethical principles that has passed easily from Conservative to Labour and from the colonial era to the present.

I also sketch an outline of the ideological system that prevents the public from seeing the reality of Britain's role in the world. This system makes it easier for elites to pursue policies in their interests and against the public interest. It is not a conspiracy; rather, the system works by journalists and academics *internalising* sets of values, generally accepted wisdom and styles of reporting.

It means that even big stories can rarely if ever see the light of day. One example is how the British government was complicit in the genocide of Rwanda in 1994 that killed a million people. Another is Britain's role in the slaughter of a million people in Indonesia in 1965 – a story as much buried as British complicity in Indonesia's invasion of East Timor in 1975. Meanwhile, the people of Diego Garcia, thrown off their islands and the subject of a decades-long Whitehall conspiracy to banish them from history, continue to seek justice in a brave struggle but remain largely unknown to the British public.

The liberal intelligentsia in Britain is in my view guilty of helping to weave a collective web of deceit. Under New Labour, many commentators have openly taken part in Labour's onslaught on the world, often showering praise on Tony Blair and his ministers for speaking the language of rights, development and global security as they proceed to demolish such noble virtues in their actual policy. To read many mainstream commentators' writings on Britain's role in the world is to enter a surreal, Kafkaesque world where the reality is often the direct opposite of what is contended and where the starting assumptions are frighteningly supportive of state power. My view is that the intelligentsia suffers from the same malady of 'elitism' as policy-makers, generally choosing to side with them, often being willingly taken in. The British liberal intelligentsia generally displays its servitude to the powers that be rather than to ordinary people, whether here or abroad.

The view has long been held that Britain 'has lost an empire and not yet found a role', in the famous words of US Secretary of State, Dean Acheson, several decades ago. Yet Britain's real role is easily discovered if we are concerned enough to look; the problem is that the results of such a search are quite unpleasant. Britain's role remains an essentially imperial one: to act as junior partner to US global power; to help organise the global economy to benefit Western corporations; and to maximise Britain's (that is, British elites') independent political standing in the world and thus remain a 'great power'.

In the final chapter, I end with some thoughts on the major challenges ahead if we are serious about changing for good Britain's role in the world – a truly necessary task, in the light of its past and present record.

PART I

THE OUTLAW STATE

For any government committed to promoting the highest ethical standards in its foreign policy, violating international law would surely be an ultimate sin. Under New Labour, however, violating international law has become as British as afternoon tea.

As the chapters in this section show, even before the war against Iraq started in March 2003, the Blair government had apparently indulged in at least six specific violations of international law: in conducting without UN authorisation the wars in Afghanistan and Yugoslavia; in committing violations of international humanitarian law in the bombing of Yugoslavia; in the illegal bombing of Iraq in December 1998; in maintaining the illegal 'no fly zones' over Iraq, a permanent 'secret' war; and in maintaining sanctions against Iraq, contributing to the deaths of hundreds of thousands of people.

Even this is only half the picture. The other half is that Britain under New Labour has been supporting, or condoning, numerous further violations of international law and human rights by its key allies, such as Turkey in its Kurdish regions, Russia in Chechnya, and Israel in the occupied territories.

The reality is that the Blair government is seriously out of control – an outlaw state, undertaking its foreign policy in open contempt for international ethical standards, including riding roughshod over the United Nations. As one of the dominating facts of New Labour's foreign policy, this is hard to miss, but it has been obscured by a web of government propaganda and media and parliament's failure to disclose the reality of state policy.

I

IRAQ:
IGNORING PEOPLE,
MAINTAINING ORDER

> It [the crisis over Iraq] does have to be resolved, yes to
> deal with Iraq, but also to ensure that the authority of
> the international order is maintained.
>
> Foreign Secretary Jack Straw

Imagine a criminal in front of a judge being asked whether he will in future obey the law, replying 'well, it depends on the circumstances' and 'it is desirable but not absolutely essential'. This is the British government's view of international law over Iraq.

By defying the UN in launching the invasion of Iraq – which has begun as I write – British leaders could hardly have displayed more open contempt for international law. Tony Blair has said starkly that 'lawful and legitimate are not necessarily the same thing'. Foreign Secretary Jack Straw has said that 'we do not regard it as absolutely essential' to secure a UN Security Council resolution that would explicitly authorise the use of force against Iraq; simply that this would be 'desirable'. Similarly, Defence Secretary Geoff Hoon, asked whether such a resolution was needed, replied: 'it depends on the circumstances'. He added: 'it is always a matter for individual member states as it is for the United

Kingdom to determine whether or not force will be used'.[1]

In fact, the circumstances under which force can be legally used are very limited under the UN charter, restricted to action taken in self-defence and collective action authorised by the security council. Tony Blair hit on a formula of saying that 'what the UN has got to be is a way of dealing with it [Iraq], not a way of avoiding dealing with it'. The message from London has clearly been: we will work through the UN if it gives us what we want and ignore it if it doesn't. Only massive public pressure made the Blair government think twice about upholding the UN charter and principles. London's position has echoed the US, whose White House Chief of Staff, Andrew Card, said that 'the UN can meet and discuss but we don't need their permission'.[2]

The government abandoned the attempt to secure a UN resolution explicitly authorising the use of force in the face of opposition from France, Russia and most non-permanent members of the Security Council. Even if London and Washington had secured that resolution, however, they have long served notice that upholding international law is not an imperative. Bribes, sweeteners and pressure were being used to bring other states on the security council into line, making a mockery of multilateral cooperation. Blair even introduced a new concept to justify ignoring the UN – the 'unreasonable veto', that could be cast by other permanent members of the security council.

Whitehall's position in 2003 echoes that over the British invasion of Egypt in 1956. Anthony Nutting, Conservative Foreign Office minister at the time, explained that Britain then refused to commit to a UN route to deal with its enemy, nationalist Egyptian president Nasser, since 'neither the security council nor the general assembly could give us what we wanted'.[3]

Open defiance of the UN is a permanent feature of British foreign policy. In the last twenty-five years of the cold war, 1965–1990, Britain cast twice as many vetoes in the security council as the Soviet Union – twenty-seven compared to thirteen, mainly to support the racist regimes in South Africa and Rhodesia. I can find no mention of this fact anywhere in the mainstream political culture, which continues to promote the myth of Britain's enduring support for the UN.

As London and Washington were insisting that Iraq comply with UN resolutions, they were themselves violating the very same. Resolutions 687 and 1284, for example, affirm the 'sovereignty, territorial integrity and political independence' of Iraq. Although the Iraqi regime is despicable, British and US policy is clearly to remove it, which obviously undermines Iraq's 'political independence' agreed at the UN. Well before the invasion was launched, Blair had said that: 'I agree entirely that a broad objective of our policy is to remove Saddam Hussein and to do all that we can to achieve that . . . If we can possibly find the means of removing him, we will.'[4]

Resolution 687 also calls for the establishment of a nuclear-weapon free zone and the 'control of armaments' in the Middle East. This is also being defied by London and Washington as the US de facto supports Israel's possession of nuclear weapons, and both the US and Britain continue to arm their allies in the region. Thus the dominating fact about the Iraq crisis has been both sides' contempt for international legal processes.

It is a myth, in my view, that Britain and the US have mainly wanted Iraq to comply with UN resolutions requiring it to be disarmed of weapons of mass destruction. Rather, their policy was initially based on punishing and 'containing' the regime, notably through a policy of sanctions. Policy then became based on overthrowing the Saddam regime. It is quite clear that Iraq has hampered and blocked weapons inspectors and has only grudgingly complied with some of the UN demands. But Iraq's disinterest in weapons inspections has essentially been matched by Britain and the US. US leaders more or less openly said that inspections were simply a tool for proving Iraq's lack of compliance with the UN so as to justify the military attack Washington was already bent on.

Evidence of disinterest in weapons inspections (ie, the UN route) was legion before the current crisis set in. In an article in *Foreign Affairs*, Rand corporation analyst Daniel Byman argued that 'an impasse over [arms] inspections is actually the best realistic outcome for the United States' and its allies. The 'most dangerous' scenario 'is the possibility that Saddam will cooperate' which could 'spell . . . the end of sanctions'.[5]

The Times reported in February 2002 that: 'Key figures in the White House believe that demands on Saddam to readmit the United Nations weapons inspectors should be set so high that he would fail to meet them unless he provided officials with total freedom.' A US intelligence official said the White House 'will not take yes for an answer'. The *Financial Times* also reported that the US' dilemma would 'grow even sharper if a diplomatic solution is devised which satisfies the UN and its arms inspectors.'[6]

US and British leaders have openly said for years that sanctions would not be lifted while Saddam was in power, whatever the status of Iraq's weapons of mass destruction. Madeleine Albright, Clinton's Secretary of State, said in 1997 that 'we do not agree with the nations who argue that if Iraq complies with its obligations concerning weapons of mass destruction, sanctions should be lifted'. Clinton also said, according to the *New York Times*, that 'sanctions will be there until the end of time, or as long as he lasts'.[7]

The British Foreign Office's view in 1994 was reportedly that sanctions could never be lifted 'whatever the degree of Iraqi compliance with UN resolutions, as long as President Saddam remains in power'. John Major had said in 1991 that Britain would veto any attempts to weaken sanctions 'for so long as Saddam remains in power'. Similarly, Malcolm Rifkind, Major's Foreign Secretary, said in 1997 that 'we won't lift the sanctions while he's in power'.

New Labour leaders were more careful not to state that this was also their policy, partly, presumably, since they were advised that such a policy was illegal – but there is little doubt that this *has* been their longstanding policy, as Blair informs us above.[8]

Rather than being an attempt by the US and Britain to uphold international law and the UN, the current attack on Iraq is better viewed as a next step in the creation of a new US-led imperial order. Initially New Labour leaders appeared to see the war as following other military adventures against Yugoslavia and Afghanistan in helping to rewrite international law to make such interventions even easier in the future. Foreign Office minister Mike O'Brien said in September 2002, for example, that 'if our peers accept that what we are doing is a proper, indeed a moral, response to the situation we face, it will become a building block for the development of international law'.[9] In other words, if we invade other countries enough times under a moral pretext, and our peers (ie, NATO allies) accept it, we will rewrite the law. This is how the new rulers of the world, in John Pilger's phrase, are trying to rewrite the rules of the game to impose their priorities. Unfortunately for Blair and Bush, some key allies this time refused to play along.

Even more frightening are US and British military plans. The past few years have seen a massive increase in 'power projection' capabilities, most recently under the cover of the 'war against terrorism'. Both British and US leaders now openly speak of using military forces as 'coercive instruments' and of using 'pre-emptive' military force worldwide, evidently to maintain US global hegemony as the sole superpower, with the junior partner in tow, described further in chapter 3.

The key overall aim is to maintain 'the authority of the international order', Jack Straw explains in the quote cited at the beginning of this chapter. This echoes the view of his predecessor, Robin Cook, who said in 1998 that a 'dominant theme' of Labour's first year in office was 'the necessity of backing diplomacy with the credible threat of force against those who challenge *international stability*.' The enemy, Straw explained in a speech to British ambassadors, are 'those who seek to undermine global stability', whether states like Iraq or terrorist groups like Al Qaida.[10]

Robert Cooper, a British diplomat despatched by Blair to become special envoy in Afghanistan, has written that 'international order is created by force, preserved by force and backed by the threat of force'. He added that 'questions about whether it is legal or not seem – at this stage in world history, at least – merely pedantic'.[11]

The outlaw state under Blair is acting according to these concerns – that the world will continue to be ruled by force, and that it will be *our* force rather anyone else's. The aim is consistent with that of British foreign policy described in this book – whereby upholding 'international order' means preserving the privileged position of Anglo-American power and ensuring that key countries and regions remain under their overall control. Moral pretexts are deployed as required.

In this light, it is worth asking why exactly Iraq under Saddam is regarded as such a threat to Western leaders. They have, after all, gone to extraordinary lengths to counter the regime – the 1993 and 1996 cruise missile attacks, the 1998 bombing campaign and various escalations of bombings in the 'no fly zones' over the past decade, and now again in 2002/03. The official answers are obviously false. Clearly, it has nothing to do with Iraqi human rights abuses against Kurds – as noted below, Britain supported Saddam during the 1980s' terror campaign against Kurds and stepped up that support after the worst of the atrocities.

Also, as noted above, the issue is only partially to do with disarming Iraq of weapons of mass destruction. If the regime does possess them and if this were the major concern, the obvious course would have been to prioritise the UN weapons inspections process, which has substantially disarmed Iraq and which was proceeding relatively successfully at the time war was launched.

Rather, the Iraqi regime is a threat to the Anglo-American conception of international order, with the previous punitive attacks against Iraq surely intended to demonstrate who's boss; but which failed to instil the proper discipline in the Iraqi regime, which continued to defy the US. The major threat posed by Iraq under Saddam is of an independent regime in a critical region that the US by definition controls.

The 1991 Gulf war following Iraq's invasion of Kuwait served notice that anyone challenging fundamental US interests would be obliterated. As then US Secretary of State James Baker told Iraqi Foreign Minister, Tariq Aziz, just before the onslaught was ordered, 'Iraq will be turned into a backward and weak state'. And so it was, as the US and Britain proceeded to destroy Iraq's civilian infrastructure, such as factories, the electricity network and water treatment facilities, committing mass violations of international law in so doing. The punishment continued with sanctions, holding the nation 'hostage', as described by UN humanitarian coordinators to Iraq, because of the failure of the Iraqi leadership to obey orders from Washington. Pentagon spokesman Kevin Bacon cheerfully said in 2000 that 'Iraq is contained . . . It has a broken economy. It is an isolated state'.[12]

The timing of the most recent US attack against Iraq is instructive. First, following Yugoslavia and Afghanistan, and now acting under a new pretext for global intervention following September 11th, the US clearly sees a greater opportunity for removing major threats to its hegemony. Second is the serious current situation concerning Middle Eastern oil.

The war against Iraq is occurring when the trio of key oil-producing states are all beyond current Western control: Iran is an official enemy while the rule of the Saud family in Saudi Arabia, a key Western ally, is facing unprecedented challenges and may even be on the brink of collapse. The controllers of 'international order' must, in this situation, ensure that the other part of the trio – Iraq, with the world's second largest oil reserves – is brought firmly into the Western orbit.

Oil is, of course, the fundamental Anglo-American interest in the Middle East, and was described by British planners in

1947 as 'a vital prize for any power interested in world influence or domination'. 'We must at all costs maintain control of this oil', British Foreign Secretary Selwyn Lloyd noted in 1956.[13]

US planners outlined in secret files at the beginning of the post-war world a 'mutual recognition' with Britain that the two countries' oil policy sought 'control, at least for the moment, of the great bulk of the free petroleum resources of the world'. The US, planners stated in 1947, should 'seek the removal or modification of existent barriers to the expansion of American foreign oil operations' and 'promote . . . the entry of additional American firms into all phases of foreign oil operations.'[14]

Over half a century later the goal is the same. General Anthony Zinni, commander in chief of the US Central Command in the Middle East, testified in Congress in 1999 that the Gulf region, with its huge oil reserves, was a 'vital interest' of 'long standing' for the US and that the US 'must have free access to the region's resources'.[15] In the current crisis, the protection of the oilfields is 'issue number one', according to a US State Department meeting on the future of Iraq reported in early 2003.[16]

Oil is designated to be controlled by Western allies in the Middle East to ensure that industry profits accrue to Western companies and are invested in Western economies. A traditional threat in the past has been that nationalist regimes would use oil wealth primarily to benefit local populations and to build up independent sources of power to challenge US domination over the region. Traditionally, such regimes have been overthrown or prevented from arising by British and US power. The declassified documents show that British and US policy has always been to support the authority of favoured repressive ruling regimes in the Gulf and has helped them counter internal challenges, as outlined in chapter 11.

The US gained greater influence over the Iraqi oil industry after the 1991 war. A quarter of Iraq's oil revenues under the UN's 'oil for food' programme currently go to Kuwait, hence indirectly to Western corporations, while sanctions serve as a way of keeping Iraqi oil off the market. A major problem with Iraq arose from its nationalisation of oil in 1972; before this, British and US oil companies had long held a three-quarters stake in Iraqi oil production. Overthrowing the regime now offers the prospect of privatising oil operations and of Western oil companies regaining their previous position. The prize is indeed great – some estimates put the value of Iraq's likely foreign oil contract awards at over $1 trillion. The prize may be even greater, however, since US control of the world's second largest oil reserves in Iraq could break Saudi Arabia's hold on the oil-pricing cartel, Opec, and set prices in the future.

The historical rivalry among countries and companies for control of this large pie is ongoing. According to one industry source, 'there is not an oil company in the world that doesn't have its eye on Iraq'. BP's Lord Browne has said that 'we would like to make sure, if Iraq changes its regime, that there should be a level playing field for the selection of oil companies to go in there.' And the Chief Executive of Chevron, Kenneth Derr, has said that 'Iraq possesses huge reserves of oil and gas – reserves I'd love Chevron to have access to', in a speech where he pronounced strong support for the sanctions that have kept Chevron's rivals at bay.[17]

US strategy is clearly to fend off Russian and French domination over Iraqi oil. Contracts with Baghdad signed by oil companies from these two countries are likely to be torn up once a pro-US government is installed, as the pro-US opposition group, the Iraqi National Congress has pledged to do if it achieves power. But Washington was willing to hold out the carrot of future French and Russian oil deals with Iraq to try to secure their backing for war. Former CIA Director James Woolsey said that 'the French and the Russians should be told that if they are of assistance in moving Iraq towards a decent government, we'll do our best to ensure the new government and American companies work closely with them'.[18] Again, both countries refused to play ball.

The new heights of state propaganda

'This is not about oil, it's about peace', Jack Straw told a reporter for the Iranian newspaper, the *Persian Morning Daily*.[19] It is obvious that the conflict is significantly about oil. However, state propaganda during the current Iraq crisis has gone much deeper: since late 2002 in particular the British public has been subject to a campaign of perhaps unprecedented heights in the post-war world.

At one level, it has been seriously funny watching the clique around Tony Blair try to work through various pretexts for attacking Iraq. It appears that the population is regarded as a giant focus group to test each new argument, a hurdle to be overcome by anything that enables elites to achieve their objectives. The Iraq crisis, to me, provides further evidence that the public is regarded as the major threat to policy-makers. The fact that the strategy emanates from a tiny clique around Blair – with major opposition from within the elite – confirms that the British political system's 'elective dictatorship' is alive and well. I return to the theme of Britain's secretive, elitist and undemocratic policy-making in chapter 13.

In 2002, ministers were mainly seizing on the argument about making Iraq comply with the UN; however, the problem here was that too many people saw little or no similar pressure being applied to Israel and other allies. Then, Saddam's human rights record was tried; however, the problem was that this appalling record is comparable to that of many regimes supported by Britain and that London had anyway backed Saddam throughout the period of the worst atrocities in the 1980s. So by early 2003, the two favourite pretexts for a full onslaught against Iraq became the regime's development of weapons of mass destruction (WMD) and the alleging of a 'link' between it and Al Qaida. Only once these two had been tried (and failed) did Blair hit on his bottom line, asserting the 'morality' of a war against Iraq.

The government's dossier on Iraq's development of WMD

published towards the end of 2002 contained all kinds of allegations. But as the *Guardian* reported: 'British government officials have privately admitted that they do not have any "killer evidence" about weapons of mass destruction. If they had, they would have already passed it to the inspectors.' On the day before Blair announced that the dossier would soon be published, a Whitehall source was quoted as saying that the dossier was based on information found up to 1998, when the inspectors withdrew from Iraq, and that there was 'very little new to put into it'.[20]

The public refused to budge, so propaganda needed to reach new heights. Towards the end of 2002, official pronouncements began to allege a link between Saddam Hussein and Al Qaida. As outlined in chapter 3, Al Qaida is the new official threat of our age to at long last replace that of the Russian hordes and act as a pretext for all manner of Western policies, notably military intervention. A truly comic episode then began. First, planners were unable to present any evidence of this link whatsoever. In October 2002, before the government appeared to formally seize on the new pretext, the *Guardian* quoted a well-placed intelligence source who, asked whether Saddam had any links with Al Qaida, said: 'quite the opposite'. The paper noted that 'the clear message from British intelligence' is that far from allying itself with Al Qaida, the Iraqi regime was distancing itself from it. This was the interpretation of the murder in Baghdad of the Palestinian terrorist, Abu Nidal, in August 2002.[21] Indeed, the Iraqi regime has been consistently opposed to Islamic fundamentalist groups (unlike London and Washington, incidentally, who can count many as allies, such as the ruling family of Saudi Arabia, the world's most fundamentalist state).

Planners then hit on a new formula: 'Terrorism and rogue regimes are part of the same picture', Jack Straw started saying around the turn of the year. The reason was that 'the most likely sources of technology and know-how for such terrorist organisations are rogue regimes'. Then, in speech after speech the same message was delivered. The assertion is plainly false since the record shows that the spread of WMD technology is likely to come as much from NATO countries as anywhere else (Germany, for example, probably provided the biggest aid to developing Iraq's WMD). But this mere truth is of course not the issue; simply asserting the link is. The media have largely taken their cue, generally reporting government assertions as serious, even if with some criticism and, most importantly, failing to ridicule them as obvious propaganda.

Since the alleged 'link' was hit upon, all sorts of imminent terrorist threats to Britain have arisen in the media, apparently the result of the 'security services' leaking unattributable stories. Examples are the supposed London underground nerve gas attack, reported threats to cross-channel ferries and the story of a tiny quantity of ricin found in the flat of a group of Algerians, together with numerous high-profile arrests. Much of the media have dutifully covered these stories, with some papers adding racist diatribes against asylum seekers now conveniently lumped into the camp of official terrorist threats. As noted by Mike Berry of the Glasgow University Media Group, Britain's foremost body critically analysing media reporting, these operations usually result in few arrests, but by then they 'have already served their purpose in helping to generate a climate of pervasive fear across the country'.[22] The message the public is meant to get is that removing Saddam will also remove a terrorist threat to us.

The wider context of ongoing state propaganda is critical to understand and little known. Judging from the abyss between its rhetoric and the reality of policy, the Blair government may have broken all postwar British records in state propaganda on its foreign policy, and is recognised as a global leader in this area. When Peter Mandelson, the architect of Blair's election victory, became a minister, he said that 'of course we want to use the media, but the media will be our tools, our servants; we are no longer content to let them be our persecutors.'[23] Everyone knows about 'spin', but this term is itself spin, while the media has only reported some aspects of it: the extent of state propaganda goes much deeper.

The Ministry of Defence has a new name for state propaganda. It used to call it 'psychological operations' but New Labour renamed it 'information support' (a change Orwell would have understood). 'But', the House of Commons Defence Committee has said, 'the concept has changed little from the traditional objective of influencing the perceptions of selected target audiences'. The aim of these operations in Britain is *'to mobilise and sustain support for a particular policy and interpretation of events.'*

In the war against Yugoslavia in 1999, the MoD identified four target audiences, according to the Defence Committee: the British public, Milosevic and his supporters, NATO allies and Kosovo Albanians. Thus the government identified the British public and Milosevic as targets; both enemies, albeit in different ways.

The Defence Committee commented that with the British public *'the prime task was to mobilise and to keep on-side public and political support for the campaign'*. It said that 'the whole campaign was designed with one and half eyes on media perceptions' and concluded approvingly that:

> Ministers could not be accused of neglecting the media aspects of the battle. From the top-down, the UK government committed its considerable media operations resources to the campaign and to the task of mobilising international and British public opinion.

Just before the bombing campaign against Yugoslavia was launched, NATO quadrupled the size of its media operation in Brussels on the advice of Alastair Campbell, Blair's director of 'communications'. The number of ethnic Albanians killed by Milosevic's forces in Kosovo was exaggerated, with the Foreign Office claiming 10,000 at the time, later revising the figure to 2,000. The bombing of Yugoslavia proceeded with an array of propaganda about good versus evil, a moral test for the future and government acting from the deepest humanitarian values (largely taken seriously, and actively promoted, by a willing media, as noted in chapter 6).

'*The campaign directed against home audiences was fairly successful*', the Defence Committee noted approvingly. It outlined Britain's role as NATO's chief propagandist, saying that the 'UK was rightly seen as the most proficient member of a generally underperforming Alliance' in media operations. It also noted that 'if anything, the UK's contribution to the war of perceptions was of more significance than its strictly military contribution'. But '*if anything, the UK's efforts to shape perceptions were less efficient than they could have been*'.[24]

So, an all-party group of MPs supported a government strategy to deceive the public, even saying it didn't go far enough – a nice illustration, perhaps, of the degree to which elected elites serve the public.

The Economist has also encouraged our leaders to mislead the public. Just before bombing Afghanistan in October 2001, it pondered on the 'requirements of the propaganda war', noting that there were critics of military action in Afghanistan even in the US. One danger was that a massive refugee exodus following bombing could be blamed on the US. 'America has to do what it can to defeat this argument', the paper noted.[25]

A new phrase for state propaganda currently popular with the liberal intelligentsia is 'public diplomacy', understood as directed towards foreign rather than domestic audiences. Mark Leonard, director of the Foreign Policy Centre, a think tank established by New Labour, is one exponent of this new, more stylish form of state propaganda. In an article for the US magazine *Foreign Policy*, Leonard explains that 'public diplomacy' is 'more important than ever' due to the 'rise of global Non Governmental Organisations (NGOs) and protest movements.' These, he explains, 'have put ever greater constraints on national governments.' So the '*last decade is rife with examples of popular perceptions, rather than governments, setting the pace for international diplomacy*' – traditionally, the great threat to elites.

He adds that 'propaganda will not persuade populations in reluctant countries to support war, but perceptions of Western motivations as imperial or self-interested can damage the chances of success'. So diplomats 'must transform themselves from reporters and lobbyists who react to issues into shapers of public debates around the world.' 'The challenge' for governments, Leonard states, 'is to move from supplying information to capturing the imagination.' Leonard goes on to advise governments thus:

> If a message will engender distrust simply because it is coming from a foreign government, then the government should hide that fact as much as possible. Increasingly, if a state is to make its voice heard and to influence events outside its direct control, it must work through organisations and networks that are separate from, independent of, and even suspicious of governments themselves. Three of the most effective mediums for this type of public diplomacy are NGOs, diasporas and political parties.[26]

In the 1991 Gulf war against Iraq, Britain and the US established a tightly controlled 'news management' system. No journalists were allowed to Saudi Arabia without official permission and, once there, were under the control of a Joint Information Bureau, run by British, US and Saudi officials. Their movement was organised, their film vetted and their copy read.

Various disinformation was provided by the government. The strength of the Iraqi army was played up, as was the degree of damage caused by an oil slick off the Kuwaiti coast – an ecological threat blamed on Iraq but which was partly caused by Western bombing of oil storage tankers. An apparent plant story was that Saddam had sent his family to Mauritania; at other times Saddam and his associates were said to be 'hiding in hotels'. The BBC reported disinformation about Iraqi soldiers surrendering and helicopter pilots defecting to Saudi Arabia. British military sources put out disinformation saying that Iraq had moved chemical weapons to the front line – part of the alleged Iraqi chemical threat well covered in the media, and that never materialised. The story of Iraqis taking babies from incubators became the most influential fabrication from the US/Kuwaiti side, and directly changed Congressional opinion in the US.

The media's tendency to report government propaganda as fact helped ensure that such disinformation was publicised then, just as the new stories are now.[27]

The *Guardian* described the 1998 bombing of Iraq by the US and Britain as involving 'a government propaganda campaign unprecedented since the end of the cold war'. There were reports of an Iraqi plot to 'flood Britain' with anthrax while briefings and leaks from Whitehall about the Iraqi regime increased as the government sensed the lack of popular support for the bombing. The government set up an 'Iraq Media Group' to coordinate propaganda across Whitehall in order 'to blacken Baghdad and prepare public opinion' for the attacks. Themes included how Saddam's regime, and not sanctions, were responsible for killing Iraqi children and how close the regime was to making biological weapons.[28]

As for the current phase with Iraq and the 'war against terrorism', no one can now say they have not been warned. A recent MoD paper freely available on its website called 'The future strategic context for defence' notes that *we need to be aware of the ways in which public attitudes might shape and constrain military activity*. It continues:

> Increasing emotional attachment to the outside world, fuelled by immediate and graphic media coverage, and a public desire to see the UK act as a force for good, is likely to lead to public support, and possibly public demand, for operations prompted by humanitarian motives.

Therefore, 'public support will be vital to the conduct of military interventions.' In future, *more effort will be required to ensure that such public debate is properly informed*.[29]

Clearly, the government has no intention of *objectively*

informing the public. So the meaning of this appears to be: first, government propaganda is key to attaining objectives and we should expect a lot more of it; second, this propaganda will tell us that the government is acting from humanitarian (rather than baser) motives. It is interesting to see a government openly committing itself to a strategy of propaganda; there are no longer any excuses for journalists simply to report government statements or opinions at face value, without ridicule.

Don't mention the war

The full-scale onslaught against Iraq began in March 2003 but the war began much earlier, although this was barely noticed in the mainstream political culture.

Britain really started the new phase of the war against Iraq in August or September 2002, when British and US attacks in the 'no fly zones' (NFZs) in northern and southern Iraq were significantly stepped up. We cannot be precise about the date since this secret war was not announced by the government and was barely reported by the media. Indeed, the continual British and US bombing of Iraq in the NFZs for well over a decade received the barest of attention in the mainstream.

In August 2002, US and British aircraft undertook nine missile and bomb attacks against Iraqi air-defence targets in the NFZs, the highest strike rate since May 2000. This was followed on September 5th with a British and US attack on an Iraqi military air-defence centre west of Baghdad involving 100 jets, reported cursorily in the *Guardian* and barely elsewhere. Further regular bombings were (sparsely) reported in October and November, in what was obviously a prelude to full-scale war and invasion. By December, the *Guardian* reported that RAF fighters based in Saudi Arabia were practising bombing runs on Iraqi targets in the NFZs.[30]

From 1991 to December 1998, the RAF flew 15,500 sorties in the northern and southern NFZs. By November 1999, US and

British forces had flown 28,000 sorties, dropping over 1,800 bombs and missiles on 450 targets.[31]

The bombing was secretly stepped up in 1998: 150 bombs were dropped on southern Iraq between December 1998 and June 2000. British aircraft dropped 0.025 tonnes of bombs on average per month between April 1991 and December 1998 and five tonnes on average between December 1998 and February 2001.[32]

This previous new phase in the war was not announced or explained to parliament; nor were the changes in the 'rules of engagement' for British and US pilots. The official argument was that they only acted defensively when fired upon by Iraqi forces on the ground, but the reality was of a gradual creep towards offensive operations.

Soon after the December 1998 bombing, President Clinton quietly sanctioned changes in the rules of engagement. This allowed US pilots to strike at any part of the Iraqi air defence system, not just those that directly targeted their aircraft. This role was escalated further when anti-aircraft batteries were attacked for locking on their radar screens to allied aircraft, even without firing. In February 1999, a US Defence Department spokesman said that the targets included missile sites, anti-aircraft sites, command and control sites, relay stations and some intelligence gathering sites. The Bush administration escalated things still further, targeting radar and command and control installations well beyond the NFZs.[33]

In early 1999, the British government conceded for the first time that the changes affected its pilots as well. It was reported that the 'self-defence' policy had been expanded into 'an active campaign aimed at fatally weakening' the Iraqi regime. Also reported was a government go-ahead to the commander in the southern zone to hit Iraqi aircraft moving north, *away from the no fly zone*.[34]

The *Guardian* also reported briefly in February 1999 on five weeks of heightened skirmishes, which had done more damage to Iraq than the four-day bombing campaign in December the previous year. US and British fighters had reportedly destroyed or damaged about forty targets since 28 December.[35]

A similar secret escalation in the war seems to have been ordered in August 2001, when fifty US and British aircraft struck missile sites, a radar installation and a military communications centre in the southern NFZ. One press report noted a recent National Security Council meeting at which President Bush called for more 'robust reinforcement' of the NFZs. It seems that the US and Britain changed the rules of engagement at will, and stepped up attacks when they so desired by always citing self-defence.[36]

The NFZs were plain violations of international law, having received no UN authorisation. London justified its patrolling of the zones – which was only rarely required, given the lack of scrutiny of the policy – by referring to UN Security Council resolution 688. This resolution, from 1991, 'demanded an end of Saddam Hussein's repression of the Kurds in the north and the Shia in the south for clear humanitarian reasons'. The purpose of the zones, the government argued, was to monitor Iraqi compliance with resolution 688. 'Such action is entirely justified within international law in response to a situation of overwhelming necessity', Geoff Hoon said in April 2000. This was the same justification the government used for the bombing of Yugoslavia, which was also illegal.[37]

According to its own argument, Britain had as much justification for its military action in the NFZs as, for example, Iran (or Iraq, for that matter) would have if it declared, say, Palestine, a 'humanitarian catastrophe' and decided to patrol the skies over the West Bank, deterring Israeli aircraft from repeatedly striking Palestinian homes.

The existence of the NFZs undoubtedly deterred the Iraqi regime from further repression of the Kurds. However, the argument that the NFZs were there for humanitarian purposes, to protect Kurds, was more or less openly refuted by British officials, at a time when increased airstrikes were acting as a prelude to full-scale onslaught. The *Guardian* noted, for example, that 'British defence sources have now given up the pretence that the southern no-fly zone is a humanitarian exercise designed to protect Iraqi Shias and Marsh Arabs.'[38]

It is unclear how many civilians were killed in the undeclared war in the NFZs. UN officials documented 144 killed by bombing in 1999. On 25 January 1999, for example, a guided missile killed more than ten people when it struck a civilian neighbourhood in Basra, according to the UN's Office of the Humanitarian Coordinator for Iraq. Baghdad claimed that 323 civilians were killed and 960 injured between December 1998 and the beginning of 2001.[39]

There was no effective parliamentary scrutiny of this secret, permanent war, as with so many other policies considered in this book. A Defence Committee inquiry into the NFZs failed to mention civilian casualties and kept to the myth that 'coalition' aircraft (ie, British and US) acted only in self-defence. It also stated that its view on the legality of the NFZs was the same as on Kosovo: 'of dubious legality in the current state of international law' but 'justified on moral grounds'. It supported the aim of 'establishing in the United Nations new principles governing humanitarian intervention'.[40]

Thus the all-party committee concluded that military action can be viewed as moral even when it is illegal, and that we should set about rewriting the law so that it supports our policy – a nice illustration of the thinking of the British political class, consistent with New Labour's attempts to rewrite international law to suit its interests in Iraq.

The irrelevance of human rights

British planners have always claimed that they are acting to support the human rights of Iraqis. They have had various recent chances to show such a commitment; how have they fared? Let us turn first to the issue of sanctions.

Sir Timothy Garden, a former Air Marshal and director of the Royal Institute of International Affairs, has written that 'the international community has had a remarkably successful policy of containing the Iraq problem', referring especially to sanctions.[41] These were imposed in August 1990 when Iraq invaded Kuwait and have been consistently renewed every six months since. The US and Britain have ensured that sanctions remain in place, defying much of the rest of the world, as report after report shows their devastating impact.

Sanctions have helped to kill more children *per month* in Iraq than were killed on September 11th. The UN estimates that 500,000 Iraqi children under five have died since 1990, as a result both of the sanctions and the effects of the Gulf War in 1990–1. Former UN humanitarian coordinator for Iraq, Denis Halliday, has said that the death toll is 'probably closer now to 600,000 and that's over the period of 1990–98. If you include adults, it's well over 1 million people.' An August 1999 Unicef report found that under-five mortality had more than doubled since the imposition of sanctions. It said in 1997 that 'malnutrition was not a public health problem prior to the embargo. Its extent became apparent by 1991 and the prevalence has increased greatly since then . . . By 1997 it was estimated about one million children under five were chronically malnourished.' Such is the reality of the 'remarkably successful policy' to which Sir Timothy Garden was referring above.[42]

Certainly not all the human suffering in Iraq is the result of sanctions; Saddam Hussein's brutally repressive regime is also responsible. But as the UN Security Council's Panel on Humanitarian Issues put it: 'Even if not all the suffering in Iraq can be imputed to external factors, especially sanctions, the Iraqi people would not be undergoing such deprivations in the absence of the prolonged measures imposed by the Security Council and the effects of war.'[43]

A July 2000 report by the UN Secretary General noted the 'suffering of Iraqi children' and the 'immediate and long term costs [of sanctions] to children, including the collapse of health and education infrastructures . . . and increased infant morbidity and mortality'. And an article in the US establishment journal, *Foreign Affairs*, estimated that Iraqi deaths from sanctions exceed the number 'slain by all so-called weapons of mass destruction throughout history'.[44]

The British government that now professes its commitment to the human rights of Iraqis has, for the previous decade, consistently rejected the overwhelming evidence about the impact of sanctions. Foreign Office minister Brian Wilson said bluntly in February 2001 that 'there is no evidence that sanctions are hurting the Iraqi people'. Tony Blair had previously informed the House of Commons that 'we reject claims that the Iraqi people are suffering because of sanctions'.[45]

To me, these are simply cold-blooded apologias for the slaughter of children. The reality is that Britain has helped to kill people by the tens of thousands in Iraq; indeed, it is likely that Britain has contributed to the deaths of more Iraqis than Saddam. London's attitude is no different to Washington's: when asked about the deaths of half a million children from sanctions as a result of the US policy of containment, US Secretary of State under Clinton, Madeleine Albright, replied that it was a 'hard choice' but that: 'We think the price is worth it'.[46]

Former UN Humanitarian Coordinator in Iraq Denis Halliday resigned in protest over sanctions and has since said that 'this policy constitutes genocide and Washington and London are responsible . . . It . . . is a deliberate policy to destroy the people of Iraq . . . We are in the process of destroying an entire society. It is illegal and immoral.'[47]

Halliday's successor in the role of Humanitarian Coordinator to Iraq was Hans von Sponeck, who also resigned in protest against sanctions. Together they have written:

> The UK and the US, as permanent members of the [UN security] council, are fully aware that the UN embargo operates in breach of the UN covenants on human rights, the Geneva and Hague conventions and other international laws . . . The two governments have

consistently opposed allowing the UN security council to carry out its mandated responsibilities to assess the impact of sanctions policies on civilians. We know about this first hand because the governments repeatedly tried to prevent us from briefing the security council about it.[48]

Many international lawyers argue that, even though the sanctions are applied by the UN (though in reality maintained by the US and British veto), they are nevertheless violations of international law. A report written for the UN by Belgian law professor Marc Bossuyt, for example, notes that 'the sanctions regime against Iraq is unequivocally illegal under existing international law and human rights law' and 'could raise questions under the Genocide Convention'. Former US Attorney General Ramsay Clark has said the economic blockade is a weapon of mass destruction, 'a crime against humanity, in the Nuremberg sense . . . The blockade is a weapon for the destruction of the masses, and it attacks those segments of the society that are the most vulnerable. Inherently, it attacks infants and children, the chronically ill, the elderly and emergency medical cases.'[49]

Sanctions against Iraq have violated the majority of the articles in the preamble of the Universal Declaration of Human Rights, while a protocol to the Geneva convention states that the starvation of children is illegal and ethically indefensible. As a signatory to the Convention on the Rights of the Child, Britain is also obligated to 'take appropriate measures' to reduce child mortality, to ensure necessary health care to all children and to combat disease and malnutrition, all of which have been exacerbated by sanctions.[50]

Whitehall has claimed that only the Iraqi regime is responsible for suffering in Iraq and Tony Blair said that 'the Iraqi authorities can import as much food and medicines as they need. If there are nutritional problems in Iraq, they are not the result of sanctions.'[51]

In response, Halliday and von Sponeck noted that in October 2001 the US and Britain were blocking $4 billion in humanitarian supplies, which was 'by far the greatest constraint on the implementation of the oil-for-food programme' (the deal whereby Iraq is allowed to sell its oil in exchange for importing food). They noted a UN report stating that the Iraqi government's distribution of humanitarian supplies was fully satisfactory and concluded that 'the death of some 5–6,000 children a month is mostly due to contaminated water, lack of medicines and malnutrition. The US and UK governments' delayed clearance of equipment and materials is responsible for this tragedy, not Baghdad.'[52]

In May 2002, sanctions on Iraq were renewed and the sanctions regime moderated in a way likely to relax the policy of holds but with potential 'dual-use' goods still needing approval. By this time $5 billion in goods were being blocked, about 90 per cent by the US and Britain. This included $4.6 billion of humanitarian supplies, according to the UN Office of the Iraq Programme.[53]

Items blocked by Britain in the 1990s included boxes of nail polish and lipsticks, consignments of paper for hospital doctors, cotton for medical use (swabs, gauze etc), water purification chemicals, a consignment of children's bicycles, and a consignment of ping pong balls from Vietnam. Drugs, various medical supplies and even such basic items as soap and syringes, have either been permanently blocked or delayed to the point where their usefulness has been eroded. Antibiotics have been held up for so long they passed their sell-by dates. The government admitted in January 2000 that it had held up the delivery of 'a number of vaccines which were of potential dual use concern'.[54]

Von Sponeck and Halliday have sought to 'encourage people everywhere to protest against unscrupulous policies and against the appalling disinformation put out about Iraq and by those who know better, but are willing to sacrifice people's lives with false and malicious arguments'.[55]

However, British policy has been met by a terrible silence on the part of parliament and much of the media. It is simply amazing that a government policy which, by credible indicators, has led to the deaths of hundreds of thousands of people has been widely met with only murmurs of objections, and sometimes outright support, in the mainstream political culture. The political class has acquiesced in the deaths of half a million children.

The second test of the British government's commitment to human rights concerns the worst atrocities committed by Baghdad against the Kurdish population in northern Iraq in the 1980s. These past brutalities are now regularly invoked by the Blair government to justify attacking Iraq. It is simply amazing that Blair is able to deploy this argument without immediate ridicule from journalists and others, in light of London's backing for Saddam at that time.

Before the country became an Official Enemy by invading Kuwait in August 1990, Western policy had been to support Saddam's Iraq since it served two useful functions: first, fighting the new Ayatollah's regime in Iran and second, brutally suppressing Kurds in Iraq: London has always opposed full self-determination or statehood for the Kurds for fear of destabilising its allies in the region, principally Turkey and Iraq.

From 1980 to 1990 Britain provided £3.5 billion in trade credits to Baghdad – critical economic support that had the effect of freeing up resources for the Iraqi military. British ministerial trade missions were regular throughout the war years and continued as Iraq used poison gas against the Iranians in 1983-4. In 1987, following the extension of export credits after UK–Iraq trade talks, a Department of Trade and Industry press release noted that 'the new facilities amounted to an expression of confidence in UK/Iraq commercial relations'.[56]

Britain sold Iraq £2.3 billion worth of machinery and transport equipment between 1981 and 1990, according to DTI figures, much of it military-related. As early as January 1981 the Cabinet's Overseas and Defence Committee, chaired by Prime

Minister Thatcher, was discussing how to 'exploit Iraq's promising market for arms'. In the 1980s, Britain exported a huge range of equipment to Saddam's war machine, including explosives, electronic surveillance equipment, a launch site for Exocet missiles, long range radio systems, pistols, rifles and shotguns, military vehicles, fast assault craft and night-vision equipment.[57]

Ministers permitted exports of much 'dual-use' equipment knowing they would be used to make weapons and help Baghdad build up its arms industry and develop weapons of mass destruction: this was clearly revealed in the Scott enquiry into arms to Iraq in the mid-1990s, brilliantly analysed by *Guardian* journalist Richard Norton-Taylor.[58] A secret June 1988 report by MoD official, Lt. Col. Richard Glazebrook, for example, warned ministers that 'UK Ltd is helping Iraq, often unwillingly, but sometimes not, to set up a major indigenous arms industry.' He stated that Britain's contribution to Iraq included establishing a research and development facility to make weapons, machinery to make gun barrels and shells, and a national electronics manufacturing complex. Taken together, the exports represented 'a very significant enhancement of the ability of Iraq to manufacture its own arms and thus to resume the war with Iran.'[59]

Machine tools from the company Matrix Churchill played a major role in this. Its final batch of exports was approved on 17 July 1990, two weeks before Iraq invaded Kuwait, sold knowing they would be used to make shells and missiles. Indeed, even after the invasion of Kuwait, Britain sold 5,000 shells to Jordan, despite knowledge that it was a diversionary route for exports to Iraq.[60]

One of the absurdities of the current crisis is that London and Washington are attacking Iraq supposedly on the basis of the latter's development of weapons of mass destruction aided by London and Washington. Exports from Britain included three tonnes of sodium cyanide and sodium sulphide, that can be used as nerve gas antidotes, delivered in April 1989, and plutonium, zirconium, thorium oxide, and gas spectrometers, all essential for nuclear technology. A 1992 UN report noted that Matrix Churchill machine tools exported to Iraq had 'technical characteristics required for producing key components needed in a nuclear programme'. An unnamed nuclear inspector told the *Independent* in November 1992 that machinery supplied by Matrix Churchill was at an engineering complex used for producing gas centrifuges and at a manufacturing site involved in producing calutrons, needed to make nuclear weapons.[61]

In March 1989, the government agreed to provide export credits to underwrite goods from Matrix Churchill that a civil servant warned were bound for an Iraqi 'chemical weapons factory'. The previous month, ministers approved another batch of Matrix Churchill exports to Iraq that included computer-controlled lathes capable of making shell casings or centrifuges for enriching uranium. In 1990, Foreign Office minister William Waldegrave approved an Iraqi order for integrated circuits capable of being customised for use in nuclear weapons, chemical and biological warheads and delivery systems. In the end this equipment was not provided because Baghdad delayed providing letters of credit.[62]

The month before Iraq invaded Kuwait, the US tried to persuade the Foreign Office to prevent Britain's export of vacuum furnaces to Iraq since they could 'enhance Iraq's nuclear or missile capabilities'. Waldegrave nevertheless approved this export but the August invasion made it academic.

Defence Intelligence Staff warned in the 1990s that there was a 'strong possibility' that British chemicals exported to Egypt were being passed to Iraq; nevertheless, many licences were granted by ministers. Exports to Egypt also included parts for ground-to-ground missiles which could be adapted to fire chemical weapons. After the Gulf War, UN inspection teams in Iraq discovered missiles of the same type fitted with nerve-gas warheads. International Military Services, a wholly owned subsidiary of the MoD, supplied chemical agent antidotes to

Jordan despite repeated warnings from the Defence Intelligence Staff that they were likely to be diverted to Iraq. Thatcher personally signed a £270 million military package to Jordan in 1985, which included the sale of 1,000 chemical warfare training suits. In fact, Britain sold Iraq 10,000 NBC (nuclear, biological and chemical) protective suits which the Iraqis might have used for their first experimental use of poison gas against Iranian troops in late 1983.[63]

This trade continued throughout the late 1980s when Baghdad was ordering the destruction of 3,000 Kurdish villages in a gruesome terror campaign (the same Kurds we now are 'defending' out of our natural humanitarianism). A key date is March 1988, when Iraqi forces used poison gas at the town of Halabja, killing 5,000 Kurds, an event now invoked to show that the Saddam regime is the personification of evil. While this is surely true, London's reaction then was instructive.

As noted above, many military-related exports were approved to Iraq after March 1988; in fact, London deepened its military support for Saddam after Halabja. First, the government expressed its outrage over the use of chemical weapons by doubling export credits for Baghdad, which rose from £175 million in 1987 to £340 million in 1988. A DTI press release of November 1988 cheerfully boasts that export credits 'are almost double those for 1987' and 'this substantial increase reflects the confidence of the British government in the long term strength of the Iraqi economy and the opportunities for an increased level of trade between our two countries following the ceasefire in the Gulf war.'[64]

Second, the government made it easier to sell arms to Iraq by relaxing the export guidelines. Five months after Halabja, Foreign Secretary Geoffrey Howe noted in a secret report to Thatcher that with the Iran-Iraq peace deal agreed in August 'opportunities for sales of defence equipment to Iran and Iraq will be considerable'. The secrecy of this policy was vital, since, as one Foreign Office official noted, 'it could look very cynical if, so soon after expressing outrage about the treatment of the

Kurds [at Halabja], we adopt a more flexible approach to arms sales.'

In October 1989 Foreign Office minister William Waldegrave noted of Iraq that 'I doubt if there is any future market of such a scale anywhere where the UK is potentially so well-placed' and that 'the priority of Iraq in our policy should be very high.' The government had already allowed numerous British companies to exhibit equipment at the Baghdad arms fair in April, attended also by arms salesmen from the government's Defence Exports Services Organisation.[65]

Third, the government only went through the motions of protest at Iraq's use of chemical weapons. For almost a year after Halabja Whitehall refused to concede that Iraq had definitely used chemical weapons, stating that the evidence was 'compelling but not conclusive'. Only in January 1989 did it admit that the evidence was 'convincing'. The US organisation Human Rights Watch recently said that when it collected evidence of abuses at Halabja and elsewhere in the Kurdish region at that time, the Foreign Office ignored it. It also said that the government was 'singularly unreceptive' to its campaign to indict the Iraqi regime at the international court of justice.[66]

Consistent with a key theme of this book that Britain tends to side with aggressors, Whitehall did manage at this time to block some chemical warfare-related exports to Iraq. A story on 26 April 1988 in the *Independent* noted that British export restrictions were preventing a group of scientists and doctors sending defensive equipment to Kurdish civilians attacked with poison gas. The report noted that 'according to the group their attempts to buy equipment have been rebuffed by companies acting on instructions from the Ministry of Defence.'[67]

Britain's backing for Saddam in the 1980s also ensured that London turned a blind eye to Iraqi assassinations of political opponents abroad, including in London – a form of terrorism, that is, at which our leaders now supposedly reel in horror.

Britain even helped train the Iraqi military under Saddam, though little is publicly known about this programme. MI6 is believed to have put Barzan Tikriti, then Saddam's chief of intelligence, into contact with former SAS officers to train Iraqi special forces at a sensitive military location in Iraq.[68]

The extent of US aid in developing Iraq's weapons of mass destruction has recently emerged in reports by the US Senate's Committee on Banking, Housing and Urban Affairs. They reveal that the US sold anthrax, nerve gas, West Nile fever germs and botulism to Iraq up until March 1992, even after the Gulf War, as well as germs similar to tuberculosis and pneumonia. Britain sold the drug pralidoxine, an antidote to nerve gas, in March 1992. US assistance included 'chemical warfare-agent precursors, chemical warfare-agent production facility plans and technical drawings, chemical warfare-filling equipment, biological warfare-related materials, missile fabrication equipment and missile system guidance equipment'.[69]

Soon after Halabja, the US approved the export of virus cultures and a $1 billion contract to design and build a petrochemical plant the Iraqis planned to use to produce mustard gas. 'The use of gas on the battlefield by the Iraqis was not a matter of deep strategic concern', Walter Lang, a former senior US defence intelligence officer recently told the *New York Times*.[70]

The third test: Forgetting Turkey

If London's support for Saddam during brutalities against Kurds is widely known, what is not widely known is a worse recent case of similar atrocities committed by our ally, Turkey, again with British backing. Tony Blair has said that Britain 'could not allow in the case of Kosovo ethnic cleansing and genocide to happen right on the doorstep of Europe and do nothing about it'.[71] But this is simply untrue, if we look at this other country on the doorstep of Europe, next door to Iraq, which further reveals the British government's attitude towards human rights.

Then Defence Secretary George Robertson said in 1998:

> I hope that the Turkish government will use their discretion and wisdom when the world community is focusing on the iniquities of Saddam and will be as generous and humanitarian to the Kurds as they have been in the past.[72]

These astonishing words were said of a Turkish government that over the previous four years had destroyed 3,500 Kurdish villages, made at least 1.5 million people homeless and internally displaced, and killed untold thousands more. Turkish abuses committed in the campaign against the PKK Kurdish organisation in the southeast of the country reached their peak in 1994–6, but have continued in the New Labour years.

In that peak period of atrocities, the British government under John Major *stepped up* arms exports to Turkey and continued trade links and normal diplomatic relations. The figures show that Britain delivered more weapons (£68 million worth) to Turkey in 1994 – the year Ankara began major offensive operations against the Kurds – than in previous years. Exports trailed off the following year and reached a new peak of £107 million in 1996. Britain also provided export credits for arms and military equipment in this period, reaching £265 million worth in 1995. British equipment was used by Turkish forces for repression, including armoured cars and the Akrep vehicle, produced locally in Turkey under licence from Land Rover, which was used by Turkish forces pursuing Kurds over the border into northern Iraq.[73]

Only eleven export licence applications for arms and military equipment to Turkey were refused between 1 January 1994 and November 1997, spanning the end of the Conservative government and the beginning of the Blair government.[74]

Atrocities substantially decreased at the end of the 1990s since the scorched earth policy succeeded in terrorising the population and pacifying the region. The PKK renounced the armed struggle in 1999 and its leader, Abdullah Ocalan, was captured by the Turkish authorities. However, abuses against Kurds in the southeast of the country are ongoing, a story now almost totally buried in the media, while Blair's claims to be acting in defence of human rights in the region go largely unchallenged.

Kurds had been forced from their homes by government gendarmes and 'village guards' whom Ankara had armed and paid to fight the PKK. This was an arbitrary and violent campaign marked by hundreds of 'disappearances' and summary executions. Villagers' homes were torched, and their crops and livestock destroyed before their eyes. As of early 2003, hundreds of thousands of people forced out of their homes by Turkish security forces in this way are unable to return to their homes. Most live in poverty and conditions of overcrowding in cities across Turkey. Local governors and gendarmerie are forbidding some returns on the grounds that villages are within restricted military zones. Others have found that village guards have occupied their lands while many are too afraid to return lest they be detained and harassed. Governors are often refusing villagers the right to return unless they sign a form relinquishing all rights to compensation. The form also contains a declaration that excuses the state from criminal responsibility for the displacements.[75]

According to Human Rights Watch, 'the government village return programme is largely fictional and most abandoned settlements remain no-go areas, in some cases occupied by government-armed village guards.' Turkish forces are continuing sporadic forced evacuations and destroying houses in the Kurdish areas. In a number of recent judgements, the European Court of Human Rights has said that security forces are responsible for house destruction, torture, 'disappearance' and extra-judicial execution in the southeast of the country.[76]

Ankara scored a major success in January 2000 when the EU decided to make it a candidate for joining the EU (to be reviewed in 2004). Since then Turkey has tried to convince the world that it is drastically improving its human rights record.

Human Rights Watch initially noted that Ankara's strategy 'consisted mainly of vague and general undertakings that were clearly designed to delay or avoid significant change'. For example, in October 2001 the government announced constitutional changes supposedly to improve human rights; but within forty-eight hours, a book by a Kurdish writer was banned, a local Kurdish politician was detained, trade unionists were indicted for preparing invitations to a meeting in the Turkish and Kurdish languages, a journalist was sentenced to twenty months' imprisonment and a magazine was shut down. By early 2002, Amnesty International was saying that 'no concrete steps have been taken at grass roots level to effect real improvement in the human rights situation.'[77]

Major human rights improvements did occur in 2002, however. In August the Turkish parliament voted to lift many restrictions on the use of the Kurdish language in broadcasting and education, ending decades of discrimination. Yet numerous restrictions on human rights remain: Turkish law continues to heavily constrain free expression, Kurdish former parliamentarians such as Leyla Zana remain in jail after a plainly unfair trial, and police torture remains systematic and widespread.

A former president of Turkey's parliamentary human rights commission has said that 90 per cent of imprisoned children have been tortured in police custody. Many lawyers and human rights defenders say the use of torture and ill treatment has increased in recent years while 'the climate of impunity for torture [has] remained unchanged', according to Human Rights Watch. It remains to be seen whether the new Turkish laws will have any effect on torture.[78]

How has New Labour reacted to this situation of horrific and ongoing human rights abuses on the doorstep of Europe and just over the border from Iraq? The government issued 101 export licences for arms and military equipment to Turkey in its first half year in office, from May to December 1997, rejecting just one application. Arms exports were worth £84 million in

1998, dropping to £9.5 million in 1999 before rising to £34 million in 2000 and £179 million in 2001.[79]

Dozens of Turkish military officers are undergoing training in Britain, as are the Turkish police, guilty of many of the worst human rights abuses. The police staff college at Bramshill even trained a chief superintendent from Northern Cyprus, brutally invaded by Turkey in 1974 and remaining under illegal occupation.[80]

Arms exports and training are to the real power brokers in Turkey, the military. The military's National Security Council does not make government policy and its role is technically an advisory one, but in reality it sets the parameters within which government policy is made. It can effectively remove prime ministers, as it did in the military coup of 1980 that instituted a bloody regime. It also did so in June 1997 when elected prime minister Necmettin Erbakan of the Islamist Welfare party was forced to 'resign' in an effective coup by the military.

A wire story just before the coup noted a classified report presented to Bill Clinton characterising Erbakan as having an 'unfriendly stance' towards the US, especially on the 'defence accord Turkey signed with the United States'. The report said that the Welfare party was threatening the country's secular status which 'was working perfectly for seventy years' and hailed the military as a 'guardian of the Turkish republics' secular character'.[81]

This effective coup against an elected leader elicited not the slightest concern from the British government, or media, as far as I can tell: testimony to the same contempt for democracy evident in the case of Russian destruction of Chechnya under elected president Maskhadov; and indeed evident throughout the post-war period (see chapter 10).

Turkish Chief of the General Staff, General Kivrikoglu, said in October 2001 that as long as there was a 'reactionary danger' – code for the threat of Islamist parties gaining ascendancy – the military would be ready 'for a thousand years' to intervene in politics. Human Rights Watch comments that 'there can be little confidence in the stability of democracy and law while the military openly threatens democratically elected politicians in this way.'[82]

Britain has consistently downplayed massive human rights violations by Iraq's neighbour, and never seriously pressed the Turkish government. London says that 'Turkey is an important partner for Britain and the EU, a NATO ally which provided vital support in the Gulf and Kosovo crises and a major market for UK exporters'. In 1998 Britain identified Turkey as 'a top emerging market' and initiated a campaign entitled 'Turkey – Positioned for Business', before tripling the number of trade missions in the country. Britain is the largest recipient of Turkish direct investment and its third largest export market.[83]

London has also aided Ankara by labelling the PKK a 'terrorist organisation', continuing Conservative policy. This supports Ankara's false framing of the conflict as a war against terrorism, and is similar to helping Russia in its framing of the conflict in Chechnya (see chapter 7). The Blair government has helpfully banned the PKK in the post-September 11th clamp-down. While the PKK certainly committed atrocities, the Turkish government has committed far more and has been systematically repressing the culture and identity of the Kurds as it has proceeded to obliterate their homes. Despite this, the House of Commons Foreign Affairs Committee can still note that because of Turkey's 'utter commitment to fighting terrorism, Turkey is an extremely valuable ally in the ongoing war against terrorism.'[84]

This echoes Ankara's special relationship with Washington. Most of the arms used by Turkey in its campaign against the Kurds were supplied by the US. Former Turkish Prime Minister Bulent Ecevit recently offered strong support for the US 'war against terrorism' because, he said, Turkey owes the US a 'debt of gratitude' since Washington 'had backed Ankara in its struggle against terrorism'.

New Labour also helped Ankara out by closing down the Kurdish TV station, MED-TV, in April 1999. In the same month, BAE struck a deal through its subsidiary Heckler & Koch to provide facilities for the production of half a million assault rifles for the Turkish army. Kamal Mirawdeli, a Kurdish poet, wrote to Tony Blair saying that 'thus, on the one hand, we were deprived of access to our language, culture and free speech through our own satellite channel; on the other you rewarded us for this by facilitating better killings of our children.'[85]

Britain under New Labour has been especially active in supporting Turkey's bid to join the EU. Robin Cook told the Foreign Affairs Committee that 'the question of rejection does not arise' – being inconceivable that Britain would invoke mere human rights atrocities to block Turkish entry.[86] While it may be true that joining the EU will force Turkey to improve its human rights performance, London's policy towards Ankara hardly betrays much concern for human rights, but rather with bringing a strategic ally firmly into the Western orbit. Past atrocities will, it can be safely assumed, remain forgotten. This contrasts to Iraq's atrocities, of which Blair reminds the British public every other day. Most media comment also ignores such atrocities: the debate on Turkish accession to the EU is confined largely to absurdities as to whether Turkey is 'too Muslim', or not, to be part of 'Europe'.

There is even more evidence of the Blair government's indifference to human rights. While Britain and the US have been patrolling the northern 'no fly zone' in Iraq supposedly to protect the Kurds, Turkey has been more or less permanently invading northern Iraq in brutal pursuit of Kurds. The 'no fly zone' allows Turkish warplanes to operate in Iraq virtually at will. Ankara launched invasions with 20,000 troops in 1992, 35,000 troops in 1995, 50,000 troops in 1997, 10,000 troops in 1998, and 10,000 troops in 2000. Turkish forces have sometimes stayed for months while destroying villages and committing widespread human rights abuses. No other country has conducted so many invasions in recent times, all with the tacit consent of Washington and London. When the US and Britain launched their full onslaught against Iraq in March 2003, Turkey already had thousands of troops in the north of the country and was poised to conduct a deeper invasion.

Britain and the US have been more directly complicit in Turkish actions. An article in the US *Air Force Times* in December 1994 noted that:

> When Turkish bombing missions . . . are being flown, the Turks ground coalition aircraft . . . Turkish military officials are privy to virtually all intelligence gathered not only from Americans but from Britain and France . . . The Turks continue to have access to information from AWACS aircraft . . . The Turks also review American and British reconnaissance aircraft data compiled during Provide Comfort flights'.[87]

RAF pilots protested in 2001 about being ordered to return to their base in Turkey to allow the Turkish air force to bomb Kurds. The *Washington Post* reported that 'on more than one occasion [US pilots] have received a radio message that "there is a TSM inbound" – that is a Turkish Special Mission heading to Iraq.' The US pilots are then required to return to base. When the pilots flew back into Iraqi air space they would see 'burning villages, lots of smoke and fire'. When Turkey invaded in December 2000, for example, most patrols in the NFZ were suspended to allow Turkey to continue bombing.[88]

The House of Commons Defence Committee asked Defence Secretary Geoff Hoon: if Britain was 'supposed to be defending those Kurds in the no fly zone, what has been your reaction in relation to Turkey when those events take place?' Hoon replied: 'It is not something that I need to react to in my present position.' He added that 'it is not something that the government is specifically aware of as far as incursions by the Turkish government is concerned.'[89]

The argument that the British government is motivated by human rights concerns in Iraq is simply laughable. Humanitarian concerns are always invoked to justify terrible policies and Britain's real role in the world has other motivations – as we see in the next chapter, by looking at the first phase in the supposed 'war against terrorism' in Afghanistan.

Finally, in terms of the international community's approach to Iraq, the issue is not whether the Iraqi regime is evil – clearly it is – nor whether Iraq's people would be better off without it – clearly they would. To me, there are two important sets of questions: first, how regimes that abuse human rights, like Saddam's (and Turkey's) arise, and how in some cases they are enabled to develop weapons of mass destruction; second, how the international community should deal with such regimes. These are big questions and brief answers cannot be sufficient. But on the first, it is clear that Britain and the US are partly (though of course not solely) responsible, as they are for helping to create many of the world's monsters, due to their basic foreign policy priorities and their conception of 'international order', described elsewhere in this book.

In answer to the second question, my view is that there is surely hope for the world if all countries are treated equally according to due processes of international law and if genuine global cooperation is seen as paramount. Following these concerns would have been a better route to dealing with the Saddam regime, together with taking all steps to encourage the Iraqi people themselves to overthrow the regime, a strategy that would have been aided by the lifting of sanctions. British and US policy generally rejects action genuinely based on multi-lateral, legal and ethical standards to cover all nations equally, including themselves and their allies, like Turkey (and many others described in this book). Although this is a far from easy outcome to aim for, it has real prospects, not least given the stupendous power now available to those who control world order. The latter's pursuit of unilateral options puts them in the same camp, ultimately, as the Iraqi regime, and is making the world far more dangerous for ordinary people.

2

AFGHANISTAN:
THE NEW UNPEOPLE

Maroff, aged thirty-eight, lived at his farm located about one kilometre from the village and told Human Rights Watch that he had witnessed the attacks, first on the Taliban military base, and then on the nearby village, from his home. When he rushed to the village the next day, he found the family compound of his relatives in ruins, and villagers digging through the rubble. Twelve bodies of his relatives were recovered from the debris of the family compound. The dead included the two sons and two daughters of his twenty-five-year-old sister Rhidi Gul: Aminullah, aged eight; Raminullah, aged three; Noorjan, aged five; and Gulpia, aged four. Rhidi Gul was recovering from serious wounds, together with her surviving one-year-old son Hamidullah, also seriously wounded in the attack. Kamno, a ten-year-old sister-in-law of Rhidi Gul, also survived the attack and was recovering from serious shrapnel wounds to the face in Quetta hospital.[1]

This is an account of the effects of a US bombing attack in Afghanistan in October 2001 in the first phase of what US and British leaders call the 'war against terrorism'. It is one of what appears to be many deliberate US attacks on civilians, in this case killing twenty-three villagers.

The image of Maroff desperately searching for lost relatives echoes the plight of New Yorkers doing likewise in the rubble of the destroyed World Trade Center. The twenty-first century opened with not one but two hideous crimes. One of them – the horrific attacks of 11 September 2001 – has been rightly condemned as an act of criminal barbarity, indefensible at every level. The other crime was the US and British response in Afghanistan.

In this chapter, I outline some of the main features of what was a very brutal onslaught, and some of the ways in which the media falsely framed it. I also address the forgotten issue of how Britain helped create the monster that struck on September 11th. Finally, I try to offer some plausible explanations of British and US strategy, beyond absurd claims of defending civilisation in the face of barbarity.

The main features of the war

To recount, briefly: following the terrorist attacks in New York and Washington, the US and its close allies took military action in Afghanistan against the Al Qaida network, and the Taliban government protecting it. After a fierce bombing campaign the Taliban regime was overthrown and the Al Qaida network dispersed from Afghanistan, although Bin Laden himself escaped. Opposition groups in the so-called Northern Alliance – tribal warlords who had effectively been the US' ground troops during the campaign – undertook brutal revenge attacks against Taliban forces and villages occupied by ethnic Pashtuns, killing hundreds and forcing thousands to flee. US and British troops were deployed on the ground to hunt down the remnants of Al Qaida and Taliban forces while an international peacekeeping force was introduced to provide stability in the Afghan capital, Kabul. A new Afghan government, more representative of the population, was established with pledges of foreign aid to support it.

The Official Story is that the war in Afghanistan was in defence of civilisation against barbarity. President Bush said it was a fight 'for all who believe in progress and pluralism, tolerance and freedom'. Tony Blair said: 'We will do it all because we believe in our values of justice, tolerance and respect for all regardless of race, religion or creed'.[2]

Almost everywhere in the mainstream media and political culture, the war was regarded as both just and having a favourable outcome: just, because the evil of September 11th, killing 3,000 people, was good cause to launch the attack on Afghanistan; a favourable outcome, since the Taliban regime was toppled, Al Qaida bases in Afghanistan destroyed, and a more representative government in Kabul created. The first phase of the 'war against terrorism' has been the subject of much rejoicing and widespread praise given to Bush and Blair for defending high values.

There is just one fact sufficient to dispel this cosy scenario – we killed more people than they did.

Almost all estimates put the number of civilians killed as a result of the bombing as greater than those killed in the attacks in the US. The real figure may even be several times greater. A *Guardian* investigation concluded that between 10,000 and 20,000 people died as an 'indirect' result of the US bombing, that is, through hunger, cold and disease as people were forced to flee the massive aerial assault. An estimate by Professor Marc Herold of the University of New Hampshire, suggests that between 3,125 and 3,620 Afghan civilians were killed by US bombing up to July 2002.[3]

The attacks in the US were horrific because of the scale of deaths of innocent, defenceless people. By the most basic values, the same applies to the people of Afghanistan. Yet their deaths have received the barest of concern from political leaders and the mainstream media, who have essentially deemed Afghan lives expendable to avenge the attack on the US.

Afghans are Unpeople, whose deaths go unnoticed – they join the East Timorese (see chapter 21), the Chagossians (chapter 22) and the children of Iraq (chapter 1) as people whose lives are valueless when they get in the way of Western policy.

The standard argument is that civilian deaths in Afghanistan were the regrettable consequence of military action that was needed to destroy Al Qaida bases and thus prevent further terrorist attacks. But this is a spurious argument since it is obvious that Al Qaida is a decentralised network. The counter-argument – that bombing Afghanistan has made it *more likely* that terrorists will attack – is equally plausible. Most of the September 11th hijackers were from Saudi Arabia, with few apparent connections to Afghanistan as such, but there were no calls to bomb Riyadh (imagine if the hijackers had been Iraqi). Rather, Saudi Arabia is a favoured ally in the 'war against terrorism'. It is obvious that at stake here are US geopolitical interests (discussed further below), more than concerns to prevent future terrorism.

The sheer number of civilian deaths in Afghanistan makes it impossible to vindicate US/British strategy, by the most basic moral standards. The reason why most commentators are happy with the war is that 'we won', which reveals how easily they abandon a professed morality in their servility to state power. Certainly the demise of the vile Taliban is welcome and the more representative government in Kabul is a major change. But against this must be set not only the devastation wrought by the US bombing – surely its dominating fact – but also the empowerment of the former warlords whose respect for human rights reaches the same lofty heights as that of the Taliban.

The Official Story has largely managed to suppress the main features of the war: mass bombing with terrifying weapons; many apparently deliberate attacks on civilians; and the use of cluster bombs leaving a legacy of thousands of unexploded shells.

The bombing campaign began on 7 October 2001. The US president received much praise in the media for not immediately lashing out after September 11th and waiting a whole month before beginning the obliteration of the world's poorest country. (The all-party House of Commons Defence Committee praised 'the measured response taken by the United States'.) More than 22,000 weapons were dropped on the country in the first six months. One in four of these missed their target.[4]

The usual fiction – that the war would involve precision targeting and the careful avoidance of civilian deaths – was stated by Tony Blair at the beginning of the war. After similar bombing campaigns against Yugoslavia and Iraq, Blair was by now acting as virtual White House spokesperson, providing the pretence of an 'international coalition' in what was clearly a US war. This role was more important than Britain's military contribution, which in the early days of the bombing campaign was token and probably of no military value. The British army did later prove useful, however, when it was called upon by Washington to replace US troops in 'mopping up' remaining Al Qaida and Taliban fighters after the fall of the major towns. This role showed that Britain was by now acting as a proxy US force, and was undertaken since 'the British public has a higher tolerance for casualties than the Americans', in the words of one British soldier.[5]

Despite public reassurances by the 'junior partner', ever more indiscriminate bombing took place as the campaign went on. The US war strategy gradually escalated from using medium-sized missiles to cruise missiles to bunker-busting 2,000 lb bombs, then to B52 carpet-bombing and finally to the devastating 'daisy cutter' bombs that destroy everything in a 600-yard radius. The city of Kandahar was reduced to rubble by US bombing.

The bombing *exacerbated* the humanitarian crisis in Afghanistan, just as it did in Kosovo (see chapter 6). According to Human Rights Watch, the airstrikes 'contributed to the humanitarian crisis, with thousands of Afghans fleeing their homes. Their flight swelled the ranks of hundreds of thousands who were already internally displaced because of drought, war, and conflict-related violence.' A quarter of a million people fled to Iran and Pakistan after September 11th while a further 200,000 fled their homes but remained inside Afghanistan.

All these people were left wandering in cold and hunger usually with no outside support, since the humanitarian effort had been blocked by the bombing too.[6]

There were many apparently deliberate attacks on civilians, which are war crimes. One example has been cited at the beginning of this chapter. A US attack on the village of Chowkar-Karez in October killed between twenty-five and thirty-five civilians. There were no military targets in the vicinity, which was a remote rural area of Afghanistan. According to Human Rights Watch, after the bombing started:

> Many of the people in the village then ran out of their homes, afraid that the bombs would fall on the homes. All witnesses stated that the aircraft then returned to the area and began firing from guns. Many of the civilians were killed from the firing. The bombing and firing lasted for about one hour.[7]

In November, at least 250 Pakistani fighters were killed in a school after trying to surrender. US warplanes hit the compound twice, after the fighters had agreed to give themselves up, devastating the main building. The *Guardian* wrote that the Pentagon's decision to bomb the school was supported by the Uzbek warlord, Abdul Dostam, 'but opposed by other local generals, who argued it would be more humane to allow the fighters to surrender'.[8] It appears that US strategy was too cruel even for 'local generals' in Afghanistan, not the most human-rights minded of soldiers.

A Red Cross compound and warehouses storing humanitarian supplies, food, blankets and oil in Kabul was hit twice by 27 October. The Red Cross called the attack a 'violation of international humanitarian law'. It pointed out that staff on the ground had seen 'a slow and low-flying plane drop two bombs on the compound, the roofs of which were painted with three-by-three meter red crosses on a white background'. In the second attack, food and non-food items intended for 55,000 people in Kabul were destroyed.[9]

The biggest single massacre was at Qali-I-Jhangi fort in Mazar-I-Sharif, when hundreds of rioting prisoners were killed. SAS and US special forces took part in the operation and directed massive aerial bombardments. Full details of the massacre have not emerged, while the US and Britain continue to resist calls for a UN inquiry.

Afghanistan's civilian infrastructure was targeted – now standard practice in the Anglo-American wars at the turn of the millennium, such as the 1991 war against Iraq, and the conflict in Kosovo. On 15 October US bombs destroyed Kabul's main telephone exchange, killing twelve people. In late October, US warplanes bombed the electrical grid in Kandahar. On 31 October, seven airstrikes were launched against Afghanistan's largest hydro-electric power station. On 18 November US planes bombed religious schools. There were several attacks on areas with no apparent military significance. On 25 October, for example, a bomb hit a fully loaded city bus in Kandahar killing between ten and twenty passengers. On 18/19 November US planes bombed the mountain village of Gluco – located on the Khyber Pass and far away from any military facility – killing seven villagers.[10]

US bombing destroyed the office of the Al Jazeera TV station in Kabul and another bomb hit a house used by the BBC a block away. I could find no evidence that the British government protested against this apparent attack on the BBC. In the first three days of the campaign US bombs knocked off the air and entirely destroyed the office of Radio Kabul. Farhad Azad of *Afghanmagazine.com* said that the Taliban had made music illegal but it was US bombs that destroyed the hidden music archive. There is little doubt that all these attacks were deliberate, recalling the attack on the Serbian Radio and Television building in Belgrade during the war against Yugoslavia (see chapter 6). Attacks on what were clearly civilian targets are therefore war crimes.[11]

Human Rights Watch appealed to the US and others to halt the use of cluster bombs immediately after the war began. It noted that in Yugoslavia there were more than 20,000 unexploded bomblets and that cluster bombs during the Kosovo war had killed between 90 and 150 civilians. Following the 1991 Gulf war there were an estimated 1.2 million unexploded bomblets, which have since killed more than 1,600 Kuwaiti and Iraqi civilians, injuring another 2,500.[12]

In spite of this, US B52s operating from the base of the depopulated British territory of Diego Garcia (see chapter 22) proceeded to drop hundreds of cluster bombs in Afghanistan. According to the UN in March 2002, Afghanistan had become littered with 14,000 unexploded bomblets. At least forty-one people have been killed and forty-six injured in Herat and nearby villages in western Afghanistan by cluster bombs that 'nestled in the soil and bided their time' long after the bombing ended there. A UN official in Afghanistan now estimates that live bombs and mines maim on average between 40 and 100 people a week.[13]

In October the US started supporting the Northern Alliance opposition groups in earnest, supplying them with food, ammunition and air support. These warlords had been so brutal in their rule over Afghanistan in 1992–95 – executing prisoners and committing rape and all variety of other atrocities – that much of the population welcomed the Taliban when it took over in 1996. Following the defeat of the Taliban, the Northern Alliance descended on villages occupied by Pashtuns, who had provided support to the Taliban, and proceeded to conduct a wave of looting, rape and ethnic killings. UNHCR estimated that 50,000 Pashtuns fled into Pakistan from January to April 2002 in fear of their lives.

By mid-2002, reports from Human Rights Watch were dispelling the notion that the Anglo-American onslaught had delivered peace and liberty to Afghans. It noted that 'ordinary Afghans are increasingly terrorised by the rule of local and regional military commanders – warlords – who are reasserting their control over large areas of Afghanistan'. 'US cooperation with certain of the warlords seems to be aggravating the problem.'

As for the situation of women, 'Afghan women of all ethnicities have been compelled to restrict their participation in public life to avoid being targets of violence by armed factions.' Especially outside Kabul, Afghan women 'continue to face serious threats to their physical safety, denying them the opportunity to exercise their basic human rights and to participate fully and effectively in the rebuilding of their country'.[14]

The media in support

These brutalities, and even more the plight of civilians fleeing the bombing, received the barest of media coverage. Television news endlessly covered the suffering of New Yorkers who lost friends and relatives; but there was almost complete silence on the similar suffering of Afghans. The media played a critical role in the designation of Afghans as Unpeople.

On 3 January 2002 the *Guardian* contained a report on Maslakh camp, housing 350,000 internally displaced people. The organisation Medialens notes that the *Guardian* had by then reported on Maslakh only twice since September 11th. By contrast, during the Kosovo war, the plight of 65,000 Kosovar refugees on the Kosovo–Macedonian border was mentioned forty-eight times. This was an average of once every two days, compared to once every two months in the case of the Maslakh refugees – a crude measure, perhaps, but an indicator of how the media takes its cue from state policy: in Kosovo, the plight of refugees was worthy of attention since Britain was supposedly defending such people; in Afghanistan, refugees were an embarrassment and a hindrance to government policy, therefore unworthy of attention.[15]

According to Medialens, US media coverage of the first American combat casualty was greater than the coverage given to *all* Afghan civilian deaths. The BBC reported the deaths of seven US servicemen by saying there would be victory in Afghanistan 'but it will be at a price'. This was in March 2002, well after estimates of thousands of civilian deaths – but these deaths, being of mere Afghans, are not worthy of being called a 'price'.[16]

Guardian editors supported the war throughout, helping to frame it largely along good versus evil lines. They delivered editorials that, as in the case of Kosovo, questioned some US and British tactics but not the overall strategy or the just nature of the bombing. At the end of October, *Guardian* editors reported on a speech by Tony Blair in Cardiff:

> The core of the speech – intellectual as well as moral – came when he contrasted the West's commitment to do everything possible to avoid civilian casualties and the terrorists' proven wish to cause as many civilian casualties as possible, a point which Jack Straw followed up powerfully in the Commons yesterday. Let them do their worst, we shall do our best, as Churchill put it. That is still a key difference.[17]

Tony Blair visited India and Pakistan at the turn of the year as tensions between the two countries rose, partly over terrorism in Kashmir. Few in the media ridiculed – but many praised – the sight of Blair telling both countries not to resort to force while his air force was helping to pummel Afghanistan. If Blair had been consistent with his own policy, perhaps he would have advised both India and Pakistan to flatten the other to defend themselves against terrorism.

Rather, the country's leading liberal newspaper regularly chose to shower unadulterated praise on the wondrous virtues of Our Leader, once saying for example:

> From the word go, Mr Blair understood what some others took time to realise, and a few still fail to grasp, that the assaults on New York and Washington were a qualitative long term challenge both to the United States and to the rest of the advanced capitalist western world . . . By his speeches, by his international diplomacy and, do not forget this point, by his

responsiveness to criticism and doubt in many quarters
that he might easily have overlooked, Mr Blair has been
in some ways exemplary . . . He deserves especial
respect for attempting to engage with the issues of
Palestine and of Islam in a serious way.[18]

By contrast, the *Guardian*'s comment pages carried many
articles critical of the war and US strategy, thanks to Seumas
Milne, the Comment pages editor. This was quite unusual in a
major newspaper in a time of war. But in the news pages the
plight of Afghan civilians was mostly ignored and relevant
background was usually not presented. And this was the *best* of
the reporting in the mainstream media.

Neither did the media – following political leaders – dwell on
the illegality of the war. The government was advised that
military action would be illegal if taken in retaliation. Only if it
could claim self-defence would it be legal. This was clearly not
the case: Blair stated clearly that 'no specific credible threat' of
terrorist action in Britain had been detected.

Guardian editors stated the day following the launch of the
war that 'it needs to be said as clearly and as unemotively as
possible at the outset that the United States was entitled to
launch a military response'. Columnist Martin Woollacott later
added: 'We have to accept that a military response of some kind
is necessary for America.'[19] Neither the editors nor Woollacott
stated whether Sudanese leaders, for example, might deem it
'necessary' to strike back at the US for the latter's 1998 attacks
on Khartoum – to cite just one example of how those on the
receiving end of Western policies are accorded a completely
different set of rights than the defenders of civilisation.

UN security council resolution 1368 called on states 'to work
together urgently to bring to justice the perpetrators, organisers
and sponsors of these terrorist attacks'. As usual, the US and
Britain interpreted this as allowing them to do what they liked;
the media followed.[20]

The option of pursuing a legal route to bringing those

responsible for September 11th to justice was never seriously considered by US leaders or the media. The latter often ridiculed the idea as hopelessly naïve but mainly ignored it, preferring to accord the US the right to bomb Afghanistan into dust. Yet, as Professor Paul Rogers of Bradford University has argued, it is possible that with the universal horror expressed over the terrorist attacks in the US, global support could have been sustained for a rigorous political and legal process of undermining support for Al Qaida around the world. He argues that 'intelligence and security cooperation would have been unparalleled. An appropriate international court could have been established under UN supervision. The existing UN conventions on terrorism would have been hugely strengthened.' Rogers also argues that what makes this route even more attractive 'is the nagging suspicion that the perpetrators of the 11 September atrocities expected a strong US military reaction and counted on it as increasing long-term support for their cause'.[21]

In November *Guardian* editors, while supporting US violence in Afghanistan, admonished those in the Israel–Palestine conflict 'who, despairing of peaceful solutions to problems, resort directly or indirectly to violence'. Also, an editorial in January stated that some members of Hamid Karzai's coalition government 'have demanded a halt to US operations'.[22] It was surely important that ministers in the new government – whose creation supposedly vindicated US strategy – were calling for a halt to military operations. But I saw no other mentions of this call in reporting, as the US and Britain continued the war.

The views of Afghan people were almost never heard in the British media. In a rare exception in the US media, the *New York Times* reported on a gathering of 1,000 Afghan leaders in Peshawar at the end of October that was 'a rare display of unity among tribal elders, Islamic scholars, fractious politicians and former guerilla commanders'. They unanimously 'urged the US to stop the air raids' and appealed to the international media to call for an end to the 'bombing of innocent people'. They urged that other means be adopted to overthrow the Taliban regime. Since these were the wrong messages, it was perhaps not surprising that Afghan voices were little heard.

An organisation that has courageously defended women's rights in Afghanistan for twenty-five years, the Revolutionary Association of the Women of Afghanistan (RAWA), issued a statement on II October saying that America 'has launched a vast aggression on our country'. It noted the US claim that only military and terrorist bases of the Taliban and Al Qaida would be struck and that actions would be targeted and proportionate but that in reality 'this invasion will shed the blood of numerous women, men, children, young and old of our country'. Later, RAWA noted that:

> The US has taken the 'Northern Alliance' into service through wooing and arming certain infamous war-lords. By so doing, the US is in fact abetting the worst enemies of our people and is continuing the same tyrannical policy against the people and the destiny of Afghanistan which successive US administrations adopted during the past two decades.[23]

A similar criticism of the bombing was conveyed by Afghan opposition leader Abdul Haq, who was highly regarded in both Washington and London and had in the 1980s visited Margaret Thatcher, then sponsoring mojahidin warlords. Just before he was killed in Afghanistan, Haq condemned the bombing and criticised the US for refusing to support his and others' efforts to create a revolt within the Taliban. The bombing was 'a big setback to these efforts', he said. The US 'is trying to show its muscle, score a victory and scare everyone in the world. They don't care about the suffering of the Afghans or how many people we will lose.' The *Guardian* ran one article by Haq, and that was pretty much it as far as the voices of Afghans were concerned. This approach was similar to that taken by the rest of the media.

Overall, the British political class acquiesced in the further destruction of a country and thousands of civilian deaths for the right of Our Ally, supported by its 'junior partner', to take whatever action it liked. It was an extraordinary performance. Let us turn to two other critical aspects of this ideological role.

Help in creating the monster

An important function of the media, especially in a war, is to present relevant background information – in this case, this would have included past US and British policy towards Afghanistan. But there was little attempt to provide such information, with only a few mentions before and during the onslaught of the covert British role in Afghanistan in the 1980s. This role makes Britain partly responsible for creating the monster that attacked on September 11th. The lack of media attention was despite sufficient evidence already in the public domain on that covert role.

More than 50,000 fighters from all over the Arab world had been trained to resist the Soviet occupation of Afghanistan following Moscow's December 1979 invasion. The US and Saudi Arabia financed this huge operation, providing around $6 billion in aid to bolster or create the mojahidin groups fighting for the Islamic cause. Most training of the mojahidin took place in camps in Pakistan and Afghanistan and most US arms shipments to the mojahidin groups were organised by Pakistan's intelligence service, the ISI. But the US also trained Pakistani and senior mojahidin commanders in the US itself. The training was in areas such as the use of explosives, automatic weapons, and remote-control devices for triggering mines and bombs, demolition, and arson. Some programmes also included training in how to stab a sentry from behind, murder and assassination of enemy leaders, strangulation and murderous karate chops.[24]

The veterans of this struggle against the Soviets – known as 'Afghanis', though most are not Afghan – now make up many of the targets of the 'war against terrorism'. 'Afghanis' have been involved in the assassination of Egyptian president Anwar Sadat in 1981, the murder of sixty tourists in Egypt in

1997, the bombing of the World Trade Center in 1993 as well as the attacks of September 11th. Russian officials claim that between 4,000 and 5,000 militants from Tajikistan passed through the camps in Afghanistan before returning to fight the Tajik government. China, Egypt, Kashmir, Azerbaijan, the Philippines and Algeria are some of the other countries where 'Afghanis' have resurfaced.[25]

Bin Laden's Al Qaida organisation grew up by drawing on the 'Afghani' network. By the mid 1980s, Bin Laden was paying with his own money to recruit and train the Arab volunteers who flocked to Pakistan and Afghanistan to fight in the jihad against the Soviets. In 1983 the Bin Laden family construction company had won a £3 billion contract to restore the holy places of Mecca and Medina in Saudi Arabia. John Cooley, an expert on Afghanistan, notes that 'delighted by his impeccable Saudi credentials, the CIA gave Bin Laden free rein in Afghanistan' to organise Islamic fighters. According to Cooley, in 1986, the CIA even helped Bin Laden build an underground camp in Khost, where he was to train recruits from across the Islamic world. The US only seems to have turned against 'its former partner Bin Laden', in Cooley's words, in 1995 and 1996, after the US suspected Al Qaida involvement in bomb attacks on US personnel in Saudi Arabia.[26]

Cooley also notes that Saudi Arabia, Pakistan and the US had by 1994 'hatched a monster of Islamic extremism, the Taliban movement'. The first Taliban was made up of mainly students of religious seminaries armed by Pakistan and some of the Afghan guerilla groups. One American observer told Cooley that:

> The Taliban began, essentially, as a kind of experimental Frankenstein's monster. They were created in the laboratories, so to speak, of Pakistani intelligence, the ISI – in order to produce a counter-force to Iran and Iranian Islamism which would be even more repugnant and unacceptable to the West and Russia than the Ayatollah Khomeini successors in Tehran.[27]

The Taliban's path to power was also partly aided by US policy. In 1988, the USSR finally agreed to withdraw from Afghanistan, but on condition that the West and Pakistan stop arming the mojahidin. But the Reagan administration broke the agreement signed in Geneva and continued the arms flow. According to Fred Halliday, a Middle East expert at the London School of Economics, 'this illegal decision . . . was the root of the subsequent chaos and fighting, which led to the triumph of the Islamist guerillas in 1992'.[28]

Afghan forces liberated Kabul in April 1992 but in May a reign of terror was initiated principally by Gulbuddin Hekmatyar, who took over as prime minister. Hekmatyar cut off Kabul and subjected it to mass bombardment, driving half a million people from the city. By summer 1993, there were estimates of 30,000 killed and 100,000 wounded in Kabul. Hekmatyar was Washington's and Saudi Arabia's favourite and carried out these atrocities with US- and Saudi-financed weaponry.[29] The atrocities committed by the Islamic guerillas who terrorised Afghanistan from 1992 to 1995 partly explain why many regarded the Taliban as liberators when they took control of Kabul in 1996.

There were various mentions in the media of CIA support for the mojahidin, but almost nothing on the covert British role.

Britain had also supported the mojahidin since the beginning of the Soviet occupation. MI6 had been authorised to conduct 'disruptive action' within the first year of the resistance campaign. A British private 'security' company, KMS, undertook training of small numbers of mojahidin commando units in Afghanistan and at an MI6 base in Oman, cleared by the Foreign Office. Ex-SAS men took over the KMS training programmes while a few other SAS veterans also trained Pakistani special forces. According to SAS veteran Ken Connor, in his book *Ghost Force*, selected Afghan fighters were smuggled into Britain disguised as tourists and trained in three-week cycles at secret camps in Scotland. Some SAS officers' role went beyond that of trainers and they were involved in scouting and back-up roles with the mojahidin.[30]

Moreover, Britain supplied at least 600 'Blowpipe' shoulder-launched anti-aircraft missiles to mojahidin groups, beginning in spring 1986. These missiles enabled the mojahidin to target Soviet military aircraft but they were also used to shoot down several passenger planes. Britain's leading expert on MI6, Stephen Dorril, notes that the ability to shoot down passenger planes 'became an acute embarrassment, as they presented a potential terrorist threat to the West'. By September 1986, when the first of the more modern US-made Stinger missiles appeared on the battlefield, Blowpipes were no longer needed. The US later spent tens of millions of dollars in a belated attempt to buy back the remaining Stinger missiles that proved lucrative on the black market.[31]

The British-supplied Blowpipe missiles were acquired by the Taliban on taking power. One news service reported two weeks into the war against Afghanistan in October 2001 that:

> The Taliban forces that now control most of Afghanistan and have harboured terrorist Osama Bin Laden still have an unknown number of the Stingers and the similar British blowpipes and Russian SA-7s, defence experts warn.

According to a Reuters report, sixty-two Blowpipe missiles were handed over to the US, along with a further 160 surface-to-air missiles, in February 2002 following the defeat of the Taliban.[32]

In the 1980s, MI6 also provided other aid to various of the Afghan warlords and factions. It supplied missiles to Abdul Haq, of the fundamentalist Hezbe-i-Islami, and also promoted ex-King Zahir Shah, seeing him as a future leader. Britain also backed a group supporting a hardline Islamic ideology led by Ahmed Shah Massoud, sending him an annual mission to see what he wanted. These missions – consisting of two MI6 officers and military instructors – also provided training to

Massoud's junior commanders. Britain supplied tactical radios made by Racal, allowing Massoud to coordinate his forces.[33]

Following attacks on US embassies in Africa in August 1998, Bin Laden became a priority for MI6. Dorril calls Bin Laden 'a creation of the CIA and MI6. They were perfectly happy to secure his support and train and arm his supporters during the covert war to drive the Soviet Union out of Afghanistan'. On the problem of what to do with the thousands of highly trained guerilla fighters after the Soviet occupation ended, one British official admitted: 'We did worry then about these wild bearded men. But there was a lot of naivety around.'[34]

The decade-long MI6 strategy to bolster the mojahidin was Britain's largest covert operation since the Second World War. With the US as the key player, the strategy helped create a globalisation of terrorism and a new terrorist threat to the West. Cooley notes that 'before the training of terrorists and guerillas became institutionalised on a large scale by the CIA and the Pakistani military during the 1979–89 Afghan war, terrorism was practised mainly by genuine liberation movements'.[35] We are now meant to accept the 'war against terrorism' as showing our shining devotion to ridding the world of an evil scourge, when it is at least partly a creation of our (US, Saudi, Pakistan and Britain's) making.

Another issue regularly passed over in the media was the mojahidin's involvement in drug trafficking. During the bombing, British leaders made much of the threat of drugs from Afghanistan on our streets, pointing out that 90 per cent of the heroin came from the country. In the 1980s, our new-found allies were doing their utmost to get these drugs to the West. The mojahidin's drug smuggling was at least condoned, and possibly actively supported, by the CIA, whose trucks and mules, which had carried arms into Afghanistan, were used to transport opium to heroin laboratories along the Afghan–Pakistan border.

A former SAS officer who covertly worked alongside mojahidin groups in Afghanistan, Tom Carew, witnessed

Pakistani involvement in opium smuggling. He says in his book that he reported this back to the CIA, who told him 'not to mention this again' and 'if you do see anything connected with opium again, just ignore it completely'. Carew notes that this 'confirmed to me that the Mujahidin were moving the opium with, at the very least, the tacit cooperation of the CIA'. It is inconceivable that MI6 were not also aware of this drug trafficking.[36]

The mojahidin's drugs output is estimated to have provided up to one half of the heroin used annually in the United States and three-quarters of that used in Western Europe.[37] Cooley notes that:

> The Afghan jihad helped to augment Afghanistan's production of drugs and ultimately, by 1998, placed the power to stifle or to increase this production in the hands of the victorious Taliban. Never has so much South Asian marijuana, opium and semi-processed opium products and heroin, reached the drug pushers, the adult addicts, the children and the general populations of the West, as in the late 1990s. Much of this was another direct consequence of the CIA's holy war of 1979–89.[38]

And, we might add, Britain's.

The known facts about past British policy in Afghanistan were rarely mentioned, perhaps being viewed as inconvenient points that didn't fit the official story. So too are more plausible explanations as to what the bombing campaign was actually about.

Plausible explanations

As I outline in chapter 6, in the Kosovo war most commentators accepted at face value Blair's and Clinton's claims to be acting for humanitarian reasons – disputing only their methods for achieving noble goals. It was almost universally accepted that there were no self-interest, strategic reasons involved in bombing Yugoslavia. I believe this was a myth and that there were major issues at stake, concerning EU enlargement and NATO expansion, as well as NATO's 'credibility'. The same has applied to Afghanistan, where the overwhelming majority of commentators bought the Bush and Blair line of defending civilisation against barbarity.

But, on more plausible reasons for the war in Afghanistan, we need only listen to President Bush. Four days after September 11th Bush spoke on US national television of a 'comprehensive assault on terrorism'. He said: 'They will be exposed, and they will discover what others in the past have learnt: *those who make war against the United States have chosen their own destruction.*' It was the same message sent to Saddam Hussein in 1990 (and again in 2003) and to Slobodan Milosevic in 1999 (perhaps these were 'the others in the past') – anyone opposing the US will be destroyed. Britain's Defence minister, Geoff Hoon, also later chipped in, saying that the bombing of Afghanistan was a 'clear message' to others.[39]

The US administration was saying, with Britain in tow as usual, that it will not tolerate major challenges to its interests and power. The war in Afghanistan was a giant act of retaliation to deliver this message, showing who's boss, not only to Afghans but to anyone else. This is a much more plausible first explanation for the bombing campaign than the notion of defending civilised values (which is quite ridiculous looking at US and British policies elsewhere).

The White House National Security Adviser, Condoleeza Rice, told Nicholas Lemann of the *New Yorker* that she 'had called together the senior staff people of the National Security Council and asked them to think seriously about "how do you capitalise on these opportunities" to fundamentally change American doctrine, and the shape of the world, in the wake of September 11th'. A senior official also told Lemann that September 11th was 'a transformative moment' because it 'drastically reduced the American public's usual resistance to American military involvement overseas, at least for a while'.[40]

My view is that the demonstration of US power in Afghanistan was much more important to Washington than capturing Bin Laden. It is surely a myth to believe – as the media have played along – that this was ever the *major* intention of US policy. If it were, a better strategy would have been to pursue the diplomatic route. The press reported several offers by the Taliban to negotiate the handing over of Bin Laden. The *Guardian* reported on 20 September that Taliban leader, Mullah Omar, was offering to hold discussions with the US. 'But the White House said it was not interested in negotiations . . . and ruled out presenting the UN with evidence of Bin Laden's involvement in the attack.' (This was reported under the misleading heading 'US prepares for long war as Taliban close path to peace'.)[41]

The *Guardian* also reported on 17 October that a senior minister in the Taliban regime had offered to hand over Bin Laden during a secret visit to Islamabad, in return for a halt in the bombing. This was the first time the Taliban had offered to hand over Bin Laden for trial in a country other than the US without asking to see evidence first of his involvement in the September 11th attacks.[42]

Now, it is very likely that the Taliban never intended to hand over Bin Laden, even if he were under their jurisdiction. But the point is that neither did the US ever show much interest in pursuing this option.

There was also a chance of removing the Taliban, after September 11th, without bombing. It was at this point that Pakistan removed its support for the Taliban, instantly cutting off its main backer. It was also reported that Pakistan was planning a coup to remove the Taliban leader. This was intended to allow moderates to take over the movement who would then join talks with the Northern Alliance on forming a coalition government. But in this solution there would probably have been a big role for Iran and Russia, who would have been involved in the negotiations to form a post-Taliban government.[43] This would clearly have been opposed in Washington as giving too much say to the US's rivals in the region – and threatening US primacy in determining the post-Taliban future.

The bombing strategy was an altogether more useful one for the US leadership. Two further factors help to explain the US resort to force. Many mainstream commentators have promoted the view that Al Qaida was attacking freedom, civilisation and our way of life on September 11th. This was a convenient way of presenting the good versus evil argument. The horrific acts of September 11th certainly pose a challenge to these values, but they cannot be explained by them. Rather, the terrorists were attacking US policy, consistent with their bomb attacks on other US targets, such as the embassies in East Africa and the warship, USS *Cole*.

Al Qaida's major target is Saudi Arabia, especially in intending to remove the US from the country and topple the ruling Saud family. Al Qaida's founding statement in February 1998 states:

> For over seven years the United States has been occupying the lands of Islam in the holiest of places, the Arabian peninsula, plundering its riches, dictating to its rulers, humiliating its people, terrorising its neighbours and turning its bases in the Peninsula into a spearhead through which to fight the neighbouring Muslim peoples. If some people have in the past argued about the fact of the occupation, all the people of the Peninsula have now acknowledged it. The best proof of this is the Americans' continuing aggression against the Iraqi people using the Peninsula as a staging post, even though all its rulers are against their territories being used to that end, but they are helpless.[44]

The war against Al Qaida and the bombing of Afghanistan is in major respects a war for control of Saudi Arabia. Bin Laden's view of the future of Saudi Arabia is even less pleasant than that of the US or Britain. But the fact is that Al Qaida represents a threat to the continued rule of the Saud family, and to Saudi Arabia's pro-Western stance. This challenge from Bin Laden – himself a Saudi, along with most of the hijackers of September 11th – is occurring when many reports suggest that the Saudi regime is on the brink of collapse, with unprecedented anti-government demonstrations and bombing attacks, coupled with long-term decline in oil revenues and falling living standards for many.

According to one report, British officials fear a coup against the current de facto ruler, Prince Abdullah, by elements in the Saud family sympathetic to Al Qaida. The Pentagon recently sponsored a secret conference to look at options if the royal family fell. The Saud family is fully aware of the challenge from Bin Laden to their rule. 'The Saudi royals have been paying off the terrorists with Danegeld for a long while' one well-placed source was reported as saying.[45]

There is no doubt how vital the US and Britain view continued 'stability' in Saudi Arabia (that is, regimes favoured by us). As noted in the previous chapter, Saudi oil was described by British planners in 1947 as 'a vital prize for any power interested in world influence or domination'. Since 1945, US and British policy in the Middle East has been largely about securing control over Saudi oil, which has meant keeping the Saud family in power (see chapter 11 and my previous book, *The Great Deception*). So keen are Britain and the US to prop up despotic rule that they currently provide 'internal security training' to the Saudi Arabian National Guard, a 75,000-strong force that protects the ruling family against any threat. Arms sales entrench the relationship further. This British support for Saudi repression involves almost complete silence on the country's horrific human rights record.

A second plausible US objective in bombing Afghanistan was therefore to remove the threat to the Saudi regime posed by Al Qaida. A diplomatic, legal route to capture Bin Laden would not have achieved this objective – the network itself needs to be destroyed. In this sense, the bombing was a continuation of the

1991 war to remove Iraq from Kuwait – to remove threats to Western control of the Middle East and to ensure that oil remains in the correct hands.

But there is a third factor which also helps to explain the US and British onslaught in Afghanistan.

In June 2000, the Strategic Studies Institute of the US Army War College published a document entitled 'US military engagement with Transcaucasia and Central Asia'. It said that the region, which includes the Caspian Sea and surrounding areas, possesses reserves of 160 billion barrels of oil and:

> will play an increasingly important role in satisfying the world's future energy demands . . . US officials publicly maintain that this region's energy sources could be a back-up to the unstable Persian Gulf and allow us and our allies to reduce our dependence on its energy supplies.

However, a recognised threat was that 'Russia could sabotage many if not all of the forthcoming energy projects by relatively simple and tested means and there is not much we could do absent a strong and lasting regional commitment [sic].' A solution proposed was that:

> Therefore, for a win-win situation to come about, *some external factor must be permanently engaged and willing to commit even military forces, if need be, to ensure stability and peace.* This does not necessarily mean a unilateral commitment, but more likely a multilateral one, e.g. under the UN's auspices but actually under US leadership. Without such a permanent presence, and it is highly unlikely that the United States can afford or will choose to make such a presence felt, other than through economic investment, Russia will be able to exclude all other rivals and regain hegemony over the area.[46]

The importance of Central Asia to US planners, and the rivalry with Russia and Iran for control of the region's oil, are clear. In 1998, Richard Cheney, now the US Vice President, said 'I cannot think of a time when we have had a region emerge as suddenly to become as strategically significant as the Caspian.' It is certainly plausible that control of Central Asian oil was a factor in deciding US strategy towards Afghanistan – to replace an unfriendly regime in Kabul and by the fact of US intervention become the major sub-regional power. As noted in the following chapter, the US has, since September 11th, established a series of new military bases in this important region under the rubric of the 'war against terrorism'.

A key aspect of the rivalry for control of Central Asian oil is the negotiations on pipeline routes to export the oil and gas to global markets. Again, Afghanistan seems to be a factor here.

Evidence indicates that the US and Pakistan started in 1994 to funnel arms and funding to the Taliban to aid their struggle against the Northern Alliance. A key reason was the Taliban's willingness to cut a deal on a pipeline route. In 1995, the US oil giant Unocal began negotiations to build a pipeline from Turkmenistan through Afghanistan and into Pakistani ports on the Arabian sea. Soon after the Taliban took power in September 1996, the *Daily Telegraph* reported oil industry insiders saying that 'the dream of securing a pipeline across Afghanistan is the main reason why Pakistan, a close political ally of America's, has been so supportive of the Taliban, and why America has quietly acquiesced in its conquest of Afghanistan'. Unocal offered to pay the Taliban regime 15 per cent for every thousand cubic feet of oil it pumped through Afghanistan.

For the first year of Taliban rule, US policy towards the regime seems to have been determined principally by Unocal's interests. Only in December 1998, four months after the US embassy bombings in East Africa, did Unocal drop its pipeline plan. But a few days before September 11th the US Energy Information Administration reported that:

Afghanistan's significance from an energy standpoint stems from its geographical position as a potential transit route for oil and natural gas exports from central Asia to the Arabian sea. This potential includes the possible construction of oil and natural gas pipelines through Afghanistan.[47]

The *Telegraph* also reported in October 2001 that 'when peace and a stable government eventually comes to Kabul, US oil companies will be looking closely at Afghanistan because it offers the shortest route to the Gulf for Central Asia's vast quantities of untapped oil and gas'. Western companies have invested $30 billion in developing oil and gas fields in Central Asia. Washington is currently proposing a $3 billion pipeline from Azerbaijan through Georgia to Turkey's Mediterranean coast. But the *Telegraph* notes that 'US companies could build a similar pipeline from central Asia through Afghanistan to Karachi at half the cost, if the next Afghan government can guarantee its security. Russia fears that is exactly what the Americans want.'[48]

There is major British interest in Central Asian oil, too, with government and companies recently exceedingly active in securing a slice of this very large cake.

The British government estimates there are fifty billion barrels of oil reserves in the Caspian. It expects the Caspian to be producing around three million barrels a day by 2010, which would meet around 15 per cent of projected additional world oil demand. There are also proven gas reserves of up to 9.2 trillion cubic metres, ranking third in the world after the Middle East and Russia. BP notes that 'the hydrocarbon reserves contained in the Caspian Sea are probably on a par with those in the UK North Sea and thus of significant global interest'.

British foreign policy in the region is basically dictated by oil company interests in securing major contracts from the local governments, many of whom are repressive with abysmal human rights records. The Foreign Office has gradually increased its presence in this key region, saying 'our posts actively promote and protect the interests of British companies already working in the region and lobby the authorities to improve the environment for business and foreign investment'. British companies have secured a major stake in Azerbaijan, Kazakhstan and Turkmenistan, mainly as part of international consortia. BP notes that the government 'have been most helpful to BP (Amoco) not only in securing commercial positions in these countries, but also in managing the path forward'.[49]

The Monument Oil and Gas company notes that 'BP-Amoco's predominant position in Azerbaijan or Monument's position in Turkmenistan would have been impossible to achieve without active and committed support from successive governments.' Especially helpful were visits by Foreign Office ministers John Battle and Derek Fatchett to Azerbaijan, which 'led to the signing of a major exploration contract in No. 10 Downing Street, where the Prime Minister played the major role'.[50]

Foreign Office minister Keith Vaz has noted that British interests are not just in winning contracts in individual countries 'but there is more than that. The South Caucasus is the gateway to Central Asia. A revival of the old Silk Road trading route would be of benefit to all of Europe and Asia.'[51]

Again, the pipeline route is critical. One oil company representative told the House of Commons Foreign Affairs Committee that there are undoubtedly large oil and gas reserves but that 'the constraining factor . . . is the pipeline routes and the ability to export . . . The key issue over the next decade is going to be generating efficient oil and gas evacuation routes and having Foreign Office help in doing that'. Washington is lobbying for pipeline routes based on its strategic interests, mainly to counter Russia and Iran. London, by contrast, says that the decisions on the pipelines are for companies, based solely on commercial considerations.[52]

These are clearly major interests which, together with the

demonstration of US power and the need to control Saudi Arabia, provide more plausible reasons for bombing Afghanistan than notions of defending civilisation. Yet these issues continue to receive little attention, the media generally preferring to play along with the Official Story of our wondrous benevolence.

3

EXPLAINING THE 'WAR AGAINST TERRORISM'

The sources of instability that affect our fundamental interests . . . are often driven more by how we, our allies and partners choose to react to particular crises, rather than the crises themselves.

House of Commons Defence Committee

The new cold war

Presenting dark threats to our way of life has long been a key way for elites to secure their goals. Stephen Dorril notes in his huge, comprehensive history of MI6 that 'the modern intelligence service's prime purpose appears to be to generate fears'. We might say the same of the world's leading governments more generally. US Defence Secretary Donald Rumsfeld describes the current official fear: 'the single greatest threat to peace and freedom in our time is terrorism'. He continues:

Today, the world does face a new threat to peace and freedom. It's not an Adolf Hitler, fascism. It's not communism. But it's one that can be as destructive as any – or all, for that matter – and one that has implications for the future that are every bit as momentous as those that we have faced in the past.[1]

The previous major official threat was from the Soviet Union during the cold war. While this threat was real in some cases, it was hugely exaggerated, and in some instances deliberately fabricated. The 'Soviet threat' served four main purposes: it provided a pretext for Western military intervention and covert action abroad as 'defence' against Soviet expansion; it allowed repressive governments to be supported on the excuse that they were bulwarks against communism; it allowed clampdowns on domestic dissent to take place by referring to infiltration by the enemy; and it allowed huge profits to be made by military industry, which produced the weapons demanded by a permanent arms race.

The Soviets used the Western threat for similar purposes. They justified their grip on Eastern Europe by saying they were protecting those countries from Western invasion and locked up political opponents by saying they were imperialist agents.

In reality, as many of the chapters in this book show, the real threat to the US and Britain in the postwar period came not from communism or the Soviet Union but from nationalist forces within developing countries. The principal 'threat' they posed was to Western control over their economic resources – the fear that a country's resources might be primarily used to benefit its people. Nationalist movements and governments were invariably labelled as communist to justify action against them. All US interventions until the invasion of Panama in 1989, and many British interventions, were justified as defending the free world from Soviet expansion.

Many features of the 'war against terrorism' mirror those of the cold war. Principally, it provides a convenient pretext for a new phase of US global intervention, backed by Britain. Almost anyone can be labelled a sponsor of terrorism and subject to US attack or other forms of US involvement in the country's internal affairs. As in the cold war, the US has divided the world into those who are with it, and those against, offering rewards and punishments as appropriate. 'Against such an enemy' as global terrorism, President Bush says, 'there can be no neutrality'.[2]

The message to Western publics is, as in the cold war, unless we do what our leaders say, we will all be incinerated: unless we confront global terrorism 'the gathering storm of terrorism will unleash its fury on us all', Donald Rumsfeld explains. 'We now know that thousands of trained killers are plotting to attack us', Bush has told Americans. Blair tells the British public the same thing, as the number of threat stories increases. As noted in chapter 1, some are apparent fabrications such as the story of an imminent gas attack on the London underground. These stories of impending doom are intended to frighten the public into giving our leaders a free hand in doing whatever it takes to destroy the ruthless enemy that seeks to kill us.[3]

The new war also gives repressive regimes (especially those allied to the West) a major pretext for clamping down on opposition groups and general dissent. It is being used by Western states themselves to counter their own domestic enemies, like asylum seekers, and to curb civil liberties. Also, like the cold war, the new war has promising consequences for arms manufacturers who will gain from increases in military spending.

The new war conveniently serves a specific purpose for the presidency of George Bush. Floundering before, with a more than shaky domestic mandate, the Bush administration seized on the new threat to pursue its conservative domestic and foreign agenda. Soon after the September 11th attacks the *Wall Street Journal* called on Bush to take advantage quickly of the 'unique political climate' to 'assert his leadership not just on security and foreign policy but across the board'. As the political scientist Thorstein Veblen wrote nearly a century ago:

> Sensational appeals to patriotic pride and animosity made by victories and defeats . . . [help] direct the popular interest to other, nobler institutionally less hazardous matters than the unequal distribution of

wealth or of other creature comforts. Warlike and patriotic preoccupations fortify the barbarian virtues of subordination and prescriptive authority.[4]

Since the collapse of the Soviet Union, there has been no obvious global threat against which the US can be seen to be 'defending' itself. US planners have done their best to deem a few rogue regimes, a few drug traffickers and, before Al Qaida, a few terrorists, as new threats. But these threats have been isolated, more easily containable, and have lacked a *global* presence that can be presented as a *systematic* threat to the West as a whole. But Al Qaida, like the Russian hordes, can surely be presented as threatening everything we hold dear, which is precisely its utility. This threat is enhanced by having an Islamic cause since, in much Western discourse, Islam and terrorism are virtually interchangeable anyway.

The list of target countries in the new war is global. 'Afghanistan is just the beginning', Bush roared to an audience of soldiers in November 2001. US Vice President Richard Cheney said at the same time that forty to fifty countries could be targeted for diplomatic, financial or military action. Secretary of State Colin Powell says that 'every nation is threatened by terrorism'. Cuba was accused by senior State Department official John Bolton of developing biological weapons, in propaganda so obvious as to be comical. He said Cuba should understand that states that fail to renounce terror and weapons of mass destruction 'can expect to become our target'. Iran also fits the bill; Defence Secretary Donald Rumsfeld has said that Iran is 'sheltering Al Qaida fighters who fled Afghanistan'.[5]

Richard Perle, a key Bush foreign policy advisor, has said that:

> This is total war. We are fighting a variety of enemies. There are lots of them out there . . . If we just let our vision of the world go forth, and we embrace it entirely, and we don't try to piece together clever diplomacy but just wage a total war, our children will sing great songs about us years from now.[6]

The message we are meant to receive is that the 'war against terrorism' is worldwide and long-lasting. 'The war against terrorists of global reach is a global enterprise of uncertain duration', the White House's National Security Strategy states. Bush warns that 'they may strike anywhere, and therefore we have got to be prepared to use our military and all the other assets at our disposal to keep the peace'.

NATO Secretary General, George Robertson, adds, helpfully: 'there is a common enemy out there'. This is while cosying up to a Russian president guilty of more terror (in Chechnya) than Al Qaida could dream of.[7]

Following the Afghanistan war the US can present the terrorist threat as having *increased*, since Al Qaida was dispersed rather than destroyed. One US official has said that 'what we're seeing now is a radical international jihad that will be a potent force for many years to come'. This is quite possibly true and was entirely predictable. Thus the predictable outcome of the immoral and devastating onslaught in Afghanistan is providing the pretext for the US to continue the same policies elsewhere.[8] It is obvious who benefits from this cycle and who therefore has interests in wheeling its spokes.

Indeed, the US National Security Strategy conveniently states that 'today's security environment' is '*more* complex and dangerous' than it was during the cold war. Interestingly, it also states that in the cold war 'we faced a generally status quo, risk-averse adversary'. This was not exactly the official line at the time, as Western publics were bludgeoned into fearing Soviet control of the world as they paid out billions to maintain 'defences' against the Russian hordes. Now that this propaganda is no longer useful, it can be discarded and the reality emerges, while propagandists move on to current official enemies.[9]

The war against terrorism is real in the sense that some groups do pose challenges to US power. And the threat of terrorism is certainly real to its civilian victims, not just in the US but in Bali, Mombasa and elsewhere as well. But the US 'response' to Al Qaida terrorism (not the correct word, given that US, and British, policy has helped to create it) is certainly not the moral one leaders claim, nor aimed principally at eradicating terrorism. It is also obvious that the states leading the new war are among the leading sponsors of terrorism, if we include the state-sponsored variety, which is far more widespread and destructive. This applies not only to the US and Britain – supporters of many of the world's worst regimes – but also Saudi Arabia, traditionally the great financier of extreme Islamic groups.

My view is that it may not work – the new threat may be easily seen through or just not materialise enough over the longer term to be of use. On the other hand, the same could have been said of the 'Soviet threat'. The absence of a major Soviet role in many areas where the US intervened (such as Nicaragua or Vietnam) was so obvious that it was truly amazing the US was able to deploy it as a pretext. Clearly, the role of the propaganda system was critical then and will be in the future.

The new interventionism

The US has already used the 'war against terrorism' to secure a major new presence in oil-rich Central Asia. In December 2001 the US Assistant Secretary of State, Elizabeth Jones, said that 'when the Afghan conflict is over we will not leave central Asia. We have long-term plans and interests in this region.' Since September 11th the US has established new bases in Uzbekistan, Tajikistan, Kyrgystan and Georgia and now has thirteen bases in nine countries ringing Afghanistan and the Gulf.[10] The US Army War College study, noted in the previous chapter, urging the US to secure a military presence in Central Asia to control oil supplies and counter Russia, has effectively been put into place.

A Kazakh government source has been quoted as saying that 'it is clear that the continuing war in Afghanistan is no more than a veil for the US to establish political dominance in the region. The war on terrorism is only a pretext for extending influence over our energy resources'.[11]

US military advisers and forces have been sent to the Philippines, Nepal, Georgia, Djibouti (for use in Yemen), and Sudan (for action in Somalia). By mid 2002, the US had 1,600 troops on a six-month deployment in the Philippines, to train troops in countering the separatist Muslim armed group, Abu Sayyaf. This deployment reintroduces a US military presence in a country from which US forces were expelled a decade ago (it also violates the Philippine constitution, which requires a treaty to be signed to establish foreign military bases). Ever since the Philippines senate refused to extend the US bases agreement in 1991, the US has been seeking to re-establish a permanent presence.[12]

US advisers have also been sent to Nepal to help the government defeat an insurgency by Maoist guerillas who declared a 'people's war' in 1996. Britain is also providing helicopters, communications equipment and training in setting up a 'military intelligence support group' with the Nepalese army. British aid to Nepal has in effect been given covertly, bypassing parliamentary scrutiny and using an obscure government 'global conflict prevention' fund.

Britain is aiding Nepal during a massive increase in violence by the army, with widespread torture, 'disappearances', the suspension of civil rights, the censorship of newspapers and arrests of hundreds of people without trial. Most of the killings have been perpetrated by those now being aided by Britain. Nepal government figures show that from 1996 to 2002, 3,290 rebels were killed by government forces while 1,360 police and army personnel and civilians were killed by the rebels.[13] The root of the insurgency lies in the failure of successive Nepalese governments to alleviate the grinding poverty of the country's rural population and to introduce land reforms long demanded by the poor. These factors explain the Maoists' popular support in many rural areas.

The British government argues that the Nepal government's struggle should be seen as part of the wider 'war against terrorism'; at the same time, Britain admits there is no evidence linking the Maoists to Al Qaida or any other external terrorist group.[14] As in the cold war, no evidence is required to support elite assertions, the mere fact of saying them is sufficient. 'Al Qaida' is now blamed for every terror and outrage, even if no evidence is presented of links to the group. It is clear that in Anglo-American official-speak, 'Al Qaida' is becoming a semantic construction designating any group that violently opposes elite interests.

The 'war against terrorism' is providing the cover for a new phase in US and British military intervention overseas. US leaders now say that 'our best defence is a good offence' and speak of 'destroying the threat before it reaches our borders'. In this, 'we will not hesitate to act alone . . . by acting preemptively against such terrorists'. The US will therefore continue to develop 'long-range precision strike capabilities and transformed manoeuvre and expeditionary forces'. US strategy is 'to project military power over long distances' with forces 'capable of insertion far from traditional ports and air bases'. US forces need to be able 'to impose the will of the United States and its coalition partners on any adversaries', including by 'occupation of foreign territory until US strategic objectives are met'. The US 'targeted killings' of six 'Al Qaida suspects' in Yemen by an unmanned CIA plane and a proposed new NATO rapid response force that would operate without the permission of the host nation, are part of the same new, imperial strategy.[15]

Along with such power projection goes 'effective public diplomacy', that is, propaganda, and 'a different and more comprehensive approach to public information efforts' that can help people to 'understand America'. And a major goal for the US in all this is ensuring global 'free markets and free trade' which are 'key priorities of our national security strategy'.[16]

British forces have in recent years been quietly reconfigured from an ostensibly defensive role to an overtly *offensive* one. Since there are no major threats to the homeland, Britain now has a 'new focus on expeditionary warfare', the all-party House of Commons Defence Committee comments approvingly. This emphasis on power projection overseas was occurring well before September 11th and was already the major feature of the government's 'strategic defence review' (SDR), concluded in 1998. September 11th has made an overt focus on military intervention overseas – a key feature of Blair's outlaw state – easier to justify.

The SDR stated that 'in the post cold war world, we must be prepared to go to the crisis, rather than have the crisis come to us'. 'For the next decade at least, the direct air defence of the UK will be a lower priority.' 'Long range air attack' will continue to be important 'as an integral part of warfighting and as a coercive instrument to support political objectives'.[17]

This 'coercive instrument' is the modern version of imperial 'gunboat diplomacy', a polite way of saying that Britain will issue military threats to countries failing to do what we (probably really meaning the US) want. Foreign Office minister Denis MacShane similarly told the Royal College of Defence Studies in 2002 that 'foreign policy and military capability go hand in hand', and that 'to have been able to order a destroyer to head for East Timor reinforces what our Ambassador says to the authorities in Jakarta where a power vacuum exists'.[18] MacShane is here claiming a benign example of the use of 'coercive diplomacy'. This use of military power to back up 'what our Ambassador says' is surely a strategy that Saddam Hussein (or Hitler) would well understand. It would be interesting to see the reaction of planners and commentators if, say, Iran were to announce that in future its foreign policy were to be backed up by 'military capability'.

British aircraft carriers 'can also offer a coercive presence which may forestall the need for warfighting, as recently in the Gulf', according to the SDR. And 'all ten attack submarines will . . . be equipped to fire Tomahawk land attack missiles to increase their utility in force projection operations'. Tomahawk cruise missiles entered service in 1998, representing 'a major step forward in capability, enabling precision attacks to be undertaken at long range against selected targets, with a minimal risk to our own forces', Defence minister John Spellar explained.[19]

The SDR goes on to outline the 'new generation of military equipment' that will be needed for this enhanced power projection, including attack helicopters, long-range precision munitions, digitised command and control systems, a new generation of aircraft carriers, submarines and escorts, the Eurofighter multi-role warplane and the development of a successor to the Tornado bomber.[20]

This is all before September 11th. By then, Blair's military interventionism had already been quite extraordinary. Post-September 11th, a Foreign Office minister referred to 'an effective doctrine of early warning and where necessary early intervention'. Foreign Secretary Jack Straw has said that 'our aim must be to develop a clear strategy to head off threats to global order and to deal with the consequences within the evolving framework of international law'. Translated, this means that Britain will conduct military interventions to preserve Western supremacy ('global order') while defying international law, and trying to change it, to make such intervention easier, as noted in chapter 1.[21]

The Defence Committee notes that 'we must . . . be free to deploy significant forces overseas rapidly', and calls for 'pre-emptive military action'. Similar to the US view, almost all areas of the world, it appears, could be the focus of British intervention. The Defence Committee states that:

> The implications of an open-ended war on terrorism – particularly one that will address the problems of collapsing and failed states which create the political space for terror and crime networks to operate – suggest that operations in central Asia, East Africa, perhaps the Indian subcontinent and elsewhere, *will become necessary as part of an integrated political and military strategy to address terrorism and the basis on which it flourishes.*[22]

An intellectual framing for the new phase in global interventionism comes from Robert Cooper, a senior British diplomat picked by Blair to be Britain's special envoy in Afghanistan. He argues for 'a new kind of imperialism, one acceptable to a world of human rights and cosmopolitan values' which 'aims to bring order and organisation'. It should be directed principally at 'failed states', countries where governments no longer have the monopoly on the use of force, or where this risk is high. Examples include Chechnya, other areas of the former Soviet Union, all of the world's major drug-producing areas, 'upcountry Burma', some parts of South America, and all of Africa. 'No area of the world is without its dangerous cases', Cooper states.[23]

The new interventionism's demands for new weapons systems is also a great boon for the arms corporations, another factor which explains elite enthusiasm for the project. September 11th itself was profitable. 'This event [is] all good things for the defence industry', commented Richard Aboulafia, senior military analyst with the Teal Group, a military consultancy, one week after September 11th. The *Economist* noted that 'as always, war is good for the makers of military hardware, and the shares of defence contractors have been soaring since the attack'. Within a few weeks of September 11th, shares in Lockheed Martin, the second largest US arms company, rose by more than 30 per cent, shares in BAE systems rose by 7 per cent, Northrop Grumman by 32 per cent and Raytheon by 40 per cent.

British companies will also profit from Bush's massive military spending increases – the biggest in twenty years, meaning that the US alone will account for 40 per cent of global military spending. BAE Systems already sells more to the Pentagon than to the Ministry of Defence, so the increases on the other side of the Atlantic will earn nice profits for some on this side.[24]

Meanwhile, the House of Commons Defence Committee and others have been calling for increases in British military spending. In July 2002, the government obliged. Gordon Brown announced an extra £1 billion a year in the military budget, the biggest increase since the cold war ended, to counter the 'urgent moral challenge' of international terrorism.[25]

The new interventionism also include a role for nuclear weapons. The US is building an arsenal of smaller nuclear weapons ('mini-nukes') for use on the battlefield. A classified Pentagon report leaked to the media identified plans to wage nuclear war against seven countries – China, Russia, Iraq, North Korea, Iran, Libya and Syria – as well as in an Arab-Israeli conflict. The US has also reversed a previous policy that it would not use nuclear weapons against states that did not possess them – now, no states are ruled out.[26]

The British government has matched the US, in a reversal of past Labour and Conservative policy. Now, Defence Secretary Geoff Hoon has stated that Britain should be prepared to use nuclear weapons even against non-nuclear states, and if British forces were attacked with chemical or biological weapons. Countries are also likely to be threatened with nuclear annihilation; Britain delivered threats to Iraq in both 1991 and 1998, saying that it would use nuclear weapons in response to Iraqi use of chemical or biological weapons. Britain also continues to refuse to adopt a 'no first use' pledge on nuclear weapons, Labour quietly dropping this previous manifesto commitment after the 1997 general election.[27]

The Blair government apparently sees nuclear weapons as war fighting weapons, not simply as a deterrent, as the myth has it. Trident has a 'sub-strategic' role, meaning it is intended for use on the battlefield as well as to deter an all-out nuclear exchange. Malcolm Rifkind, Defence Secretary under Thatcher, asserted that because the threat of an all-out nuclear assault might not be 'credible', it was important to 'undertake a more limited nuclear strike' to deliver 'an unmistakeable message of our willingness to defend our vital interests to the utmost'. The Blair government similarly says that 'the credibility of deterrence . . . depends on retaining the option for a limited nuclear strike'. Geoff Hoon said in March 2002 that 'I am absolutely confident, in the right conditions, we would be willing to use our nuclear weapons.' He publicly repeated Britain's willingness to use nuclear weapons three times in one month in early 2002.[28]

The government even says in the SDR that nuclear weapons are to deter '*any* threat to our vital interests'. Such 'vital interests' include not only Britain's survival but its international trade and dependence on 'foreign countries for supplies of raw materials, including oil'.[29]

The Labour government keeps one nuclear submarine on patrol at all times, with forty-eight nuclear warheads. This is called the 'minimum necessary' to provide for Britain's 'security'. It is an argument that anyone – perhaps Saddam Hussein – might use for acquiring nuclear weapons, in fact with more reason, given a greater likelihood of being attacked (that is, by us).

The government has no intention whatsoever of abolishing its nuclear weapons, even though all nuclear weapons states are required to move towards disarmament under the Non-Proliferation Treaty. While paying lip service to this treaty, the government is actively defying it. In late 1998, a draft resolution was under discussion at the UN called 'Towards a nuclear weapons free world: The need for a new agenda'. The government said that 'we oppose the current draft of this resolution . . . since it is inconsistent with maintaining a credible nuclear deterrent'. Meanwhile, it says it wants Trident to remain in service for thirty years and that 'we intend to . . . design and produce a successor to Trident should this prove necessary'. And it is also developing a new generation of 'mini-nukes' in a massive £2 billion project.[30]

This is occurring at a time when Iraq is targeted for destruction by the US and its junior partner supposedly for attempting to acquire weapons of mass destruction.

Britain displayed its customary attitude to international law following the Advisory Opinion of the International Court of

Justice in 1996. This stated that the threat or use of nuclear weapons would generally be contrary to the rules of international law. Conservative Defence minister Nicholas Soames said that 'we do not believe the court's advisory opinions will have any implications' for British policy.[31] Neither does the most recent government of the outlaw state.

Curbing domestic enemies

The 'war against terrorism' is also providing a pretext for states, usually Western allies, to crack down on internal dissent. In chapter 10, I outline how British foreign policy is largely based on supporting elites who promote British and Western interests, especially commercial interests. These favoured elites are regularly brutal and repressive of demands for greater political participation and human rights. Britain, contrary to myth, generally sides with the elites against more democratic forces. The new war is a new-found ally in this process.

According to Human Rights Watch, 'the anti-terror campaign led by the United States is inspiring opportunistic attacks on civil liberties around the world'. Countries such as Russia, Uzbekistan, China, India and Egypt 'are using the war on terror to justify abusive military campaigns or crackdowns on domestic political opponents'.[32]

Russian President Vladimir Putin has embraced the 'war against terrorism' to defend Russian brutality in Chechnya while Britain and the US have virtually abandoned even the pretence of concern for the plight of Chechens, as outlined in chapter 7. The Chinese government has similarly used 'anti-terrorism' to pursue new draconian and often brutal measures to counter political agitation in Xinjiang province. Israeli Prime Minister Ariel Sharon, meanwhile, has referred to Arafat as 'our Bin Laden'.[33]

US military aid to repressive regimes has been significantly stepped up since September 11th. Tajikistan has been rewarded for its support of the new war by the US lifting an eight-year arms ban. Uzbekistan, a truly gruesome dictatorship, is receiving $43 million in military aid, while the Philippines is to get $100 million. Sanctions imposed on Pakistan and India for conducting nuclear tests have been lifted and US military cooperation with Indonesia has been extended. Overall, the US arms export process has been made easier.[34]

Western governments are similarly using the 'war against terrorism' to curb civil liberties and erode international law. Britain has been leading the international community in promoting a legal definition of terrorism that may stifle domestic political dissent. According to Amnesty International, the UK's Terrorism Act of 2000 'may contravene UK obligations under international human rights law' in terms of the rights to liberty, a fair trial and freedom of association. Plotting the overthrow of a foreign government from Britain became a criminal offence – meaning surely that Blair should immediately lock himself up, given his plans for Saddam.

On seeking to curb the rights of asylum seekers, Britain has been surpassed only by Australia. Australian Prime Minister John Howard built his candidacy for re-election in November 2001 around his summary expulsion of asylum seekers who had reached Australia, in blatant violation of international refugee law.[35]

Human Rights Watch has issued a challenge to the US and its allies in the 'war against terrorism', saying that 'they must decide whether this battle provides an opportunity to reaffirm human rights principles or a new reason to ignore them'. 'Unfortunately, the coalition's conduct so far has not been auspicious . . . Its leading members have violated human rights principles at home and overlooked human rights transgressions among their partners'. Human Rights Watch then says:

> In Egypt, Saudi Arabia and many of the other countries where Osama Bin Laden strikes a chord of resentment, governments restrict debate about how to address

society's ills. They close off avenues for peaceful political change. They leave people with the desperate choice of tolerating the status quo, exile, or violence . . . The West has quietly accepted this pattern of repression because, in the short term, it seems to promise stability, and because the democratic alternative is feared. In an environment in which the political centre has been systematically silenced, these governments can credibly portray themselves as the only bulwark against extremism.

Although the correlation is not always neat, these experiences suggest that the appeal of violent and intolerant movements diminishes as people are given the chance to participate meaningfully in politics and to select from a range of political parties and perspectives . . . But if the West continues to accept repression as the best defence against radical politics, it will undermine the human rights culture that is needed in the long run to defeat terrorism.[36]

However, the US and Britain are not only tolerating, but in many cases actively promoting, the repressive policies of favoured elites. The long-term consequences may be immense.

But there are good reasons for this strategy to continue, seen from the perspective of US and British elites. The context is one where many parts of the Islamic world are offering serious resistance to US global hegemony, whether economic or military. Islamic radical forces are the major barriers to total US domination of the Middle East. As in Egypt, the 'war against terrorism' is a new pretext for rolling back further the greatest sources of resistance to US power within many Middle Eastern countries. The new war may therefore be seen as a way of helping to contain and control the Islamic world – a surely naïve and dangerous view, as it is more likely to generate more violent opposition.

Defence Secretary Donald Rumsfeld explains that the US has

to do what it can 'to encourage the moderate Muslim voices' who 'aspire to enjoy the blessings of freedom and democracy and free enterprise'. 'One possible model for the aspirations of the Muslim world for democratic progress and prosperity', Rumsfeld continues, is Turkey – a country that has killed, displaced and repressed hundreds of thousands of its citizens in the past decade. Rumsfeld also describes the 'larger war' beyond that against terrorism, a 'battle of ideas' to show that 'free markets and open societies do improve lives'.[37]

Both US and British ministers have tried to use the 'war against terrorism' for still other purposes. For example, both US Trade Representative Robert Zoellick and Britain's Trade Secretary Patricia Hewitt have tried to push their agenda of ever greater trade 'liberalisation' on developing countries by saying that we should 'fight terror with trade' (see also chapter 9) – surely showing, at least, that the promotion of the 'war against terrorism' has a truly comical side. At the ministerial meeting of the World Trade Organisation in Qatar two months after September 11th, the US and the EU, led by Britain, tried to add new policy areas to the WTO's trade rules. This was in the face of opposition from almost all developing countries. This agenda – to achieve new global agreements on investment and government procurement – aims to open up more areas of national economies to control by Western transnational corporations. Promoting global 'free trade' is identified by the US as a key part of its global 'security' strategy, alongside the 'war against terrorism' and part of the 'battle of ideas' referred to by Donald Rumsfeld.

It is clear that the 'war against terrorism' is a key part of promoting traditional US foreign policy aims. Its goal is to achieve through military and political intervention what global economic 'liberalisation' (see chapter 9) aims to achieve through economic policy – continued US supremacy in the global system, intended to benefit US elites, transnational businesses and allies closest to the US.

The primary threats to be countered in this strategy are

independent forces acting as barriers to US domination. These are mainly radical Islamic groups and enemy governments, in the case of the 'war against terrorism'; states pursuing economic strategies independently of the US and the multilateral institutions, in the case of the 'global liberalisation' project; and also the 'anti-globalisation' movement that is mobilising public opinion towards alternatives in the global economy.

This strategy is all very dangerous, in my view. The 'war against terrorism' is already creating new enemies, making the world a more insecure place, and curbing our own rights in democratic societies. And it is a myth that increases in military spending make us more secure; the opposite is the case. As one British Ministry of Defence official has noted, it is 'because of Western conventional dominance that state adversaries will use unconventional means'.[38]

The US and Britain helped to create the globalisation of terrorism in the first place, by funding and training a generation of fighters for action in Afghanistan. The current priorities in US and British foreign policy are surely creating their own future monsters.

A British parliamentary committee recently noted that 'the sources of instability that affect our fundamental interests . . . are often driven more by how we, our allies and partners, choose to react to particular crises, rather than the crises themselves'.[39] The major threats to us, the public, come more from our own policy-makers than from the official threat.

The other face of terrorism

Huge media attention is being paid to the Al Qaida network and other terrorist groups and their gruesome deeds. But there is one category of terrorism that is excluded from this debate. There is a much simpler way of countering some terrorism, at least, and that is by changing policy closer to home. If we were honest and serious, this is where the 'war against terrorism' might begin.

During the onslaught against Afghanistan, Britain's Chief of Defence Staff, Admiral Sir Michael Boyce, said that the bombing will continue 'until the people of the country themselves recognise that this is going to go on until they get the leadership changed'. Boyce was echoing Tony Blair during the Kosovo war. Two weeks into the bombing of Yugoslavia in April 1999, Blair said that 'we will carry on pounding day after day after day, until our objectives are secured'.[40]

These comments in two wars fit very well with the British government's definition of terrorism:

> Terrorism is the use, or threat, of action which is violent, damaging or disrupting and is intended to influence the government or intimidate the public and is for the purpose of advancing a political, religious or ideological cause.[41]

The recent onslaught against Afghanistan, together with the previous strikes against that country and Sudan, and now the bombing of Iraq, shows that the recent phase of US and British global intervention, under the cover of a 'war against terrorism', is in effect involving a war of terrorism by those claiming to defend the highest values. There is nothing surprising in this. The US has a long history of practising terrorism and supporting states conducting it.

US attacks against Nicaragua in the 1980s, condemned by the International Court of Justice, fall into this category, as does CIA training of contra guerillas in terrorist activities. The US currently harbours Cubans attacking Cuba and human rights abusers like Emmanuel Constant, the leader of paramilitary forces in Haiti responsible for thousands of murders in the early 1990s, whose extradition the US is refusing. The notorious US army training school in Fort Benning, Georgia, known best as the School of the Americas, trained dozens of Latin American military officers who went on to become their countries' worst killers. US training of the mojahidin in a variety of assassination techniques was noted in the previous chapter.

One of the major terrorist acts of the 1980s was the car bombing in Beirut in March 1985. The bomb was placed outside a mosque timed to explode when worshippers left, and was aimed at killing Sheikh Fadlallah, the Shia leader accused of complicity in terrorism. Around eighty people were killed, including women and children, and over two hundred wounded, while Fadlallah escaped. The bombing was organised by the CIA and Saudi agents with the assistance of Britain's MI6.[42]

The idea that Britain is a supporter of terrorism is an oxymoron in the mainstream political culture, as ridiculous as suggesting that Tony Blair should be indicted for war crimes. Yet state-sponsored terrorism is by far the most serious category of terrorism in the world today, responsible for far more deaths in many more countries than the 'private' terrorism of groups like Al Qaida. Many of the worst offenders are key British allies. Indeed, by any rational consideration, Britain is one of the leading supporters of terrorism in the world today. But this simple fact is never mentioned in the mainstream political culture. The official 'war against terrorism' is being framed according to elite priorities, excluding a large chunk of reality from public awareness.

I consider state-sponsored atrocities backed by Britain in several chapters in this book. They include Russia, Israel, Saudi Arabia and Turkey, all of whom have escaped significant international censure partly due to British protection of them. Russia – an extraordinarily close British ally under Putin – is worthy of particular note, given not only its gross brutality in Chechnya but also the evidence that its security forces may have been involved in bombing apartment blocks in Moscow, as noted in chapter 7. There is a litany of further examples of past British support for the world's very worst regimes. For example, Britain was happy to count Iraq under Saddam and Iran under the Shah as allies in the 1980s while they assassinated political opponents in the West, including in Britain itself, not to mention British support for Baghdad during the atrocities committed against Kurds in northern Iraq.

Britain has also traditionally been the chief apologist for US terrorism around the world. As outlined in the next chapter, Britain consistently supported US violence against Nicaragua and also, contrary to myth, largely in Vietnam. London also offered reflexive support to the US raid on Libya in 1986 as easily as it did for the US strikes against Sudan and Afghanistan in 1998, all acts of terrorism under most definitions of the term.

Further, a long history has been buried. British government involvement in assassinating foreign leaders is virtually an elite tradition. The best-known assassination attempts were against Egyptian president Nasser in the mid-1950s, an independent nationalist regime that threatened British power in the Middle East. In one attempt, MI6 injected poison into chocolates destined for Nasser, but they failed in the end to reach him. Nerve gas, an SAS hit squad and firing a poisoned dart from a cigarette packet were considered but either rejected or stalled.

There is also evidence that MI6 planned the assassinations of Indonesian president Sukarno in the 1950s, Ugandan president Milton Obote in 1969, Albanian President Enver Hoxha in 1948 and Cypriot guerilla leader Colonel Grivas in the late 1950s. According to Kenneth Younger, a Foreign Office minister in the Attlee government and a former senior MI5 officer, Britain also gave serious thought to assassinating the Mufti of Jerusalem and Indian nationalist leader, Chandra Bose. These did not proceed to the planning stage because 'nothing would be gained by making martyrs of such people'.[43]

In 1998, Archbishop Desmond Tutu revealed recently uncovered letters from South Africa's Truth and Reconciliation Commission that implicated British, US and South African agents in the death of UN Secretary-General Dag Hammarskjold in 1961. Hammarskjold died when his plane exploded before landing in Rhodesia on a trip to mediate a peace agreement between Congo and the breakaway province of Katanga. The letters described meetings between MI5, the CIA and a South African military front company and plans to place TNT in the wheel bay of the aircraft.[44]

Former MI6 officer, Richard Tomlinson, revealed that MI6 also planned an assassination attempt against Yugoslav president Slobodan Milosevic. Conceived in 1992, MI6 put forward three options in a paper entitled 'The need to assassinate President Milosevic of Serbia'. These were: to train a Serbian paramilitary group to carry out the assassination; to send in an SAS team to kill him with a bomb or sniper ambush; or to kill him in a road crash to be staged during a visit to Geneva, such as by disorienting Milosevic's chauffeur using a blinding strobe light as the cavalcade passed through one of Geneva's motorway tunnels. It appears that the plan was not carried out. As noted in chapter 6, NATO aircraft specifically targeted Milosevic for assassination during the Kosovo war.[45]

Britain set up pseudo-terrorist 'counter gangs' in Palestine in the 1940s and Aden in the 1960s, consisting of former terrorists and loyal tribesmen (in the case of Aden) led by British officers disguised as locals. They were sent out in twos and threes to target those suspected of terrorism against British and local targets. In Palestine the squads were given a free hand to kill Jewish terrorists seeking an end to British rule and were 'able to adopt methods close to those adopted by the Jewish terrorists, but such methods quickly became a political embarrassment', Stephen Dorril notes. In the mid 1960s, an MI6 officer noted that his organisation was helping to train local security services in the Middle East to detect threats to their regimes and arranging where required their 'neutralisation' by 'surrogates'. 'Killer squads' were also used in the colonial war in Malaya.[46]

Former SAS officers have also conducted terrorism. Veterans often maintain contact with the government and unofficially promote British policy, as when former SAS officers trained the Afghan mojahidin with the clearance of the

Foreign Office. As one SAS officer once noted, the SAS is 'the only agency whose job is to go out and zap people'. In the 1950s and 1960s, many former SAS officers were recruited by the racist Rhodesian regime's Central Intelligence Organisation. Some ran a campaign of bombings and assassinations in Zambia against Rhodesian nationalists in the 1970s, including assassination attempts on Robert Mugabe.[47]

The London connection

The media's burying of the past and present British role in supporting terrorism is all the more amazing in the light of recent revelations about Libya and Northern Ireland.

Former MI5 officer David Shayler first alleged in 1998 that there was British support for an assassination attempt against Colonel Qadafi. Then, in February 2000, a secret MI6 cable was leaked and published on the internet. The cable, dated December 1995, revealed MI6's knowledge of an attempt to overthrow Qadafi in a coup scheduled for February 1996. 'The coup plotters would launch a direct attack on Qadafi and would either arrest him or kill him', the cable stated. 'One officer and twenty men were being trained especially for this attack' while the coup plotters had obtained 250 British pistols. 'The coup plotters expected to establish control of Libya at the end of March 1996', they would form an interim government and 'would want rapprochement with the West'.

The cable also recognised that the coup plotters 'had some limited contact with the fundamentalists, whom a military officer described as a mix of Libyan veterans who served in Afghanistan and Libyan students'. The leader of the coup plotters was Abdal Muhaymeen, 'a veteran of the Afghan resistance who was possibly trained by MI6 or the CIA', Dorril comments. A recent book by two French authors, *Bin Laden: The Forbidden Truth*, claims that MI6 was in contact with 'Osama Bin Laden's main allies' in the plot.[48]

This coup plot went ahead, but failed to kill Qadafi, instead killing six innocent bystanders. Shayler asserts that the coup plotters were funded by MI6. He states that:

> We need to know how around £100,000 of taxpayers' money was used to fund the sort of Islamic extremists who have connections to Osama Bin Laden's al Qaida network ... By the time MI6 paid the group in late 1995 or early 1996, US investigators had already established that Bin Laden was implicated in the 1993 attack on the World Trade Center. Given the timing and the close connections between Libyan and Egyptian Islamic extremists, it may even have been used to fund the murder of British citizens in Luxor, Egypt, in 1996.[49]

The British establishment has naturally denied all involvement in the coup/assassination. Robin Cook said that the story was 'pure fantasy'. But the Metropolitan Police appear to believe otherwise, and began an investigation into the case, presumably believing there was sufficient prima facie evidence. Meanwhile, Shayler has been hounded by the authorities and arrested while newspapers have been ordered by the government to hand over any material they have in relation to him.

Media coverage has been minimal given both the seriousness of the issue and that we are supposedly in the midst of a 'war against terrorism'. There was a BBC *Panorama* programme on the Qadafi plot and a spattering of press articles at specific times in 2000 and again in 2002, surrounding Shayler's court case. Aside from this, the story rarely surfaces and is simply never mentioned in the numerous articles on the 'war against terrorism'. I searched the parliament database to see if our elected representatives were interested in whether the government had engaged in terrorism, and found just four mentions of the plot to kill Qadafi – all in February 2000, when the leaked MI6 cable was revealed; nothing since.

Perhaps MPs could look at a speech in the House of Commons by Foreign Office minister Ben Bradshaw in March 2002. He said that 'there is no moral distinction between an attacker who kills civilians or parliamentarians and a state that wittingly provides the resources that facilitate such a terrorist attack'.[50] Quite right, and what could this possibly have to do with Britain?

Neither have journalists and parliamentarians allowed British involvement in assassinations in Northern Ireland to upset the view that Britain is purely devoted to fighting terrorism. There is a long history of British collusion with loyalist paramilitary groups in Northern Ireland engaging in 'targeted assassinations' of suspected IRA members. 'What we need to do is to use the methods the terrorists use in order to overcome [the IRA]', Northern Ireland Secretary James Prior said in 1981.[51]

The European Court of Justice ruled in May 2001 that Britain had violated 'the right to life' of eleven people killed by security forces and one person killed by a paramilitary group between 1982 and 1992. More revelations about the security forces' involvement in the murder of Belfast lawyer Pat Finucane emerged in the months following September 11th. The British army's Force Research Unit, the centre of covert collusion with paramilitary groups, is suspected of involvement in up to fifteen murders. These are the modern variants of the British death squads operating in Ireland during the Irish War of Independence. Then, police and soldiers in plain clothes were used to assassinate members and sympathisers of Sinn Fein.[52]

If Britain were currently serious about countering terrorism, perhaps it might also have arrested Henry Kissinger while he was visiting Britain in April 2002. French and Spanish judges were asking the British government to allow them to question Kissinger about his role in crimes against humanity in Chile under the Pinochet regime. The government declined. Amnesty International notes that 'as well as being a violation of the UK's obligation under the European Convention [on Human Rights], the reported refusal by the Home Office to cooperate with the French and Spanish authorities is inconsistent with its obligations under general principles of law' recognised by the UN.[53]

The Kissinger issue is perhaps a small indication of the government's strong commitment to avoid fighting terrorism when conducted by our allies. It also highlights the special relationship between London and Washington, to which we now turn.

4

BIG BROTHER, OUR FAVOURITE ALLY

> The world should be grateful that the most powerful nation in all history wields its military and economic might so benignly.
>
> The *Financial Times*, 30 December 2000

British elites have many special relationships, often with brutal regimes like those in Saudi Arabia, Turkey and Indonesia. Under Blair, London has also cultivated a markedly special relationship with Russia. Common among these relationships is British support for repressive ruling elites and effective backing for their crushing of internal dissent, through arms exports, trade relations, diplomatic support and apologias for human rights abuses. With the US, however, the special relationship with Britain is different in its core and defining principle.

The essence of this special relationship is British support for US aggression. It dates back to the end of the Second World War when British planners recognised their role of 'junior partner in an orbit of power predominantly under American aegis'.[1] The 'junior partner' role was adopted by British elites as a way of preserving some 'great power' status and of organising the global economy according to Western interests. The most recent phase under Blair shows the essence of the relationship to be not only alive and well but reaching new, quite extra-ordinary, depths.

The Washington–London axis is not only special to the two elites; it has been a pillar of world 'order' for over five decades. The two leading Western powers have, since 1945, colluded to shape the global economy and much of international affairs to their interests. The US has clearly led the strategy, which in the early postwar years meant replacing British power with its own, notably in the Middle East; the relationship has been a competitive as well as a collaborative one.

The British role in helping to shape world order according to US power – essentially imperial power – is usually under-estimated. It is Britain that plays the secondary role in supporting the family elites in the Gulf states, which maintains the traditional Middle East order and the global oil regime. It is Britain that is the loudest voice for promoting and deepening economic 'liberalisation' in the global economy, in order to benefit Western (in fact, primarily US and British) businesses. And it is Britain that often plays a secondary role to the US in shaping the parameters of action of the UN Security Council. Britain's role should not be overstated and its world influence has certainly declined over the past decades, but in these key ways Britain's foreign policies remain important to shaping the global order, essentially in alliance with the US.

This chapter presents a brief overview of some aspects of the special relationship. Other features necessarily run through the rest of this book – notably in the chapters on Iraq, Afghanistan, the war against terrorism and the Middle East.

British support for US aggression – the long history

Under Blair, history is repeating itself. There is a long history of British backing for US aggression and covert action – from the overthrow of the Guatemalan government in 1954 to the bombing of Libya in 1986 to the invasion of Panama in 1989, which I reviewed in a previous book, *The Ambiguities of Power*. I have covered other Anglo-US covert operations in other parts of this book – the 1953 overthrow of the Iranian government by MI6 and the CIA (see chapter 14) and joint complicity in the Indonesian bloodbath of 1965 (see chapter 20).

Britain sent troops to overthrow the democratically elected government of British Guiana in 1953 (see chapter 17), an intervention that was strongly backed by the US. The following year, Britain returned the favour by supporting the US overthrow of the government of Guatemala. The US organised and financed an invasion of the country to remove democratically elected President Jacobo Arbenz, under what was to become the usual pretext of the international communist threat. The reality was that Arbenz's land reform programme, which redistributed hundreds of thousands of acres to landless Guatemalan peasants, threatened the position of the country's largest landowner, the US-owned United Fruit Company.

With the invasion under way, Guatemala took complaints about US aggression to the UN. There, Britain (and France) aided Washington by abstaining on Guatemala's request for the Security Council to consider its complaints, and thus the request was rejected. This prompted President Eisenhower and Secretary of State Dulles to express satisfaction with the British 'willingness to cooperate in regard to the UN aspect' of US policy, saying that this cooperation had contributed to the 'happier situation in Guatemala'. With the threat of UN action removed, the US got on with removing the government.[2]

A new ruling junta took over, repealed the land reforms and the expropriation of United Fruit Company land, and eliminated the threat of independent, nationalist development. With Guatemala's popular democratic experiment overturned, the way was paved for a succession of regimes that ensured that wayward socio-economic priorities would not be pursued. These regimes' response to the popular movement seeking to reduce the grinding poverty of the majority was its physical extermination, amounting to around 100,000 deaths by government forces over the next four decades.

Britain publicly backed the US overthrow. The declassified files reveal that some British planners had some private misgivings about the way the US had removed Arbenz – that is, by organising an overt military invasion – but not the fact of it. The British position was that 'we should be happy to see Arbenz disappear but would not exert ourselves to remove him'. The Foreign Office noted:

> If the Americans had quietly worked for the overthrow of the Arbenz government, but nevertheless preserved the decencies of international justice, I think a different impression would have been left behind about the whole affair . . . We are glad Arbenz has gone, but, like Henry I with Becket, we do not like the circumstances attending his removal.[3]

This memorandum failed to elucidate how it was possible for the US to 'overthrow' the government while preserving international justice. Anthony Eden later recalled in his memoirs that:

> Anglo-American solidarity was of overriding importance to us and to the West as a whole. I believed that even if we did not entirely see eye to eye with the United States government in their treatment of the Guatemalan situation, we had an obligation as their principal ally to go as far as we could to help them.[4]

Jumping forward a decade, it is commonly believed that Britain failed to support the US war against Vietnam, and the official history is that British troops did not take part. It is true that Britain publicly refused to commit troops. But it did much else to back the US in its terrible onslaught.

In fact, Harold Wilson approved US requests for MI6 to help the US in Vietnam. Britain's SAS secretly took part in the war where they were attached to Australian and New Zealand SAS squads. An MI6 team of Malays and tribesmen from Borneo was also despatched on a tour of duty among ethnic Montagnards in South Vietnam.

Britain conducted secret air flights from Hong Kong to deliver arms, especially napalm and five-hundred-pound bombs. MI6 also assisted the Malayan government to transfer arms and other military supplies secretly to South Vietnam. British counter-insurgency experts were also seconded to Saigon as part of a British Advisory Mission. Some soldiers were seconded to Fort Bragg, home of the US special forces, and then inducted into the US army. Britain trained US, Vietnamese and Thai troops at its jungle warfare school in Malaya in the late 1960s, and for several years one of Britain's leading counter-insurgency experts, a veteran of the war in Malaya, advised the Nixon regime on Vietnam policy.

Britain's major contribution to the US was intelligence. This took various forms, including forwarding intelligence reports to the Americans from MI6 station heads in Hanoi. The British monitoring station at Little Sai Wan in Hong Kong provided the US with intelligence until 1975. The US National Security Agency coordinated all signals intelligence in Southeast Asia, and Little Sai Wan was linked to this operation. Its intercepts of North Vietnamese military traffic were used by the US military command to target bombing strikes over North Vietnam.[5]

At the diplomatic level, the Macmillan, Douglas-Home, Wilson and Heath governments all effectively supported the US war to varying degrees. Conservative governments were especially enthusiastic but Labour leaders were also consistently sympathetic to basic US objectives and most of its actions. Despite occasional criticism of some specific US military strikes, one will search in vain for British government statements questioning the US' basic right to conduct the war or questioning its supposed noble, moral motives. Britain often acted, as now, as an apologist for US atrocities. The Wilson government after 1964 refused to break with its ally even as the scale of US terror rose to unprecedented heights.

The myth that the South Vietnamese were being 'defended', and with the best US intentions, has been long-standing, and was often promoted by British governments. Prime Minister Douglas-Home, for example, informed the House of Commons in March 1964 that in recent talks with President Johnson 'I reaffirmed my support for United States policy which . . . is intended to help the Republic of Vietnam to protect its people and to preserve its independence.'

The US 'strategic hamlet' programme was intended to control the population and deprive the liberation movement of support – in the course of which Vietnamese peasants were herded with violence into thousands of villages surrounded by concentration-camp-style fortifications. The British saw this programme as a justifiable, defensive operation. 'The "strategic hamlet" programme', then Lord Privy Seal Edward Heath noted in 1963, 'is giving improved security to villagers and a chance to build up again the traditional system of Vietnamese village councils and communal activity.' The US was drawing on the British practice of 'villageisation' in Malaya that was equally brutal (see chapter 16); a British expert served as an adviser during the US version in Vietnam.[6]

The aggressor in Vietnam was never regarded as the US, by definition. In 1962, as US aircraft were bombing South Vietnam and spraying chemical defoliants over the Vietnamese countryside, the British Foreign Office minister could still state that 'the threat to peace in Vietnam does not arise from United States action but from the policies of the North Vietnam government'.

In March 1965 Harold Wilson could state: 'We fully support the action of the United States in *resisting* aggression in Vietnam.' This 'resisting' of aggression by then involved major escalations in the bombing of North Vietnam such as the beginning of the Rolling Thunder bombing campaign, lasting for most of the year, as well as the widespread use of napalm and chemical poisons.[7]

As the terror mounted following these escalations, the

Labour government became more guarded in public in expressing support for US policy, arguing that its position as co-chair of peace negotiations precluded it from taking sides. In the numerous discussions of Vietnam in the House of Commons in the second half of the 1960s, Labour governments refused to condemn basic US policy, expressing only occasional opposition to specific acts, for example over the horrific saturation bombing of Hanoi and Haiphong in 1968.

The Heath government was even more supportive. When the US launched another saturation bombing campaign in April 1972, in response to North Vietnam's intervention in the South, the Foreign Office minister declared that the 'American reaction is understandable', with Heath noting that this 'surely is an attitude to be respected'. In response to a parliamentary question noting that US violence was causing the destruction of houses, numerous civilian casualties and 'pellet bombs dropped on individuals', the Foreign Office minister replied that 'it is not for us to make protests about individual types of weapons used'.[8]

During the Christmas 1972 US terror bombing of cities, meanwhile, the *Observer* reported that 'the British government has no intention of joining in the international condemnation' of the US. While the Foreign Office was saying nothing in public, 'private comments leave no doubt that British official thinking supports Mr Nixon's action'.[9]

US aggression in Central America in the 1980s was also strongly supported, this time by the Thatcher government. 'We support the United States' aim to promote peaceful change, democracy and economic development' in Central America, the Prime Minister stated in January 1984; by this time, the US aim of destroying the prospects for peaceful change and economic development were abundantly clear. This was evidenced in US backing of the murderous regimes in El Salvador and Guatemala and in the CIA's creation of a contra terrorist army to operate against the Nicaraguan government under the Sandinistas. British apologias sometimes reached astounding heights. The Foreign Office minister stated in 1985 – several years after contra operations had begun devastating Nicaragua – that 'the American government have stated time and again that they are seeking a solution by peaceful means to the problems of Central America'.[10]

With a probable nod and a wink from Whitehall, the British private 'security company', KMS, trained some of the contras. KMS also organised the destruction of the El Chipote arms depot in the centre of Managua, and KMS helicopter pilots flew with the contras in Honduras. The company also recruited soldiers for the gun-running operation to the contras directed by Oliver North, helping to deliver planes full of military equipment into Nicaragua.[11]

London also used its diplomatic weight to back US positions. Foreign Office documents leaked in 1985 referred to Britain's policy of helping to block loans to the Nicaraguan government and said: 'We shall need to stick to our present line of claiming that our opposition is based on technical [that is, rather than political] grounds' – 'If we can find them!', another Foreign Office official appended to the note. Whitehall could not bring itself to support international law, and abstained on the UN vote condemning the US for mining Nicaraguan ports. The World Court's judgement that US actions in Nicaragua were illegal made no difference to British support. Throughout the US war, Britain preferred to maintain what Thatcher called 'the fundamental alliance between Great Britain and the United States'.[12]

In November 1983 Britain and West Germany were the only EU states to abstain on a UN resolution expressing 'deep concern' at the human rights atrocities of the US-backed regime in El Salvador, which by then had reached staggering proportions. In 1984, London instructed its World Bank delegation to stop 'opposing or abstaining on all proposals' and to support all 'developmentally sound projects' in El Salvador. It then reintroduced a small aid programme to the country and offered military training in Britain to a few Salvadorean military officers.

Britain was the only European government not to send observers to the 1984 elections in Nicaragua, won by the Sandinistas. Though the elections were regarded by independent observers as free and fair, Foreign Secretary Geoffrey Howe's view was that 'free and fair elections could not be regarded as having taken place'. 'In El Salvador', Howe assured the House of Commons, 'a real transfer of power took place; but that was not the position in Nicaragua.' In other words, the wrong side won.[13]

Britain and the US were the only major donors that gave more aid to Nicaragua in the last few years of the brutal Somoza dictatorship than in the first few years under the Sandinistas. This was despite a British government minister's recognition that Nicaragua under the Sandinistas had 'a good record in the spending of development aid'. According to the British chargé d'affaires in Managua, Nicaragua had a 'very impressive record on social development', one which was 'amazing' in comparison with El Salvador and Honduras; yet the latter received 100 times more British aid than Nicaragua.[14]

Other US acts of aggression in the 1980s were also strongly supported by Britain. Britain allowed the US to use its bases for the 1986 bombing of Libya, described by Thatcher as an act taken 'in self-defence'. Britain was the only major state to support publicly the US invasion of Panama in 1989. Only the 1983 invasion of Grenada caused a ripple of concern in Whitehall, since Washington invaded a commonwealth country with the barest of consultation with London. But ministers were careful not to criticise the US invasion in public, in contrast to the condemnations from virtually all other states.

The current phase

The special relationship has reached new depths under New Labour. The Blair government is certainly comparable to Thatcher's in the level of its support and apologies for US aggression. But New Labour has surpassed even Thatcherite

Conservatives, in terms of the joint resort to violence with our favourite ally. There has been no other time in postwar – and earlier – history that Britain has so regularly conducted military interventions as junior partner to the US, as in the repeated bombing of Iraq and the wars in Yugoslavia and Afghanistan.

When President Clinton ordered cruise missile attacks against Sudan and Afghanistan in August 1998, Blair offered reflexive British support. These attacks came two weeks after 224 people had been killed by bomb blasts at American embassies in Nairobi and Dar es Salaam. The US attacked the Al Shifa pharmaceutical plant in Khartoum, claiming that it was producing nerve gas for use in possible terrorist attacks. Donald Anderson, former US ambassador to Sudan, conceded later that 'the evidence was not conclusive and was not enough to justify an act of war'. The US never provided the 'evidence' it claimed it had, while Sudan's proposal for the UN to investigate was vetoed by the US.[15]

Tony Blair stated that 'I strongly support this American action against international terrorists.' He explained that 'our ally, the United States, said at the time of the strike against Al Shifa that they had compelling evidence that the chemical plant was being used for the manufacture of chemical weapons materials' – and so that was enough. Privately, however, it was reported that some British officials and ministers thought the strikes counter-productive, though they never said so publicly.[16]

As for violating international law, Britain's Attorney General – the government's top legal officer – explained that 'the legality of the US action against the Al Shifa factory in Khartoum is a matter for the United States', perhaps a bit like saying that Yugoslav intervention in Kosovo was a matter for Yugoslavia or, an even closer parallel, that Iraqi action in Kuwait was a matter for Iraq. This somewhat contrasts with the government's statement in a later human rights report that: 'blatant contempt for international law can never be regarded as an internal matter'. This double-think is possible, and normal, since it is obvious that international law, and human rights, are simply tools to be wielded in support of elite objectives, and discarded when not of use.[17]

As a result of the attack on Sudan, a *Boston Globe* report estimated that tens of thousands of people had died from malaria, tuberculosis and other treatable diseases. The bombing had destroyed the life-saving medicines in the factory which produced 90 per cent of Sudan's major pharmaceutical products. Sanctions against Sudan made it impossible to import the necessary quantity of medicines to cover the gaps left by the destruction of the plant. Germany's ambassador to Sudan, Werner Daum, wrote that:

> It is difficult to assess how many people in this poor African country died as a consequence of the destruction of the Al Shifa factory, but several tens of thousands seems a reasonable guess.[18]

So, perhaps tens of thousands of people died as a result of this US attack, fully backed by the British government, and which followed a long list of other violations of international law reviewed in the previous chapters. All of this occurred before September 11th. We should, therefore, already have ridiculed the stance of Blair, Bush and others as they professed their commitment to civilisation versus barbarity on September 11th.

The current phase of British soldiers standing shoulder to shoulder with the US military comes when it is crystal clear that our primary ally is in fact the world's greatest outlaw state. Under Bush, the US could hardly demonstrate greater open contempt for the international cooperation to which Britain is rhetorically committed. The Bush administration has scuppered the biological weapons convention, torn up the anti-ballistic missile treaty, rejected the international criminal court, backed off signing the landmine treaty, undermined the small arms treaty and refused to sign the climate change treaty. It remains the protector of Israel, the supporter of repressive Middle Eastern Arab regimes, the new-found ally of totalitarian regimes in Central Asia, and the leading architect of a fundamental reshaping of the global economy to empower Western corporations.

After September 11th, US foreign policy has become so overtly imperial that it is common even for mainstream commentators to recognise this. Britain's primary ally is now an unleashed global hyperpower with no rival, bent on violence against states that seriously oppose it and working largely outside the international law to which it is rhetorically committed. Meanwhile, British leaders continue to steadfastly praise the US for remaining committed to the values it is openly demolishing, indeed continuing to offer unstinting support. Tony Blair notes that 'I find working with President Bush extremely easy and we do see eye to eye on the big geopolitical issues of the day.' Jack Straw adds that 'the United States has always acted in a manner that is consistent with international law, it just has'.[19]

Britain under Blair is so clearly the leading apologist for US foreign policy, that the relationship seriously resembles that between the former Soviet Union and its satellite republics of Belorussia and Ukraine. These two entities were allowed to keep separate seats at the UN throughout the postwar period, and were allowed separate votes. But in practice it was clear to all that they were client states of Moscow. Britain, in its major foreign policies, is now largely a US client state while its military has become an effective US proxy force. Although some differences over foreign policy remain, this degree of British subjection to US imperial power is altogether new.

This heightened proxy role is one of several elements that New Labour is adding to the traditional US–British special relationship. In Afghanistan British forces played the role of a US proxy force by providing specialist troops to hunt down Taliban and Al Qaida operatives when Washington asked for British help. Britain stepped in when the major fear in Washington was of too many US troops being killed in these operations.

However, in any military intervention the US is likely to undertake, and in the cases of Kosovo and Iraq, British forces are not really needed for military purposes. Rather, Britain provides a token military commitment, its more useful function being to uphold the pretence of an 'international coalition', where only the US and its faithful 'junior partner' are seriously interested in military action.

A second role is that British ministers and officials are acting in effect as US diplomats – as international coalition builders in support of US strategy. At the UN, the US and Britain often work hand in glove. Over Iraq, London and Washington have worked extraordinarily closely, first to ensure that sanctions are maintained and now to try to outmanoeuvre the opposition (that is, most of the world) in securing UN acquiescence in military intervention against Baghdad. It is British ministers, notably Blair himself and Foreign Secretary Jack Straw, who fly around the world to drum up support for the Anglo-US line on Iraq and, previously, Afghanistan. Similarly, it was largely British ministers and diplomats who manoeuvred to secure 'NATO' support for bombing Yugoslavia, when it was largely an Anglo-American operation.

The *Wall Street Journal* described Blair on the eve of the war against Afghanistan as the 'newest US ambassador'. It said that 'Mr Blair has emerged as America's chief foreign ambassador to members of the emerging coalition' to combat terrorism. Blair 'has become a self-appointed adviser on Mr Bush's top team of doves and hawks' and 'can travel when Mr Bush is reluctant to leave home'.[20]

But the third British role is just as important. Britain under Blair has overtly become chief public propagandist for 'Western' strategy. As noted in chapter 1, during the Kosovo war, Britain's propaganda contribution to the 'NATO' campaign was probably far more important than its military contribution. New Labour is the recognised international expert on propaganda directed to Western publics. This involves both media 'spin' and some unprecedented intellectual justifications for Anglo-US wars, as articulated in ministerial speeches. In Kosovo, Afghanistan and Iraq, Blair has articulated 'allied' strategy in trendier language more designed to win over the media and placate public opinion than the more blunt (and less media-savvy) US administration.

It is a myth that, as some have argued, Britain has generally restrained the US. The reality is generally the opposite, that British support for the US has empowered it to secure its objectives more easily, as evidenced in the three British roles noted above. Over Iraq, Britain, it appears, simply helped persuade the Bush administration to give the appearance of following a UN route, even after the US said it intended to launch an attack with or without UN support. Again, the British government was acting more like Bush's public relations adviser.

All this is not to say that British elites support everything the US does. There are various public areas of disagreement between London and Washington, for example over Iran and some aspects of trade, as there have always been. And in private many British ministers and diplomats have major concerns about various US policies. Some of these, notably policy towards Israel, are sometimes seen as a liability to Western interests. But for the most part these are disagreements over tactics and presentation of policy. On most of the big strategic issues, there is common purpose on objectives.

I think it is a mistake to see Britain simply as a 'poodle' of the US, as though Britain slavishly follows Washington for the sake of preserving a special relationship. The situation is in reality more serious. Most client states feel bound by their masters; Britain is different in *choosing* to support US actions and in being willingly subservient. Many of the worst US policies are supported by British elites because the latter agree with the US quite independently, not simply out of loyalty to a special relationship. Those elites acted with complete disregard for moral standards when they ruled the globe so it is hardly surprising that their successors give the same latitude to the US.

When British elites really disagree with the US they are often not afraid to say so in the strongest terms. When the US imposed tariffs on imported steel in early 2002, the British government was enraged. Trade Secretary Patricia Hewitt said in the House of Commons that the US action was 'wholly unjustified' and 'quite the wrong response'. It was also a 'clear breach' of the US' 'free trade' obligations in the World Trade Organisation as well as being 'in clear disregard of international opinion'. Hewitt also said that 'we are not prepared to allow the United States to try to dump its problems on the rest of the world'.[21]

The difference in this case is of course that US actions on steel imports threaten Britain's commercial interests. By contrast, pummelling foreign countries such as Afghanistan are worthy objectives, in line with British elites' own interests, in fact as British as Sunday cricket.

Basic support for US foreign policy has traditionally been a pillar of British foreign policy shared across the British elite. The ideological system reflects this view in its reporting on the US.

Criticism of US foreign policy in the mainstream media has tended to be only in areas where US policy *differs* from Britain's. On issues where the two elites agree, the core of the special relationship, there tends to be stunning obedience to elite ideology. The idea of the US as an ultimate defender of high principles is regularly put, rarely challenged and almost never – as is surely justified – ridiculed. US leaders' claims to be acting morally are regularly reported at face value with little or no critical comment. Television news can be distinctly embarrassing in this respect, but so too is much of the print media.

Just as important is what is *not* reported. The argument is sometimes made that the British media are generally critical of the US. But compared to the reality of US foreign policy, what passes for criticism is generally superficial only. The range of US policies undermining human rights around the world, especially support for repressive regimes, is regularly unreported. US economic policies, as in the World Trade Organisation, which are capturing the global economy to benefit US corporations, also go systematically uncovered. Reporting on US military interventions usually focuses on the tactics used, rather than exposing more plausible objectives, and comment is invariably restricted to the practicalities of whether it will be in the interests of US elites. The simple reality that the US is a consistent violator of global ethical standards had been little mentioned in the mainstream, although such comments have risen under Bush, where, as noted, it is seriously hard to miss. No other state in the world – with the exception of Britain itself – is given such latitude by the British media to commit international crime.

In the right-wing press the US is generally seen as a wondrous defender of all that is good in the world. An editorial in the *Financial Times* the day after the US attacks against Afghanistan and Sudan in 1998 noted that 'committing violence deep inside a distant state is not an action to be undertaken lightly' since a number of risks are involved. 'The only question', it continues, 'is whether the threat posed by the terrorists to US and international security is large and imminent enough to justify running such risks.' So international law is not an issue, only the pragmatic calculation (by the US itself, that is) about whether the threat outweighs the risks. It is unimaginable that the *Financial Times* would provide this framing in the case of Iran or Iraq (or even France and Germany) carrying out some attack abroad on what it deemed 'terrorist targets'.[22]

There is also amazing apologia for US policies in the liberal press; the idea that it is systematically critical of US policy is a myth. The *Guardian*'s Polly Toynbee once remarked on, for example, 'America's new found sense of responsibility for universal human rights' at the end of the Clinton administration. An earlier report by Martin Walker covered a speech by President Clinton at the UN, who said that many leaders who had just spoken at the same podium would return home to 'walk over the basic rights of people and nations. It is up to us to stop them.' There was no hint of irony in reporting this, and no mention of the fact that the country that leads in walking over other nations' rights – by a large margin, in modern times – was the one delivering the speech.[23]

Columnist Martin Woollacott has proved to be one of the primary apologists for US power. In one article, Woollacott notes that the recent phase in US interventionism is on balance 'a good development', in a world order 'that needs America's capacity to enforce as a last resort'. He convinced himself at the end of the Clinton administration that 'Clinton's worst sin in international affairs was probably procrastination, followed by over-cautiousness about what the American public would bear and by a failure to manage an admittedly difficult congress.'[24] Worst sin? What, worse than bombing Sudan and Iraq, or supporting state terror in Colombia or Israel? This is Clinton's 'worst sin' seen from *within* an elite agenda.

In his columns, Woollacott regularly plays the role of 'independent expert' – preparing the intellectual ground for elite policy or retrospectively justifying it. For example, when Kofi Annan negotiated a UN agreement with Saddam Hussein in February 1998 that forestalled a US/British military attack on Iraq, Woollacott warned: 'are we beating the retreat from intervention?' Interventions are seen by some as likely to make a bad world worse or as a hangover from Western imperialism, Woollacott noted. But 'the truth is that intervention is, at its best, nothing more or less than action based on the conviction that it is worth trying to set the world to rights, and without that we are nothing'.[25]

The consensual elite view is that the US is essentially benign. This is captured in the term 'global policeman', with its allusion of keeping order and maintaining the law in a world of criminals. The *Financial Times* has described the US as a 'reluctant global policeman', implying that it is the criminals that force the US to adopt unwillingly an interventionist role in the world.[26] To me, the *FT* is here expressing the modern version of the imperial concept of 'the white man's burden'. The term 'global policeman' doesn't exactly capture the idea that the same country is the world's leading international criminal.

Even past mass murder in Vietnam has subsequently been regularly excused. Geoffrey Wheatcroft, writing recently in the *New Statesman*, for example, refers to the US' 'idealistic war-waging to make the world safe for democracy' and the fundamental US commitment to 'the defence of freedom'. 'The US had no material motive in Southeast Asia', Wheatcroft explains. 'Kennedy liberals . . . would have been unable to sleep at night if they had not intervened on behalf of civilisation and justice.' These levels of support for the Official History of our ally do not always apply, but neither are they rare.[27]

There is a phrase for anyone lunatic enough to believe that the US is less than wholly supportive of ethical standards globally – 'anti-American'. This term of abuse is regularly used by mainstream commentators of anyone who criticises US foreign policy.

Let us be clear about this. There are numerous aspects of American domestic society to admire, notably its enshrinement of individual freedoms and rights, which probably surpass any other country. But the deep poverty and inequality in US society is abhorrent, as are the key aspects of its foreign policy, which are systematically abusive of other people's human rights. One leitmotif of US history is consistent interventions to overthrow or undermine progressive governments that offer good development prospects for their people, such as in Guatemala, Iran, Chile and Nicaragua. The US' most fundamental role in the world is organising the global economy and key regions to benefit US business, a strategy that has further impoverished dozens of nations and which holds large regions of the world hostage to US commercial interests. The current phase of US global intervention under the rubric of the 'war against terrorism' is further imposing the US elite's will on much of the planet, in support of often repressive local elites. Amnesty International could say in 1996:

> Throughout the world, on any given day, a man, woman or child is likely to be displaced, tortured, killed or 'disappeared', at the hands of governments or armed political groups. More often than not, the United States shares the blame.[28]

This reality of US foreign policy has been analysed by a large range of analysts such as Noam Chomsky, Gabriel Kolko, Edward Herman, Walter La Feber, Michael Klare, Michael Parenti, William Blum and others. Their analysis should be uncontroversial. That it is usually seen as 'radical' shows just how ideologically supportive of the state institutions the British mainstream political culture is.

The veil of deceit that obscures much of the reality of US foreign policy, cast by the mainstream media and others, prevents a more accurate understanding of our primary ally's real role in the world. In turn, this allows British elites to pursue policies supportive of the US, binding an important relationship which has been so destructive to people's lives over the past decades, and continuing today.

5

ISRAEL: SIDING WITH THE AGGRESSOR

It is a fact that we have killed 14 Palestinians in Jenin, Kabatyeh and Tammum, with the world remaining absolutely silent.

Israeli defence minister Ben Elizer,
14 September 2001[1]

Foreign Secretary Jack Straw was told in an interview on BBC Radio 4 that more Palestinians than Israelis had been killed in recent violence. Straw replied:

Well they have, although one doesn't want to get into this kind of arithmetic. There is no direct moral equivalence between people who are the direct victims of terrorism, who are entirely innocent, and those who are taking part in conflict.[2]

This comment revealed the British government's understanding of the conflict – in essence, the Palestinians are the primary aggressors and Israel the victim. The reality is mainly the opposite, and, in accordance with traditional practice, Britain has chosen to side with the primary aggressor.

In the Jenin massacre in April 2002, the Israeli army killed around the same number of people (fifty-two) as Yugoslav forces did in the Racak massacre in Kosovo three years earlier. The latter, as noted in chapter 6, elicited the unqualified outrage of British leaders, who used it as sure-fire proof of the evil of the Milosevic regime. A few days after the release of a UN report on Racak, NATO began its bombing campaign. After Jenin, however, Britain barely raised an eyebrow.

Israel 'committed war crimes in the military operation in the Jenin refugee camp', with many civilians 'killed wilfully or unlawfully', according to Human Rights Watch. The Israeli army used Palestinians as 'human shields' and indiscriminate and excessive force. A fifty-seven-year-old wheelchair-bound man was shot and run over by tanks, and a thirty-seven-year-old man was crushed in the rubble of his home when Israeli soldiers refused to allow him time to leave before a bulldozer destroyed it. US-supplied helicopters fired anti-tank missiles into the camp, failing to distinguish between military and civilian targets, hitting many houses where there were no Palestinian fighters. 140 buildings were levelled and more than 200 severely damaged. Israel also blocked emergency medical access to Jenin camp, and soldiers repeatedly fired on Red Cross ambulances, in one case shooting a nurse who had come to the assistance of a wounded man.[3]

Israeli actions in Jenin were so gross that Britain could not entirely ignore them. Britain's Defence Attaché in Israel conducted an official report – not made public – concluding that the Israelis used 'excessive and disproportionate force'. Britain did publicly criticise Israeli actions, along with the rest of the international community. Foreign Office minister Ben Bradshaw claimed that it was due to a British initiative that the UN endorsed a fact-finding mission to Jenin (that was blocked by Israel).[4] But it appears that Britain's motivation for this was to support Israel in light of the contending views about the number of deaths, some initial claims of which reached into the hundreds. After the massacre, Jack Straw told the *Today* programme on Radio 4 that he phoned his Israeli counterpart, Shimon Peres, and that:

> I said to Shimon, it was very important for Israel and for Israel's reputation in the world that this fact-finding mission should be admitted as soon as possible . . . If you have nothing to hide, let's get this fact-finding mission in as soon as possible. I'm quite sure, knowing Kofi Annan as I do, that he will be able to make arrangements to ensure that the legitimate concerns of the Israeli government can be met.

Straw related that Peres told him that while Israel would accept the fact-finding mission it could not allow individual soldiers to be interviewed without any involvement by the Israeli government. Straw then said, paraphrasing Peres' remarks, that 'these circumstances are very special because the Israeli defence forces are operating not in their own territory but in the occupied territories of the Palestinian Authority'. Amazingly, Straw is here endorsing Israel's argument that it is entitled to special treatment precisely because it is occupying territory![5]

When Ben Bradshaw was asked whether the International Criminal Court might be brought to bear against Israel, he replied that 'in the case of Israel, being a country that has respect for the rule of law, we would expect it to carry out its own investigations'.

Britain publicly criticised the Israeli re-invasion of the occupied territories begun in March 2002. London supports the creation of a 'viable' Palestinian state alongside Israel and adheres to the international legal position that Israeli settlements in the West Bank are illegal (Bradshaw adding that 'the vast majority would have to go' in any peace deal). It has also said that it would expect East Jerusalem to be the capital of a Palestinian state.[6] These positions are in line with the international consensus.

But Britain is doing nothing to bring any of this about; indeed, its actual policies are undermining its public positions to the extent that the latter appear largely for public relations. The Blair government has consistently failed to identify Israel as the primary aggressor and has refused to seriously press Israel to change policies that are systematically violating international law through its occupation of the West Bank and Gaza. Instead, London acts as a de facto condoner of Israeli aggression as trade links are stepped up and arms exports are subject to minimal disruption, as outlined further below. The Blair initiative, taken in early 2003, to organise a conference in London to discuss the Israeli–Palestinian conflict, is easily explained as needing to be seen to be doing something on Palestine to better justify the obliteration of Iraq. The minimal efforts made to argue the Palestinian case appear mainly intended to placate world opinion. The balance sheet is clearly a pro-Israel strategy, amounting to complicity in human rights atrocities.

All this is despite Britain's obligation – along with the rest of the international community – to take action against Israel under the terms of the Fourth Geneva Convention. This obligates all parties to 'respect and ensure respect for' the Convention's human rights articles, numerous of which Israel is systematically violating. London easily ignores such obligations under international law while it professes its undying commitment to the same in the case of official enemy, Iraq.

Tony Blair has personally been very careful not to condemn Israel outright. The customary formulation is to blame 'both sides' for the violence, as though guilt is equally shared. By doing this, the British government is ignoring the gross imbalance in the fact that Israel is occupying Palestinian territory. The 'both sides' formulation is a propaganda victory for Israel.

When George Bush declared Israeli Prime Minister Ariel Sharon a 'man of peace' – while Israel's invasion of the West Bank was in full swing – Blair was asked repeatedly by Jeremy Paxman on BBC's *Newsnight* whether he agreed that Sharon was such 'a man of peace'. Blair was unable to state the obvious and said that he believed Sharon wanted peace over the long term. Two months earlier, Sharon had declared that 'the

Palestinians must be hit and it must be very painful: we must cause them losses, victims, so that they can feel the heavy price'. Blair's line matched the Foreign Office view – stated in October 2000 – of avoiding 'attempting to apportion blame for recent events'.[7]

Britain does not find it difficult to identify some leaders as incarnations of evil, such as former Yugoslav President Milosevic and Zimbabwean President Robert Mugabe, not to mention Saddam Hussein. Britain has exerted huge diplomatic pressure to expel Zimbabwe from the Commonwealth and to press the EU to condemn and marginalise the Mugabe regime. By contrast, with Israel Britain is unable even to identify the primary aggressor, let alone take any significant action against it. Sanctions against Israel, unlike against Milosevic and Mugabe, are not even a serious option – sanctions are largely unmentionable in the mainstream media, whose framing of policy options is largely set by the priorities of the state.

The British position of apportioning equal blame to both sides sometimes reaches hysterical depths, as when Blair declared to the House of Commons that:

> The Israelis must allow a state of Palestine, secure in its own borders. And in exchange the Palestinians and the whole Arab world must recognise and respect Israel's borders.[8]

In fact, the Palestinians and the Arab world have recognised Israel's borders and right to exist for some time. Only the first of Blair's sentences is correct – something that our Israeli ally is refusing to implement.

Even more amusing, if it weren't so tragic, was Blair's statement that 'I agree UN resolutions should apply here [Israel] as much as to Iraq. But they don't just apply to Israel. They apply to all parties' – meaning the Palestinians.[9] Thus the Palestinians are equated with Israel in terms of implementing UN resolutions, numerous of which Israel is defying while occupying the territory of the other side.

Britain's pro-Israel stance while Tel Aviv continues to defy the UN is sufficient to ridicule the Blair government's professed commitment to upholding UN security council resolutions in the case of Iraq. But few commentators fall about laughing when Whitehall insists on Iraq upholding UN demands, and fewer still mention that the issuer of the demand is himself head of an outlaw state guilty of numerous violations of international law in the past few years.

In recent months, more than five times the number of Palestinians have been killed by Israel than vice versa. The number of Palestinians living below the poverty line is around 65 per cent, which has doubled since the new phase of the Palestinian uprising began. The rise in poverty is mainly due to the Israeli policy of 'closures', imposing harsh restrictions on Palestinian freedom of movement and in effect confining Palestinians to a siege situation and the freedom of a glorified prison camp. In late 2002, round-the-clock curfews were affecting about one million Palestinians. The horrific suicide bombing attacks, which are clearly completely indefensible and grotesque, arise from the frustration of a brutally oppressed people and are clearly more responses to Israeli aggression and occupation, rather than vice versa.

Robin Cook said that to play a part in brokering a future peace deal 'we have to retain an even-handed approach'. This 'even-handed approach' is towards a government engaged in 'a long term project which will complete the destruction of a Palestinian administration, paralysed for eighteen months by Israeli bombardments and blockades', in the *Guardian*'s Suzanne Goldenberg's words. The March 2002 re-invasion of the occupied territories was Israel's largest military offensive since the invasion of Lebanon two decades ago.[10]

However, it is a myth that British policy is 'even-handed'. Blair's personal envoy, Lord Levy, has close ties to the Israeli Labour party and has helped develop 'a strongly pro-Israel line from No. 10', according to the *Guardian*. The paper also describes Foreign Secretary Jack Straw as 'a strong defender in public of Israel'.[11] With the invasion of the West Bank under way and with Israel laying siege to Yasser Arafat's head-quarters, the *Guardian* reported that 'the foreign secretary, Jack Straw, yesterday pleaded for greater public sympathy for Israel's position in its conflict with the Palestinians'. Straw has also written that 'whether one agrees with the stance of the Israeli government is not the point. What is important is to understand the huge pressures on them.'[12]

Blair applies a similar apologia for Israeli assassinations of Palestinians – 'targeted killings' in the Israeli term. Britain's condemnation of these acts – completely illegal under inter-national law and akin to terrorism – is usually immediately qualified. For example, in November 2001, Blair stated in Jerusalem:

> I understand the pressures that Prime Minister Sharon is under, the pressure that he feels and the position of Israeli people who have seen their citizens killed by terrorist acts. I believe it is important that any measures that are taken in relation to security are measured and proper in accordance with international law, but let us be absolutely clear, we are never going to get back into a process again unless the violence and killing every-where stops.

This statement was carried in a press release by the Israel embassy in London, understandably since it apologises for the 'pressures' Sharon is under and adopts the Israeli line that the suicide bombings must stop first, as though the Palestinians are the primary aggressor responsible for the political impasse, when the opposite is the case.[13]

Indeed, Britain has been so concerned not to condemn or punish Israel, that in December 2001 it abstained on a UN resolution criticising Israel, saying that the wording did not sufficiently criticise the Palestinians. Britain was the only EU state to abstain, which is an instance of how some British policies are worse under Labour than under the Conservatives, who at least voted to condemn Israel in such resolutions in the past.[14]

Britain has also led the way in supporting US 'leadership' in the peace process and ensuring that the EU offers no alternative, arguing that 'the European Union role has been to complement the [US] leadership'.[15] This occurs at a time when it is clear that the Israeli government has no interest in the creation of a viable Palestinian state or a peace agreement on anything other than Israeli terms, and after the US gave Sharon a de facto green light to invade the West Bank. The US effectively backs the Israeli strategy, even if there are some US concerns over Israeli tactics.

When President Bush gave a speech demanding that Arafat stand down as chair of the Palestinian Authority, to which he had been elected, Blair unusually appeared to distance himself from the US. He said that 'it is up to the Palestinians to choose their own leaders' (that is, as we arm and step up trade with the aggressor trying to destroy them). But the *Guardian* reported that 'Mr Blair tried to minimise the split by emphasising his disappointment with Mr Arafat's political leadership, and agreeing that the peace process might be easier if the Palestinian Authority president stood down.' Britain then called for new elections for the Palestinian Authority.[16]

If British policy were even-handed perhaps it would arm the Palestinian Authority so that British equipment could be used against Israeli forces. It could also establish high-level military contacts with Palestinian security forces engaged in operations against Israel. Perhaps it might also designate Palestine as one of a handful of 'target markets' worldwide for British exports, and deliver speeches in favour of greatly expanded trade at a time when atrocities mount. Or it could agree with its EU partners a beneficial trade and aid agreement (the EU's association agreement) with a clause saying that all parties must support human rights – and then refuse to call for its suspension when human rights are being clearly violated. But this is the reality of current British policy only towards Israel.

In 1999, Britain sold Israel £11.5 million worth of arms, and in 2000, £12 million. This almost doubled to £22.5 million in 2001, as Israeli aggression mounted during the year. Supplies include small arms, grenade making kits and components for a range of equipment such as armoured fighting vehicles, armoured personnel carriers, tanks and combat aircraft. According to the Israeli newspaper *Haaretz*, military officials in Israel say that it's military purchases from Britain are not especially large 'but some are critical items of equipment'. The level of violence undertaken by the recipient appears of little concern to London. Throughout the Palestinian uprising against Israel, the Blair government has been busy approving licences for arms and military equipment: 297 export licences were granted between January 1999 and November 2000; 300 from January 2001 to April 2002; and twenty were issued in March 2002 when Israel invaded the West Bank.[17]

BBC Radio 4's *World at One* programme in August 2001 reported a senior Israeli Ministry of Defence official confirming that British equipment was being used in the occupied territories. Armoured landrovers and British personnel carriers were 'ferrying IDF troops into occupied territories' [*sic*]. Britain was also supplying components, including transponders, for Bell Huey helicopters, which back up the front-line Apache helicopters that regularly assault Palestinian targets in the West Bank.[18]

The British government disclosed in March 2002 that Israel had modified Centurion tanks sold between 1958 and 1970 to be used as armoured personnel carriers by the army. This broke Israeli 'assurances' to London that British equipment would not be used. However, Jack Straw told parliament that the Israelis:

> did not however accept that this [i.e. the Centurions] was a breach of the assurances given and they have not committed to stop using the armoured personnel carriers in the occupied territories . . . We also have questions about other possible breaches of the assurances with regard to equipment supplied under previous administrations.[19]

It was also revealed in 2002 that Israeli Merkava tanks have been equipped with cooling systems made by a British company, and that were last supplied in 1996. And British equipment, including missile trigger systems, was being used in the US-made Apache helicopters supplied to Israel. The Blair government also allowed the export of British components for US F16 warplanes sold to Israel, which have also been repeatedly used against Palestinians. Also reported was that Israel was upgrading British Jaguar bombers made by India under licence to enable them to carry nuclear weapons.[20]

The approval of the F16 spare parts deal occurred *after* press reports noted in 2002 that the British government had begun delaying the approval of arms-related exports to Israel. A number of export licences were apparently blocked and being considered on a case-by-case basis. But the 'embargo' to which some commentators refer covers only some types of equipment; the government is continuing to reject a formal arms ban despite the public knowledge that British equipment has been used, that Israel has not promised to stop using such equipment, and that there may be other equipment being used not already acknowledged. Judging by previous cases – such as the mythical arms 'embargo' to Indonesia in 1999 that simply delayed all exports for a few months before continuing as normal – Britain may also be delaying the supply of military equipment to Israel until public attention on Israeli aggression dies down.

These supplies show that the government's arms export 'guidelines' are largely for public relations purposes, as discussed further in chapter 8, and to be taken seriously only by the most ideologically disciplined of observers. Military-related exports to Israel violate almost all the guidelines in a flagrant way: Israel is occupying territory, is guilty of gross human rights abuses, and refuses to sign any international treaty regulating nuclear weapons, all of which should invoke formal arms restrictions by Britain. Meanwhile, the government admits that it 'has not placed specific limitations or end-use conditions on licences for exports to Israel'.[21]

Arms exports are just part of a much wider military and commercial relationship with Israel. Britain has a Memorandum of Understanding on Defence Material Cooperation signed with Israel in 1995, the details of which have never been made public. The British government noted in April 2000 that 'during the past year there have been numerous meetings between MoD and Israeli officials in the UK and a wide range of issues were discussed'. Britain's police have brought Israeli bullets and the MoD has purchased Israeli grenades, shells and military avionics.

Overall, the British embassy in Tel Aviv noted recently a 'flourishing relationship' between the two countries. 'Britain is a good friend of Israel', it says, and 'our two prime ministers are in regular contact and have a good working and personal relationship'. 'Significant UK investment in Israel continues to grow.'[22] This was just before the spat between Sharon and Blair over Britain's invitation to Palestinians to attend the London conference, which incensed the Israeli leadership.

Israel is one of fourteen 'target markets' worldwide for the Department of Trade and Industry. 'One of the main aims of the target market campaign is to encourage more British companies to look at the possibilities offered in the Israeli market', Trade Secretary Patricia Hewitt explained to the British–Israel chamber of commerce in January 2002. The previous year, British trade with Israel reached a record £2.5 billion. 'And what of the future for trade?', she asked, 'well, it looks bright.' The DTI says that 'Israel is a remarkable success story for British exporters'. It is the second largest customer in the Middle East after Saudi Arabia.[23]

Much media reporting has essentially followed the government line on Israel. The country's leading independent media analyst is the Glasgow University Media Group (GUMG), which has consistently exposed the distortions of mainstream media reporting over the past three decades. One of its recent reports, by Greg Philo, begins by saying that 'if you don't understand the Middle East crisis it might be because you are watching it on television'. Philo notes that the history and origins of the Israeli–Palestinian conflict are rarely addressed in the media. The reason is that to do so would be controversial, since Israel is closely allied to the United States and there are very strong pro-Israel lobbies in the US and Britain. But, with little discussion on the background, the accounts focus only on day-to-day events in which it can appear that the 'normal' world is disrupted only when Palestinians riot or bomb.

The Israeli viewpoint nearly always dominates. Palestinian bombings are usually reported to be 'starting' a series of events to which Israel 'responds'. For example, one *Newsnight* piece asserted: 'Dozens of Palestinians and Israelis have been killed in a relentless round of suicide bombings and Israeli counter-attacks.' Philo found no reports saying Palestinians 'responded' to Israeli attacks.

According to the GUMG report, Israelis were allowed to speak twice as much on TV news as Palestinians and there were three times as many headlines that expressed the Israeli view compared to the Palestinian. There was only muted criticism of Israeli violence, while the fact that there are powerful forces in Israel opposed to any peace settlement was rarely reported. Language such as 'murder', 'atrocity' and 'savage cold-blooded killings' were used to describe Israeli deaths, but not Palestinian. 'This difference in the language is noteworthy', Philo writes, since from the beginning of the intifada 'nearly ten times as many Palestinians had in fact been killed as Israelis'.[24]

There are only a few exceptions to this general pattern of reporting on Israel. One outstanding exception is the *Independent*'s Middle East correspondent, Robert Fisk, who not only reports reality but also bravely takes on fellow journalists in failing to. Fisk has written that 'we are reporting this terrible conflict as if we supported the South African whites against the blacks'. He notes that 'rarely since the second world war has a people been so vilified as the Palestinians. And rarely has a people been so frequently excused and placated as the Israelis'.[25]

Fisk also writes that 'the Israeli line – that Palestinians are essentially responsible for "violence", responsible for the killing of their own children by Israeli soldiers, responsible for refusing to make concessions for peace – has been accepted almost totally by the media'. He cites as an example of distorted reporting that the BBC cannot even call it murder when committed by Israeli forces: according to one BBC report, undercover Israeli soldiers 'shot dead a member of Yasser Arafat's Fatah faction yesterday in *what Palestinians called an assassination*'.[26]

The *Economist* has noted that 'violence is not one-sided. It has, in point of fact, been initiated by the Palestinians . . . Israel's aim is to stop them'. This is the general framing. The same report also rejected the notion that the US role in the Arab-Israeli conflict has been 'one-sided and excessive'. It concludes that the US record 'is not the record of a superpower with no interest in peace and justice'. The article was entitled 'the unblessed peacemaker', referring to the US.[27]

That the US is regarded as an 'honest broker', a 'mediator' or even, as above, a 'peacemaker' is generally accepted and widely put across the mainstream. Where reporting does point out that the US is not wholly impartial, it is usually expressed in mild terms like US 'bias' towards Israel. Rarely is US policy directly seen as the major problem. Most criticism of the US is about Washington not engaging *enough* in the peace process. But the US has been seriously engaged for some time – giving a green light to Israeli aggression, supplying Israel with the arms to carry it out and ensuring international action is impossible by vetoing UN resolutions, etc.

But it is Britain's role that has been given even more serious ideological treatment. Television news cannot mention the simple fact that Britain is in effect condoning violence by Israel (or anyone else), by definition. Neither can the press, so far as I can tell. The range of (growing) British trade links with Israel promoted by the government has been barely mentioned. Even the supply of British arms-related equipment has escaped much scrutiny and concern. There have been few mentions of the levers that could be used to pressure Israel, such as Britain's bilateral links or multilateral levers like suspending the EU's association agreement with Israel or boycotting goods exported illegally by Israel from the occupied territories.

In Kosovo, the media's role was crucial in lending weight to the government's policy of demonising Milosevic and undermining his regime through sanctions and finally bombing. With Israel, there is little demonising of Sharon in the media and few, if any, calls to undermine him through British policies.

6

KOSOVO: ANTI-HUMANITARIAN INTERVENTION

We will carry on pounding day after day after day, until
our objectives are secured

Tony Blair, 12 April 1999[1]

The December 1998 US and British attacks on Iraq were
followed by weeks of bombings in a secret escalation of the war
in the 'no fly zones' of northern and southern Iraq. Then
Britain took to war again. In March 1999, NATO forces,
primarily British and American, began pounding Yugoslavia
and Kosovo from the air. The bombing lasted eleven weeks
until June, causing massive damage not only to Yugoslav
military forces but also the country's civilian infrastructure. The
official reason for the war against Yugoslavia was 'to curb
Milosevic's ability to wage war on an innocent civilian
population' in Kosovo, and to 'prevent an impending
humanitarian disaster', Tony Blair explained.[2]

The war against Milosevic's Yugoslavia has been the subject
of huge debate in the political mainstream, due to the
government's framing of the war as a new kind of military
action taken to defend humanitarian values. The liberal press –
notably the *Guardian* and the *Independent* – backed the war to

the hilt (while questioning the tactics used to wage it) and lent critical weight to the government's arguments.

The Kosovo war to me revealed the extraordinary nature of British mainstream political culture and how willingly deceived it generally is by government rhetoric on its moral motives. In my view, the claim that the war was fought in defence of human rights is so absurd as to defy belief. This was already clear at the time, but it is even clearer now. This important episode needs to be reviewed not only because it further highlights British contempt for international law and ethical standards, but also because one aspect of the Kosovo war was indeed new – Western leaders discovered anew that 'humanitarianism' could be a successful pretext for military intervention and that the mainstream political culture would buy it.

Precipitating humanitarian disaster

The claim that the war was fought for humanitarian purposes rests on the belief that the bombing prevented a humanitarian disaster. This claim is illusory, since it is clear NATO bombing *precipitated*, rather than halted, large-scale 'ethnic cleansing'.

NATO leaders claimed before the bombing began that 'genocide' was taking place at the hands of Milosevic's forces in Kosovo. Foreign Office minister Geoff Hoon claimed 10,000 Albanians had been killed; US Defence Secretary William Cohen even spoke of up to 100,000 military-aged men missing. Other figures in the tens of thousands were bandied around.

However, in the year before the bombing, according to NATO sources following the war, about 2,000 people had been killed in Kosovo and several thousand had become internally displaced. A British government memorandum written after the NATO bombing says that 10,000 people were killed in Kosovo in 1999 – Foreign Secretary Robin Cook confirmed that only 2,000 of those deaths occurred before the bombing, meaning four times as many occurred after. These were deaths on both sides of the conflict between Yugoslav forces repressing ethnic Albanians, and the Kosovo Liberation Army (KLA).[3]

The mass deaths alleged to be taking place before the bombing seem to have been a NATO fabrication. Documents since released by the German Foreign Office and German regional administrative courts – used in deciding the status of Kosovar refugees in Germany – provide a completely different picture of Kosovo before the bombing. One report from February 1999 notes that 'the often feared humanitarian catastrophe threatening the Albanian civil population has been averted'. In the larger cities 'public life has since returned to relative normality'.

Most killings in Kosovo before the bombing were the result of fighting between Yugoslav forces and the KLA, rather than 'ethnic cleansing'. A German report exactly a month before the bombing stated that:

> Events since February and March 1998 do not evidence a persecution program based on Albanian ethnicity. The measures taken by the armed forces are in the first instance directed towards combatting the KLA and its supposed adherents and supporters.

UN special envoy Jiri Dienstbier has said that 'before the bombing Albanians were not driven away on the basis of ethnic principle. [They were] victims of the brutal war between the Yugoslav army and the Kosovo Liberation Army.'

According to US diplomat Norma Brown, an aide to the Director of the Observer Mission in Kosovo, 'there was no humanitarian crisis [in Kosovo] until NATO began to bomb . . . Everyone knew that a humanitarian crisis would arise if NATO started to bomb.'[4]

The mass refugee exodus from Kosovo began only after the bombing commenced. The British government has stated that before the bombing there were 'over 200,000 internally displaced people in Kosovo and nearly 70,000 refugees (Kosovo Albanians and Kosovo Serbs)'. These are already big numbers; it is clear that the situation was appalling for ethnic Albanians before the bombing as they faced severe repression and human rights abuses by Yugoslav forces and as a result of the war. But soon after the NATO bombing began, Milosevic implemented a campaign that forced more than 850,000 Kosovars over the borders, mostly into Albania and Macedonia.[5]

Yugoslav forces took advantage of the NATO bombing to implement this more terrifying campaign. It had begun on 19 March, but it was only with the NATO bombing that commenced on 24 March that the regime's attacks were massively stepped up. A study by the Organisation for Security and Cooperation in Europe (OSCE) notes a 'pattern of expulsions and the vast increase in lootings, killings, rape, kidnappings and pillage once the NATO air war began on March 24' and that 'the most visible change in the events was after NATO launched its first airstrikes'. The study states that once the OSCE monitors left Kosovo on 20 March and in particular after the bombing campaign began, Yugoslav soldiers and paramilitaries 'went from village to village and, in the towns, from area to area, threatening and expelling the Kosovo Albanian population'.[6]

General Naumann, Chairman of NATO's Military Committee in 1999, said on Channel 4 that the humanitarian disaster 'may have been accelerated by NATO, and definitely some of the atrocities which happened were caused by NATO bombs, since [these provoked] this vendetta feeling'. It is interesting that the indictment of Milosevic by the Hague war crimes tribunal refers to a long list of crimes committed by Milosevic, all of them after the beginning of the NATO bombing.[7]

The House of Commons Foreign Affairs Committee concluded in its inquiry into Kosovo that:

> It is likely that the NATO bombing did cause a change in the character of the assault upon the Kosovo Albanians. What had been an anti-insurgency campaign – albeit a

brutal and counter-productive one – became a mass, organised campaign to kill Kosovo Albanians or drive them from the country . . . The withdrawal of the OSCE monitors combined with the Serbs' inability to inflict casualties upon NATO during the bombing campaign led to an intensification of the assault on the Kosovo Albanians.[8]

The Defence Committee concluded in an October 2000 report that 'all the evidence suggests that plans to initiate the air campaign hastened the onset of the disaster'. It said that 'whilst the strategy did in the end result in Milosevic withdrawing his forces from Kosovo, it did not achieve its aim of averting a humanitarian disaster'.

In its report, the Defence Committee criticises the British government for telling the public that a humanitarian disaster could be prevented solely by using air power. Indeed, this was the major criticism of NATO from within the political mainstream – that ground forces should also have been used, or at least not ruled out. But what the Defence Committee fails to realise is that by saying that the government failed to prevent the humanitarian disaster it is undermining the government's whole rationale for launching the bombing campaign in the first place.[9]

The evidence also suggests that NATO leaders knew that Milosevic would launch such a campaign if they attacked, but still went ahead.

The *Guardian* reported on 28 April that 'MI6 is understood to have warned that bombing would accelerate ethnic cleansing.' Pentagon planners told the *New York Times* they had warned Clinton that Milosevic was likely to attack the Kosovars if faced with airstrikes. Pentagon spokesman Kevin Bacon said that 'we were not surprised by what Milosevic has done'. 'I think there is historical amnesia here if anyone says they are surprised by this campaign.'[10]

There is much more evidence from the media. The *Washington*

Post of 1 April said that for weeks before the NATO bombing campaign, CIA Director George Tenet had been forecasting that Yugoslav forces might respond by accelerating ethnic cleansing in Kosovo. The *Sunday Times* of 28 March reported the views of General Shelton, Chairman of the US Joint Chiefs of Staff, noting that 'air strikes might provoke Serb soldiers into greater acts of butchery'. Airstrikes alone, Shelton stated, 'could not stop Serb forces from executing Kosovars'. The report also said that 'Britain's ambassador to Belgrade had been making a similar argument in a flood of cables to London.'[11]

Indeed, three days into the bombing, on 27 March, the NATO Commander General Wesley Clark said that it was 'entirely predictable' that Serb terror and violence would intensify after the NATO bombing. Shortly afterwards Clark said: 'The military authorities fully anticipated the vicious approach that Milosevic would adopt as well as the terrible efficiency with which he would carry it out.'[12]

During the bombing, Foreign Secretary Robin Cook gave evidence to the Foreign Affairs Committee. Cook refused to admit that NATO actions had escalated the atrocities, claiming that the ethnic cleansing had already begun. But he also said:

> We anticipated, therefore, the spring offensive; that it would be accompanied by ethnic cleansing; we did not have any intelligence to suggest he was going to load up whole trains and run a shuttle train deportation from Pristina to the Macedonian border.

At the very least, Cook is admitting that the government was not surprised by Milosevic's actions, only the scale of them. He added that if NATO had not begun to bomb, the Milosevic regime would likely have acted as it did anyway.[13]

The Foreign Affairs Committee concluded that 'it does seem, therefore, that there were pieces of information which were available to the USA' and which should have been available to Britain 'that indicated that the internally displaced in Kosovo were about to become refugees'.[14]

On the basis of Cook's evidence, alongside the press reports, it appears very likely that the government knew that Milosevic would launch such a campaign once NATO attacked. If so, the subsequent bombing campaign was in callous, perhaps even criminal, disregard for human suffering.

There is also the issue of 'Operation Horseshoe'. Two weeks into the bombing, the German Foreign Office said it knew of a plan by Milosevic to 'ethnically cleanse' Kosovo. NATO leaders seized on this to justify the bombing and to say that the attacks and expulsions now taking place would have taken place anyway. The plan received widespread media coverage. But it appears that 'Operation Horseshoe' was a fabrication. A retired German Brigadier General and now OSCE consultant, Heinz Loquai, states in his book, *The Kosovo conflict: The road to an avoidable war*, that the German Foreign Office culled the story from Bulgarian intelligence reports and turned it into propaganda, even coining the name 'Horseshoe'.[15]

There is another massive hole in the government's argument that NATO was trying to prevent a humanitarian disaster: many military strategists and others openly said that this was not their policy.

In launching the bombing, NATO Secretary General Javier Solana said that NATO's actions were 'directed towards disrupting the violent attacks being committed by the Serb army and special police forces and weakening their ability to cause further humanitarian catastrophe'. But this was immediately contradicted by a source in Britain's Ministry of Defence, who told the *Guardian* that 'air strikes in this situation are a political weapon but it will not stop the Serbs killing Albanians in Kosovo'. 'It will not provide a military solution.'[16]

Three weeks into the bombing Wesley Clark said that 'you cannot stop paramilitary murder on the ground with aeroplanes'. A week later, he said that the NATO operation 'was not designed as a means of blocking Serb ethnic cleansing. It was not designed as a means of waging war against the Serb forces in Kosovo. Not in any way. There was never any intent to do that. That was not the idea.' . . .[17]

Britain's military commander, General Sir Charles Guthrie, also told the press that 'NATO's air assault was never likely to stop Serbian forces killing ethnic Albanians in Kosovo.' A year after the bombing US General Harry Shelton said that 'the one thing we knew we could not do . . . we could not stop the atrocities or the ethnic cleansing through the application of our military power'.[18]

So the situation at the beginning of the bombing campaign appears to be that NATO, led by the US and Britain, launched military action knowing that it would provoke a brutal ethnic cleansing campaign by Milosevic. This occurred in stark fashion, with immense consequences, which then enabled NATO leaders to claim that they were acting to prevent the humanitarian catastrophe that they had provoked. With bombing under way, military figures publicly refuted political leaders' whole justification for the war, by saying that the military strategy could not prevent the humanitarian disaster.

There was one other reason given for going to war: to preserve NATO's 'credibility'. Blair said the day before launching the bombing that 'to walk away now would . . . destroy NATO's credibility'. Robin Cook said that 'I think its [NATO's] credibility would have been undermined if we had failed to act in this case.'[19]

NATO leaders had long searched for a new mission for the organisation after the collapse of the Soviet Union, and NATO's fiftieth anniversary was due on 23–5 April 1999. As war raged in Kosovo, Blair delivered a speech in Chicago outlining some principles of 'humanitarian intervention', that he termed a 'doctrine of the international community'. The speech was widely praised as showing our leader's commitment to the highest values, while NATO forces were committing violations of international law in Kosovo, after having launched an illegal war. In reality, the speech was a justification for the war. British and US leaders have always delivered fancy speeches when they are about to pulverise enemies; George Bush's 'new world order' speech, for example, was delivered to justify the onslaught to 'liberate' Kuwait in 1991. In the Chicago speech, Blair explained the meaning of 'credibility':

> One of the reasons why it is now so important to win the conflict is to ensure that others do not make the same mistake in the future. That in itself will be a major step to ensuring that the next decade and the next century will not be as difficult as the past. If NATO fails in Kosovo, the next dictator to be threatened with military force may well not believe our resolve to carry the threat through.[20]

This is frightening stuff. As Noam Chomsky has pointed out, Blair is acting like a mafia don. When a shopkeeper fails to pay protection money the goons despatched do not simply take the money, they leave him a broken wreck, so that others will get the message.[21] The head of the Outlaw State is in my view here delivering a similar message to those threatening the bosses of world order.

International law and war crimes

The war supposedly fought to defend humanitarian values was done in plain violation of international law. Robin Cook said that 'the legal basis for our action is that the international community states do have the right to use force in the case of overwhelming humanitarian necessity'. In fact, express authorisation by the UN Security Council is needed to launch military action. The war also violated the NATO treaty, Article 5 of which says that force can be used only in self-defence.

Britain also prevented consideration of the case at the International Court of Justice (ICJ). Yugoslavia brought proceedings against several NATO members, including Britain, to the ICJ in April 1999. Whitehall chose not to contest the substantive issue and argued the procedural point that

Yugoslavia had accepted the court's compulsory jurisdiction too late for Britain to be required to deal with Yugoslavia's complaint. The Foreign Affairs Committee concludes that 'the decision to rely on a technicality to prevent the International Court from deciding the issue does suggest a concern that the judgement would not have been favourable'.[22]

NATO was guilty of numerous violations of international law in the bombing. This is now (and pretty much then, as well) conveniently forgotten as we move on to other targets in defence of civilised values.

Five hundred Yugoslav civilians are known to have died in ninety separate attacks, according to Human Rights Watch. It established sixty-two of the targets in those ninety incidents. In nine of these sixty-two, civilian deaths 'were a result of attacks on non-military targets that Human Rights Watch believes were illegitimate'. These included the headquarters of Serb Radio and Television (RTS) in Belgrade, a heating plant and 'seven bridges that were neither on major transportation routes nor had other military functions'. Human Rights Watch concluded that NATO violated international humanitarian law since it:

> conducted air attacks using cluster bombs near populated areas; attacked targets of questionable military legitimacy, including Serb Radio and Television, heating plants and bridges; did not take adequate precautions in warning civilians of attacks; took insufficient precautions identifying the presence of civilians when attacking convoys and mobile targets; and caused excessive civilian casualties by not taking sufficient measures to verify that military targets did not have concentrations of civilians.[23]

Amnesty International said in its report one year after the bombings that 'NATO forces violated the laws of war leading to cases of unlawful killings of civilians.' The bombing of the headquarters of RTS, which left sixteen civilians dead, 'was a deliberate attack on a civilian object and as such constitutes a war crime'. 'In various attacks . . . NATO forces failed to suspend their attack after it was evident that they had struck civilians.' However, 'no proper investigation appears to have been conducted by NATO or its member states into these incidents'.[24]

Throughout the bombing, NATO expressly targeted Milosevic and other elected government officials for assassination. On 22 April 1999, a NATO airstrike demolished Milosevic's residence, with four bombs striking the living room, dining room and bedroom. When asked during a television interview if this attack indicated that Milosevic was a target, former Pentagon official Ronald Hatchett replied 'certainly he was . . . there's no question about the fact that that was what we were trying to do in striking that house'.[25]

The prosecutor of the International Criminal Tribunal for the Former Yugoslavia (ICTFY), Carla del Ponte, has refused to accept that NATO deliberately targeted civilians in the campaign. But Amnesty held to its view that the attack on the RTS was a war crime. The ICTFY declined to investigate possible violations because 'either the law is not sufficiently clear or investigations are unlikely to result in the acquisition of sufficient evidence to substantiate charges against the high level accused or against lower accused [sic] for particularly heinous offences'. In other words, the tribunal was not expecting NATO to provide such evidence.

The ICTFY report also noted that if the attack on RTS 'was justified by reference to its propaganda purpose alone, its legality might well be questioned' – but this was exactly the explanation given to Amnesty by NATO. British ministers have consistently defended the attack on the radio and television station as a 'legitimate military target'.[26]

Various groups of lawyers have compiled dossiers against NATO leaders. One group, led by Professor Michael Mandel, sent to the Tribunal a dossier accusing NATO of 'grave violations of international humanitarian law' including 'wilful killing'. It noted an estimated $100 billion damage and the destruction of, or serious damage to, dozens of bridges, railways and railway stations, major roads, airports, including civilian airports, hospitals and health care centres, television transmitters, medieval monasteries and religious shrines, hundreds of schools, thousands of dwellings and civilian industrial and agricultural facilities.[27]

The Tribunal's refusal even to investigate NATO actions shows how in reality it is a political tool of NATO (that is, the US and Britain). The Tribunal is funded by the US and its allies and staffed with their approval, and depends on them for their information and support. Comparable crimes have received completely different treatment by the Tribunal: for example, Serb leader Milan Martic was indicted for launching a rocket cluster-bomb attack on military targets in Zagreb in 1995; but NATO's cluster bomb raid on Nis in May 1999, far from any military target, has simply been ignored. After persistently trying to make the case to the Tribunal for investigating NATO war crimes, Mandel eventually gave up when it became clear 'that the tribunal was a hoax'.[28]

There was massive bombing of civilian infrastructure. Human Rights Watch noted that:

> We are concerned that NATO bombed the civilian infrastructure not because it was making a significant contribution to the Yugoslav military effort but because its destruction would squeeze Serb civilians to put pressure on Milosevic to withdraw from Kosovo.

Such military force against civilians is a clear violation of international law.[29]

Two weeks into the NATO campaign a group of Yugoslav NGOs made an appeal to stop the bombing. They noted that 'for two weeks now the most powerful military, political and economic countries in the world have been killing people and destroying military and civilian facilities'. The NGOs said they had fought against 'every war-mongering and nationalistic policy, and for the respect of human rights, and particularly against the repression of Kosovo Albanians', insisting on the restoration of autonomy for Kosovo. 'Throughout this period', they noted, 'Serb and Albanian civil society groups were the only ones to retain contacts and cooperation. The NATO intervention has destroyed everything that has been achieved so far and the very survival of the civic society in Serbia.'

Similarly, the director of the Belgrade Centre for Human Rights and a former Vice Chair of the Human Rights Committee, Professor Vojin Simitrijevic, wrote that:

> The air strikes erased in one night the results of ten years of hard work of groups of courageous people in the non-governmental organisations and in the democratic opposition, who have not tried to 'topple' anyone but to develop the institutions of civil society, to promote liberal and civil values, to teach non-violent conflict resolution . . . The Kosovo problem will remain unresolved and the future of democracy and human rights in Serbia uncertain for many years.[30]

NATO forces have also left a deadly legacy of thousands of unexploded shells. Human Rights Watch notes that 'the use of cluster bombs raises questions of humanitarian law' and that they are dispersed over a large area 'creating a grave lingering danger for the noncombatant civilian population'. The 'high dud rate of cluster bomb sub-munitions turns these weapons effectively into anti-personnel landmines that do not distinguish between combatants and noncombatants, detonate on contact, and may lie undisturbed for years after a conflict has ended until someone happens upon one'. Because of their appearance, 'children are particularly drawn to the volatile live remnants'.[31]

Half of all British bombs dropped were cluster bombs – 531 of them. The White House quietly restricted the US use of cluster bombs after civilian deaths in the city of Nis on 7 May, for which it blamed a technical fault. But Britain continued to use them, arguing that the technical fault didn't apply to its own cluster bombs. During the war, between ninety and 150 civilians were killed by these bombs, according to Human Rights Watch.[32]

The Ministry of Defence admits to a failure rate of 5 per cent for the 147 bomblets in each bomb, but the real figure may be at least double that. According to the Defence Committee, this means that the RAF left between 4,000 and 10,000 unexploded bomblets on the ground in Kosovo. Another 151 people were killed or injured by unexploded bomblets within a year of the end of the bombing.[33]

NATO was in search of a pretext to start the campaign against Milosevic. In the negotiations in Rambouillet, outside Paris, in March, NATO needed to present Milosevic as totally unwilling to pursue a diplomatic outcome to the crisis. The Yugoslavs were consequently presented with a plan that was impossible to accept. The Rambouillet text drawn up by NATO called for military occupation and political control of Kosovo by NATO and effective military occupation of the rest of the Former Yugoslavia at NATO's will. Appendix B noted that 'NATO shall enjoy, together with their vehicles, vessels, aircraft and equipment, free and unrestricted passage and unimpeded access throughout the FRY including associated airspace and territorial waters.'

The former Canadian ambassador to Yugoslavia later said that 'the insistence of allowing access to all of Yugoslavia by NATO forces . . . guaranteed a Serbian rejection'. A senior US administration official told the media at Rambouillet that 'we intentionally set the bar too high for the Serbs to comply. They need some bombing and that's what they are going to get.'[34]

The Foreign Affairs Committee concludes that:

> One interpretation of the oral evidence given to us by FCO officials is that they never really believed that Milosevic would sign at Rambouillet, but that . . . 'we had to go through a process', presumably with the aim of promoting unity among the international community

in favour of military action by showing that Milosevic was unwilling to negotiate . . . Unless Milosevic could be blamed for the collapse of the talks, it would be difficult to justify the use of force against him.[35]

There may have been a chance to secure a diplomatic solution. The Serbian National Assembly responded to the US/NATO ultimatum on 23 March. It rejected the demand for NATO military occupation but called for negotiations leading 'towards the reaching of a political agreement on a wide-ranging autonomy for Kosovo . . . with the securing of a full equality of all citizens and ethnic communities'. This possible opening was ignored by NATO and barely reported in the media.[36]

During the war, US and British leaders managed to ignore or deflect all potential peace deals except those purely on their terms. On 14 April, for example, Germany proposed a six-point peace plan that was consistent with 'NATO's' demands on Milosevic. The plan called for the withdrawal of Yugoslav forces from Kosovo alongside a twenty-four-hour pause in the bombing. This plan was immediately rejected by the US and Britain, who insisted that Milosevic withdraw before a bombing pause. The press reported that 'the US and Britain are unwilling to stop the bombing temporarily because it might prove hard to restart'.[37] With the rejection of the German plan, and also moves by France to present other plans, it was clear that the 'NATO' demands were those of the US, backed by Britain.

On 22 April following talks between Milosevic and Russian Foreign Minister Viktor Chernomyrdin, the latter announced that Milosevic had agreed to an 'international presence in Kosovo under United Nations auspices' if NATO stopped the bombing. He reiterated the Serbian National Assembly proposals of 23 March.[38] These diplomatic openings were also ignored by NATO and the bombing continued.

On 3 June, the Kosovo peace accord was signed. The US/NATO abandoned their demands for full military occupation and substantial political control of Kosovo. The Rambouillet wording that has been interpreted as calling for a referendum on independence for Kosovo was also missing. Serbia agreed to an 'international security presence with substantial NATO participation'. Kosovo was to be under the control of the UN Security Council. The outcome of 3 June suggests that diplomatic initiatives could have been pursued on 23 March.[39] The deal that concluded the bombing campaign was in many ways better for Yugoslavia than that offered to Milosevic at Rambouillet and also better than that demanded by NATO during the campaign. There was no requirement, for example, to permit NATO transit rights through Serbia.

With the bombing campaign over, what happened to the immense humanitarian impulses that had supposedly motivated Tony Blair, Bill Clinton and others to act in March 1999? The answer is evident. By late 2000 more than 210,000 ethnic Serbs had been forced to flee Kosovo, most of them in the first few weeks of the NATO troop deployments as agreed in the peace accord. According to British government sources, this figure was three times greater than the number of refugees outside Kosovo before the bombing, which supposedly promoted NATO's 'humanitarian' intervention. This was more 'ethnic cleansing', in percentage terms the 'largest in the Balkan wars', according to Jan Oberg, Norwegian director of the Transnational Foundation for Peace. Around 1,000 Serbs and Roma were murdered or went missing after mid-June under 'ethnic cleansing' by the Kosovan Liberation Army (KLA). This time, however, these abuses elicited no calls for action to prevent a humanitarian catastrophe and no grandstanding speeches. The media were not required to offer their support, so also remained largely quiet.

In this case, massive human rights abuses took place under the very noses of NATO troops. 'Immediately following NATO's arrival in Kosovo, there was widespread and systematic burning and looting of homes belonging to Serbs, Roma and other minorities', Human Rights Watch noted. It said that 'the international community is partially to blame for the postwar violence' with the UN and NATO failing 'to take decisive action from the outset to curb the forced displacement and killings'. The most significant reason for this 'is the lack of political will. Senior NATO and UN officials know that persons linked to the former KLA . . . are implicated in violence and in criminal activities, but they have chosen not to confront them'. Human Rights Watch noted a 'culture of impunity' in the province. 'It took almost a year before international officials' including NATO Secretary General Lord Robertson 'were finally willing to concede that attacks against minorities in Kosovo were systematic in nature'.[40]

In this case, no bombing campaign was required to act in defence of human rights; with thousands of forces on the ground, simple arrest procedures would have been largely sufficient. If, that is, there had been the slightest interest in protecting human rights in Kosovo. The simple conclusion is that defending human rights was never the motive for the war against Yugoslavia. It is a truism to state – and the rest of this book provides further evidence – that 'human rights' is simply a convenient pretext to be deployed to promote policies to achieve other objectives.

Motives imagined and real

The media performed a critical role by taking British/NATO rhetoric largely at face value. The war was portrayed as good versus evil, civilisation versus barbarity, and every newspaper except the *Independent on Sunday* took a pro-war line. Some individual commentators opposed the bombing. But overall the mainstream media revealed themselves once again in war as more a part of the campaign than independent commentators. In particular, there was almost no questioning, let alone ridiculing, of the notion that Britain was fighting for human rights. Virtually the only serious issue debated was whether air power alone could achieve the highly moral objectives assumed by our leaders, or whether the ground troops were also needed.

Philip Hammond, a media lecturer at South Bank University, notes that 'the refugee crisis became NATO's strongest propaganda weapon, though logically it should have been viewed as a damning indictment of the bombing. The hundreds of thousands of Serbs who fled bombing were therefore determinedly ignored by British journalists, just as most of the killings, kidnappings, beatings and torture of Kosovo Serbs after the war were not deemed newsworthy.' After the bombing, journalists went to extraordinary lengths to praise NATO and managed to overlook the fact that there was not the humanitarian disaster on the scale that the NATO leaders claimed, until the bombing started.[41]

Some media comment reached staggering levels of support for state policy. The *Guardian*'s Polly Toynbee claimed that 'there was nothing in this for anyone, no political gain for any leader, no glory, only the certainty that Milosevic's monstrous ethnic cleansing had to be stopped'. It was an 'honourable cause' and 'a brave and probably only chance for the West collectively to create a more ethical foreign policy', showing a 'purity of motive, freedom from self-interest'.[42]

Jonathan Freedland wrote in the *Guardian* that it was 'a war fought in pursuit of a humanitarian aim. The prize is not turf or treasure but the frustration of a plan to empty a land of its people'. It was 'a noble goal'. The *New Statesman*'s John Lloyd wrote that it showed that 'the most powerful states are willing to fight for human rights'.[43]

The *Guardian*'s Hugo Young similarly explained that 'what this action is about, for better or for worse, is humanitarian impulse'. 'It wasn't part of cold war geo-politics. There was no oil. It asserts a principle that is new and, progressively, admirable: the moral imperative to stop dictators brutally punishing and exterminating national ethnic groups.'[44]

In fact, Young was writing four days after his newspaper reported the massacre of dozens of people in Liquica, East Timor. The perpetrator was our ally and favourite arms recipient,

Indonesia. But neither the *Guardian* nor any of the other mainstream newspapers seemed troubled by this (or any other) rather obvious example of the complete indifference to human rights that the British government really has.

If anything, there was more (albeit minuscule) critical comment in the right-wing press than in the *Guardian* and *Independent*. Unusually, a *Spectator* editorial a year after the bombing came remarkably close to the reality. It referred to NATO war crimes and 'its criminal terror-bombing campaign'. It said that NATO's 'policy was to destroy Serbia's civilian infrastructure' and that 'deliberately to destroy civilian targets with the intention of rendering the daily life of a population impossible is a clear breach of the very international law which Mr Clinton and Mr Blair claimed to uphold'.[45]

Interestingly, one year after the war the *Guardian* had somewhat changed its position. During the war it had given complete ideological backing to the British government, saying it was 'a test for our generation'. Now it said that 'the code name "humanitarian intervention" which its proponents gave was not, of course, the whole truth. *No countries go to war on the basis of altruism*'. This simple truth could now be stated – and completely undermines the *Guardian*'s position at the time. But it still held to the view that the bombing was legitimate.[46]

The amazing thing the media managed to avoid – with near 100 per cent discipline – was comment on whether the government might just have had any motives other than purely humanitarian. Commentator after commentator accepted the humanitarian rationale and the notion that Britain had no interests in the region since 'Kosovo had no oil'. Now that the *Guardian* has discovered that 'no countries go to war on the basis of altruism', perhaps it might be able to speculate on more plausible explanations for the bombing campaign against Yugoslavia.

The first plausible explanation is the other one provided by NATO leaders – 'credibility'. I believe this is certainly true, as noted above. But there was little attempt in the mainstream media to explain the meaning of 'credibility' and how it fell just a little short of the humanitarian motives also claimed.

But there were other obvious Western strategic objectives at the time, such as expanding NATO eastward and organising Eastern European economies to benefit Western business. These are complementary strategies geared to bringing the former Soviet bloc countries into the Western orbit. NATO's expansion is meant to ensure Eastern Europe's reliance on the US and its European allies for 'security', including lucrative arms purchases. NATO expansion is seen as an important enough strategy in NATO capitals to risk incurring Russia's wrath as its former enemy seduces former Soviet satellites and moves its alliance borders closer to Russia.

The US ambassador to NATO, Alexander Vershbow, explains that NATO is 'an alliance of 19 democratic, market-oriented countries'. NATO membership provides to new allies 'the security and stability that is a key element for participation in the multi-trillion global economy – by reassuring investors that these are stable countries worthy of long-term commitment'. Therefore, 'continued NATO enlargement is an essential part of the Alliance's strategy for unifying and stabilising Europe'.[47]

The economies of Eastern Europe, the object of huge Western 'advice' and pressure after the collapse of Soviet control, have been organised according to much of the same neo-liberal economic ideology that devastated the developing world – privatisation, deregulation and liberalisation. Poverty in many Eastern European countries has shot up; absolute poverty now affects 15–20 per cent of the population across most of the region, and is as high as 40 per cent in Romania, according to the World Bank.[48] Those profiting from Eastern Europe's restructuring have included a new entrepreneurial and often criminal class, as well as Western businesses which have gained from a more favourable investment climate. In this strategy, the West has supported the most radical economic 'reformers' and undermined both the revamped communist parties and more progressive alternatives.

Robin Cook told the *New Statesman* just after the end of the bombing of Yugoslavia that 'our key tasks [in southeast Europe] are first of all to increase trade, open up their markets and help them with economic progress, [and] to intensify the integration with European structures'. Europe Minister Keith Vaz has similarly noted that 'Southeastern Europe . . . needs to attract investors by creating a favourable climate for investment.'[49]

The basic strategy to 'open up their markets' also applies to Kosovo and Bosnia. The EU's economic strategy in the Balkans is based on 'a special and demanding contractual relationship', EU Commissioner Chris Patten explains. 'In exchange for the assistance we offer', Patten notes, 'they will need to work hard on economic reform in order to build solid market economies capable of competing freely and openly with member states.' The Rambouillet text had stated that 'the economy of Kosovo shall function in accordance with free market principles'. Later, the British government said that the international community was aiming to create a Kosovo where 'prosperity is based on free markets'. Britain and the EU were aiming to develop Bosnia as 'a business-friendly, single economic space', including by eliminating inter-entity trade barriers.[50]

In November 2001, Foreign Office minister Baroness Symons gave a speech at the Confederation of British Industry directed at new Yugoslav President Kostunica, who was on his first visit to the UK. She said that in 1990 Yugoslavia was Britain's fastest growing trade and investment partner in central and eastern Europe, but that Milosevic ruined all that. Now, however, there were again lots of business opportunities. She said that 'Britain can continue to benefit from the reconstruction of Yugoslavia,' the country her government had recently bombed. And she announced that Britain was to restart negotiations with Yugoslavia on bilateral investment promotion and protection.[51]

It is certainly plausible that these concerns about bringing southeast Europe firmly into the Western security and economic orbit played a key role in British and NATO strategy to undermine and help remove Milosevic. The regime in Belgrade was brutal and repressive; it was also one of the few countries with a reconstituted communist party in power and had essentially continued Yugoslavia's traditional stance of remaining independent of East and West. Its more independent domestic policies posed the last real barrier to openly expressed British, EU and US aims in Eastern Europe, which amount to returning the region to its historical status of de facto client area of the West.

Final questions concern the costs of the war in Kosovo and what the alternatives might have been. One alternative might have been the diplomatic solution that NATO was never seriously interested in exploring, as noted above. Supporters of the war argued that Milosevic would have launched his campaign of 'ethnic cleansing' anyway, without NATO bombing. We can never know, but the chances are that such a campaign would have been less devastating had it not been conducted under the shroud of NATO bombing. The effects of NATO bombing were at least 500 civilians killed and up to 10,000 unexploded cluster bomblets left by Britain alone, not to mention the damage to the country's infrastructure, impact on people and civil society attempts to promote peaceful resolution of tensions in the Balkans. It is true that ethnic Albanians could return to Kosovo following the NATO 'victory' but this return was accompanied by expulsions of ethnic Serbs.

Then there are the consequences of the world's powerful states again using force illegally to impose themselves on official enemies. One lesson from such actions to be drawn by dictatorships and perhaps more benign governments, not to mention terrorist groups, is that if you want to defend yourself against the world's powerful states, you'd better acquire weapons of mass destruction. It is inconceivable that NATO would have bombed Yugoslavia if Belgrade had possessed functioning weapons of mass destruction. Former Soviet leader Mikhail Gorbachev said at the end of NATO's bombing campaign against Yugoslavia that:

Smaller countries – among them 31 'threshold' states capable of developing nuclear weapons – are looking to their own security with growing trepidation. They are thinking they must have absolute weapons to be able to defend themselves or to retaliate if they are subjected to similar treatment.[52]

The 'balance sheet' is complex and not cut and dried. But a number of things are clear: the launching of the war was illegal; NATO conducted violations of humanitarian law and war crimes; NATO actions precipitated rather than prevented a humanitarian catastrophe; political leaders like Blair and Clinton probably knew what the terrible consequences of launching the bombing campaign would be, but still went ahead; and therefore British and US leaders' claims to be acting from humanitarian motives were mythical. Yet these facts have consistently been suppressed or forgotten (if they were ever mentioned) in the mainstream, while the war over Kosovo has gone down in history as a great victory for humanitarian values.

In some ways the Kosovo war was – as the *Guardian* claimed in a different sense – 'a test of our generation': a test of whether British foreign policy planners abide by international law and ethical standards in their role in the world; and of whether British mainstream political culture is able to see through a new generation of 'humanitarian' propaganda by leaders. The test was failed on both counts.

7

CHECHNYA:
A CHRONICLE OF
COMPLICITY

The liberation of Kosovo and the message it sent to regimes that disregard human rights will come to be seen as a defining moment in modern history
> The government's annual report on human rights
> 1999[1]

One can only imagine the thoughts of the officials who wrote this. As Britain exuded outrage at Milosevic's crimes in Kosovo, its Indonesian ally was directing paramilitary groups in a terror campaign in East Timor (see chapter 21), while Turkey was continuing repression throughout its Kurdish regions. Three months after the end of the bombing of Yugoslavia, Russia launched a ferocious campaign in Chechnya eliciting the barest of concerns by Western leaders.

What was required in these cases was nothing so dramatic as military intervention, or mobilising the public to support a full-scale war, but simply to turn off the tap of support, be it on arms, trade, investment or diplomacy. The list of human rights abusers supported by Britain is long enough to make simply ridiculous the idea that the government suddenly became devoted to human rights in Kosovo in March 1999.

In the Blair government years, a number of horrific massacres of civilians have occurred elsewhere. One was in January 1999 when Serb special forces killed forty-five people in the town of Racak, Kosovo. The official report into Racak was released on 17 March 1999, the head of the Finnish investigating team calling the massacre 'a crime against humanity'. Foreign Office minister Tony Lloyd said that 'we do quite clearly condemn [the Racak massacre] as a crime against international law, but specifically as a war crime'. He added that 'only the most forthright condemnation is fitting for what did take place there'.[2]

NATO leaders seized on the Racak massacre to prove that the Milosevic regime was evil, and it provided the pretext for the military intervention that NATO was bent on. 'Spring has come early', was reportedly what US Secretary of State Madeleine Albright told National Security Adviser Sandy Berger, on hearing of the massacre. Racak was consistently reported in the media. According to the *Independent* it 'set in motion the events which led to NATO's air campaign'. The *Observer* noted that it was 'the massacre that lit the touchpaper of the war with Yugoslavia'. A week after the official report into Racak, NATO bombing began.[3]

British leaders, and the media, have reacted somewhat differently to a range of other massacres of comparable size elsewhere. In Liquica, East Timor, in April 1999 – as NATO was bombing Yugoslavia – fifty-two people were killed in attacks by a paramilitary group created and supported by the Indonesian army. For at least six hours thousands of men, women and children seeking sanctuary were subjected to automatic gunfire and tear gas.[4]

On 6 September 1999 in Suai, East Timor, at least fifty people were massacred in a church where 100 people had taken refuge. The church was attacked directly by members of the Indonesian army and police as well as militias, commanded by an Indonesian lieutenant. One priest was stabbed and hacked to death, and at least two other priests were murdered. Twenty-six bodies were loaded on to a truck by the commander of the attack and buried across the border in West Timor.[5]

At Bumi Flora in the Aceh province of Indonesia on 9 August 2001, dozens of armed men dressed in camouflage uniforms entered one of the housing areas of a rubber and palm oil plantation, and shot thirty men and a two-year-old child to death.[6]

On 24 February 2001, fifty-one bodies were discovered in the village of Dachny, less than a kilometre from the main Russian military base in Chechnya. Sixteen of the nineteen bodies that could be identified were last seen in the custody of Russian forces, many in civilian clothing, blindfolded and with their feet or hands bound. According to Human Rights Watch:

> The mass 'dumping site' – the bodies were dumped along streets in the village and in abandoned cottages over an extended period of time – provides striking evidence of the practice of forced disappearances, torture and extrajudicial execution of civilians by Russian federal forces in Chechnya.[7]

These massacres provoked no calls for action in defence of human rights and no grandstanding speeches about the principles of military intervention. The reason is obvious – they were perpetrated by our allies.

Britain probably has more leverage over these allies than it ever did over the Milosevic regime, but these massacres provoked no changes in British policy. Since they were not noticed by political leaders, neither were they noticed by the media – there are only one or two media mentions of these other massacres, compared to a stream of reporting on Racak. I also did a search on the Houses of Parliament database. There were sixty-eight mentions of Racak compared to six mentions of Liquica, none of Suai and none of Dachny.

Let us now look closer at the Russian actions in Chechnya that began soon after the war over Kosovo.

Moscow in Chechnya, London in denial

An eight-year-old Chechen boy called Ali Makaev, living in a Chechen refugee camp in Ingushetia, wrote in a school essay:

> I do not know if Putin has a heart. But if he did he would not have started such a war. Putin thinks that human life is worth fifty kopecks. He is deeply mistaken . . . I'd like Putin to know that we are also human beings.[8]

This is a description of one of Tony Blair's greatest allies in the early years of the new millennium. The Blair–Putin relationship has been one of the most extraordinary developments in British foreign policy in recent years. It is instructive that the Foreign Office claims this relationship as a great success for the country's foreign policy; in reality, it means British complicity in some of the worst horrors of our time.

The background to the current phase in the Chechnya conflict was the Russian invasion of the territory from 1994–96, when Moscow sought to destroy Chechen demands to establish a fully independent republic. Though Chechen forces eventually managed to defeat Russia, the latter slaughtered between 60,000 and 100,000 Chechens, wounded hundreds of thousands more and left a deadly legacy of millions of landmines scattered across the territory. Russian forces used artillery and rocket barrages to destroy Chechen villages and towns, deliberately targeting civilians, and razing most of Chechnya to the ground. The Chechen capital Grozny was destroyed over new year 1995. Anatol Lieven, an analyst at the International Institute for Strategic Studies in London, notes that the 1996 victory of the Chechen separatist forces was 'one of the greatest epics of colonial resistance in the past century' in a context of Russian imperial rule in the Caucasus.[9]

A treaty eventually signed granted Chechnya de facto independence though Moscow refused to grant full independence.

The agreement also recognised that a popular referendum should be held in Chechnya in December 2001 to determine the ultimate fate of its independence. Russia's attack on Chechnya in 1999 was a violation of the 1996 treaty and sought to avenge its defeat and reimpose Moscow's will over the territory.

September 1999 – three months after the end of the bombing of Yugoslavia – marked the beginning of the new phase of the conflict. Then, bomb explosions ripped through apartment blocks in Moscow killing around 300 people. The Russian government immediately blamed Chechens for these attacks and within days Moscow had deployed 50,000 troops in Chechnya and begun airstrikes, which soon drove 185,000 civilians from their homes. It quickly became obvious that Russian war strategy involved both heavy indiscriminate bombing and deliberately targeting civilians. Cities and villages began to be bombarded while Chechnya was encircled by Russian forces, which cut off all gas and electricity supplies.

Let us consider a brief chronology of further Russian actions in Chechnya, alongside the response of the Blair government.

1999

Following the invasion, the EU adopted a 'common strategy on Russia' but this 'contained very weak language on human rights and the rule of law', according to Human Rights Watch. In October the EU presidency expressed only limited concern for civilians in Chechnya.

The city of Grozny was ferociously bombed for three straight months from November 1999 to February 2000 and 'was essentially treated as one enormous military target'. Most people had left by then but between 20,000 and 40,000 remained, many too poor or sick to leave. 'These people were given little thought as the Russian military machine obliterated the city', Human Rights Watch noted. The attack on Grozny levelled the city with massive indiscriminate bombing, turning it into a wasteland, with thousands dead.[10]

The *Guardian*'s Maggie O'Kane wrote that 'usually in war there are some rules. But in Chechnya, no one is saying sorry or even pretending that they are not dropping 1,000 lb bombs on houses, hospitals and schools.'[11] Russian forces denied aid agencies access to the area, and engaged in systematic looting and plundering from homes, and destroyed power stations and industrial plants. Billions of roubles in assets were probably taken.

Blair wrote to then Prime Minister Vladimir Putin (Boris Yeltsin was still president, resigning on 31 December) urging Moscow to halt its advance on Grozny. The US described Russia's 'indiscriminate' use of force against civilians as 'indefensible'.[12] In December, the IMF postponed a £400 million loan to Russia and the EU agreed to freeze some aid. But it was already clear that the West was not going to impose any tough measures against Russia. Therefore, Russia paid little attention, proceeding to obliterate the city.

The ferocious obliteration of a defenceless city was not enough to provoke British leaders to do anything other than go through the motions of protest – mild protest at that. Britain failed to use any of its bilateral levers with Russia (see further below) to pressure the aggressors at this time. Human Rights Watch correctly noted that while Yeltsin was in power Britain 'was unwilling to use this relationship as leverage to secure better human rights compliance by the Russian government'.[13]

In fact, it was Russia not Britain that used the levers available to press the other side. The Ministry of Defence noted that 'our developing military relationship, based on high level contacts and exchanges, suffered a setback' in 1999 – not due to British pressure over Chechnya, but because of Russian opposition to the attacks on Iraq in December 1998 and on Yugoslavia. Russia had begun 'by scaling down contacts and then cancelling all bilateral military events planned with the UK'. One programme that survived had been launched in 1995, involving Britain retraining nearly 10,000 retired Russian officers for future employment at eight centres in Russia.

'During 1999, we offered to extend this programme' and agreed to establish two new centres, the MoD notes.[14] The military conducting gross atrocities in Chechnya was the same that Britain was bending over backwards to court.

2000

Entering into 2000, with Grozny in the process of being flattened, Foreign Office minister Keith Vaz assured the House of Commons that 'we have repeatedly raised with the Russians our concerns about their bombing campaign in Chechnya'. However, on the same day, Defence minister Geoff Hoon also said:

> Engaging Russia in a constructive bilateral defence relationship is a high priority for the government. Russia remains the highest priority in our 'Outreach' programme of defence assistance to central and eastern Europe countries. We wish to continue to develop an effective defence relationship with Russia.[15]

In a 63-paragraph-long Foreign Office memo to a parliamentary inquiry into British relations with Russia, dated 27 January 2000, Chechnya is not mentioned once. The memo simply says that 'we still have some concerns' on human rights and that 'there are also significant weaknesses, both in policy and implementation, in the [Russian] government's treatment of vulnerable groups and its obligation to protect their rights'. There was a supplementary memo provided, fifty-four paragraphs long, on the 'FCO's role in promoting British interests in and relations with Russia'.[16] Again, no mention of Chechnya. The issue was, quite simply, off the radar screen.

Foreign Secretary Robin Cook told the Royal Institute of International Affairs on 28 January that Russian 'conduct in Chechnya is unacceptable and has produced grave humanitarian suffering. Nor, without a political settlement, will it produce their own stated objective of defeating the terrorists.'

Here, Cook was accepting Moscow's official line for its actions – 'defeating the terrorists', an all-too-obvious mask, as we see below.[17]

In February, the House of Commons Foreign Affairs Committee noted that 'none of these strong messages [that it believed Britain was delivering to Russia] achieved any meaningful change in Russian attitudes or actions in Chechnya'.[18]

The reality of the 'strong messages' was shown by Channel 4 news, which reported on 23 February 2000 that Cook, in his visit to Russian Foreign Minister Ivanov, said he 'understood' Russia's problems in Chechnya. Cook delivered Britain's 'frank concerns' over Chechnya, before also saying that 'it is equally important that we retain a relationship with Russia that enables us to work together constructively'. Cook also said of Vladimir Putin, who had by now become acting president: 'I found his style refreshing and open and his priorities for Russia are ones that we share.'[19]

On the same day that Cook was saying that Britain and Putin shared the same piorities, the *Guardian* reported Human Rights Watch saying that at least sixty-two people had been killed earlier in the month in one of the worst massacres. Survivors described how around one hundred Russian soldiers systematically robbed and shot civilians on the southern outskirts of Grozny in a two-day rampage in which troops raped civilians, threw grenades into basements where people were hiding and executed anyone who tried to resist looting. 'This is the single worst massacre of civilians that we have documented so far', Human Rights Watch commented.[20]

Keith Vaz gave a further speech in March 2000 to a 'political and economic prospects in the Caspian Sea region' conference. His only mention of Chechnya was to refer to the 'appalling footage of fighting in Chechnya, with terrible consequences on both sides'. (The 'both sides' formula being customary in apologising for the crimes of our allies, as with Israel and Turkey.)[21]

A week before a visit by Tony Blair to Vladimir Putin, the *Observer* revealed the slaughter of 363 people in the village of Katyr Yurt. Eyewitnesses said that Russian troops offered to give villagers safe corridor but then proceeded to use rockets against them. One witness was a doctor who had operated on hundreds of patients without anaesthetics, medicines or electricity during the bombardment. He said:

> First they hit the village, then gave the civilians a corridor and they were shot. They didn't bring the dead to us, only those in agony. They brought 10 bodies, to check if they were alive or not: one baby among them, grown ups, teenagers, some without both legs, burnt with traumas to the head, stomach.[22]

Blair met acting President Putin in Russia on 11 March 2000. They went to the opera together while Cherie was taken to the Hermitage museum in St Petersburg by Lyudmila Putin. Human Rights Watch said:

> This is absolutely the wrong signal to be sending, making a private visit to the opera at a time when war crimes are being committed with impunity by Russian forces in Chechnya . . . There are mass executions of civilians, arbitrary detention of Chechen males, systematic beatings, torture and, on occasions, rape. There is the absolute and systematic and rampant looting of Chechen homes by Russian troops; these acts need to be condemned in the strongest possible terms.[23]

Asked about the risk of being seen to be backing Russia in Chechnya, a British government spokesman said: 'You can't plan your international diary according to the ups and downs of fighting on the ground.'[24]

The *Observer* noted that 'Blair's visit and the cordial tone of the meetings with Putin is being seen as a coup for the Russian leader' which marked a 'broad seal of approval' for him. Blair said that it was a 'privilege' to be in St Petersburg and that 'we've had a very good and full discussion . . . I want to say how much I have enjoyed that dialogue'. Britain also continued to offer public support for the Russian line, a Downing Street official saying that 'there is a terrorist insurrection on their territory'.[25]

Indeed, Britain offered specific help to Russia on this visit. The press reported that Blair agreed to despatch a team headed by David Miliband, the head of the Downing Street policy unit, to advise Putin's new government on how it could 'best handle a well-established bureaucracy and civil service to push through its wishes'. Blair also agreed to send a top Treasury official to Moscow to advise on economic reform. Blair's calls for investigations into human rights abuses and comments that Russian actions in Chechnya should be 'proportionate' could only have been drowned in this context.[26]

Later in the month, in response to a parliamentary question on Chechnya, Blair repeated that he had told the Russians their actions needed to be 'proportionate' and urged access for human rights observers. At the same time, he had also discussed the 'prospects for the Russian economy and British investment in it. I made clear the need to improve conditions for investors.'[27]

It would be hard to express milder criticism of Russia than Britain did at this time, while courting the Russians in virtually every other field. After weeks of indiscriminate bombardment of civilians with massive human rights abuses ongoing, the most that a Downing Street spokesman could say ahead of the next Blair–Putin meeting was: 'We have recognised that the Russians have a security problem. Any use of force should be proportionate and mindful of the need to reduce the risk to civilians.'[28] It was hardly surprising that Putin made Britain his first destination after becoming president.

Ahead of the next meeting in April, Human Rights Watch wrote to Blair imploring him to press human rights concerns on Putin. It said that 'your failure to condemn the war crimes committed by Russian forces and to call for accountability' would undermine the Council of Europe's parliamentary assembly, which had just voted to strip Russia of its voting rights. 'Britain must play a critical role in maintaining pressure on the Russian government to curtail abuses by its forces in Chechnya, and to punish' those guilty of human rights violations.[29]

Blair met Putin on 13 April. His speech showed that he failed to condemn the violations in Chechnya and repeated the formula that Russia was simply responding to terrorism: 'I can understand Russia's need to respond to the threat of force from extremists and terrorists.' He added that 'I am also clear that the measures taken should be proportionate and consistent with its international obligations' – weeks after Grozny had been levelled. He said that Russia should allow humanitarian access by international organisations, and there are no military solutions. 'But I believe that the best way . . . is through engagement [with Russia] not isolation.'[30]

Resolutions of the UN Commission on Human Rights in 1999 and 2000 condemned Russia for its actions in Chechnya and called on it to undertake investigations into 'all violations of international humanitarian law and human rights'. According to Human Rights Watch, 'Russia has blatantly resisted implementation of both resolutions, challenging the authority and credibility of the Commission and the UN human rights mechanism . . . Not a single high level commander has had to answer for atrocities.'[31]

2001

Coming into 2001, numerous unmarked graves containing people last seen in Russian custody continued to be discovered, with Dachny only the largest. About 140,000 people forced to flee from Chechnya remained in neighbouring Ingushetia, many in squalid conditions. In March, Human Rights Watch reported 113 documented 'disappearances' since September

1999. It described a 'dirty war' in Chechnya, with 'mass violations of human rights' by Russian forces who were also detaining thousands of people, most without access to lawyers.[32]

A human rights organisation based in Grozny, the Lam Centre for Pluralism, also reported in March on the terrible conditions in the mountain region of Chechnya. People were living in half-destroyed houses while 'nothing is left of the regional capital of Itum-Kale except ruins and piles of trash'. The regional hospital now operated out of a private home with patients cared for 'either outside or in tents'. School buildings had been completely destroyed and children were studying mainly in unheated tents.[33]

After the terrorist attacks in the US on September 11th, Britain, NATO and the EU virtually abandoned all pretence of concern at Russian atrocities in Chechnya. Blair said that 'Russia has impressed many by her willingness to set history aside and to align herself solidly with the international coalition against terrorism.' The German Chancellor said that Russia's war against Chechnya should be 're-evaluated' in the light of the 'war against terrorism'. NATO Secretary General Lord Robertson stated that 'we have certainly come to see the scourge of terrorism in Chechnya with different eyes'; Russia and NATO are 'trusting friends and brothers-in-arms'.[34]

At the same time, Muscovites were asked in an opinion poll: 'What do you think most influenced Vladimir Putin's declaration of firm support for the struggle against international terrorism?' The highest number – 44 per cent – said: 'to reduce criticism by the West of actions by Russian forces in Chechnya'.[35]

By October 2001, Blair was exuding praise for Putin in unprecedented terms. In a joint press conference in Moscow he said that 'I would like to pay tribute to the strength and leadership of President Putin at this time.' Britain and Russia were 'working through problems in the spirit of friends and true partners'. This was Blair's eighth meeting with Putin in under two years. This, Blair noted, was 'a very good indication of the strengthening relationship, not just between Russia and Britain, but a strong personal relationship too, which I greatly value,' he added. The relationship today is of Russia as 'a partner and a friend'. It was thus Blair that proposed the creation of a Russia–North Atlantic Council to bring Moscow closer to NATO – one of the post-September 11th rewards for Moscow's good behaviour in supporting the 'war against terrorism'.[36]

At another joint press conference on 22 December 2001 Blair was asked if Chechnya had been discussed. He said it had, and that Putin had told him of the 'political initiatives being taken there, but it is important to remember that whatever cause people have, terrorism is not the way to pursue it', mentioning only acts of terrorism carried out against Russia. This was Blair's only mention of Chechnya in the press conference. No wonder Putin could say of Russia's attempts to deal with 'terrorism' (meaning Chechnya) that 'we felt and we saw and we knew that our voice was being heard, that the UK wanted to hear us and to understand us and that indeed we were being understood'.[37]

During 2001, the EU tabled a draft resolution on Chechnya at the UN Commission on Human Rights in Geneva but then tried to negotiate a much weaker chairman's statement. Human Rights Watch said that:

> UK prime minister Tony Blair and German chancellor
> Gerhard Schroeder undermined the European Union's
> efforts in Geneva, repeatedly praising President Putin's
> leadership but neglecting publicly to raise abuses in
> Chechnya, including Russia's failure to comply with
> EU-sponsored resolutions.

At two EU–Russia summits Chechnya was discussed behind closed doors and the EU said nothing in public.[38]

Following September 11th into 2002, the Parliamentary Assembly of the Council of Europe concluded in a report on Chechnya that 'no tangible improvement of the human rights situation in the Chechen republic could be observed during the past year'. A US State Department report said that Russia's human rights record was 'poor in Chechnya, where the federal security forces demonstrated little respect for basic human rights and there were credible reports of serious violations, including numerous reports of extra-judicial killings by both the government and Chechen fighters'.[39]

Human Rights Watch noted that 'civilians in Chechnya continued to suffer from ruthless sweep operations by Russian troops and from abusive guerilla tactics employed by rebel fighters'. In April it released another report documenting eighty-seven new cases of 'disappearances' in Chechnya since its last report in March 2001, noted above. This meant there had been more than 200 documented cases in Chechnya since September 1999, but there were a further 793 missing persons as of December 2001. The Russian human rights organisation, Memorial, documented 992 people murdered by the security forces from 1999 until January 2002, but said that the true figure was probably double that.[40]

May saw NATO agreeing to allow Russia into its new twenty-member council, giving Moscow an important new role in NATO policies. Jack Straw commented that this was 'the funeral of the cold war . . . Fifteen years ago, Russia was the enemy, now Russia becomes our friend and ally.'[41]

At the same time the human rights organisation, the Institute for Democracy in Eastern Europe, was describing conditions in Grozny. For the 275,000 residents of the city there was no water or electricity while from time to time the gas was turned off. It said that Russia 'has done practically nothing to restore the Chechen living quarters in Grozny', so the city was 'completely unsanitary' with the majority of hospitals and clinics 'in shambles or undergoing repair'. Eighty per cent of able-bodied citizens were unemployed and had no means of subsistence.[42]

In August four international human rights organisations wrote to the UN's Sub-commission on Human Rights to say that:

> Contrary to the recent declaration of Vladimir Putin, the situation in Chechnya is far from normalising. Cleansing operations undertaken by the Russian military forces, indiscriminate arrests, summary executions and torture are happening daily. And the first victims are the civilians.[43]

By late 2002, Britain's apologia for Russian terrorism in Chechnya had reached staggering heights. In a media interview in October, Tony Blair said that in view of the 'terrorism coming from extremists operating out of Chechnya . . . I have always taken the view that it is important that we understand the Russian perspective on this.' He added that it was important that Russia's territorial integrity be upheld and that 'I have always been more understanding of the Russian position, perhaps, than many others.'[44]

This came a week after a further (futile) attempt by Human Rights Watch to urge Blair to press Putin on human rights abuses in Chechnya. It noted that over the previous year the situation in Chechnya had not improved, that Russia 'continues to give the military in Chechnya a free hand to violate some of the most fundamental principles of international human rights and humanitarian law' and that not a single senior military commander had been held to account for atrocities. By this time, Russia had 80,000 troops in Chechnya (whose population totals 500,000), with reports indicating that this number would be beefed up still further.[45]

When Chechen terrorists took dozens of people hostage in a Moscow theatre, Putin ordered special forces to storm the building. 150 hostages were killed in a Russian operation for which Blair was one of the first leaders to congratulate President Putin. The hostage-taking offered a propaganda coup to Putin, who was able to continue to portray Chechens as simply terrorists and who continued to refuse to enter into a dialogue to negotiate a political settlement.

One press report in the same month outlined the continuing grisly details of atrocities in Chechnya over recent months: a massacre of twenty-one men, women and children – bound together and then blown up – in July; the bodies of six men found in September, naked with plastic bags over their heads; discoveries of numerous other mass graves; townspeople being forced to watch women being raped by soldiers, and sixty-eight men who protested being subsequently handcuffed to an armoured truck and raped too.[46]

One might imagine the Western abuse and condemnation that would have been heaped on the Soviet Union had it done what Russia has done in Chechnya. It would have been further proof of the 'empire of evil' and used by the hardliners in Washington and London to build more weapons and cut off contacts with Moscow. It would have been used to contrast with the West's shining devotion to human rights. Regular media coverage would surely have followed and the issue would have become a common talking point.

Instead, as the above chronology shows, British policy has been a series of de facto apologias for Russian atrocities, of accepting the Moscow line, and of refusing to use any levers to press Russia.

Britain has willingly gone along with Russian propaganda that the war in Chechnya is predominantly about fighting terrorism. September 11th was a godsend for Moscow and made it easier for leaders like Blair to apologise for Russian actions. But Blair, Cook, Straw and others were toeing the Russian line well before September 11th.

Russian forces may have been defeated in Chechnya in 1996 but the territory emerged devastated, with massive poverty and deprivation. Elections held in 1997 were won by Aslan

Maskhadov with 65 per cent support, but the institutions of a modern state collapsed and government has in practice bordered on anarchy. Maskhadov's attempts to create a largely secular order in Chechnya have been opposed by some Chechen military commanders. Some of the latter, such as Shamil Basayev, hero of the 1994–96 war, formed alliances with 'Wahabi' Islamist extremists who sought to turn Chechnya into an Islamist republic and who led an attack on the neighbouring Russian republic of Daghestan in August 1999.

The warlords in the territory, together with Islamic extremists, have been responsible for kidnappings and murders. Basayev and some other Chechen military leaders were trained in the mojahidin camps in Afghanistan in the 1980s and Basayev in particular had close contacts with high level officers in Pakistan's International Security Service, ISI, which organised the mojahidin, and which also helped train the Chechen rebel army. But the Russian propaganda line has essentially tried to depict all Chechens as terrorists. In reality Chechen society is too secular to justify Putin's claim that it acts as a base for Bin Laden-style fundamentalism. Putin's official spokesperson, Sergei Yastrzhembsky, admitted in late 2001 that there were only 200 Islamic mercenaries fighting in Chechnya.[47]

It is clear that the principal Russian objective in Chechnya is to defeat the prospects for full independence for the territory. Emil Pain, a former adviser on nationality affairs to president Yeltsin, states that:

> The main goal of the Russian army is not a struggle with terrorism but a desire to keep Chechnya within the [Russian] Federation . . . For a struggle with terrorists a completely different tactic is needed: the concentration of the efforts of small mobile groups of Special Forces and of a network of agents.[48]

As the respected military analyst of the weekly *Moscow News*, Pavel Felgenhauer, has noted, the Russian dilemma in

Chechnya is 'the fact that the separatists are actively supported by a significant part of the populace while, it appears, the overwhelming majority sympathise with them'.[49]

The line that Russia is *fighting* terrorism is being promoted even when evidence has emerged of Russian security services involvement in the Moscow bombings that provided the pretext for the Russian invasion. No convincing evidence has emerged of Chechen involvement in the bombings. The *Independent* obtained video evidence from a Russian officer testifying to the involvement of the FSB, the Russian security service, and the GRU, military intelligence, in the explosions. In September 1999 the Russian police discovered that FSB agents had planted explosives in the basement of a block of flats 100 miles south of Moscow. Various prominent figures have provided evidence of official Russian involvement in the bombings.

According to former Soviet political prisoner Vladimir Bukovsky:

> Evidence exists that entire apartment districts of Moscow were blown up by the special services in order to incite hatred against the Chechens. Chechnya was used for political goals. It permitted Putin and the KGB to return to power . . . What the Russians are doing in Chechnya is no less a crime than what Milosevic did in Kosovo, but Milosevic is in the Hague while Putin for some reason is not.[50]

Former Russian interior minister and prime minister Sergei Stephashin has said, according to British journalist Patrick Cockburn, that: 'Russia made its plans to invade Chechnya six months before the bombing of civilian targets in Russia and the Chechen attack on Daghestan which were the official pretext for launching the war.' Stephashin said that the plan to invade Chechnya had been worked out in March 1999 and that he had played a central role in organising the military build-up before the invasion.[51]

In this light, our ally may be directly responsible for

terrorism, in Moscow as well as in Chechnya, a fact that has troubled neither New Labour's propagandists nor, apparently, most of the mainstream media.

Chechen President Maskhadov's proposals to negotiate a political settlement have been repeatedly rejected by Putin. General Sergei Babkin, commander of the pro-Moscow Chechen security services, told reporters that the FSB's strategy towards Maskhadov's ministers was that 'our conditions . . . remain unchanged: if you want to live, surrender; if not, that's your problem'. Putin's preference is for war rather than political negotiation – perhaps a quality that endears him to Blair and Bush, judging by their own records, and despite their lip service to the need to negotiate a political settlement.[52]

Peace overtures from Maskhadov have also been rejected by the G8 states. In June 2002, for example, Maskhadov wrote to G8 leaders saying that 'I am writing to bring the tragedy in Chechnya to your attention and call on you to do everything possible to stop this senseless war', proposing a halt to military action and the renewal of negotiations between a Chechen representative and the Russian government. Commenting on this appeal, Maskhadov's special representative, Akhmed Zadaev, said that 'a halting of the conflict depends much on the good will of the US administration'. However, the newspaper *Kommersant* reported that in meetings with Putin several weeks after the Chechen appeal, President Bush 'did not touch upon the Chechen theme'.[53]

Putin's whole presidency partly owes its fortunes to being the strongman wanted by the military to reassert control over Chechnya. Nikolai Fedorov, president of the autonomous republic of Chuvashia, recently said that the war was part of a process in which 'a strongly centralised Bolshevik Russia is being built'; it was also 'criminal' and 'hopeless, with no end in sight'.[54]

British indifference to atrocities in Chechnya is especially striking in view of the fact that President Maskhadov has been democratically elected. Robin Cook admitted to a parliamentary inquiry that Maskhadov had been 'elected by the people of Chechnya, admittedly not quite by the same detailed standards that we apply ourselves, but it was held to be a reasonably free and fair election'.[55] This inconvenient fact is rarely raised by the government. Neither has it troubled too many journalists – there are very few mentions of the Russian strategy of destroying a democratically elected presidency in Chechnya but all too many simply buying the line of fighting 'terrorists'.

It is instructive that Britain is prepared to antagonise Moscow over bombing Iraq and Yugoslavia, which were bitterly opposed in Moscow. But it has not even lifted its little finger for the sake of mere Chechens. For them, Britain has even refused to support calls for an international inquiry into human rights abuses. Foreign Office minister Ben Bradshaw noted in April 2001: 'The UK has not called for an international inquiry into allegations of human rights violations in Chechnya' – Russian crimes now reduced to 'allegations'.[56]

The deceit maintained by the government is that Britain has few levers with which to press Russia into stopping the worst of the abuses. The standard line has become that the only option is all-out war with Russia, as when Robin Cook admonished those calling for stronger British protests by saying: 'Are you really suggesting that we go to war with Russia?'[57] The media largely plays along with this absurd fiction that there is nothing short of war that Britain can do.

There are levers available, but we do not know if they could be effective since Britain has never had any intention of using them. For reality to dawn, one only need read a Foreign Office memo submitted to a parliamentary inquiry in January 2000. This outlines the range of contacts Britain has with Russia, many of which could be regarded as important levers: £30 million annual aid from the Know How Fund; a Training Management Initiative, an aid scheme to support Russian private sector managers; military assistance and training under the 'Outreach' programme; exports to Russia of £296 million in 1999 and imports of £763 million; and a line of £500 million in export credit guarantees available to exporters to Russia. Britain is also the fifth largest foreign investor in Russia and signed a Partnership and Cooperation Agreement on trade and investment in 1997.[58]

The aid programme is an obvious lever, especially as it claims to support human rights activities. The Foreign Affairs Committee says that the programme's 'first priority is the promotion of good government, human rights and free, independent and responsible media'.

Robin Cook was asked in parliament in December 1999:

> What advice is the Foreign Office giving to British companies at the present time preparing bids for alternative oil pipelines to duplicate or perhaps replace the pipeline which passes close by Grozny?

He replied:

> We do not have the temerity to offer advice to financial companies or to oil companies on this question. This is a matter that we are leaving entirely to their commercial judgement.[59]

Rather than pressing Russia, the Blair government has been doing the opposite – actively stepping up contacts, especially with the Russian military. The MoD notes that in early 2000 'the Russian Ministry of Defence indicated that it was willing to re-commence a defence relationship with the UK'. It said that Britain had a 'new defence relationship with the Russians'.[60]

At the same time, Britain has been engaged in bringing Russia into Western structures in order to 'develop Russia as a comfortable, willing partner in the global economy and in global security'. According to the British government, Russia needs to be 'open to the West, attracting Western investment and working together to resolve regional conflicts' not retreating into 'chauvinist isolation' – the threat of Russian nationalism.[61]

A key British and Western aim has been the economic recolonisation of Russia in the post-Soviet era, shaping the Russian economy to benefit Western business interests. British policy is to 'make Russia a more attractive market for foreign companies and investors to do business in', Trade Secretary Patricia Hewitt explains. This has involved promoting the usual array of privatisation, deregulation and 'shock therapy' under the auspices of Western advisers and the International Monetary Fund. Foreign Office minister Mike O'Brien told a Russian business and banking conference in London that the Russian authorities were 'taking a clapped out old communist economic system and driving it forward into the twenty-first century with remarkable skill'.[62]

O'Brien's description is truly amazing, even by traditional British standards of apologia for human suffering at the hands of allies. The fact is that the Russian people have in the past decade been plunged into gross impoverishment by their own leaders, aided by the advice of international institutions and the new liberalisation theologists in Britain and elsewhere. Poverty has skyrocketed as the country has undergone an unprecedented economic collapse. The Russian population fell by three million in 1992–96 alone as a result of higher death rates and lower birth rates. This was an even greater fall than in the civil war of 1918–20, when the population fell by 2.8 million. Between 1991 and 1998 overall agricultural and industrial production fell by half.

A form of oligarchic capitalism has been established in Russia where financial flows, the mass media, raw material resources and political influence have become concentrated in the hands of a few dozen families, while a new criminal class has gained huge wealth. This has occurred under an increasingly authoritarian and centralised political system of which Putin is the current apogee.[63]

A priority for the international community should have been to help post-Soviet Russia establish a democratic political system and an economy that benefits people, after decades of totalitarian tyranny – but these have never been British goals.

The threat of Russian 'chauvinism' to which Cook referred is surely real – and the West, with Britain in the lead, could hardly have contributed to its likely emergence more than by pushing on Russia traditional 'neo-liberal' economic policies, with entirely predictable effects. At the same time, US/British military interventions elsewhere have, if anything, strengthened militaristic voices in Russia. Britain can hardly claim the excuse that over Chechnya it is suddenly discovering the need not to contribute to 'chauvinist' forces in Russia; its general policies have aided the rise of a new authoritarian despotism.

The 'double standards' involved in the West's condoning of Russian actions in Chechnya compared to bombing Yugoslavia supposedly in defence of human rights were so obvious that some media comment was inevitable. But usually this inconvenient comparison was quickly dealt with. The fact is that Russian crimes in Chechnya are worse than Yugoslav crimes in Kosovo. Though Putin is one of Tony Blair's favourite leaders, presiding over a grim chronology of Russian atrocities in Chechnya, Blair's rhetoric on human rights continues to be taken seriously, on policy towards Russia as elsewhere.

8

LABOUR'S REAL POLICY ON ARMS EXPORTS

My people have suffered terribly from the effects of armaments made in countries far from our shores . . . I appeal to the government of the United Kingdom, and its allies, to consider the dreadful consequence of this so-called defence industry. Please, I beg you, . . . do not sustain any longer a conflict which without these sales could never have been pursued in the first place, nor for so very long.

East Timor's Bishop Belo[1]

Bishop Belo said in the speech in Westminster noted above that British arms exports were 'sustaining' the conflict in East Timor. He was, tragically, only scratching the surface of the British arms exports industry.

In the business of death, Britain is truly a global player. It is the world's second largest arms exporter (after the US), with a full quarter of the global trade, selling around £5 billion worth of arms to 140 countries.

The story of arms exports under the Blair government is one of complicity in massive human rights abuses in several countries, exacerbating regional tensions in areas of conflict and violating its own and the EU's (already very elastic) guidelines. Although British arms exports receive occasional critical media coverage, usually as 'exceptions' to otherwise benign government policies, the overall picture is much more serious than usually presented.

The message to the arms companies

The Blair government has been saying two things on arms exports, depending on the audience. First, there is the message to the public.

British governments know that arms exports are not terribly popular. In a 1998 survey, 41 per cent of people said they were against *all* arms exports, rising to 47 per cent among women.[2] The government therefore tries to convince the public, first, that a 'responsible' arms trade is possible and second, that Britain has one. The problem is that both are plainly untrue, which makes it a little harder.

Many in the media appear to have taken seriously the idea that Labour is trying to adopt a more 'ethical' policy on arms exports than the Conservatives. But there is a more interesting side to the Blair government's rhetoric on arms exports: in reality, it barely even claims to promote a policy much different to the Tories. The government has only ever promised a 'responsible' and 'properly regulated' arms trade. This pales by comparison with the grandiose rhetoric on foreign policy overall, where Labour leaders claim they want to make Britain a 'force for good' in the world – no small task – or Blair's grand 'doctrine of international community'. These are purely fabricated propositions that bear no relation whatsoever to actual British policy in the world. But where arms exports are concerned, propagandists have only been working on the sidelines – the government has never really promised that much by way of a more 'ethical' policy.

So, the government's second message is to the arms manufacturers and related businesses within British military industry. To them, the message has been crystal clear – business as usual on arms exports, with no major difference from the Tories. Indeed, this has been the overwhelmingly stronger message of the two, despite the gullibility of the media.

The strategy of business as usual is seriously hard to miss. Labour has bent over backwards and double to reassure military industry of its support. Three months before winning the 1997 election, Tony Blair said in the internal newsletter of BAE Systems – Britain's biggest arms company – that a Labour government would be:

> committed to creating the conditions in which the defence industries can thrive and prosper. Winning export orders is vital to the long term success of Britain's defence industry. A Labour government will work with the industry to win export orders.

This followed Labour's election manifesto, proclaiming support for 'a strong UK defence industry, which is a strategic part of our industrial base as well as our defence effort'.[3]

Six months into the new government, Defence Minister Lord Gilbert told parliament of plans to 'involve industry in the concept phase of new systems that we need to procure'. This was to be a partnership involving military industry designing systems for tasks outlined by the government. 'Industry has responded extremely enthusiastically to our initiatives in that way', he said. He added that 'its export achievements are quite remarkable', shown by the fact that 'the British defence industry obtained nearly one quarter of the world defence market last year'.[4]

A year into the new government, Defence Secretary George Robertson confirmed again (he really didn't need to, by now) that 'the defence industry is in very safe hands', mentioning the 'importance of the British defence industry, which I spend much of my time helping when visiting foreign lands'.[5]

This message could not fail to be heard loud and clear by industry. Nicholas Oliver, director of Procurement Services

International, said on television one month after Labour's election victory that 'Mr Blair's view is that the type of equipment that the Conservatives have given export licences to would present no difficulty for the Labour government.' Oliver was referring to Indonesia, an obvious candidate for any major change in arms exports policy. Yet even here it was understood there would be no change.[6]

The beneficiaries of business as usual are of course arms corporations, notably the two largest, BAE Systems and GEC-Marconi, who benefit from massive government subsidies. There are various estimates as to how much, but it is likely to be close to £1 billion a year in taxpayer support to companies to develop new weapons systems and promote exports. Around a third of government export credits are for arms exports. The heavily subsidised arms industry is one of the few areas in the British economy not exposed to the wonders of the 'free market'.[7]

On balance, it is likely that the arms industry costs the taxpayer money. Britain's military industry is not as important to the economy as its supporters claim. Around 90,000 jobs are linked to arms exports and military procurement supports around 10 per cent of manufacturing employment, but this represents less than 2 per cent of total employment. Military spending often diverts resources away from more profitable civilian uses while subsidies are a direct cost to taxpayers. Many academic studies conclude that military spending has a negative effect on economic growth and that reductions in military spending can improve economic performance.[8]

Labour established a new Defence Diversification Agency (DDA) in 1999 – but it had already allayed any fears of the arms companies that it would do anything so radical as convert military into civilian industry. Defence Secretary George Robertson reassured them that 'we are talking about defence diversification and not defence conversion. We are not in the business of running down defence production facilities and converting them to purely civilian use.' The DDA has been concerned as much with exploiting civil technology for military use as vice versa, and anyway has a minuscule budget of £2 million a year.[9]

British arms corporations occupy a special place within the elite. As well as receiving massive subsidies from the taxpayer to secure often huge private profits, MI6 routinely passes commercial intelligence to them. Former MI6 officer Richard Tomlinson has said that in 1993 MI6 helped BAE (then called British Aerospace) win a £500 million deal to sell Hawk jets to Indonesia by supplying details of a competing bid from French manufacturer Dassault. Similar intelligence was passed to BAE to help it win orders for Tornado fighters and Hawks as part of a £1.7 billion package with Malaysia. This was linked to the Pergau dam 'aid' package of £234 million in which the Conservative government was found to have acted illegally.[10]

New Labour clearly has a special relationship with the big arms manufacturers. BAE's Chairman, Sir Richard Evans, has been described by the *Observer* as 'one of the few businessmen who can see Blair on request'. The Labour party also holds nearly 30,000 shares in BAE Systems, which is reported to have donated £5,000 to Labour funds in 1998 and 2000 and sponsored a ministerial question-and-answer session at the 1999 party conference. Labour also has more than 45,000 shares in GEC and Vickers, according to a report by the Campaign Against the Arms Trade.

Then there is the 'revolving door' between government and the corporations. For example, Raytheon systems, the British subsidiary of giant US arms corporation Raytheon, appointed Sir Robert Harman-Joyce as chairman in 2000; he retired from the Ministry of Defence in 1999 as chief of defence procurement. Former Conservative Defence minister, Lord Freeman, is on the board of Thomson-CSF, a huge French arms manufacturer.[11]

There are good reasons, therefore, for business as usual, and it soon became obvious that nothing would change with the new government in 1997. 'There'll be differences at the margins, but little more', one well-placed official said during the new government's review of arms exports criteria a month after taking office.[12]

The guidelines eventually announced by New Labour confirmed this. They state that export licences will not be issued 'for the sale of arms to regimes that might use them for internal repression or external aggression'. Except that the word 'might' was substituted for 'are likely to', this was identical to the formula used by the Conservative government.

The guidelines are clearly more intended to promote than prevent arms exports. They say that 'full weight should be given to the UK's national interests when considering applications for licences'. These 'national interests' are listed as the effects on Britain's security interests, on the relationship with the recipient country, the effect on economic and commercial interests and the protection of the UK's strategic industrial base.[13]

Both the Scott report on arms to Iraq and even the Green Paper produced by the Conservatives in 1996 had specifically addressed the need for arms exports to avoid contributing to human rights abuses. But the Labour government refused to simply ban exports to countries abusing human rights, saying instead that specific arms exports should 'avoid contributing to internal repression'.

According to Neil Cooper, an expert on arms exports at the University of Plymouth:

> Judged solely on its own language Labour's arms sales policy is actually less ethical than its own policy in the eighties, less ethical than that of a number of other states, less ethical than the EU code, less ethical than Scott and less ethical than the Green Paper on export controls produced by the Conservatives.[14]

The government also worked avidly to water down the EU code of conduct on arms sales that was eventually adopted in

1998. Nordic countries, for example, had wanted a permanent blacklist of countries with poor human rights records. Instead, the EU code adopts much of the same language as the British guidelines.

That the new EU code was also riven with qualifications was noticed by three senior retired British military officers. They argued for tighter restrictions on arms exports than the EU code, since European troops have faced 'military equipment supplied by their own governments in peacekeeping operations in Somalia, Rwanda and Bosnia'.[15]

In outlining these guidelines the government was in effect announcing – for all to hear – that nothing would change. Note that we are still dealing with the *publicly stated guidelines* on arms exports, not actual policy. The point I am making is that the government is not in reality even *pretending* to implement an 'ethical' policy on arms exports. It has been more concerned with reassuring military industry of continuing government support.

Even where it might have been easier to adopt more 'ethical' policies, government policy has frankly been embarrassing. For example, New Labour has made a lot out of its decision to ban landmines in support of the international treaty doing so. When the *Guardian* first reported the ban under the heading 'Britain bans use and sale of mines', it also wrote that this had been delayed until 2005 as a concession to the military, because 'adequate alternative weapons would not be readily available earlier'. Military officials said that 'alternatives, such as better surveillance techniques and more advanced conventional bombs, including mortars and shells, were being developed'. The *Financial Times* reported the military's belief that it would have alternative 'area denial' weapons by 2005 to 'replace land mines'. The government has also decided to proceed with the procurement of a vehicle-launched scatterable anti-tank mine ordered by the last government (anti-tank mines not being covered in the landmines ban).[16]

My view is that the guidelines (and actual policy) are enabling the government to make four clear pledges to its major audience and intended beneficiaries – the arms corporations. This is the government's real policy on arms exports. These pledges are being tragically borne out in practice and the human consequences are severe.

Pledge one – We arm both sides in conflicts

Britain is currently arming around fifty countries undergoing major conflict or civil war, to the tune of hundreds of millions of pounds. It is traditional British practice to arm both sides in a conflict. The Campaign Against the Arms Trade has noted that:

> Arms companies within the UK are thriving upon deliberately supplying opposing warring states. Not only are they allowed to do this but, as events like DSEI [an arms exhibition] show, the UK government is actively involved in promoting the opportunity to do it. The government routinely secures arms contracts with both sides of a confrontation through subsidies, promotions, arms exhibitions and ministerial visits.[17]

Britain provided military equipment to both Iran and Iraq during their war in the 1980s. An array of equipment went to Iraq, the favoured location. But MI6 worked with an Iranian-born arms dealer, Jamshid Hashemi, to help supply foreign arms to Iran, in direct violation of the government's guidelines banning weapons to both countries. In one deal with Iran, MI6 sanctioned the supply of fifteen British-made motorboats reinforced to carry heavy machine guns. The boats, exported via Greece, were used against civilian shipping in the tanker war in the Gulf in the mid-1980s.[18]

Britain currently arms Greece and Turkey, countries that have come close to war in disputes over Cyprus and sea boundaries. It also provides arms-related equipment to both China and Taiwan, both poised for serious confrontation. In the past it has armed Israel and Lebanon, while Israel was occupying the south of Lebanon.

Britain is now arming both Pakistan and India as tensions rise on the Indian subcontinent and an all-out war is a real prospect. The government has rejected repeated calls to stop the arms flow. Indeed, arms exports have been *stepped up* as tensions have increased. In 1999, for example, £8.3 million worth of arms was supplied to India and £1.5 million to Pakistan. In 2000, nearly 700 export licences worth £64 million were approved to both countries. Britain sold £122 million worth of arms to India and £17.5 million to Pakistan in the two years up to February 2002. This was often for similar equipment, including combat helicopter parts, aircraft radar and small arms. Export licences continue to be issued as India mounts its largest military build-up in thirty years along the Kashmir line of control, as Pakistan tests new ballistic missiles, and as both deploy tactical nuclear weapons near their border.[19]

In January 2002, Tony Blair visited India and Pakistan saying that 'we can have a calming influence' and warning of the 'enormous problems the whole of the world would face if things went wrong'. Behind the scenes, Blair was pushing to sell India sixty Hawk aircraft at a cost of £1 billion. British lobbying for this deal has been ongoing throughout the crisis on the Indian subcontinent. The Hawks can be used as ground attack aircraft and would be used to train Indian pilots to fly fast jets, including Jaguar bombers previously sold by Britain. These Jaguars (126 of which are being produced in India under licence) are capable of being adapted to carry nuclear weapons. The media has reported that plans are under way to upgrade their performance with Israeli help.[20]

Blair's visit was one in a long line of lobbying by British officials. After a visit to India in late 2000 Defence minister Geoff Hoon said he hoped the Hawk deal would go ahead and that he envisaged 'all manner of further collaboration with BAE Systems' and India.[21]

Six weeks after Blair's lobbying mission, British arms

companies attended an arms fair in New Delhi, where Britain had one of the biggest pavilions, funded with support from the DTI. With official blessing, British arms companies were offering India howitzers, anti-aircraft guns, missiles and tanks. It was reported to be likely that the same delegations would visit Pakistan's state-sponsored arms fair later that year.[22]

It can hardly be doubted that arms exports to India and Pakistan might be used in combat. The government issued a licence to Vickers to export tank spare parts to India; these tanks were subsequently lined up on the border with Pakistan. In response to a letter from Edward Garnier MP, Foreign Office minister Peter Hain wrote that 'while there is a theoretical risk that India might use tanks offensively in the future, the criteria make clear that this is not sufficient grounds to refuse an application'.[23]

So much for Britain's export guidelines. The government states that it will 'not issue an export licence if there is a clearly identifiable risk that the intended recipient would use the proposed export aggressively against another country, or to assert by force a territorial claim'. 'The need not to affect adversely regional stability in any significant way will also be considered.'[24]

Britain has sold to Pakistan mortars, armoured personnel carriers, combat aircraft, production equipment for assault rifles and machine guns. London has not let Pakistan's nuclear tests (conducted in July 1998) or the overthrow of a democratically elected government (in October 1999) seriously get in the way. 'No informal embargo, freeze or moratorium on exports of arms and military equipment to Pakistan was ever in force', the government has said.[25]

No export licences were, however, issued to Pakistan for a while after the coup and a de facto moratorium may have been in place. By January 2000, the *Guardian* reported a debate in Whitehall on whether the government should resume normal business with Pakistan. It published leaked minutes of a meeting which noted 'the Whitehall consensus in favour of processing outstanding export licence applications to Pakistan' but that Clare Short and Robin Cook were opposed. It noted eighty outstanding licence applications and that 'exporters are becoming increasingly impatient and suspicious'.[26]

The inevitable happened. In July 2000 the government announced that a number of licences to Pakistan had been approved. Some had been refused and the export of small arms and ammunition would be blocked.[27] But it meant pretty much business as usual.

High British principles were also absent regarding the murderous war in the Democratic Republic of Congo (DRC), which claimed three million lives until a tentative peace accord was reached in July 2002. Britain sold arms to Zimbabwe, Namibia and Angola, who intervened to support the DRC regime, at the same time as supplying Uganda and Rwanda, who were fighting the DRC and its allies. Representatives from opposing sides (Uganda and Angola) were invited to a major British arms exhibition in September 2001. The International Institute for Security Studies in Pretoria said that 'Britain is inflaming the situation by arming both sides.'[28]

The worst aspect was arming Zimbabwe. The Mugabe regime had been a standard destination for British arms exports, including machine guns, ammunition and, in the 1980s and 1990s, around a dozen Hawk aircraft, together with military training. The Foreign Affairs Committee notes that in the government's annual reports on arms exports for 1997 and 1998 'no indication was given . . . that any particular special [arms exports] regime was being applied to exports to Zimbabwe'.[29]

In other words, Mugabe's appalling human rights record was not relevant to government policy in this period. It only mattered once Mugabe started threatening white farmers with forcible expulsion from their farms.

Britain continued arms exports to Zimbabwe after August 1998, when it intervened in DRC's civil war. From this point on Zimbabwe deployed British-supplied Hawk aircraft to devastating effect. The Foreign Affairs Committee commented that 'it is not disputed that the Hawks have been used in the intervention in the DRC'. The context was a brutal one. According to Amnesty International, in December 1999 over 600 civilians were killed in the northwest of the country by indiscriminate bombing by DRC government forces and their allies. Dozens more were killed in targeting towns like Goma, Kisangani and Uvira from May 1999.[30]

An export licence for military-use signals equipment spares was granted in October 1998 and licences were also granted in November 1998 for components for British Canberra, Hawk, Hunter and Islander aircraft in Zimbabwe. In May 1999 a licence was granted covering components for military vehicles and in June 1999 for military air traffic control radar. Only one licence was refused from the beginning of Zimbabwe's intervention in the DRC until February 2000.

The Foreign Affairs Committee notes that the export licences provided in late 1998 and early 1999 'may well have been used to supply spares for military equipment used for intervention in the DRC, including aircraft spares'. It also notes that British policy 'represented an open door for the export of military material to Zimbabwe, primarily aircraft and aircraft weapon spares, but also radars, military computers and military vehicle spares', potentially for use in the DRC.[31]

'We have made it clear that there can be no military solution' to the conflict in the Congo, Foreign Office minister Tony Lloyd said in December 1998. 'Britain is working hard for peace', he told the House of Commons, presumably without laughing, as the government continued to arm Zimbabwe.[32]

Whitehall also ignored the EU. In June 1999, following the failure of efforts to secure a ceasefire in the DRC, the EU presidency called for 'rigorous application' of the EU code of conduct on arms exports by member states. This prompted no noticeable change in London which continued to issue export licences, apparently breaching its own and the EU's guidelines.

Following press reports in January 2000 of Whitehall

disagreements on issuing licences for Hawk spares the government announced a 'tightened' policy on arms exports on 9 February 2000. But then it got worse.

On 24 February 2000 seven outstanding licence applications for Hawk spares were granted. This was done in the full knowledge that Hawks had already been used in the DRC and would be used again. Without these spares it had been widely reported that two of the Hawks would be unable to operate. This decision was taken against the recommendation of Foreign Secretary Robin Cook and was a further clear breach of the export guidelines, which claim that the government will not supply equipment that can be used for aggressive purposes.

Only in May 2000 did Britain finally announce an arms embargo, following state-sponsored violence in Zimbabwe. Five of the seven licences for the Hawk spares were revoked, but two had already been processed. So the Zimbabwean air force had already received some spares critical to resume Hawk operations in the grotesque war in the DRC.

Pledge two – We arm human rights abusers

The British government is complicit in massive human rights atrocities through its current arms exports. Whichever way you look at it, the Blair government has blood on its hands.

Robin Cook once described small arms as 'the basic method of mass killing over the past decade'.[33] Indeed, the vast majority of people killed in wars are victims of small arms, about two million over the last decade alone.

Britain has exported small arms to dozens of countries, issuing 1,500 small arms licences in the Labour government's first year in office alone. These basic methods of mass killing have gone to countries such as Israel, Zimbabwe, Sri Lanka, Colombia, Pakistan, Saudi Arabia, Morocco, Egypt and Turkey – all states that are highly repressive or at war with their own people or others.[34]

Government policy, as noted above, is not to stop exports to human rights abusers, merely to 'take into account respect for human rights'. Clearly, not much is taken into account in this long list of gruesome governments.

The government's claim that it will not allow exports to regimes that 'might use them for internal repression' is simply a lie; there is no other way of putting it. British military exports go to governments repressing their people *all the time*. There are many examples, but I will consider two in some detail – Indonesia and China.

Indonesia

The government's 1998 annual report on human rights contains a photo of Robin Cook shaking hands with President Suharto of Indonesia. It is meant to be an example of where Britain pursues 'constructive engagement'. This is true in the sense that Britain had engaged constructively with the brutal Suharto regime for thirty-five years, providing it with military, economic and political support to continue repressing people and conduct violence and terror in Aceh, West Papua and East Timor (see chapter 21). The basis of British policy towards Indonesia is support for the central government in Jakarta, which, following the fall of Suharto in 1998, remains guilty of gross atrocities in Indonesian provinces seeking self-determination.

Let us look at known cases of British-supplied arms being used for repression.

• In April 1996 Scorpion light tanks supplied by the British firm, Alvis, were used against students in south Sulawesi, killing three and injuring many others protesting against bus fare increases and military brutality. Despite this, a few months later the Conservative government issued further licences for Scorpions.

The Blair government refused to revoke the licences for this agreement to sell fifty Scorpions and related equipment.

- Scorpions were again used in Jakarta in May and November 1998 in incidents killing eighteen protesters.

The Labour government also refused to revoke licences for seven Tactica water cannon agreed in December 1996.

- Tactica water cannon supplied by British arms company GKN in the 1960s were used in Bandung in June 1996 against people protesting at the deaths of the students in south Sulawesi. Eyewitnesses said that tear gas was used in the water cannon.[35]
- These water cannon were also used against street protesters in May 1997 to break up an election march, where they were filmed spraying water over the crowd.[36]
- Water cannon were again used in February 1999 against workers in Surabaya, East Java, dispersing discoloured liquid to suppress workers' rights to free assembly.[37]

Other British-supplied armoured cars have also been used:

- In December 1999 and July 2000, Saladins (Alvis-made armoured cars exported in the 1960s) were used in Ambon in incidents where more civilians were killed.[38]

There are thus eight known occasions since 1996 that British-supplied armoured vehicles have been used for repression in Indonesia, six of them occurring under the Blair government. Yet dozens of these vehicles have been delivered to Indonesia under Labour. The 'assurances' provided by Jakarta to the effect that equipment will not be used for internal repression are clearly laughable. But in the case of the water cannon, the government has admitted that it has not received any assurances anyway.[39]

The fact is that any arms or military-related equipment going to Indonesia might be used for internal repression in one way or another. As Amnesty International has said: 'Indonesian armed forces are focused primarily on combatting internal dissent rather than external threats. Their role is to monitor and suppress violent and peaceful dissent throughout Indonesia'. In March 1997, General Tanjung announced that his forces would shoot on sight any violators of electoral law. He also said that any opposition to the government would be 'sliced to pieces'. In February 1999 a shoot-to-kill policy to quell civil disturbances was ratified by parliament. All this must be well known to those issuing export licences.[40]

It must have been especially helpful to the Indonesian authorities to have acquired from Britain a sophisticated surveillance system to monitor protesters as well as traffic and criminal suspects.[41]

Further support to Jakarta comes from Heckler & Koch, a subsidiary of BAE Systems. It has supplied to Indonesia machine guns produced in Turkey which are used by the Indonesian police and the Kopassus special forces. Defence Secretary George Robertson described the commander of Kopassus, General Prabowo, as 'an enlightened officer, keen to increase professionalism with the armed forces and to educate them in areas such as human rights'. In fact, Prabowo is known in East Timor as an 'enthusiastic torturer who killed at least one independence leader', according to the *Independent*. He gained his reputation by using torture and murder and organising bands of civilian thugs, the forerunners of the 'militias' that have terrorised East Timor. Despite this, Kopassus officers were allowed by the British government to attend a post-graduate course in defence studies at Hull University. Another fifty Indonesian military officers have been trained in the UK under Labour.[42]

On coming to power, the Blair government had the option of revoking the licences for the sale of Hawk aircraft agreed in 1996. This was the simplest of decisions for a government with even a remote commitment to an improved arms exports policy. Hawk aircraft have been regularly used against the civilian population in East Timor, according to East Timorese leaders and other eyewitnesses. While in opposition, Robin Cook said in 1994 that Hawk aircraft 'have been observed on bombing runs in East Timor in most years since 1984'.[43]

But New Labour refused to revoke the licences, allowing the Hawks to be delivered. It said that revoking the licences was not 'realistic or practical', and that it legally had to honour its commitment. This was simply not true. Legally, the government could have stopped the sale but, in the words of the House of Commons Foreign Affairs Committee, it 'would be obliged to demonstrate that its policy towards that country had indeed changed in such a way as to require revocation'.[44] Since Labour has never had any intention of changing British support for Jakarta, this option was effectively closed.

So, in addition to processing 125 licences outstanding from the Conservatives, Labour has proceeded to issue dozens more. Taxpayers may also be pleased to know that they pay for the RAF to train Indonesian pilots in using the Hawks. By July 1998 five instructors and twenty-four student pilots had been trained.[45]

As well as being used to intimidate the population in East Timor in the Blair years (see chapter 21), Hawks play other useful roles for Jakarta. In 2000, Hawk aircraft conducted a series of operations over towns in the province of West Papua, similarly designed to frighten local people and intimidate supporters of independence.[46] In fact, the British government agreed with the Indonesian authorities that Hawk aircraft could be used in military exercises in the skies over West Papua. The Indonesian military doubled the number of Hawks stationed in the province from three to six, as it intensified its campaign of repression.

British complicity in Indonesia's brutal war in West Papua has gone largely unreported. Since 1969 at least 100,000 West Papuans have been killed or disappeared as a result of Indonesia's military occupation. Conditions worsened in 2001 when Indonesian forces attacked civilians in areas where rebels of the Free Papua Movement are active, engaging in indiscriminate and excessive force against pro-independence demonstrators.[47]

Britain has extensive business interests in West Papua, with

Rio Tinto, the world's largest mining company, set to own 40 per cent of the Freeport copper and gold mine, the world's largest, and BP set to initiate a large gas project in the territory. In June 2001, British ambassador Richard Gozney made a statement supporting Indonesian military operations in West Papua, apparently since they would ensure protection for a nearby BP site that he was visiting.[48]

Britain expresses strong support for Indonesia's campaigns to suppress self-determination, just as it effectively backed Indonesia's invasion and subjugation of East Timor for a quarter of a century. According to the *Jakarta Post*, Defence Minister Geoff Hoon said on a visit to Singapore that the Indonesian government should 'respond appropriately to separatist movements'. The press reported that when Tony Blair visited Indonesian President Wahid in February 2000, he also pledged British support for Indonesia's 'territorial integrity'.[49]

Achieving 'territorial integrity' also comes at a grave price for people in Aceh province. The Indonesian military's war against self-determination there has escalated dramatically since the fall of Suharto. In 2001, over 1,500 people were killed as Indonesia stepped up repression and brutality, conducting an all-out offensive to crush 'separatists'. It was reported in July 2002 that Hawks had been used in Aceh. Indonesian reports said that ten Hawks were used to 'restore order', in the words of Indonesian air force commander Colonel Djubnedi. Tens of thousands of troops are now stationed in Aceh, guilty of all manner of violations well-documented by human rights groups.[50]

The standard British government response to Indonesian brutality is to say: 'We call on *all* sides to show restraint', in the words of Foreign Office minister Derek Fatchett.[51] London is thus unable to identify the aggressor and unwilling to take action against it, just as with Israel, Russia, Turkey and others.

Sales of an array of military equipment to Indonesia continue, including components for combat helicopters and aircraft, naval equipment, machine gun spares and military imaging equipment. Only a small number of applications for equipment such as armoured cars and sniper rifles are being refused. Total British arms exports to Indonesia have gone down over recent years due to Indonesia's economic crisis, rather than any change in British policy.

Just as Tony Blair dismissed the appeal by Bishop Belo cited at the beginning of this chapter, so he also ignored the appeal of Indonesia's most prominent prisoner of conscience, Muchtar Pakpahan, a trade union leader imprisoned for organising pro-democracy protests. One month after Blair's election, Pakpahan said from a guarded hospital room in Jakarta: 'I hope that he [Blair] will stop selling weapons to Indonesia, weapons which are used for human rights violations.'[52]

China

The case of China provides further insight into the government's policy of exporting military equipment at all costs.

The EU imposed an arms embargo on China in 1989, shortly after the Tiananmen Square massacre. It called for 'interruption [by EU states] . . . of military cooperation and an embargo on trade in arms with China', but the precise meaning of this was left to individual member states to interpret. Within months of the ban the Conservative government allowed GEC-Marconi to export radar equipment for Chinese fighter aircraft – on the grounds that this was 'non-lethal' equipment rather than arms. Britain thus helped to undermine the message of disapproval intended by the embargo. Continuing sales (some in violation of Britain's own interpretation of the ban) and growing military links between Britain and China have continued into the Labour years, exposing the token nature of the British 'embargo'.

Britain interprets the embargo as covering lethal weapons but not 'non-lethal' military equipment. In reality, this distinction is often meaningless. 'Non-lethal' traffic control systems were exported to China and used during the Tiananmen Square massacre to photograph protesters and help police capture dissenters. Licences for the same traffic control technology have since been granted, which is now in use in Lhasa, Tibet, occupied by China.

Military equipment supplied to China amounted to £32 million in 2001 and includes military aerospace components, surveillance equipment, laser sighting and targeting equipment, components for combat aircraft, military electronics, communications and navigations equipment, military explosives and test equipment for small arms ammunition. These significant pieces of equipment may help China launch an assault on Taiwan as well as contribute to internal repression. Some countries have banned virtually all military items to China, but Britain naturally does not stoop this low. The US embargo is much tighter, covering all military goods with only some exceptions.

But British policy goes even further, directly wooing the Chinese military, despite the fact that the EU embargo calls for 'interruption . . . in *military cooperation*' as well as arms exports. The man who commanded the Tiananmen Square massacre, General Chi Haotian, who became China's Defence Minister, was a guest of the government in January 2000, visiting John Prescott and Geoff Hoon. China has been invited to arms exhibitions in Britain, and in May 2000 a seventy-strong Chinese military delegation visited the MoD in London and several British military installations, where they were shown the Eurofighter.[53]

As with Indonesia, the government says it pursues 'constructive engagement' with China on human rights, claiming this is the only way to produce results. The actual results are clear: in recent years the Chinese authorities have clamped down even more on dissenters and threats to 'stability', and human rights violations have increased, as Amnesty International, Human Rights Watch and the US State

Department have all reported. Beijing is currently using the 'war against terrorism' as a cover for more repressive internal policies, arresting, for example, 10,000 people in its 'strike hard' anti-crime campaign. In 1999, Amnesty International had already told a parliamentary inquiry that 'the current situation in China is perhaps worse than at any time since the post-Tiananmen clampdown'. The Free Tibet Campaign also criticises the British government, saying that the 'human rights dialogue' is failing to halt a worsening of the situation in Tibet.[54]

Britain is much keener on providing support to the Chinese elite. When Chinese President Jiang Zemin visited Britain in October 1999, human rights issues were not raised publicly while police denied protesters the right to peaceful assembly. Officers illegally seized Tibetan flags and other banners at human rights protests in an outrageous display of support for the visitors.

Similarly, pro-democracy activist and former prisoner of conscience, Wei Jingsheng, visited Britain and accused Robin Cook of being 'two faced' after Cook cancelled planned photo calls and the Foreign Office tried to prevent Wei meeting the press. He criticised Britain for leading the EU in blocking support for a UN resolution on China's appalling human rights record. The Blair government is the first since 1989 not to support such a resolution. Wei said that the Chinese government will respond to public pressure, not the UK's private 'engagement'.[55]

The priorities are obvious. The DTI states that 'China is one of the fastest growing markets in the world, offering huge trade and investment opportunities for British companies.' In a speech at London Export's Chinese new year lunch, Foreign Office minister Baroness Symons outlined British support for China's accession to the WTO and the need for China 'to remove some onerous requirements for foreign investors'. These are the important things; she failed to say anything at all about any human rights problems.[56]

Pledge three – We arm countries that others stop supplying

One standard defence of British arms exports is that: 'if we don't supply them, someone else will'. But the truth is more like: 'we will export as soon as someone else stops'. Again, this is standard practice.

Britain's massive contract to re-equip the Saudi armed forces (called Al Yamamah, worth around £50 billion) was secured once the US restricted exports to Saudi Arabia following pressure by the Israeli lobby. After India and Pakistan conducted nuclear tests in 1998, the US imposed military sanctions; Britain refused to impose formal embargoes and has in effect exploited the gap. 'Twas ever thus. In 1992 the US cut off military and economic aid to Pakistan, and asked it to return eight frigates when their leases ran out, in protest against Pakistan's development of nuclear weapons. Britain stepped in and supplied Pakistan with six frigates.[57]

The US imposed a military embargo on Indonesia following the atrocities in East Timor of September 1999, and which remained in place through 2001. The EU imposed an embargo for only four months, ending in January 2000, following which Britain resumed arms sales. Most of Indonesia's US-supplied F-16 and F-5 fighters were grounded for want of spare parts. However, Britain has helpfully continued the supply of Hawks, which partly compensated for the lack of the US aircraft.

Pledge four – We arm even the very poorest countries

At the October 2001 Labour party conference, Tony Blair pledged to help heal a 'scar on the conscience of the world' by addressing poverty and conflict in Africa. Some commentators fell over themselves eulogising Blair's vision (see chapter 18). Three months later the value of British arms to Africa was revealed to be a record – four times that of the previous year. In

2001, Britain exported around £400 million of arms to Africa according to the Campaign Against the Arms Trade.[58]

These arms go to the very poorest countries, many of which are enduring conflicts Blair said he wanted to address. Small arms have been exported to, for example, Botswana, Egypt, Eritrea, Gambia, Kenya, Malawi, Morocco, Nigeria, Sierra Leone, South Africa, Tanzania, Zambia and Zimbabwe. Around a fifth of Africa's debt comes from arms purchases, meaning that Britain's arms push directly adds to Africa's huge debt burden, which Blair also claims to want to reduce.

Arms exports can also counter any beneficial impact that aid might have, skewing scarce government resources away from badly needed social programmes, enhancing the military's role in society (and therefore undermining more democratic government) as well as being used in conflict. The British attempt to get India to spend £1 billion on Hawk aircraft is equivalent to ten years' bilateral aid.

It does look like a concerted arms push to the poorest countries. Under New Labour Britain has delivered 86 per cent of all its arms exports to developing countries (up from 84 per cent in 1993–96). No other country apart from China delivers a higher proportion of arms to poor countries. Under the Conservatives, arms to Africa made up 1.6 per cent of all British arms to the Third World; by 2000 that had grown to 19 per cent.[59]

In January 2000, Tony Blair took advantage of a 'family holiday' in the Seychelles to act as salesman for BAE Systems in South Africa. A deal agreed in 1999 was for South Africa to purchase £4 billion in military equipment from European companies. BAE Systems is the largest contractor in the deal, and is due to sell Hawk aircraft (yes, more of them) worth around £1.6 billion. Blair led a delegation to South Africa to lobby for the BAE bid shortly before it was awarded.

This is a deal the poor of South Africa can ill afford. In a country with massive poverty levels, it is worth twice the government's housing budget and over one hundred times the amount spent on combating HIV/AIDS, from which five million South Africans suffer. But it will be tremendously profitable to BAE Systems and those in South Africa accused of the usual corruption and nepotism in signing the deal.

Two weeks after Blair led a seventy-strong British delegation to the World Summit on Sustainable Development in South Africa in September 2002, the British government sponsored arms companies to attend an arms exhibition in Pretoria. The DTI described South Africa as an 'under exploited and newly emerging target'.[60]

Violating the export guidelines

The arms exports 'guidelines' are mainly for public relations purposes, to convince people there is a 'responsible' and 'well regulated' arms trade. Nothing could be further from the truth.

A clear indication is that, as the government admits, 'no formal procedures exist for routinely monitoring the use that is made of British defence equipment, once exported'.[61] It rejects repeated calls to establish such legislative checks on end use. Meanwhile, all arms exports to Saudi Arabia under the massive Al Yamamah deal are completely exempt from export licensing. This means that Britain really cares not a hoot what happens to them or whether they break any of its supposed guidelines.

Equally clear is that the government has little intention of sticking to its own, or the EU's, already very weak guidelines, which are being violated at every turn. Let us take, for example, the EU Code of Conduct on arms exports, to which Britain is legally bound.

Britain has exported arms to Morocco, illegally occupying the Western Sahara, while the EU code states that arms will not go to countries to enable them to 'assert by force a territorial claim'. British equipment also goes to Israel – in illegal occupation of the West Bank and Gaza – and to Turkey – illegally occupying northern Cyprus. The supposed distinction between arms exported for legitimate 'self-defence' and those which might be used for repression or aggression often simply does not exist. Human rights abusers and those illegally occupying territory regularly use equipment which has ostensibly been supplied for self-defence, such as aircraft and trucks for ferrying troops, as instruments of repression.

The licensing of Hawk spares to Zimbabwe (which enabled Hawks to be used in the DRC) and Indonesia (used in East Timor), and arms to India and Pakistan (for possible use between the two) fly in the face of the EU criteria forbidding exports 'if there is a clear risk that the intended recipient would use the proposed export aggressively against another country'.

Other EU criteria forbid 'exports which would provoke or prolong armed conflicts or aggravate existing tensions or conflicts in the country of final destination'. Hawks supplied to Indonesia (used in West Papua) and arms supplied to Sri Lanka (which London acknowledges are used against the rebel Tamil Tigers in a brutal civil war) appear to depart from these criteria.

The EU criteria also call on member states to 'exercise special caution and vigilance in issuing licences' to 'countries where serious violations of human rights have been established by the competent bodies of the UN, the Council of Europe or by the EU'.[62] Yet British arms continue to flow to Indonesia (armoured cars persistently used), Turkey (vehicles used against Kurds), the Gulf states (arms supplied to the 'internal security' forces) and many others.

Other EU criteria call on member states to 'take into account' the recipient's record on its international commitments, including 'its commitment to non-proliferation'. Yet Britain continues to provide arms to Israel, India and Pakistan, all with functioning nuclear weapons, and to Iran, suspected of developing them.

A simple question – why do British governments all push arms exports and in particular arm human rights abusers? Arms exports are clearly profitable for the military industry, but this is not the only reason for such exports; it is a myth to believe that the choice is simply between 'profits' and 'morals', as the debate is usually framed. There is a third factor in explaining

Whitehall's support for arms exports which goes to the heart of Britain's role in the world – *of support for favoured elites.*

Supplying British arms to persistent human rights abusers who use them to promote repression is so systematic as to be, in my view, virtually government policy. I say 'virtually' because it is not so much explicit as a reflex on the part of policy-makers. I argue in Part II that British foreign policy is largely based on support for often repressive elites who promote British commercial or political interests. Britain has regularly gone to extraordinary lengths to install and keep such elites in power, including by covert action and military intervention. But exporting arms to foreign armies, as well as training their soldiers, are also key aspects of this strategy.

Both arms exports and military training have long been recognised as performing a number of functions. They can help favoured elites to maintain 'internal security' (ie control the domestic population); enhance the domestic power of the military (often undermining democratic forces); and cement links with current and future political leaders likely to emerge from within the elite.[63]

According to leaked papers from the British embassy in Jakarta in the early 1990s, referring to British military training schemes:

> The position of the armed forces in Indonesian society is such that its members are important decision-makers and opinion formers . . . Up to 40 per cent of the participants in Indonesia's political fora are drawn from the armed forces and they are a target for support under FCO schemes in Indonesia.[64]

According to the Ministry of Defence, military training plays a very important role in 'the promotion of British influence and standing overseas and in support to wider British interests including defence sales'. It says that 'some care must be taken to avoid giving the impression that our relationship is purely based on defence export marketing opportunities'.[65]

New Labour continues to offer military training to many of the world's worst human rights abusers, as did the Conservatives before them. Nearly 4,000 military personnel from over one hundred countries are currently being trained in Britain. These include such well-known defenders of democracy and human rights as Bahrain, China, Egypt, Indonesia, Israel, Morocco, Oman, Saudi Arabia and Turkey. British armed forces are also serving in around one hundred countries, including all those just mentioned.[66] It is no surprise that these also tend to be the same countries that are key recipients of British arms.

Under New Labour, Britain has if anything beefed up its military training programmes. It has, for example, established a new 'defence diplomacy' programme – to provide allies with short-term training teams, seconded personnel and a scholarship scheme – and a new scheme called ASSIST (Assistance to Support Stability with In-Service Training), which, it claims, promotes 'respect for civilian government and practices, the rule of law and international human rights standards'.[67] The argument that training helps improve human rights practices is simply a fig leaf for which there is little evidence. Britain has been training the armed forces of many human rights abusers for years; many have become more, not less, repressive.

On the surface, it would be easy for a government remotely committed to 'ethical' policies to halt all this: it could simply stop training armies with abominable human rights records. But even this minuscule step has not been taken.

PART II

ELITES AND THE GLOBAL ECONOMY

The official story is that British policies are helping to make globalisation work for the poor and to eradicate poverty globally, while supporting democratic groups and governments. The reality, however, is quite different.

Under New Labour Britain is helping to organise the global economy to benefit a transnational business elite while pursuing policies that are often deepening poverty and inequality. New Labour has, in fact, a very grandiose project, not – as it claims – simply to *manage* globalisation, but actively to push an extreme form of economic 'liberalisation' globally.

The Blair government is also continuing the British tradition of undermining countries' ability to pursue *independent* development strategies which might be successful. It is basing its foreign policy on propping up many repressive elites, especially in the Middle East, while undermining many democratic, popular forces. The reality is that the British government regularly views democracy abroad as a threat – which matches how it increasingly sees the public in Britain. These policies are being decided in an elitist and increasingly undemocratic decision-making process in Britain, which in its foreign policy is, I argue, akin to a totalitarian state.

These policies are harming people all over the world. Even

though this is hard to miss – and is shown in the following five chapters – it is largely being missed, because most commentators in a position to see have willingly swallowed New Labour's extraordinary rhetoric. I believe that the Blair government's worldview is actually very frightening. And if planners have their way in matters concerning the global economy, to which I turn first, things will look even more frightening in the future.

9

TRADING OFF INTERNATIONAL DEVELOPMENT

We want to open up protected markets in developing countries.

Trade Secretary Patricia Hewitt

The new liberalisation theologists

According to Tony Blair, 'real development can only come through partnership. Not the rich dictating to the poor. Not the poor demanding from the rich. But matching rights and responsibilities.'[1]

This is Blair's world – where the poor majority have no right to make demands on the rich minority. Yet this is a world where half the population lives in poverty, on an average of $2 a day, while the richest few dozen individuals command more wealth than hundreds of millions of people. In this situation, are the poor really not entitled to be 'demanding from the rich' rather than simply 'matching rights and responsibilities'?

Blair's view is echoed by Chancellor Gordon Brown, who has outlined a 'global new deal' based on the poorest countries and the richest countries 'each meeting our obligations'. The poorest countries' 'obligations' are 'to pursue stability and create the conditions for new investment'. The richest countries' obligations are 'to open our markets and to transfer resources'.[2] One might think that the world's poorest countries have no 'obligations' to us, after centuries of exploitation and enduring extreme poverty due partly to an international economic system that plainly disadvantages them. But no – those with few schools, health services and little safe water are deemed by New Labour to have 'obligations' to us – and those obligations are about helping our companies to make more profits (creating 'the conditions for new investment').

The Blair government's rhetoric stresses the need to 'make globalisation work for the poor' and calls for fairer trade rules – especially in the World Trade Organisation (WTO) – which will allow developing countries to benefit more from globalisation. Clare Short, the Secretary of State for International Development, has led this process and constantly stresses Britain's commitment to reaching the 2015 international development targets that seek to reduce global poverty. But Gordon Brown (on debt) and Tony Blair (on Africa) have also led new initiatives that appear to many to show a government serious about tackling global poverty. In the media and academia, the government's 'development' policies have received little short of unadulterated praise. Britain is regularly seen as one of the most progressive voices for change in areas of the global economy to benefit developing countries, even as a 'champion of the poor'.

It is an extraordinary view. Because, putting the progressive rhetoric aside, government ministers have also made plain their other goals – which are more plausible and confirmed by their actual policies. This is easy to spot, if we bother to look.

Britain's basic priority – virtually its raison d'etre for several centuries – is to aid British companies in getting their hands on other countries' resources. As Lord Mackay, then Lord Chancellor, revealed in the mid-1990s, the role of MI6 is to protect Britain's 'economic well-being' by keeping 'a particular eye on Britain's access to key commodities, like oil or metals [and] the profits of Britain's myriad of international business interests'. This traditional task of foreign economic and 'development' policy continues to be pursued by New Labour, shielded by high rhetoric (and outlined further in chapter 10).[3]

The basic goal is to break into foreign markets. Trade Secretary Patricia Hewitt says that 'we want to open up protected markets in developing countries'. Referring to India and China's emergence as among the biggest economies in the world in the next twenty years, she says that 'we must be in there'. A new WTO round of international trade negotiations 'is the best way of ensuring that our businesses can benefit from, and contribute to, future economic growth anywhere in the world'.[4]

'Opening up markets and cutting duties around the world' will 'create new opportunities for our service sectors', Hewitt adds. Similarly, Trade Minister Baroness Symons assured a big business lobby group on services that the government was committed 'to work with you to bring those [trade] barriers down'. She said that 'there is still a lot to be done in India – and other markets – to facilitate market access for industry.'[5]

Former Trade Secretary Margaret Beckett wrote in the *Financial Times* that a key objective of the Department of Trade and Industry is 'to continue developing the conditions, at home and abroad, in which British business can thrive'. 'Britain's businesses need to be able to trade throughout the world's markets as easily as they can in home markets without facing high tariffs, discriminatory regulations or unnecessarily burdensome procedures.'[6]

Securing business' access into foreign markets is the aim of economic 'liberalisation'. Under New Labour, Britain has been perhaps the world's leading champion of trade 'liberalisation', which it wants to see applied in all countries. Policies like import tariffs and subsidies, raised by governments to protect their markets from competition that can undermine domestic industry or agriculture, are seen as essentially heretical for developing countries ('trade-distorting', in the theology). 'Trade liberalisation is the only sure route' to economic growth and prosperity for developing countries, Tony Blair says with religious conviction.[7]

The rich North's aim is to 'lock in' all countries to the global, legally binding WTO agreements that require countries to promote economic 'liberalisation'. The WTO has become in effect an organising body for the global economy. Northern countries have succeeded in adding to the WTO's remit issues – like investment, services, intellectual property rights and agriculture – that go well beyond trade and which aim to make domestic economic policy-making subject to global rules. Peter Sutherland, former Director-General of the WTO, for example, has said that an aim of the trade negotiations was to extend liberalisation 'to most aspects of domestic policy-making' affecting international trade and investment.[8]

The promotion of this 'one-size-fits-all' economic ideology mainly benefits transnational corporations (TNCs). One of the sacred principles of WTO agreements is that they require governments to give equal treatment to foreign as to domestic companies in increasing areas of domestic economic policy. TNCs benefit most from the easiest access to markets and the lightest government regulation of their activities, precisely the British government's main aims in its global economic policies. As the Chief Trade Economist of the World Bank has said: 'The dynamic behind the WTO process has been the export interests of major enterprises in the advanced trading countries.' The purpose of global trade policy, explained Lawrence Summers, a former World Bank chief economist and Clinton administration official, is to 'ensure viable investment opportunities for OECD companies'.[9]

New Labour's project goes much deeper even than global trade 'liberalisation'. Essentially, only minimal government regulation should be allowed to interrupt the free flow of capital around the world which, the argument goes, is good both for business and for 'development'. Thus Britain – while stressing its intention to simply 'manage' globalisation better – is actually promoting a much grander project. It has been a leading advocate of the WTO setting rules in new areas of domestic policy-making, and is actively seeking to deepen globalisation to an extreme form of worldwide economic 'liberalisation' that will turn the global economy into a playground for corporations. In alliance with like-minded governments, like the US, this amounts to a reshaping of the global economy based on a fundamentalist economic ideology. It is also a major attack on democratic decision-making since the WTO rules massively restrict the ability of governments to promote policies in their own national interests.

TNCs and big business pressure groups have long lobbied for rules enabling them to act globally with the fewest restrictions. Many WTO agreements, like the agreement on services (GATS) and on intellectual property (TRIPS), would not be in the WTO at all without lobbying by big business. The US company Cargill, the world's largest agribusiness corporation, reputedly wrote the first draft of the US government's negotiating position on agriculture, which turned into the WTO's agreement on agriculture.[10]

A great myth is that this is a 'free trade' agenda. 'Free trade' is a gross misnomer, and really means 'corporate control'. Global markets in most commodities and many industries are controlled by a handful of corporations. 'Free trade' means freedom for them to control these markets even more tightly. Trade 'liberalisation' generally means other countries opening up their economies to be dominated by transnational business interests.

British elites have been using propaganda on free trade for centuries. In the Elizabethan era, the argument for 'free trade' was made wherever English shipping called. According to the text of Queen Elizabeth I's standard letter of introduction to Eastern princes, God had so ordained matters that no nation was self-sufficient and that 'out of the abundance of ffruit which some regions enjoyeth, the necessitie or wante of others should be supplied'. Thus 'several and ffar remote countries' should have 'traffique' with one another and 'by their interchange of commodities' become friends. 'The Spaniard and the Portingal', on the other hand, prohibited multilateral exchange and insisted on exclusive trading rights.[11]

New Labour has created a new instrument for promoting these interests – the Department for International Development (DFID). Established from the old Overseas Development Administration, which was part of the Foreign Office, DFID was given full Cabinet status with Clare Short as International Development Secretary. In designing and managing aid projects, it seems that DFID has somewhat better focused British aid on poverty eradication, with more and better aid going to the poorest countries. But DFID's role in the international institutions goes beyond a narrow focus on aid and includes a strong influence on Britain's global economic policies and on its overall policy towards developing countries, which have far greater impact than its aid programme. The great change brought about by New Labour is that an extremist economic project is being pursued under a great moral pretext – that global 'liberalisation' will promote 'development' and 'poverty eradication'. This is not a government conspiracy to mislead the world – the new liberalisation theologists actually appear to believe it.

To some, the fact that DFID and the DTI agree on promoting this project is evidence of 'joined up government'. This is true in the sense that DFID is promoting the DTI's agenda for it, and is an equally strong advocate of 'liberalisation' across the global economy. If the Conservatives ever achieve government again, they would be wise to retain this new department – it is simply too useful in serving elite purposes.

DFID has in effect become big business's biggest ally. A variety of initiatives have been established, and numerous speeches made, to reassure business of the benefits of Labour's policies, and emphasising that business is a 'partner' in development. Indeed, DFID has not hidden the fact that it acts as a high level global lobbyist for big business. Consider Clare Short's speech to business leaders at Lancaster House in April 1999:

> The assumption that our moral duties and business interests are in conflict is now demonstrably false . . . I am very keen that we maximise the impact of our shared interest in business and development by working together in partnership . . . We bring access to other governments and influence in the multilateral system – such as the World Bank and IMF . . . You are well aware of the constraints business faces in the regulatory environment for investment in any country . . . Your ideas on overcoming these constraints can be invaluable when we develop our country strategies. We can use this understanding to inform our dialogue with governments and the multilateral institutions on the reform agenda.[12]

So, DFID is offering itself as an instrument for business to shape the policies of multilateral institutions and developing country governments. This is at least an honest admission, and has been the subject of various other speeches by DFID and DTI ministers.[13]

DFID policy is to help minimise the risks for private investors in developing countries and 'to develop an investor friendly environment' and 'a more favourable business environment'. DFID's new Business Partnership Unit is a first point of contact for business and looks at 'ways in which DFID can improve the enabling environment for productive investment overseas and how we can contribute to the operation of the overseas financial sector'. DFID is also working with the World Bank's 'Business Partners for Development Programme', involving governments, businesses and some NGOs in the water, transport and extractive industries sectors. Its bilateral aid programmes 'provide governments of developing countries with the advice and expertise to help attract private finance'. It also supports the World Bank's Private-Public Infrastructure Advisory Facility, which provides 'advice' on regulatory frameworks to attract foreign investment.[14]

Domestically and internationally, the government is actively campaigning for the minimum regulation of business. Clare Short says that:

> By far the best approach is for enterprises themselves to ensure that they respect the rights of workers, protect their health and safety and offer satisfactory conditions of employment . . . Voluntary codes . . . are often more effective than regulation.[15]

It might be thought astonishing that a Labour leader believes that businesses should be left to themselves to ensure they respect the rights of workers!

But not if the strategy is to act as a great protector of transnational business. Britain is home to many of the world's biggest TNCs, many of which have been implicated in the worst cases of human rights abuse, environmental degradation and undermining workers' rights. The wide range of TNC abuses that are occurring in the New Labour years include Premier Oil's involvement in forced labour with the Burmese junta; BP's financial stake in Sudan, where the army is burning down villages and killing thousands to facilitate oil production; and British American Tobacco's use of 'contract farmers' in Brazil, involving unsafe use of pesticides and farmers' virtual bondage to the company. Yet the government rejects legally binding international regulation to ensure that companies abide by the minimum ethical standards in their overseas operations. Trade minister Stephen Byers has referred to the government's 'presumption against regulation'; 'regulation will only be introduced where absolutely necessary and where all other avenues have been pursued.'[16]

Labour's rejection of legally binding regulation to protect people contrasts starkly with its vociferous support for legally binding WTO rules that benefit business – a sure sign of where its priorities lie. An obvious agenda for any British government remotely concerned with development would be to rein in the worst aspects of TNC activities. Labour has chosen the opposite route – working to empower TNCs and actively lobbying in their favour.

I can find no statement where the government has seriously criticised TNCs for the harmful effects they have on the world's poor. Addressing poverty eradication without tackling big business is a bit like addressing malaria without mentioning mosquitoes. Labour's promotion of big business interests in Britain has provoked some (justified) media coverage. Its far more serious capitulation to big business globally has gone virtually unnoticed.

The link between Labour's domestic and global agendas seems to be to 'liberalise' economic policy-making from the nasty interference of democratic politics. 'I believe it is right to take these decisions out of politics', said Chancellor Gordon Brown, on making the Bank of England 'independent' (that is, no longer subject to political control) a few days after coming into office. In November 2001 Brown spoke of introducing a new domestic competition regime 'with decisions taken out of the hands of politicians and truly independent of the political process'. 'Monetary policy run independently of government' is how Blair put it. Labour leaders here are *boasting* about removing democratic control over decisions on economic policy.[17]

'I want Britain to be the best competitive environment for business in the world,' Brown has said, boasting of cutting corporation tax to the lowest rate of 'any major industrialised economy'. The government is committed to 'labour market flexibility', no return to 'old fashioned attitudes, no protectionism' and 'no outdated restrictive practices'. 'Britain still has one of the most lightly regulated labour markets in the world', Blair happily told the Confederation of British Industry.[18]

While New Labour has sought to remove political control over economic policy, it has been happy to put business leaders in charge of political matters. Head of BP, Sir David Simon, for example, became Minister for European Competition and Martin Taylor, head of Barclays Bank, became head of Gordon Brown's welfare reform task force.

Britain's biggest businesses have won huge government contracts while donating employees to work in government departments. In March 2000, the *Observer* reported that BAE Systems, which is winning multi-billion military contracts from the MoD, had eight staff working for free inside the MoD; construction giants Kvaerner, Ove Arup and Bovis, which stood to make millions from roadbuilding programmes after a change in government transport policy, all had key staff working in the Department of Transport; BP had paid for British employees to work in the British embassy in Washington and on the Foreign Office's Middle East desk; and British Telecom, which successfully lobbied to be removed from tighter regulation under the Utilities Bill, had two staff inside the DTI. Price Waterhouse Coopers had staff in the Foreign Office, the DTI, the MoD, the Cabinet Office and the Department of Health. The Treasury employed the 'free' services of Price Waterhouse Coopers, Ernst and Young and Pannell Kerr Forster, all of whom have earned huge consultancy contracts from the department. In 1998, the Foreign Office revealed in an answer to a parliamentary question that it currently had seconded staff from BP, British Nuclear Fuels, Standard Chartered Bank, Taylor Woodrow, Brown and Root, Barclays, BT, Nat West, Ernst and Young, HSBC and Rolls Royce, and many others.[19]

None of my analysis is from an 'anti-business' perspective per se. Certainly, small-scale business plays a vital role in local economies and in my view is central to democratic society because a proliferation of smaller enterprises means that economic power is more widely dispersed. But New Labour's agenda is very different, amounting to the unprecedented empowerment of transnational big business, through reshaping the rules of the global economy. British governments have always worked in alliance with big business, but the Blair government's domestic and global priorities take this alliance to new heights.

This is what Thomas Frank has called 'market populism', where businessmen are seen as public servants and the box office as a voting booth. The corporatisation of society is leaving almost every sector of life open to control by profit-making companies that lack any real accountability to the public and are outside of democratic control.[20] So in Britain, so throughout the world.

The scale of corporate power is shown by the fact that the world's largest 200 corporations control a full quarter of global wealth. Never before in human history has such a small number of private corporations wielded so much power. Increasingly, whole economies – in the North as well as the South – are being geared to cater to the demands of transnational capital. Ministers see their role simply as administering these demands, while preparing their citizens for the cut-throat international competition ahead through 'education'. Politicians aid this attack on democracy by removing many instruments they could use to control it.

In some ways we are witnessing the re-emergence of the 'chartered government' of the colonial period. In the seventeenth century a number of English colonies were founded by private companies, who were given full control over the area they occupied subject to the authority of the Crown. These companies were pretty much free to exploit the resources of the territory as they wanted. In many countries, corporate power is so great that they resemble these chartered governments.

The chief enforcer of this project is no longer Western armies but the various levers Northern governments use and especially the WTO, using not military power but legally binding agreements that it will be almost impossible to reverse. We are in danger of entering – if we have not already – an era of Corporate Absolutism, a modern variant of absolute monarchy in the past.

The predictable effects

What have been the effects so far of the global 'liberalisation' project that Britain is championing?

Let us take the example of Haiti. There, thousands of poor rice farmers have been put out of business and thrown further into poverty by subsidised rice from the US entering the local market. One rice farmer interviewed by the development NGO Christian Aid, Fenol Leon, said that 'unless something is done to protect us from cheap rice imports, I don't think there's a future for us – we'll all be wiped out'. Farmers have been forced to leave their land and many have become economic migrants, some trying to find work in neighbouring Dominican Republic, others fleeing to the US. Philippe Michel, the head of a local NGO, said; 'You wake up in the morning hungry. You've got nothing for your children to eat. What do you do? Some people have taken to the boats, others have committed suicide.'[21]

In Haiti's case, the global trade rules allow the people of the Western hemisphere's poorest country to be made poorer by the trade policy of the hemisphere's richest country. WTO rules and other agreements that the Haitian government has been obliged to sign, along with a sheer lack of resources, make it extremely difficult to raise barriers to protect farmers from the devastation wrought by these subsidised exports from the US.

This story is repeated all over the world. Cheap food imports are undermining poor farmers' food security and livelihoods in Mexico, Gambia, Brazil, the Philippines, Guyana, Sri Lanka and many other countries, affecting untold millions of poor people. Although urban consumers can gain from cheap food imports, the costs to the poorest farmers are often devastatingly greater.

These impacts are entirely predictable, and have been occurring for centuries, as when colonial Britain ensured that cheaper goods from Lancashire destroyed the Indian hand-looms industry, causing starvation and untold misery for millions of poor Indians. Then, as now, British governments champion the so-called 'free trade' agenda.

Various UN reports show the effects of the WTO agreements. The United Nations Development Programme calculated that the least developed countries would be worse off by $600 million a year as a result of the Uruguay round of trade negotiations concluded in 1994. A UN General Assembly report states that 'cheap food imports are threatening local food production' and that in the majority of least developed countries 'there are no safeguards to protect fragile industries from abusive competition, and this has resulted in the closure of many domestic industries, worsening the situation of unemployment.'[22]

The UN Sub-Commission on the Promotion and Protection of Human Rights has called the WTO 'a veritable nightmare' for developing countries. In its view:

> The assumptions on which the rules of WTO are based are grossly unfair and even prejudiced. Those rules reflect an agenda that serves only to promote dominant corporatist interests that already monopolise the arena of international trade.[23]

Even Clare Short admitted that the world's poorest continent – sub-Saharan Africa – would face 'a small welfare loss' as a result of the Uruguay Round agreements.[24] But this has not stopped Britain arguing for more of the same policies.

The previous phase of the 'liberalisation' project was in the 1980s and 1990s, when the 'structural adjustment programmes' of the World Bank and IMF imposed trade liberalisation and privatisation on most of the planet. The results were often devastating, with health and education services collapsing in many countries, farmers being forced into deeper poverty through price falls and the urban poor being made increasingly desperate by cuts in food subsidies. It is no coincidence that the HIV/AIDS pandemic swept through the poor world during this period, as cutbacks in government health spending left many countries unable to cope with the disease. The same period also saw the world's poorest countries' share of world trade halve from an already minuscule 0.8 per cent in 1980 to 0.4 per cent in 2000.

The prices of many food and agricultural commodities, on which many countries depend for their survival, declined to their lowest level for decades, some to their lowest level for 150 years. Much of this was due to the World Bank's insistence on countries pursuing export-oriented strategies that increased global competition and pushed prices down. Devastation has been wrought in many communities dependent on the production and export of these commodities.

The South Commission has noted that globalisation 'is proceeding largely for the benefit of the dynamic and powerful countries'. In twenty-two of the forty-nine least developed countries – the poorest countries on the planet, where 600 million people live – national wealth per person either declined or was stagnant through the 1990s. Between 1988 and 1993 (according to the most recent available figures) the incomes of the poorest 80 per cent of the world's population fell; while the richest 20 per cent saw their incomes increase. The richest 1 per cent saw their incomes rise the fastest. In Africa, the poorest half of the population became even poorer in 1988–93, according to the World Bank. This is increasing poverty and inequality on a very large scale. Not all can be laid at the door of global 'liberalisation' – many populations in developing countries are also victims of their own governments – but much surely can.[25]

It is clear that the very richest are becoming richer and the very poorest are becoming poorer. Meanwhile, hundreds of millions of people in both North and South are experiencing much greater job insecurity (and stress) and worsening public health and education services, even as incomes rise for many. There are certainly many people benefiting from ever-deepening global 'liberalisation' and life is not exactly all doom and gloom for many people in richer countries. But the principal beneficiaries tend to be the already wealthy, especially the super-wealthy, and those in senior positions within, or associated with, transnational business.

We do not need to look far for the impact of structural adjustment programmes, since the Thatcher government effectively imposed one on Britain. One result was the astounding rise in child poverty. A UNICEF study in 2000 noted that the number of children in Britain living in poverty rose from 1.4 million twenty years ago to more than three million now. Nearly 33 per cent of children live in poor households – where weekly income is less than half the national average.[26]

Two decades of Conservative rule left Britain with the worst poverty record in the developed world, according to the OECD. Poverty affected 20 per cent of the population between 1991 and 1996. This was a worse record than even the US – where 14 per cent were affected – and compares with 10 per cent in Germany and 7 per cent in Sweden. A UN report found that a fifth of adults in Britain were functionally illiterate and that 13.5 per cent were permanently living in poverty, a worse record than all other developed countries except the US and Ireland.[27]

In the winter of 2000/1, more than 20,000 old people died of cold-related illness in England and Wales, according to Help the Aged. This was the number of excess deaths compared to the average for the summer and autumn months and followed an estimated 26,000 deaths in the winter of 1990/1.[28] These are Third World-scale deaths that are due considerably to poor, inaccessible public services and low incomes of the most vulnerable – partly the result of government economic priorities under the same model foisted on developing countries.

According to UNCTAD, the UN's trade body, 'the efficacy of the economic reforms on which so many lives and livelihoods now hang, is, and must remain, *an act of faith*'.[29] Unfortunately, it is one that Labour's liberalisation theologians are pursuing with real vigour.

The 'veritable nightmare' of the future?

If a prize were to be given for exploiting September 11th for one's own ends, then Trade Secretary Patricia Hewitt would surely be one of the front-runners. An aide to Transport Secretary Stephen Byers suggested in an internal memo that the government take advantage of September 11th to push through some unpopular policies; the aide and Byers were hounded by the media for weeks, contributing to Byers' eventual resignation. By contrast, Hewitt said something worse openly – that the attack on the World Trade Center 'was also an attack on global trade'. 'So we must respond by launching a new trade round' and 'fight terror with trade'.[30] Thus the dead of September 11th were being used to push further 'liberalisation' on the world's poor.

At the WTO's ministerial summit two months after September 11th, in Doha, Qatar, the British government led the way in pushing for a 'new trade round'. Britain had a tricky task to perform. On the one hand it was continuing the line of wanting to 'make trade work for the poor'. At the same time, it arrived in Qatar determined to force developing countries to 'agree' to add new issues, such as investment and government procurement, on to the WTO agenda – something to which almost all were completely opposed. The problem is that the natives just don't see what's good for them. As Clare Short said before Doha, 'much remains to be done in order to secure developing country support to launch a new Round'.[31] Developing countries were clearly right in arguing that agreements in these areas would benefit only the rich countries and their corporations. And that they lacked the capacity to negotiate new agreements when they were already so overstretched in trying (largely in vain) to defend their interests in the existing negotiations.

It was a hard act of double-think to perform but the government managed, aided by the fact that there were virtually no mentions in the media of the government's strategy and why it might be important to the world's poor. Rather, the media preferred to parrot the government's line – by now, embarrassingly absurd – about 'making trade work for the poor'. At public meetings in Doha, meanwhile, Clare Short managed to vilify those who failed to accept total 'liberalisation' by saying they were supporters of Burma and North Korea.

Post-Doha, and in the run-up to the next WTO meeting in Cancun, Mexico in 2003, British planners have a definite agenda for the future. A key British aim in the WTO is to secure a global agreement on investment that would require all governments to give 'equal treatment' to foreign as to domestic businesses in many important economic policy areas. This would be a disaster for many developing countries – all successful developers in the past have strongly discriminated in favour of their domestic companies, nurturing them to become competitive, to aid national development. If foreign companies are treated equally, an important development policy is removed and local markets can be dominated by foreign enterprises. In turn, profits can simply be repatriated back to the home country and poor countries drained of scarce resources.

Britain is pushing for 'treating inward investors exactly the same as domestic investors – ownership of the company should not be relevant to the application of national laws and regulations'. This is, of course, exactly what Britain's businesses want – unfettered access to the world's markets for investment. The aim of a global agreement, Baroness Symons explains, is to 'help lock in individual countries' own investment reform efforts' – that is, ensure they promote the 'one-size-fits-all' model.[32]

Britain was one of the strongest supporters of the proposed Multilateral Agreement on Investment (MAI) that Northern countries tried to negotiate in the OECD. If passed into law, the MAI would have massively increased the power of corporations over elected governments, greatly expanding their investment rights all over the world. Most worryingly, the MAI would have given companies the power to sue governments for the loss of profits if governments enacted laws discriminating against them, and to be compensated for any losses. Despite this, Clare Short told parliament that a report commissioned by DFID 'concluded that the MAI could have a positive developmental impact'.[33] The MAI proposal was eventually scuppered in 1998, partly due to an NGO campaign against it.

The government did not give up, however. After the talks collapsed, it immediately said that 'it is better to start afresh in another forum' than the OECD given its 'long-standing objective' of pursuing investment negotiations in the WTO.[34]

Asked by a parliamentary committee whether an international investment agreement was needed, Trade Minister Brian Wilson replied that:

> As to whether there is a demand from UK companies for some such agreement, I can assure you that this is a subject that is raised with us very regularly by UK companies which invest abroad.[35]

The government is also acting as an ally to big business in the ongoing WTO negotiations on services. Trade Minister Baroness Symons has told members of International Finance Services London – a big business pressure group – that Whitehall is seeking 'an international trading environment in which UK business can compete and thrive'. She added: 'I hope you will view this government as your greatest ally in moving that agenda forward', including through the WTO. After the Qatar ministerial, Symons said that the WTO negotiations 'offer a huge opportunity to European and British businesses'. In services, 'we need to continue to ensure that the UK's key offensive interests are reflected'.[36]

Services are big business to Britain, which is the second largest exporter of services in the world, amounting to £67 billion in 2000, and the fourth largest importer. Symons notes that for Britain 'trading services internationally is of far greater importance than it is to a number of countries', which explains why to New Labour's liberalisation theologists 'open markets are a major economic interest and essential to our own economic performance'.[37]

Campaigners have forced some attention on the scandal of GATS, the WTO's General Agreement on Trade in Services.

Supporters of the global 'liberalisation' project would ultimately like to require all countries to allow foreign business equal access to all domestic markets for services – including health and education, as well as tourism and financial services. The European Commission has described GATS as 'first and foremost, an instrument for the benefit of business'. A British government memo leaked in 2001 showed a DTI official complaining that the case for GATS was 'vulnerable' when campaigners asked for 'proof of where the economic benefits lay' for developing countries.[38]

Currently, the WTO rules do not formally require developing countries to 'liberalise' their services sectors; each country is technically free to decide for itself whether or not to do this. The British government says that: 'Naturally, looking at our own export interests, we would hope that countries *could be persuaded* to liberalise their services markets through negotiation of balanced benefits'. On this matter 'governments with export interests such as the UK will often be guided by the advice they receive from business'.[39]

What being 'persuaded' actually means was discovered by Christian Aid. It found that in Ghana, the British government was in effect tying the release of British aid to Ghana's government privatising its water services. DFID was withholding £10 million in aid for the expansion of water supply in the city of Kumasi until company bids for the leases of Ghana's urban water supplies as a whole had been received. DFID had commissioned the Adam Smith Institute – a wholesale supporter of privatisation – to 'advise' the British government on restructuring the water sector in Ghana. British water and construction companies have been waiting in the wings to take advantage of privatisation.[40]

The difference between developing countries 'choosing' and 'being forced' to accept the Northern countries' agenda is wafer thin. A huge number of levers are used by Northern countries to secure their goals. Indeed, by the time that the WTO formally requires developing countries to liberalise all services sectors, this may have already happened in practice, thanks to pressure outside the WTO, as in Ghana. As Baroness Symons explains, privatisation 'is a growing phenomenon worldwide . . . This is occurring quite independently of the GATS negotiations'.[41]

And this is just in Ghana. The government is pressing for the privatisation of water supplies and other services across the planet. DFID's chief civil servant notes that 'we are . . . extending our support for privatisation in the poorest countries from the power sector in India to the tea industry in Nepal'.[42] A new trilateralism of government, business and NGOs is being established to push this agenda. DFID, for example, has established a group involving British water companies and some development NGOs to press for global water privatisation. The NGOs are being seriously co-opted, in my view, in a process aimed at private companies getting their hands on critical public infrastructure. It is not that major reforms of such services are often not needed in developing countries, just that handing over effective control to foreign multinationals – as is often occurring – is a very particular strategy with obvious beneficiaries.

The drive for worldwide privatisation includes, of course, Britain. Here, the Private Finance Initiative – involving 'public-private partnerships' – is transferring ownership and control of much of the economy's infrastructure, including schools and hospitals, to private business, a key aspect of what George Monbiot calls 'the corporate takeover of Britain'. The same is happening globally.

Another 'new issue' to look out for in the future is 'public procurement', that is, government spending. Depending on the country, this amounts to between 3 and 12 per cent of GDP, so is a massive market that transnational business is keen to access. Britain notes that 'government procurement represents a sizeable slice of economic activity' and 'this in itself is a strong argument for including purchases by governments in the multilateral rules system'. If public procurement were 'liberalised', all governments could be required to give equal treatment to foreign companies in government spending contracts, thus removing an important tool to promote national development.[43]

The high-point of propaganda on 'development' has come following the Doha ministerial. Ministers now refer to the outcome of the summit as the 'Doha Development Agenda' – a description of global liberalisers' plans for total control of the world economy while offering a few scraps to the poor. In Doha, developing countries had to fight the EU and the US hard to only just manage to delay (until the next summit) 'agreement' on adding the new issues on to the WTO's remit. One or two important gains were made by developing countries since they remained united in the face of an onslaught by the liberalisation theologists, including the British government. But the declaration at the end of the summit simply calls for the ever onward march of more liberalisation, with no acknowledgement of any adverse impacts on anyone. The phrase 'Doha Development Agenda' has now entered the lexicon and is regularly used without speech marks, not only by ministers but also in the media, and even by some NGOs. It has become a Fact, since it has been so designated. In reality, it shows that 'development' can largely be translated as 'corporate control'.

There are several ways in which the New Labour government claims it is making globalisation work for the poor (wits with somewhat greater insight suggest it could be described as 'making the poor work for globalisation'). One is by 'opening up our markets' – championing the removal of the EU's trade barriers to exports from poor countries. Certainly, blocking these exports at the same time as forcing open their markets is gross hypocrisy, and Britain has been outspoken on this. But the reality is that this 'market access' is being offered as a sweetener for poor countries to do likewise – open their markets even further to exporters from the North. For example, according to former Trade Minister Richard Caborn, access to EU markets 'is the message we need to hammer home if we are to get the developing world to agree to another round of WTO talks', that is, further liberalisation.[44] It is a myth that mutual liberalisation creates a level playing field from which all countries will benefit equally; rather, it is mainly TNCs who will gain, poised as they are to take advantage of newly opened markets.

There are two camps among Northern governments. In the first are those pressing economic liberalisation for others while practising protection themselves. These countries, like France and Ireland who defend the big farm subsidies in the EU's Common Agricultural Policy, could be termed the 'hypocrites'. In the second camp are those pressing for 'liberalisation' everywhere – the 'extremists'. Britain is one of the leading voices in this camp.

Another way in which Britain claims to be helping developing countries is by 'capacity building' aid to help developing countries better participate in the trade negotiations. But the small amount of aid Britain gives is mainly to help those countries implement agreements they have opposed in the first place. The government says this aid is given 'in order to help them understand their rights and implement their commitments under international trade agreements' and to enable them 'to adjust to any social and economic changes which further liberalisation may bring'. Of a recent £20 million package in such aid to developing countries, £6.5 million was specifically earmarked to help them negotiate the new issues that they opposed including in the WTO.[45]

A third area where the government is often praised is in the area of increases in overseas aid. New Labour has increased the aid budget significantly, from a low point at the end of Conservative rule. But aid is still being used to press developing country governments into promoting the 'correct' macro-economic policies, which can completely undermine the positive impact that better aid could have. For example, Gordon Brown's widely praised aid initiative in December 2001 – for rich countries to increase their aid by $50 billion a year – is conditional on developing countries pursuing trade 'liberalisation' and 'creating a favourable climate for investment'.[46] The government has abolished formal tied aid – aid given on the specific condition that it is used to buy goods from the donor – which is a positive step; but as the Ghana water privatisation case shows, the imposition of its priorities continues using various other levers.

On debt relief, Britain has a more positive record than most other creditor governments. It was largely public pressure – notably through the Jubilee 2000 debt campaign – that pushed the government into its more progressive stance. But its record is not as fantastic as many believe. First, debt relief is also conditional on countries pursuing policies under the global liberalisation project – a reward for developing countries promoting policies that will further impoverish them, and a bit like a doctor offering a patient an aspirin at the same time as injecting them with a deadly disease. The fact that debt relief is such a lever over developing countries plausibly offers one explanation for why New Labour has become keen on it.

Second, not much debt relief has actually been granted. Britain's agreement to write off the bilateral debt owed to it by the poorest highly indebted countries was a very small step. These countries were paying Britain only around £40 million in debt service in 1999. (This decision, announced with great fanfare, was much praised – it was reported on the front page of the *Guardian* under the heading 'Britain ends third world debt'!)

The G7 countries promised at the Cologne summit in 1999 to cancel $100 billion in debt; only around a third of this has been cancelled, while Africa continues to pay back $15 billion a year in debt service, about the same as it receives in aid. Meanwhile, some countries are expected to pay higher interest rates under the World Bank's much-vaunted current debt relief scheme than before. For Zambia, one of the world's poorest countries, this amounts to twice as much in debt repayments as it spends on health.[47]

Even if we accept that there are some positive aspects to these policies, they are completely dwarfed by the wider government agenda. The same goes for the role of Clare Short in government. It is true that in some debates between government departments, Short has spoken out against several of Blair's and the DTI's policies, such as on a few proposed arms exports. But these are minor in the big picture where DFID, and Short personally, have been leading champions of the global 'liberalisation' project.

Outside any effective media and parliamentary scrutiny, the British government is pursuing a set of policies affecting the lives of hundreds of millions of people in a project to reshape the global economy for many decades to come. Its extremist economic policies in support of the WTO fly directly in the face of UN agencies, not to mention a multitude of civil society organisations and people around the world. The UN is highlighting the serious adverse effects of these policies, and calling for fundamental changes, such as the removal of the WTO's policy restrictions and holding impact assessments, before further liberalisation goes ahead. These are being rejected by New Labour, while it professes an unadulterated commitment to international development. This is a further example of the contempt with which British elites in reality view the concept of multilateral cooperation and the UN, except when they can use it to achieve their fundamental priorities.

10

THE THREAT OF DEMOCRACY

> We have to devise techniques for bringing influence to
> bear upon other countries' internal decisions.
>
> Treasury memorandum, 1945

My view is that the 'war against terrorism' and the project to
promote global economic 'liberalisation' are two sides of the
same coin. Western elites' main enemies in both strategies are
independent forces outside of Western control, some malign,
some benign. To illustrate this, it is important to see that the
roots of current globalisation lie in US, and British, economic
planning following the end of the Second World War. Elite goals
were crystal clear, and we would be wise to understand them if
we are concerned about peering through current rhetoric.

The roots of globalisation

US leaders incessantly outlined their global economic goals
during, and following the end of, the Second World War. The
basic goal of US foreign policy was to create an 'open door' in
trade and investment where US companies were to be able to
secure access to other countries' markets. The State

Department noted that 'our foreign policy is aimed at achieving the kind of world community in which trade and investment can move with a minimum of restrictions and a maximum of security and confidence'. This meant that 'efforts should be made to develop climates attractive to private investment'. Given massive US power in the early postwar years, US plans were for nothing less than control of the world economy.[1]

The economies of key countries and regions were to be organised to benefit Western, primarily US, business interests. The key regions for the US were Latin America; areas under European colonial control – such as Africa and Southeast Asia; and the Middle East, due to the importance of oil in the global economy, and the interests of US oil corporations. The overarching goal was – and remains, as noted in the previous chapter – for business to secure access to and control over other countries' resources.

A 1950 British Foreign Office document noted that Africa 'is an important source of raw materials in peace and war' that enables the UK to 'both earn and save dollars'. Southeast Asia was 'a substantial economic asset and a net earner of dollars', with the colony of Malaya alone having a surplus of $145 million in 1948. In the Middle East, British officials recognised that 'United Kingdom oil companies have made large net profits since the war', with £50 million by the Anglo-Iranian Oil Corporation in Iran in 1948.[2]

The first postwar Labour administration under Clement Attlee is adulated by many Labour supporters as the most radical and successful Labour government. The reality is that in foreign policy, it continued the imperialist policies of its predecessors, sometimes deepening them under the guise of its 'internationalist' rhetoric. Attlee and his Foreign Secretary, Ernest Bevin, initially conceived the idea of establishing Britain as a 'third force' between the United States and the USSR. This involved a vast scheme for joint Western European exploitation of resources in the colonies. It aimed at establishing 'an African Union under European auspices' in which, Bevin observed, 'it would be necessary to mobilise the resources of Africa in support of West European Union'. He said in 1948 that the need was 'to develop the African continent and to make its resources available to all' (that is, us). The US 'is very barren of essential minerals and in Africa we have them all'. Bevin's aim for the Middle East, meanwhile, was to develop 'a prosperous producing area which would assist the British economy and replace India as an important market for British goods'.[3]

This plan was supported by the Chancellor of the Exchequer, Stafford Cripps, who noted that 'the development of our African resources in particular is . . . of prime importance and must be a major consideration in planning our economic activities'. Field Marshal Montgomery claimed that British living standards could be maintained by Africa's minerals, raw materials, land and cheap coal. The only problem was that the African was 'a complete savage' incapable of developing these resources himself.[4]

The 'third force' idea was formally abandoned by 1949 when it had become obvious that Britain and Europe could offer no such counter to the US and USSR. But the basic strategy of using colonial resources to benefit Britain remained and became standard practice.

The declassified files of the early post-war years show that Colonial Office planners were aware that they were grossly exploiting the colonies: 'the Colonial territories are helping so much on [Britain's] balance of payments', one file from 1951 reads. The Attlee government drained the then colonies of millions to help Britain's post-war economic recovery. Bevin believed that the possibility of presenting (naturally, unfairly) British policy as exploitation was 'almost endless'. So he suggested that 'care and preparation' would be needed to present British policies as promoting development. Clare Short and other ministers have taken up this baton today.[5]

The US backed the continuation of European colonial rule and exploitation in Africa. In 1948, the US Policy Planning Staff said that Britain's plan for 'the economic development and exploitation' of colonial Africa 'has much to recommend it'. This was because 'the United States realises the importance to her own economy, in peace and war, of many British colonial resources and the possibilities of their further development'. The US did expect, however, that 'equal economic treatment will be given to American capital and American nationals who engage in trade in the African colonial areas'. The countries of Southeast Asia were also recognised as 'rich in natural resources and certain countries in the area at present produce surplus foodstuffs'. Indochina, US planners noted, could be a 'most lucrative economy'.[6]

These early postwar priorities were pursued throughout the postwar period. Britain's aim under 'decolonisation' – a misleading term, implying that Britain voluntarily gave up formal control over its colonies, when the reality was that it was forced out of many – was to ensure that 'independent' countries continued to allow British companies to exploit their economic resources, as shown in the chapters on Malaya, Kenya and British Guiana. Rich pickings could be had – provided ultimate control over key countries and regions, and the international economy as a whole, could be maintained, by military interventions or covert operations if necessary. British military and covert interventions in Kuwait (1961), Egypt (1956), Iran (1953), Oman (1957 and 1964), North Yemen (1960s), for example, as described in other chapters, were all intended to keep resources in the correct hands. Similarly, the host of US interventions since 1945 served mainly to defend business interests and to ensure that other governments pursued pro-Western economic strategies. As noted elsewhere, Soviet policy was sometimes a factor but the Soviet threat was generally exaggerated or fabricated in order to justify interventions which would achieve these other goals.

Current globalisation, including especially the agreements of the World Trade Organisation, is in many ways the fruition of this long-standing foreign policy goal. The WTO agreements are novel in that they are global and legally binding, essentially requiring all countries to pursue a 'neo-liberal' economic model. By so doing, they increasingly obviate the need for Western military intervention or covert action in as many countries as previously. Throughout the postwar period, both Soviet power and the strength of nationalist voices in the Third World made such far-reaching global agreements impossible. Under globalisation, Third World elites have mainly thrown in their lot with their Northern counterparts.

The threat of independent development

The major forces previously opposing these Western economic goals in the Third World were nationalist, often popular forces. They were sometimes allied or sympathetic to the USSR and China, but just as much, not. The chapters on Iran, Indonesia, British Guiana and Kenya show that British governments clearly saw threats to their interests as arising from nationalist groups opposed to continued British exploitation of resources. They offered popular alternatives to address the grinding poverty in which most people lived. These policies usually included land reform to benefit the rural poor, economic reforms to tax the rich more, greater regulation of, and some-times takeovers of, foreign enterprises and more resources devoted to health and education services for the poor. Nationalist forces were surely not always benign, but in many cases they did offer alternative development paths that generally would have been better for most people than the British-backed strategies.

British planners usually presented these as 'Communist' threats, often as part of Moscow's grand design. I do not believe this was usually a planned conspiracy as such; rather, such propaganda came from an unconscious internalisation by planners of 'what works best' in achieving their objectives.

A Foreign Office paper from 1952 – called 'The problem of nationalism' – articulated the primary threat. It noted two kinds of nationalism – 'intelligent and satisfied nationalism' and 'exploited and dissatisfied nationalism'. The wrong nationalism is likely to 'undermine us politically' and undermine the UK's position as a world power. Specifically it means:

> (i) insistence on managing their own affairs without the means or ability to do so, including the dismissal of British advisers; (ii) expropriation of British assets; (iii) unilateral denunciation of treaties with the UK; (iv) claims on British possessions; (v) ganging up against the UK (and the Western powers) in the United Nations.[7]

The threat is therefore of countries 'managing their own affairs'. One US State Department adviser, referring to Latin America, once said: 'economic nationalism is the common denominator of the new aspirations for industrialisation. Latin Americans are convinced that the first beneficiaries of the development of a country's resources should be the people of that country'.[8]

Now, in British (and US) doctrine, it is simply not on that a country's resources primarily benefit the people of that country. The world's resources are to primarily benefit commercial elites, not people. This aim is clearly shown both in the formerly secret documents and in current plans for the WTO, outlined in the previous chapter.

For example, a Treasury memorandum of 1945 stated that Britain should ensure a 'rapid and non-autarkic economic growth' in the middle and low income countries, since this would expand world trade. It then warned of 'the danger to us of *autarkic industrialisation undertaken for its own sake*'. But there was a 'real difficulty' of avoiding this since it depended on 'decisions on internal policy in the countries concerned'. Therefore, 'we have to devise techniques for bringing influence to bear upon other countries' internal decisions'.[9]

Thus the danger was of development for national purposes over which Britain would have no control. British strategy was to counter this, and instead promote trade that would benefit

British commercial interests. The 'internal decisions' upon which it all depended are now increasingly made under the global rules of the WTO, thus achieving a long-standing aim.

The US documentary record is also rich in showing the threat of independent development to US elites. For example, a 1949 National Security Council study stated that the US should find ways of 'exerting economic pressures' on countries that do not accept their role as suppliers of 'strategic commodities and other basic materials'. In 1954 a State Department official warned that Guatemala:

> has become an increasing threat to the stability of Honduras and El Salvador. Its agrarian reform is a powerful propaganda weapon; its broad social program of aiding the workers and peasants in a victorious struggle against the upper classes and large foreign enterprises has a strong appeal to the populations of central American neighbours where similar conditions prevail.

The US soon organised the overthrow of the government and replaced it with one that understood the correct priorities. The same fear convulsed US planners with the success of the popular revolutions in Cuba and Nicaragua. Secretary of State George Shultz once noted, for example, that if the Sandinistas in Nicaragua 'succeed in consolidating their power', then 'the countries in Latin America, who all face serious internal economic problems, will see radical forces emboldened to exploit these problems'.[10]

Currently, and sticking to Latin America, one US enemy is Venezuelan president Hugo Chavez, an independent leader who has criticised US foreign policy and challenged US oil companies. Chavez's wayward ideas have been met with apparent US involvement in an attempted coup. It would be predictable if a similar fate also awaited Ignacio da Silva, known as Lula, the recently elected president of Brazil and head of the Workers Party.

The fear of independent development goes back much further into history. Two hundred years ago, British elites feared the success and spread of the ideas of the French Revolution in 1789. The call for 'liberty, equality and fraternity' had an explosive appeal that carried across borders. Britain became the most determined of the governments engaged in the counter-revolutionary war against France. The radical, republican agitation that arose in England following the French Revolution was met with a pogrom and severe legal repression, with Tory mobs, conniving with the magistrates, often looting and burning the houses of radicals and dissenters.

This period saw increasing threats to the position of the British aristocracy through the establishment of what historian A. L. Morton described as the first definitely working class political organisation, the Corresponding Society. This Society drew on the ideas of Thomas Paine's *Declaration of the Rights of Man*, which put forward the novel idea that politics was the business of all the people rather than simply a ruling elite, with the test of government being whether it pursued 'life, liberty and the pursuit of happiness'. Paine's expression of the principles of the French Revolution drew great support among the British working class.

The government's response was to enact draconian laws to suppress dissent, banning public meetings and making the Corresponding Society illegal. *The Rights of Man* was banned and Paine himself escaped trial by fleeing to France. Over the next few years, the government continued to suppress dissent and frequent strikes and bread riots broke out. Morton comments that 'the whole country was covered with a network of barracks' while 'the industrial areas were treated almost as a conquered country in the hands of an army of occupation'.[11]

The key way in which the threat of independent development is currently being countered is through multilateral organisations, especially the trade agreements of the WTO. According to the United Nations Development Programme, 'the new [trade] rules are highly binding on national governments and constrain domestic policy choices, including those critical for human development'. The UN's main trade body, UNCTAD, states that 'many WTO members will not be able to emulate the development strategies pursued successfully by many countries in the past'.[12]

Policies banned under the WTO rules include many pursued by East Asian countries in successfully eradicating poverty. Cambridge economist Ajit Singh states that openness, international competition and close integration into the world economy – all urged by New Labour's liberalisation theologists – 'were not in fact practised by either Japan or the Republic of Korea, the two most successful East Asian countries'. From the 1950s to the 1970s Japan imposed 'draconian import controls' and was 'far from being open or closely integrated into the world economy'. Other heretical policies pursued were a highly protected internal market, discouragement of foreign direct investment and heavy government intervention in all spheres of the economy.[13] Many of these policies could not now be legally pursued.

Indeed, while half the world lives in poverty, the WTO rules championed by Britain and the US are in effect preventing developing countries from promoting their own development. As noted in the previous chapter, these rules restrict countries' ability to raise tariff barriers to protect themselves against the cheap imports that are undermining local producers. They also heavily restrict countries' ability to regulate foreign investors to contribute to national development. Some types of government subsidies to agriculture – the lifeline of most poor people – have been banned altogether. And many industrial subsidies – successfully used by some countries to nurture local business through 'infant industry protection' – are now also banned.

The WTO's agreement on intellectual property and patents, TRIPS, is a case of massive corporate protectionism – giving private companies the ability to take out monopoly patenting rights over natural resources such as plant varieties and seeds. The evidence suggests that these patents are likely to reduce poor farmers' access to affordable seed, make local agriculture dependent on imported inputs and enable biotech companies to control local species. TRIPS has been described by UNDP as 'a silent theft of centuries of knowledge from developing to developed countries'.

Before TRIPS, most industrial countries, including Britain, developed their own industries by copying innovations from elsewhere. But now, according to UNDP, 'tighter control [of intellectual property] under the TRIPS agreement has closed off old opportunities and increased the costs of access to new technologies'. UNDP also says that:

> The privatisation and concentration of technology are going too far . . . Poor people and poor countries risk being pushed to the margins of this proprietary regime controlling the world's knowledge . . . From new drugs to better seeds, the best of the new technologies are priced for those who can pay. For poor people, they remain far out of reach. Tighter property rights raise the price of technology transfer, blocking developing countries from the dynamic knowledge sectors. The TRIPS agreement will enable multinationals to dominate the global market even more easily.[14]

Northern governments use various other levers to counter independent development and promote global 'liberalisation'. The receipt of loans from the World Bank and IMF, debt relief and bilateral aid are all conditional on southern governments pursuing the correct policies. The 'agreements' the EU is making with developing countries on 'regional free trade areas' are likely to be even more extreme than the WTO rules in pressing developing countries to 'liberalise' their economies. These levers are pushing in the same direction to achieve a global economy that works for the primary benefit of transnational business. And they are all being justified by reference to 'poverty eradication'. Much current 'development policy' is effectively geared to *preventing* development.

In summary, in the earlier postwar period, the major threat of nationalism was countered by a mix of economic policies, covert action to remove wayward governments and outright military intervention. The constant pretext was the Soviet threat. The chief proponents of the nationalist threat were 'radical' governments (that is, those independent of the West) and liberation movements.

In the era of globalisation, independent forces are being countered primarily by economic instruments like the WTO and by military/political strategies like the 'war on terrorism'. The latter is aimed at bolstering friendly regimes (under the guise of anti-terrorism) and provides a cover for a new phase of global intervention to remove unwanted governments. There are a variety of proponents today of alternative strategies: the global pro-democracy movement, labelled the 'anti-globalisation' movement; governments promoting alternative types of capitalism (such as China, Malaysia and other parts of Southeast Asia); and (often extremely brutal) Islamic regimes and groups in the Middle East. The first offers the brightest prospects, to which I return briefly in the final chapter.

The democratic threat

Popular, democratic forces are more of a threat than a promise to British governments. It is a myth that British governments generally promote democracy abroad. The reality is quite the opposite. Britain tends to support any government that promotes its fundamental interests, which are to maximise its political influence in the world and to make the global economy enrich British, and Western, commercial interests. Given that many popular, nationalist and/or democratic forces oppose these aims, Britain systematically sides with elites, often repressive ones who will keep such democratic forces in check.

If, as the myth goes, Britain generally supports popular, democratic forces struggling against elites, why did Britain not support the African National Congress and instead choose to back successive apartheid regimes in South Africa?; why did it not support a succession of progressive movements in Latin America struggling against US-backed elites, but chose to side with the US in undermining them?; why didn't it support the various popular African movements like the MPLA in Angola or Frelimo in Mozambique?; why doesn't it support popular movements like the Zapatistas in Mexico?; why have New Labour ministers been so critical of – and often tried to ridicule – the 'anti-globalisation' movement? Why have they supported the repressive regime in Bahrain rather than its more democratic, popular opposition?

Britain gave its total support for Indonesian ruler, General Suharto, until the mid-1990s when he began opposing economic policies imposed by the IMF. At this point, the West began to seek his removal and suddenly discovered he had been murdering Indonesians and East Timorese for three decades. Zimbabwe's Robert Mugabe was supported during atrocities committed by the army in the 1980s and afterwards, until the point when the started threatening white-owned farms. Now, the British government has suddenly discovered his regime is repressive and abusive of human rights.

Similarly, the Saddam Hussein regime was given British backing while he gassed and otherwise murdered tens of thousands of the Kurds throughout the late 1980s. This backing suddenly ceased when he disobediently invaded Kuwait in 1990, at which point he was transformed overnight into a new Hitler. Various Turkish regimes kill Kurds and depopulate their villages by the thousands while Britain barely bats an eyelid and extends diplomatic support for Turkey's entry into the EU.

The list goes on. British support for repressive elites is so generalised that promoting repression is an ordinary element of British foreign policy. Neither is British foreign policy about promoting 'national interests'. What *national* interests are being promoted when Britain supports sanctions that kill children in Iraq or adopts a pro-Israel line in the Middle East, or as in the past, overthrows governments in British Guiana and

Iran, or, arms Indonesian generals and sides with economic elites in Russia and South Africa? The interests being promoted here – outlined further in the following chapters – are those of British elites.

Put crudely, British 'foreign policy' is in reality a fancy term for supporting elites overseas. Britain ensured the continuation of its empire by creating new (or sustaining old) elites in the conquered territories who would manage colonialism in British interests. British rule in colonial India was based on support from the army of sepoys, native princes and landowners who thus owed their privileges to British authority. Britain destroyed the village community, the social base of the life of the mass of the population, and created instead a new oppression by those princes and nobles.[15]

Towards the end of formal colonialism, Britain set about creating elites that would do Britain's bidding after independence; some attempts were successful – as in Kenya, described in chapter 15 – while some failed. Britain remains a 'great power' (second order, these days), partly because it is an important ally to some key ruling elites. This is especially true where Britain's commercial interests are great, such as in the Gulf, where favoured ruling families manage oil under overall Western control. The Gulf includes some of the world's worst authoritarian regimes, which are partly propped up by British policy. Here, British elites barely even pretend to support more liberal political forces, so total is their support for the existing rulers.

Under globalisation, however, something new in human history has emerged – a *transnational* elite. It consists mainly of business and political leaders, together with senior technocrats from North and South, mainly the US, and is organised around the major actors in the global economy – the 200 largest corporations which control a quarter of the world's wealth. This elite is the champion of the global 'liberalisation' project that seeks a fundamental reshaping of the world's economy. It is a new, often personally stupendously wealthy and powerful global 'overclass'.

The new transnational elite acts on behalf of itself, not the nation state from which its individuals and companies come. This applies even, in fact especially, to US business elites, who are the clear leaders of the global liberalisation project. The elite has an annual meeting at the World Economic Forum in Davos, Switzerland, every January, attended by a few thousand specially invited business leaders and a handful of academics, journalists and international NGOs.

Most southern elites are no longer challenging US power. Instead, they see themselves as junior partners in the transnational elite, concerned with creating the best local conditions for transnational capital. This often means pitting country against country in increasing competition between them, resulting in a 'race to the bottom' in standards, lower wages, less regulated capital and reduced workers' rights.

The role of national governments is no longer seen by the transnational elite as formulating national policies; it is simply to prepare citizens to take advantage of 'opportunities' presented by globalisation and to administer policies favoured by the transnational elite. These policies – or rules – usually emanate from the multinational institutions (such as the WTO and the World Bank) that the elite controls. As noted in chapter 9, this, of course, is a massive, conscious undermining of democratic decision-making.

The new transnational elite ultimately wields political power but the underlying power lies with the demands of the global market economy. Political leaders are deploying their influence to deepen the economic power of the transnational elite, and in so doing are in effect disenfranchising themselves politically. There is little that is 'inevitable' about globalisation, just like there is little 'natural' about 'free trade'. 'Free trade' rules and globalisation itself have been brought about by massive government intervention. Elected governments, working together, can choose to regulate globalisation, to a very large extent, if they want. But political leaders like Tony Blair are choosing to abandon the ultimate political control they have.

The transnational elite has both an economic and a political project. The economic project is global 'liberalisation', which seeks total mobility of capital and completely 'liberalised' markets everywhere for trade, investment, services and much else. It eliminates most state intervention in the economy and most means to regulate businesses to promote national development goals and ethical standards. Its political project is to promote governance systems that will deepen such global liberalisation. In this, governments can be straightforwardly repressive, but they are tending to be elitist forms of democracy, that have been called 'polyarchy'.

Polyarchy is generally what British leaders mean when they speak of promoting 'democracy' abroad. This is a system in which a small group actually rules and mass participation is confined to choosing leaders in elections managed by competing elites. Those who win in elections then become largely insulated from the public so that they can 'effectively govern'. Between elections, groups who control the state are largely free from serious accountability to the public. Polyarchy has been described as a form of 'consensual domination' where (competing) elites control the state while popular forces and civil society groups are subject to the hegemony of the elite.[16]

In contrast to polyarchy stands 'popular democracy', where public participation is much greater and civil society groups are able to use the state to promote their interests. Here, mobilisation within civil society would be the principal way in which political power is exercised.

The elitist understanding of 'participation' in policy-making is instructive here. The World Bank responded to massive criticism of its economic policies in the 1980s and 1990s by launching a new initiative to promote the 'participation' of civil society in formulating government policies in developing countries. Governments are now required to hold formal consultations with civil society groups in order to draw up a national development strategy, which will then receive World Bank funding. These processes are now taking place in most countries where the World Bank is 'aiding' governments. But real participation is generally non-existent, as numerous recent studies show. It is not people's involvement in policy-making that is being promoted. Rather, civil society groups are being consulted to ratify decisions on policies being made by elites. In most countries there are few opportunities to shape policy, still fewer to implement alternatives.

Much of the blame for this should go to Southern elites who often have no intention of allowing the public to deflect them from their policies. But much is also to do with the conception of democracy emanating from the World Bank and the transnational elite.

Western governments support and work through civil society groups and non-governmental organisations to promote the polyarchic and neo-liberal economic agenda, using aid programmes to support local and Northern NGOs. Some of this aid can help the emergence of a more vibrant and influential civil society. But most aid in fact goes to more elitist organisations with reformist rather than radical agendas. Much aid to NGOs is intended to substitute for the state's role in providing public services. The involvement of transnational business, especially in public services, is increasingly being encouraged. Many NGOs have been co-opted while popular, radical alternatives have been closed off.

This is perhaps not surprising. Although they may seem independent and critical of government policy, most northern NGOs receive government funding and are afraid of criticising government policy outside of narrow limits. My experience is that almost all are so conservative in their basic political outlook and are themselves run undemocratically along polyarchic lines, that they could barely spot the difference between polyarchy and popular democracy anyway.

In the earlier postwar period, the West propped up a series of straightforwardly repressive elites who did its bidding – dictators such as Mobutu in Zaire, Suharto in Indonesia, the Shah in Iran and so on. These authoritarian regimes provided the crucial 'favourable investment climates' for Western business. Support for repressive regimes – especially in the Middle East and Gulf – remains a cornerstone of British and Western foreign policy, and is deepening under the 'war against terrorism'. However, under globalisation, polyarchy has been seen as a better guarantor of Western interests in most parts of the world.

Promoting authoritarianism had previously meant the West supporting right-wing political forces, often the extreme right. Under polyarchy, the centre-right or even the centre-left can be the favoured parties. The West has backed the emergence of polyarchic political systems in, for example, Russia and other Eastern European countries, the Philippines, Chile, Nicaragua, South Africa and Haiti. These countries have all discarded authoritarian regimes but what has emerged are systems that have staved off more radical change towards popular democracy, largely preserved the social order and the role of elites and are promoting economic policies favoured by the advocates of global liberalisation.

Take South Africa. The betrayal of South Africa, as it emerged from decades of institutionalised racism to black majority rule under the African National Congress (ANC) has been one of the most tragic episodes of recent years. Following apartheid, the advocates of global liberalisation – inside and outside the country – have created a South African economy geared to offering a generally favourable climate for investment by business. At the same time, the threat of radical change that might have principally benefited the majority of the population living in poverty has been staved off.

Britain's former Foreign Office Minister, Peter Hain, noted that 'where South Africa was once the reactionary pariah of Africa, now it is the radical and progressive model'. Identically, another former Foreign Office Minister, Tony Lloyd, noted that South Africa's 'economic and political success acts as a model and a catalyst for other sub-Saharan African countries'.[17]

The reality of South Africa's 'success' has actually been

persistent poverty, under which most South Africans continue to live. 100,000 jobs in the public sector and over 500,000 in agriculture have been lost in recent years. The group that has gained most, apart from whites who have retained their control of much of the economy, has been the black middle class – 20 per cent of black wage earners now take home nearly two-thirds of all income brought in by black workers. These effects derive from the 'neo-liberal' economic strategy imposed by the South African government with the support of the World Bank, International Monetary Fund, foreign businesses and governments such as Britain.

From the mid-1980s the issue for the US was not so much whether apartheid would be dismantled but how South African capitalism and the interests of the transnational elite in the region could be preserved following a transition period. US analyst William Robinson notes that 'the US objective was not to disregard the ANC or Mandela, but to check the growing radicalism among the black population by developing counterweights to popular leadership through US political and economic aid programmes'.[18]

In Mandela's last month in prison in 1990 the ANC was still saying that 'the nationalisation of mines, banks and monopoly industries is the policy of the ANC and a change or modification of our views in this regard is inconceivable'.[19] But by the time the ANC had achieved power in 1994, free enterprise and property rights were enshrined in every major economic policy statement as well as in the Constitution itself.

A somewhat progressive economic and social strategy – the Reconstruction and Development Programme (RDP) – was ditched within two years, as the government adopted 'neo-liberal' policies that pleased foreign investors and that geared South Africa towards a more favourable investment climate. Many of the RDP's promised reforms were never delivered and some reversed. Critical policies for the poor – such as building millions of housing units for the urban poor, radically improving terrible urban municipal services like water supply, and adopting a radical land reform programme – were undelivered or abandoned.

South Africa expert Patrick Bond notes that 'the consequences of a market-centred approach to low-income housing delivery were disastrous' in the ANC's first term. 'The effect of the neoliberal policy was to transfer state resources that should have gone into public or social housing, into the private sector, with little to show for it in return. Massive incentives found their way to banks and developers.'

A key role has been played by the World Bank and the IMF. Bond notes that 'the persuasive power of World Bank/IMF intellectual arguments . . . was partly to blame for the fact that a decades-old liberation movement disappointed its constituents' entirely reasonable aspirations within months of coming to state power'. He notes further that 'there were probably no more effective advocates for the interests of rich, white South Africans in post-apartheid South Africa than the quiet, smooth bureaucrats of the World Bank'. In virtually every area of social policy, Bank staff have worked behind closed doors and advocated policies that entrenched status quo wealth and power relations. The World Bank has been an important player in the post-1994 market-driven housing and land policies: the 'user pays' approach to water delivery, the increasing privatisation of infrastructure and services, and the cuts in spending on education, health and social welfare.

On his visit to South Africa in January 1999, Tony Blair said that Pretoria's economic strategy 'has set South Africa on a course to tackle the needs of the disadvantaged while retaining the confidence of the markets'.[20] Blair was referring to the Growth, Employment and Redistribution Strategy (GEAR), which promotes a restricted role for the state in redistribution, the restructuring of trade and industrial policies towards a more export-oriented strategy, market-led reforms to create an environment favourable to foreign investors, and privatisation across the board. The GEAR is based on regarding government spending as excessive and corporate tax rates as too high. It was not surprising that then deputy president Thabo Mbeki could bait journalists in 1996 to 'call me a Thatcherite', while a leading South African newspaper, the *Mail and Guardian*, dubbed Finance Minister Trevor Manual as 'Trevor Thatcher'.[21]

'We have no doubt about South Africa's attractiveness as a business partner for UK companies', Trade Secretary Patricia Hewitt notes. British companies are currently the largest investors in South Africa, amounting to £11 billion.[22]

Britain's Department of Trade and Industry noted that business 'opportunities exist across the board and include privatisation/restructuring of the ports, railway, power and water sectors, consultancy, telecoms and IT/electronics, the environment and water, healthcare, tourism, creative industries and agriculture'. Also, 'South Africa's healthcare sector offers significant opportunities for UK business' while 'there are many more opportunities for UK water utilities and contractors to win future business'.[23]

Thus the 'elite transition' in South Africa has preserved much of the wealth relations and economic order under apartheid. It is continuing to offer Western businesses an attractive climate for investment as the top priority for economic policy, rather than policies to primarily address mass poverty.

II

OUR ALLIES, THE GULF ELITES

Why do we support reactionary, selfish and corrupt governments in the Middle East instead of leaders who have the interest of their people at heart?

Stafford Cripps, Chancellor in the
Attlee government, 1945–51[1]

Former SAS officer, Peter de la Billiere, the commander of British forces in the 1991 Gulf War to eject Iraq from Kuwait, makes an extraordinary comment in his personal account of the war. He notes Saudi Prince Khalid telling him of his need to ensure that the Saudi ruling family remained in power after the war, to which de la Billiere replied:

> I fully understood the Prince's difficulties and sympathised with him, but my understanding attitude was not entirely altruistic. As we, the British, had backed the system of sheikhly rule ever since our own withdrawal from the Gulf in the early 1970s, and seen it prosper, we were keen that it should continue. Saudi Arabia was an old and proven friend of ours, and had deployed its immense oil wealth in a benign and thoughtful way,

with the result that standards of living had become very high. It was thus very much in our interests that the country and its regime should remain stable after the war.[2]

The 'system of sheikhly rule' in Saudi Arabia to which de la Billiere casually refers is one that systematically imprisons, tortures or beheads all political opponents in one of the world's most repressive states. That a military commander can write of Britain's interests in the continuation of Saud family rule says a lot, to me, about the values of British elites. That it can be said in a best selling book without creating a furore says a lot about the deafening silence on Britain's complicity in massive human rights abuses in the Middle East.

British policy in the Middle East is based on propping up repressive elites that support the West's business and military interests. This is having two outcomes. The first is that Britain is often undermining the prospects for the emergence of more popular and democratic governments. The second is that it is helping to fan the flames of religious extremism that is often the only alternative available to those being repressed. Britain's role in the region is far from benign and is, frankly, dangerous to its inhabitants as well as – perhaps increasingly – people in Britain and the West. These are truisms about all British governments, but New Labour is continuing the policy, indeed with real enthusiasm.

The importance of Britain's role in the Middle East should not be underestimated. Although the US is clearly the major power in the region, Britain has an array of close diplomatic and military relations with the regimes in Oman, Bahrain and Kuwait and it has the world's largest arms deal with Saudi Arabia, whose brutal internal security forces it is continuing to train. Britain has been responsible, with the US, for the continuation of sanctions against Iraq and the policing of the 'no fly zones' over the north and south of the country. It is traditionally the only major country to have actively and unequivocally supported US violence in the region, as in the 1991 Gulf war against Iraq, in various missile attacks, and in Afghanistan. London has also traditionally been a primary apologist for massive human rights atrocities in Turkey and is a current diplomatic champion of Turkey's attempts to joint the EU (see chapter 1). Britain under Blair has also played an extraordinary role in adopting a pro-Israel position in the context of increasing violence in the occupied territories (chapter 5).

There has been no greater myth since September 11th than that everything has changed as a result. Rather, in the post-September 11th world, Britain – and the US – have continued their traditional policies of supporting the existing repressive regimes in the Middle East. The only change appears to be a deepening of this support as many states use the 'war on terrorism' as a new cover to repress their people, as noted in chapter 3.

Robert Fisk, Britain's most outstanding journalist on the Middle East, has noted that:

> In Egypt, I have catalogued the systematic torture of Islamist prisoners by the state security police; conducted dozens of interviews with torture victims in Cairo, Assiut and Beni Suef and identified the floor of the Lazoughli Street police headquarters where electricity is used on prisoners. The Egyptians have both denied the evidence and pointed out that they are fighting 'international terrorism'. But gross human rights abuses have merely grown worse. Britain and other Western governments have put no pressure on the Egyptians to halt these practices. President Mubarak is called the West's most faithful Arab friend.[3]

The pattern of human rights abuses is the same across the Middle Eastern regimes supported by Britain and the West, where torture, discrimination against women, the complete suppression of dissent, free speech and association and the banning of political alternatives are all the norm.

Britain's current commitment to the Gulf regimes is so great that, according to the Ministry of Defence, 'all of the [Gulf] countries have an expectation that we would assist them in times of crisis'.[4] All six states in the Gulf Cooperation Council – Bahrain, Kuwait, Oman, Qatar, Saudi Arabia and the United Arab Emirates – have military officers being trained in the UK while all (except Bahrain) are housing British military forces.

The fundamental Western interest in the region is of course oil, outlined in chapter 1 and elsewhere. An additional factor is that the Gulf elites should spend their stupendous oil incomes on Western arms or invest the revenues in the Western banking system. Repressive Middle Eastern elites understand these priorities, and also that their role in this system helps keep them in power locally; the West could withdraw its support for them if they got any wayward ideas.

The policy of supporting elites in the Gulf, and aiding their internal repression, is long-standing, as I outlined in my previous book, based on declassified documents.[5] The Gulf sheikhdoms were largely created by the British to 'retain our influence' in the region. Policy was to defend them against external attack but also to 'counter hostile influence and propaganda within the countries themselves'. Training their police and military would help in 'maintaining internal security'. The US shared these concerns, noting that British and US interests in the region could be preserved by recognising the challenges to the West and 'to traditional control in the area'. US planners based their policy on supporting the 'fundamental authority of the ruling groups'.[6]

The chief threat to these regimes was never Soviet intervention but what the Foreign Office called 'ultra-nationalist maladies'. The Cabinet Secretary, Norman Brook, told the Prime Minister in 1961 that 'we are fighting a losing battle propping up these reactionary regimes' in the Middle East. The declassified documents show that British planners recognised that they were opposed to the 'rising tide of nationalism' and 'the force of liberalism'.[7] Thus, along with support for repressive elites has been more or less permanent opposition to popular regimes or groups in the Middle East. In 1957, the Foreign Office identified the danger of the existing rulers 'losing their authority to reformist or revolutionary movements which might reject the connexion with the United Kingdom'.[8]

The same goes today. The West has continually failed to support the democratic rights of the Kurds in Iraq and Turkey, preferring brutal regimes to keep order from Baghdad and Ankara. The West opposed Yasser Arafat 'in opposition', when the Palestine Liberation Organisation was more a popular, legitimate representative of the Palestinians; until recently at least, it supported Arafat as Chairman of the Palestinian Authority when his rule had become increasingly repressive.

Britain and the US have also generally refused to offer support to opposition groups in repressive regimes which are advocating peaceful, political change, such as the Muslim Brotherhood in Egypt and the Committee for the Defence of the Legitimate Rights of the Saudi People in Saudi Arabia. Egyptian President Nasser in the 1950s and 1960s – popular, nationalist – was an official enemy; current Egyptian President Mubarak – repressive, unpopular – is official friend.[9] There are many other examples. Only in Iraq does Britain support opposition groups posing alternatives to the current regime and even there the West appears more interested in a similarly repressive replacement.

London and Washington have throughout the postwar period connived with Middle Eastern elites to undermine popular, secular and nationalist groups which have offered some prospect of addressing the key issues in the region – the appalling levels of poverty and undemocratic political structures. Postwar US planners, for example, recognised that 'among increasing numbers of Arabs there is . . . a conviction that we are backing the corrupt governments now in power, without regard for the welfare of the masses.'[10]

With the undermining of these secular, nationalist opposition groups, the field has been left open for anti-Western Islamic groups to offer themselves as the major political alternatives.[11]

Britain and the West are not anti-Islam, in my view. They quite happily support Islamic extremists in power when they do the West's bidding – as in Saudi Arabia, the most 'fundamentalist' of all ruling elites. It is when groups cross the line in threatening fundamental Western interests that they become official enemies. However, the 'Islamic threat' is likely to prove increasingly useful to British and Western elites in coming years.

Liberal, more democratic or popular groups and regimes – in the Middle East as elsewhere – are generally viewed as a threat; our allies are repressive regimes. This simple truth about British policy cannot be expressed in the propaganda system. Let us consider two examples in more detail.

Supporting Saudi repression

Under New Labour Saudi Arabia remains a key British ally, the recipient of huge quantities of British arms, while London remained virtually completely silent on human rights abuses. But the British government is not only complicit in failing to speak out, it is more actively contributing to domestic repression.

In Saudi Arabia there is no freedom of association and expression, peaceful anti-government demonstrations are banned, women are pervasively discriminated against and there are no moves 'towards a more open and tolerant society', according to Human Rights Watch. The regime practices torture and corporal and capital punishment, with over 200 people beheaded during 2000 and 2001. There are no political parties, non-governmental organisations, trade unions or independent local media. The ruling family's refusal to allow any institutions outside its control puts the family 'beyond public reproach and accountability'. No one in the country dares report on human rights abuses, while international human rights organisations are banned from entering.[12]

New Labour has continued the British tradition of saying

nothing critical of Saudi human rights abuses. The strongest statement I have found – in a report to parliament – is that the government 'has concerns about the human rights situation in Saudi Arabia', without outlining what any of these are. It adds, presumably with a straight face, that it 'believes that a patient and discreet dialogue with the Saudi authorities is the best way to make progress'.[13] The rest is complete silence.

According to Human Rights Watch, there were 'no discernable improvements' in Saudi Arabia's human rights record in 2001 or, we might add, 2002.[14] This indicates that London's policy of private consultations is hardly paying off – even if we accept that there is any effort at all in trying to make it do so.

Former Foreign Office Minister Peter Hain admitted to a parliamentary committee in November 1999 that he had not 'publicly said anything' about human rights abuses since becoming the minister responsible for policy towards Saudi Arabia. When the committee asserted that Britain's policy was being dictated by trade interests, Hain simply replied: 'There is always a balance to be struck' and that the government had to determine 'how we can best achieve better human rights in any particular country'.[15]

Instead of publicly criticising the regime, Hain chose effusive public sycophancy. At a speech in front of Crown Prince Abdullah in June 2000, Hain said he was delighted by the Prince's presence in London 'which we like to think is your second home'. He praised Saudi Arabia for having 'balanced its obligations' to Islam 'with the secular pressures of commercial and economic change' with 'great dignity and skill'. There was one area in which Hain said Saudi Arabia needed to change: 'the investment climate in the kingdom is in need of modernisation'. He implored the Saudi regime to 'please do your best to open up as many sectors as possible to foreign investors'.[16]

Tony Blair counts Saudi Arabia as 'a good friend in the international coalition against terrorism'. The Prime Minister has 'no doubt at all that in the future those ties and that relationship will become even stronger still'. The Ministry of

Defence notes that 'Saudi Arabia has been our most important ally in the Gulf region, and our largest defence sales markets in the world.'[17]

The government's silence on human rights abuses should be seen in the context of the torture of British citizens arrested by the Saudi authorities. David Mornin was arrested five months after Hain's speech in connection with a series of bombings in Riyadh and Khobar on what strongly appeared to be trumped-up charges. Held in solitary confinement for eight weeks with the light burning constantly, Mornin said that:

> They flung me off the walls, punched me in the gut, kicked me in the ribcage . . . they hammered me. They threatened to gang rape my wife, to plant drugs on her, they said they would take me to the desert and cut my throat and leave me there . . . They kick you awake, make you sit down, then stand up about every 15 minutes . . . They hung me from bars above the door by my handcuffs so I was just off the balls of my feet for 24 hours at a time. They did that on four occasions.[18]

It is simply not the done thing in mainstream political culture to dwell on – or even mention – the repression and human rights abuses of our Saudi ally. This is despite the fact that it is hard not to pay attention to it – there are, after all, 30,000 British citizens living there.

It doesn't seem to matter how bad things get. In 1988, for example, a Saudi government-appointed religious body issued a fatwa, sanctioning the execution of members of opposition political parties.[19] This fatwa issued by our ally caused a good deal less attention – that is, none – than that issued against Salman Rushdie by our enemy, Iran. In the latter case, the fatwa usefully signalled all kinds of evil things about Islam and fitted nicely the government's designation of Iran as official enemy.

But New Labour is also actively contributing to the defence of the Saudi regime. Britain currently has a military mission that is providing 'internal security training' to the Saudi Arabian National Guard (SANG). The 75,000-strong SANG is specifically designed to defend the royal family from social unrest and military coups from the regular forces. The military mission is 'providing advice on such issues as officer training and developing basic military skills, and in more specialised areas such as anti-terrorism', a parliamentary committee notes. The MoD states that 'short-term training teams from the UK have been conducting low level internal security training for the SANG at UK expense'. Following the bombing in Khobar, teams were deployed in 1996, Spring 1997, Autumn 1998 and February 2000. 'All were a success', the MoD notes. Further teams are to be deployed over the next two years, it stated in March 2000.[20]

The British programme runs alongside a much bigger US operation. The most recent five-year US/Saudi contract is worth $831 million and involves 280 US government personnel and 1,400 staff of a private company, the Vinnell corporation. The US programme notes that the SANG 'is responsible for defending vital internal resources (oil fields and refineries), internal security, and supporting the Ministry of Defence and Aviation'. US personnel 'are directly involved in all aspects of SANG's force expansion and in helping to develop a total army'.[21]

This training makes Britain and the US direct allies of the Saudi royal family's retention of power against all-comers, a practical means of support for the regime championed by Peter de la Billiere, mentioned above. I can find almost no mention of this fact anywhere in the mainstream media. Neither is there any apparent concern in Westminster.

British training of the SANG is long-standing, going back decades. But almost nothing is known about it, partly because the British elite's relations with the Saudi elite are shrouded in secrecy, and subject to hardly any scrutiny.

A sign of the closeness between London and Riyadh is that during the 1991 Gulf War against Iraq, MI6 helped organise the Kuwait resistance in liaison with the Saudis. A training camp for volunteers was set up in eastern Saudi Arabia, involving members of the SAS, while Britain also provided machine guns. As with the aid given to the Afghan mojahidin, MI6's activities were a smaller vision of a similar CIA programme. Journalist Mark Urban quotes one person involved in this programme as saying that the guerilla training 'always had limited objectives, and its real value may have been as a long-term political gesture' – presumably, a gesture of support for the existing regimes.[22]

Selling arms is a further important aspect of the special relationship with Riyadh. This is not just about profits and supporting British military industry; arms exports also help to 'keep the goodwill of the king and other important Saudi Arabs', it was recognised by the US State Department in 1947.[23]

Britain's Al Yamamah arms contracts, signed in 1985 and 1988 and worth up to £50 billion, are not so much arms deals as a re-equipment of Saudi Arabia's military forces. These contracts involve dozens of Tornado and Hawk fighter and trainer aircraft, minehunters, associated infrastructure and arms, and support equipment including spares. One official linked to the deals admitted that Britain had beaten France's rival bid by gaining intelligence about which Saudi officials they intended to bribe and by outbidding them. A former MI6 station chief told BBC's *Panorama* that MI6 informed British businessmen about what the foreign competition might be.[24]

An investigation into the Al Yamamah deals by the National Audit Office is likely to show massive bribery and corruption. But the British administration that is committed to 'open government' has maintained its predecessor's refusal to make the report's findings public. This would likely embarrass our Saudi friends and no doubt a few British officials too.[25] The reluctance of British governments to publicise details of the deals may have been another reason why the Saudis chose to buy from Britain in the first place.

It is thought that about 15 per cent of the costs of the Al Yamamah deal went into the private bank accounts of Saudi princes and their associates.[26] Indeed, given that the weapons acquired by Saudi Arabia are far in excess of its defensive needs, it is plausible that the princes signed the deals precisely to receive massive bribes.

There is a further important aspect to the Al Yamamah deals: all the arms are exempt from export licensing by the British government. This means that there are no restrictions on the use or deployment of the arms under the deal.[27] Britain has simply washed its hands of any use the Saudi regime may want to put its weapons to. As noted in chapter 8, the bulk of this British arms trade with Saudi Arabia only arose from the then reluctance of the US to supply the regime.

When Jonathan Aitken, a former government minister, was imprisoned for perjury, the media were happy to dub him a liar and a con-man. This was due to his lying about a hotel bill paid by a Saudi prince, with whom Aitken had built up close business relations over many years. But, as the Campaign Against the Arms Trade has pointed out, the real scandal is that a man who for many years was in effect a servant of Saudi royalty was appointed to ministerial office. Moreover, Aitken was made minister for British 'defence procurement' (that is, the arms trade), the most important customer of which was the family of his former business connections. It is likely that these connections were instrumental in ensuring that Al Yamamah contracts continued in the 1990s.[28]

Bahrain – siding with the rulers

Bahrain has provided a good test case for how seriously New Labour would address human rights abuses committed by traditional British allies, and for whether it would be prepared to support opposition groups calling for greater political participation in the political system. Would New Labour be any different or continue business as usual?

A month after Labour came to power – in June 1997 – Human Rights Watch published a report on Bahrain entitled *Routine abuse, routine denial*. It noted that human rights abuses in Bahrain were wide-ranging, especially in the denial of fundamental political rights and civil liberties such as freedom of expression and association. The group said that there was a particular responsibility on Britain to take a lead since 'many abusive practices derive from the policies pursued by Great Britain prior to independence in 1971.'

Under the Conservative government, Britain's approach to these abuses had been similar to that of the US, Human Rights Watch noted: London only expressed concern 'in very general terms' about human rights practices and raised the issue only on a confidential basis. But this approach 'can no longer be regarded as adequate or sufficient'. It called on the newly elected British government to:

> make clear to the government of Bahrain, both publicly and privately, that persistent and recurrent human rights violations will affect negatively the depth and quality of relations with the United Kingdom, including military and security relations.[29]

The Blair government's reaction was immediately clear. A month following the report, Foreign Office Minister Derek Fatchett expressed support for the Bahraini regime's 'shura' system of consultative councils appointed by the Emir. Fatchett described this system as a 'respected and accepted' form of constitution and that the 'Bahraini shura council is not perfect but we should not write it off'.[30]

Britain rejected Human Rights Watch's suggestion to make clear that military relations would suffer as a result of human rights violations. Instead, London conducted another round of military talks with Bahrain in November 1997, addressing 'issues of mutual defence interest and bilateral defence relations'.[31]

When asked in a parliamentary question the extent to which the government believed that human rights were violated in Bahrain, Fatchett simply replied: 'we take seriously any abuse of human rights wherever it might occur' and said he regularly raised human rights with Bahraini ministers.[32] This signalled a continuing policy of supposed private diplomacy that Human Rights Watch had labelled not 'adequate or sufficient'.

The British government's support for the shura system has been in direct defiance of liberal and Islamic groups in Bahrain demanding greater political liberalisation. Since 1994, there has been a growing popular movement to press the regime to become more open, to allow greater political participation and to restore the constitution suspended in 1975. The constitution had been established in 1973 and consisted of a national assembly with thirty elected members and fifteen nominated government ministers. Major demonstrations have occurred together with mass petitions. By October 1994, 25,000 prominent people had signed a petition to the Emir calling for political liberalisation, including the greater involvement of women in the political process and the need to address the country's economic problems, like unemployment and inflation. The Bahraini people were not asking for the Earth, calling neither for the overthrow of the Emir nor even for full democracy.

The response of the Bahraini regime after 1994 was to crack down hard on all demonstrations by indiscriminate arrests and arbitrary detention of several thousand people, by abuse and torture of prisoners, deporting leaders and tightening restrictions on all forms of meetings and public expression.[33] Reserve Bahraini military forces were called up and even columns of special Saudi National Guards – as noted, also trained by Britain – crossed into Bahrain in support of the authorities.[34]

In May 1998, the *Financial Times* reported that the Bahraini government 'continues to crack down on the slightest sign of dissent'. It noted that five women had been given a three-month suspended jail sentence for nothing more than 'chanting slogans against the existing political system'. Thousands of people had been jailed.[35]

Major changes occurred in 2001 and 2002, however, under

the new Emir – Hamad Al Khalifa – who had taken over on his father's death in 1999. In February 2001, all political prisoners were pardoned and the state security law and state security court, which severely suppressed basic freedoms, were abolished. The following February, the kingdom of Bahrain was proclaimed, with the Emir declaring himself king. Municipal elections were held in May 2002 and parliamentary elections in October 2002. Most importantly, the king announced the restoration of parliament, with the creation of a lower house – consisting of forty elected members – and an upper house – a shura or consultative council, of forty members appointed by the king.

These are significant improvements for Bahrainis, but major brakes on democratic freedoms remain. Most important is the fact that the new parliament is less powerful than the old one suspended in 1975. The appointed upper house is far more powerful than the elected chamber, meaning the King retains overall control. According to the Bahrain Freedom Movement (BFM), a major opposition group based in London:

> Many Bahrainis thought they were going back to the 1973 constitution, with a single legislative chamber boasting wide powers. Instead the king promulgated a new constitution creating an appointed upper house that can effectively block anything the elected parliament does.

The BFM also notes that 'the government is aiming for a namesake parliament with the occasional ritual of elections' and that 'real and effective state power is vested in the traditional monarchy'. Public rallies have also been prohibited while access to opposition internet sites have been blocked.[36]

Britain has chosen to side very firmly with the rulers, both before and after the (limited) political opening of the last two years. It has rejected Human Rights Watch's call to use its close military and political ties with the Bahrain regime publicly to press it to end abuses, and also failed to express any (that I can find) public support for the calls of the popular protest movement. Rather, it appears simply to have seized on the king's recent initiatives. Foreign Office Minister Mike O'Brien has expressed Britain's welcome for 'progress towards constitutional monarchy and a democratic state', even saying: 'Bahrain is in many ways providing a lead to show that it is possible to create a more democratic state in the Middle East that can participate in the international community with its head held high'.[37]

Britain continues to arm and train the regime and exports arms to 'all units of the Bahraini security forces, including the Bahrain Defence Force and the Bahrain National Guard, whose forces have received some training from the Ministry of Defence'. That training is 'tailored to Bahrain's requirements', a parliamentary committee notes, while the MoD describes Bahrain as 'a key regional ally of the UK'.[38]

'The relationship between Britain and Bahrain is special', Trade minister Baroness Symons told a 'Doing business in Bahrain' seminar, before praising the regime for the 'wise way in which Bahrain has used its oil wealth'.[39]

Policy has changed hardly a jot since 1965 and 1966, when Britain put down demonstrations against the regime, then a colony in all but name. The *Economist* correctly noted at the time that 'the British have no sympathy with the notion of political organisations in Bahrain'.[40] London's priorities clearly change little.

Whitehall bears even greater responsibility for repression in Bahrain, however. Bahrain's internal security services are riddled with Britons, with around a dozen in mainly senior roles. It is only the most prominent, Ian Henderson, who has received some (minimal) media coverage. Henderson, a British national and a former colonial official in Kenya, had been Director General of the Public Security Directorate, the Criminal Investigations Directorate (CID) and the State Security Directorate (SSD), from 1966 until 1998, before taking up the role as adviser to the interior ministry until July 2000.

With reputed direct access to the Emir and the Prime Minister, opposition groups have accused Henderson of 'masterminding a ruthless campaign of repression'.[41]

Henderson's CID and SSD 'have for many years been responsible for gross human rights violations', especially torture under interrogation, according to Amnesty International. Methods at the security service HQ apparently included pulling off fingernails, using dogs to attack prisoners and sexual assault. One prisoner said that 'they trussed me up like a chicken for fifteen minutes. The take you and bend you double and handcuff you. They insert a wooden rod and they suspend you'.[42]

A Channel 4 news story suggested that Henderson had been personally involved in torture sessions. One pro-democracy activist, Hashem Redha, said that Henderson 'tortured me one time. He kicked me and shook me two times. He said "if you like to be hit, we can hit you more than that"'. Another torture victim now in exile claims that Henderson repeatedly visited him while he was a prisoner in the 1980s. He says of his tortures that:

> They hit me with cables all over my body. They put a rope on my legs and hung me, and put cloth in my mouth so I couldn't cry out. A British man came in and advised me to cooperate. I thought that everything would stop because he was British. I told him they were torturing me, but he just sat and watched what they were doing. He ordered the torture.

His torturers later told him the Briton was Henderson.[43]

The Labour government has deliberately allowed Henderson to escape justice. Under a 1998 law, the government can arrest in Britain anyone involved in torture anywhere in the world. Henderson was allowed, however, to take a new year holiday at his home in Devon in December 1999. As Amnesty International has said:

The UK government, under international law, has an obligation to conduct in inquiry into Henderson's role in the use of torture in Bahrain. A superior who knew or who should have known subordinates were committing human rights violations and took no steps to ensure punishment of those responsible and stop the abuse, is criminally responsible. Also under international law torture is a crime against humanity when committed on a widespread or systematic basis.[44]

Henderson has consistently denied that he had been involved in torture and told the *Independent* that the allegations were 'laughable' and that the charges against him were made up by opposition groups from Bahrain to attract media attention.[45]

After a joint *Independent*/Channel 4 investigation, the then Home Secretary Jack Straw announced that an investigation had begun into Henderson by the Metropolitan Police, who were in receipt of papers alleging torture. At the time of writing, the investigation is pending. The history of Conservative and Labour governments' acquiescence in repression presided over by Britons for nearly four decades provides little optimism that justice will really be sought.

12

THE FORGOTTEN PAST
IN THE MIDDLE EAST

> The Political Resident has recommended that the three
> villages concerned . . . should be warned that unless
> they surrender the ringleaders of the revolt they will be
> destroyed one by one by bombing.
>
> Foreign Office memorandum on Oman, 1957

Western military intervention in the Middle East is the current
subject of huge media coverage; but the relevant background is
not. There is an extraordinary record of British military and
covert intervention in the region that has been forgotten and
consigned to the memory hole. This past puts into perspective
the current government's claims to be defending the highest
principles in the region. The chances are that if this past were
better known the public would simply fall about laughing when
a British prime minister now invokes democracy, human rights
and international law when speaking of British intervention in
Iraq and Afghanistan.

As noted in the previous chapter, Britain's primary concern
is to defend the autocratic rulers of the Gulf and elsewhere in
the Middle East against any external or internal opposition,
however liberal or democratic, to ensure that pliant regimes are

in charge. The major reason is to secure control over the region's oil, which in turn helps ensure that the global economy functions under effective Western supervision.

I came across a story at the Public Record Office (PRO) showing the extraordinary lengths to which British planners have been prepared to go to defend favoured regimes, to which I turn first.

Kuwait – Defence of a regime

The 1991 Gulf War against Iraq was not the first time Britain had conducted a military intervention in support of Kuwait; Britain also intervened in Kuwait thirty years before. Then, Britain was desperate to protect its oil business interests, and to solidify its relations with the Kuwaiti regime. The formerly secret files suggest that British planners engaged in a giant conspiracy – by deliberately fabricating an Iraqi threat to Kuwait to get the Kuwaiti regime to 'ask' Britain for 'protection'.

Business interests were extensive. Kuwait was then the world's third most important oil-producing country, with around one quarter of the world's known reserves. British Petroleum (BP) had a 50 per cent interest in the Kuwait Oil Company while Shell, in which the British government had a 40 per cent interest, had been granted a Kuwait concession in January 1961.

Britain was also the largest state investor in Kuwaiti oil, which provided around 40 per cent of Britain's oil supplies. Furthermore, Kuwait's sterling reserves accounted for about one third of total British sterling reserves and by 1961 Kuwait had invested £300 million in British banks, providing a very significant lever over the British economy.[1]

British planners recognised the 'vital importance of Kuwait to our Middle East oil interests' and 'the advantages to this country, both in supplies and in the balance of payments, which flow from the operations of the British companies in an independent, affluent and friendly Kuwait and from Kuwait's readiness to accept and hold sterling'.[2]

Indeed, according to 1958 US documents, the UK's 'financial stability would be seriously threatened' if Kuwaiti and Gulf oil were not available to Britain 'on reasonable terms', if Britain were 'deprived of the large investments made by that area in the UK' and if sterling were 'deprived of the support provided by Persian Gulf oil'.[3]

On 20 June 1961, Kuwait achieved nominal independence from Britain but with agreement that Britain would come to Kuwait's defence if the latter requested it. That the Kuwaitis agreed to this defence commitment after independence was a success for the British government. A year earlier, under pressure from growing Arab nationalist sentiment throughout the Middle East, the Emir had indicated a desire to end completely British protection of Kuwait. During the independence negotiations, leading Kuwaiti figures had also supported ending British guarantees after independence.

In fact, after the 1958 coup in Iraq – in which a repressive British-backed monarchical regime was overthrown by Arab nationalist forces – Britain 'advised' the Kuwaiti Emir to 'request' military assistance, but the 'offer' was rejected. With independence, therefore, Britain had secured a formal protection agreement but its real solidity was questionable.[4]

British fears were expressed in secret files two months before independence:

> It is clear that, as the international personality of Kuwait grows, she will wish in various ways to show that she is no longer dependent upon us. *But we must continue to use the opportunities which our protective role will afford to ensure so far as we can that Kuwait does not materially upset the existing financial arrangements or cease to be a good holder of sterling.*[5]

Events then proceeded as follows. On 25 June, five days after the announcement of Kuwait's independence, Iraqi leader Abdul Karim Qasim publicly claimed Kuwait as part of Iraq.

Five days after this, at 8 am on 30 June, the Emir, after receiving information that Iraq might invade Kuwait, formally requested British military intervention. At midday Britain acceded to the 'request' and on the morning of 1 July British forces landed, eventually numbering around 7,000.

But the alleged Iraqi threat to Kuwait never materialised, as the files show.

On 26 June – one day after Iraq had claimed Kuwait – the Foreign Office noted that 'Qasim's decision appears to have been taken on the spur of the moment' and 'on present indicators it seems on the whole unlikely that Qasim will resort to military action'. The following day the British embassy in Washington reported that the US State Department viewed Qasim's claim as a 'postural move' only – 'They do not (repeat not) believe that he intends further action'. David Lees, the Commander of the British air force in the Middle East in 1961, later wrote that the British government 'did not contemplate aggression by Iraq very seriously'.[6]

On 28 June, the British embassy in Kuwait discounted 'the possibility of an Iraqi engineered internal coup in Kuwait'. Equally, the consulate in Basra near the Kuwait border noted that 'no (repeat no) reliable informant has seen or heard any unusual troop movements'.[7]

But then, also on 28 June, Britain's ambassador in Baghdad, who had not previously reported any unusual troop movements or war preparations, cabled London: 'My most recent information reveals Qasim's intentions to build up in Basra a striking force suitable for an attack on Kuwait.'[8]

On 29 June the Foreign Office changed its tune. It noted that 'there are now indications, still somewhat tenuous but pointing unmistakeably at preparations by Qasim to reinforce his troops near Basra with a tank regiment'. 'The latest information shows Qasim to be making preparations which would enable him to make a very early military attack.'[9]

The ambassador in Baghdad did not state the source of the 'most recent information'. And how could the Foreign Office's 'indications, still somewhat tenuous', point 'unmistakeably' to war preparations? The key is that the information purporting to indicate an Iraqi threat came exclusively from the British embassy in Baghdad. Its assessment was based on alleging the movement of a tank regiment from Baghdad to Basra, near the border with Kuwait. However, the PRO files also contain reports from the British consulate in Basra, which give a different assessment.

Earlier on the same day that the Foreign Office reported the movement of this tank regiment, the consulate in Basra stated that 'in the last 48 hours there have been no (repeat no) further clear indications of intended aggressive action'. Security patrols were normal and Iraqi civilian aircraft were continuing to fly to Kuwait. Furthermore, even on 1 July – that is, after the Kuwaiti request for intervention and the British decision to intervene – the Basra consulate reported that 'evidence so far available in Basra area does not (repeat not) indicate that an attack on Kuwait has been under preparation'.[10]

In fact, eleven days after the British intervention a Ministry of Defence report stated that it was 'unlikely' that any tanks had been moved to Basra between 29 June and 4 July. On the contrary, Qasim had ordered a reduction of military activities to a minimum, precisely to avoid any misinterpretation of Iraqi intentions.[11]

Belief in an Iraqi threat might simply be put down to an intelligence failure, but this appears infeasible. At the time, RAF photo-reconnaissance squadrons based in Bahrain could provide detailed analysis of troop movements. British assessments of Iraqi troop movements in the Basra area had taken place on an almost regular basis before. Moreover, there is evidence that the instructions given to commanders leading the British intervention were not geared to responding to any real Iraqi aggression. Also, the size of Britain's initial intervention force was unlikely to have been able to defend Kuwait from any Iraqi attack.[12]

The evidence suggests that the Emir was simply duped into

'requesting' intervention by the British. His information on the supposed threat came almost exclusively from British sources. London was certainly eager to intervene. The Foreign Office noted on 29 June that 'we are taking a number of preparatory measures to place ourselves at the highest state of readiness in case it becomes necessary for us to introduce forces, at the Ruler's request, into Kuwait'. It also instructed the embassy in Kuwait to inform the Emir of preparations against an Iraqi attack and that 'in order to enable our forces to move quickly enough if and when the danger appears imminent we need to have a formal request from the government of Kuwait'.[13]

'The moment has come' for the Emir to request our assistance, the Foreign Secretary stated. 'We think the ruler should make this request forthwith', the Foreign Office informed the Kuwait embassy. By the morning of 30 June, the Foreign Office declared that it needed the request 'as soon as possible'. Finally, it was Lord Home who asked the Emir to make a formal request for British assistance.[14]

Britain's 'political agent' (i.e. ambassador) in the Gulf, John Richmond, was not impressed with London's instruction that he 'encourage' the Emir to request assistance. He thought the intelligence reports were 'too shallow and unclear' and took no account of the fact that 'the Iraqis might verbally threaten Kuwait but they will not invade'. Richmond was rebuked by his bosses in London and told to 'keep quiet', while the Foreign Office and MI6 thought that military action would 'enhance Britain's position in the region'.[15]

Former Defence Secretary Denis Healey provides the official version of the intervention in his autobiography, saying simply that: 'in 1961 our intervention in Kuwait had saved oil facilities vital to the West from falling into the hands of General Kassim, the half-crazed military dictator of Iraq – with no loss of life'.[16]

In reality, the files strongly suggest that Britain knew there was no Iraqi threat but had already decided to move troops into the area. The threat was deliberately fabricated to achieve this end. Intervention could reassure friendly Middle Eastern regimes that were key to maintaining the British position in the world's most important region. The Prime Minister's foreign policy adviser said that letting go of Kuwait would mean that 'the other oil sheikhdoms (which are getting richer) will not rely on us any longer'.[17] Most important, the intervention reaffirmed the Kuwaiti regime's reliance on British protection, preserving the close relationship vital to London due to its commercial interests in the country.

Oman – supporting the depths of repression

Britain's closest ally in the Gulf has traditionally been Oman. In the war in Afghanistan, it provided crucial logistics and base facilities for British forces, which at the time had just been conducting military exercises with the Omani armed forces. British officers commanded the Omani military forces until the mid-1980s and there remains all kinds of close military cooperation. The current sheikh, Qaboos, owes his fortunes to the British, who installed him in a coup that overthrew his father in 1970.

The recent history of British support for Omani elites is not at all widely known. But it throws further important light on how Britain has been prepared to support the most vile regimes if its interests are protected. Let us take two British interventions in Oman – one beginning in 1957, the other in 1964.

In 1957, British forces were despatched to Oman to defend the extremely repressive Sultan's regime, which had been in power with constant British backing since 1932. The Sultan had several thousand slaves, used as bodyguards, who were forbidden all contact with the native population. There was no pretence of any political openness and neither was there any economic development to speak of, except for the Sultan's entourage. The main city did not even have a public electricity supply until 1971 when a small power station began to function. There were hardly any schools, while diseases were rampant, contributing to an extremely high number of child deaths.

This regime was in effect run by the British. It was as closely controlled by Britain as any formal colony, with Britons serving as commanders of the armed forces, Secretaries for Financial Affairs, Foreign Affairs and Petroleum Affairs in the government, and Director of Intelligence. Britain was therefore responsible for the repression. The feudal justice system imprisoned opponents in barbaric conditions, subjecting prisoners to torture, starvation and inhumane treatment while British advisers stood by.

Resources were in the correct hands. A British bank had held a monopoly in Oman since 1948 and the management of Oman's oil company – Petroleum Development (Oman) Ltd (PDO) – was British, the managing director being probably the most powerful man in the country after the Sultan. PDO was managed by Shell, which had an 85 per cent interest in Omani oil. With almost all Oman's income deriving from this source, 'the oil revenues were paid into the Sultan's account, and he in turn released a proportion to the exchequer', Oman analyst John Townsend notes.[18]

The British intervened to quell a revolt in the north of the country by the Omani Liberation Army, which was backed by an unusual alliance of King Saud of Saudi Arabia, US oil company Aramco and Egypt's nationalist president Nasser. The SAS fought a covert guerilla war while the Royal Air Force engaged in systematic bombing and shelling of rebel villages and strongholds, attacks against the civilian population in the areas under rebel control, and the destruction of livestock and crops.

At the beginning of the operations in 1957, Britain's Political Resident in Bahrain recommended bombing in support of the Sultan 'to show the population the power of weapons at our disposal'. This would help 'to inflict the maximum inconvenience on the population so that out of discomfort and boredom they will turn against the rebel minority'. There would be no ground troops at this stage and the rebels would be 'impotent against aircraft'; they could be bombed free of reprisal.[19]

After the rebels had eventually been pushed back to three

villages on the Jebel mountain the Foreign Office noted that 'the Political Resident has recommended that the three villages concerned . . . should be warned that unless they surrender the ringleaders of the revolt they will be destroyed one by one by bombing'.[20]

In January 1959 the British Air Ministry stated that RAF bombing was aiming to prevent the rebels holding out in the mountains by attacking their defensive positions and 'their means of existence, including the cultivation, animals and water supply of the local population assisting them'. David Lees, later to become Air Chief Marshal, spoke in his account of the campaign of the relentless bombardment 'against simple agricultural tribes' continuing week after week, admitting it was 'a terrifying experience'.[21]

The SAS operation to take the Jebel mountain is customarily presented as one of which Britons should be proud, showing the superhuman skills of their famous SAS. In reality, British 'success' was mainly due to inflicting terrifying violence. In fact, most of the villagers on the Jebel mountain were pleading to surrender before the SAS arrived. These methods ensured Britain defeated the rebels by 1959.

By 1960 a UN committee had been formed to investigate the situation in Oman. One report concluded that 'a serious international problem' had arisen from 'imperialistic policies and foreign intervention' in Oman:

> Had it not been for the possibility of oil being discovered in the interior, the action taken by the United Kingdom might well have been less drastic and much damage, destruction, human suffering and loss of human life might have been avoided.

In December 1965 the General Assembly passed a resolution recognising Oman's right to self-determination, stating that this was being prevented by Britain's colonial presence, and calling upon Britain to withdraw.[22] Britain naturally brushed aside such UN calls.

By 1964, Britain was countering another revolt against the Sultan's extreme repression – known as the Dhofar Rebellion, by the Popular Front for the Liberation of the Occupied Arab Gulf. The rebels' proclamation of June 1965 – calling for the liberation of Dhofar province – was, according to Townsend, 'the product of an economic and social frustration inflamed by a mindless political repression'. Even by 1970 the Omani regime forbade smoking in public, playing football, wearing glasses, shoes or trousers, having electricity or importing medicine, eating in public or talking to anyone for more than fifteen minutes. The Sultan's response to the rebel proclamation 'was not an alternative programme with proposals for reform or economic assistance . . . but simply the use of even greater force'.[23]

Britain removed the Sultan in a 1970 coup. Prime minister Harold Wilson sanctioned it and it was carried out shortly after the Heath government took power in the June general election. A detachment from the Omani army surrounded the Sultan's palace and British-flown aircraft from the Omani air force dropped teargas bombs, providing cover for a military advance. British officials had organised everything but expressed 'amazement' at suggestions in the *Guardian* that they might have had anything to do with the coup. Britain installed the old Sultan in the Dorchester hotel in London where he died two years later.[24]

The new Sultan was immediately surrounded by British advisers and officers, including a four-man SAS unit entrusted with his personal protection. Under the cover of a 'British army training team', an SAS unit organised irregular forces to fight the rebels, and British forces numbered 1,000 by 1974. They included a psychological operations units that undertook leaflet drops and radio broadcasts to guerilla-held areas.

Customary methods were used in countering the rebels. One British army officer stated that they 'burnt down rebel villages and shot their goats and cows. Any enemy corpses that we recovered were propped up in a corner of the [main city's

market] as a salutary lesson to any would-be freedom fighters';
tactics reminiscent of those used in Malaya.[25]

A military contingent was also later sent by the Shah of Iran,
taking time off from terrorising his own population to help out
with other necessary Western duties. Jordan – whose pro-
Western regime had been bolstered by a 1958 British military
intervention – also sent military advisers to Oman, while the
US provided counter-insurgency aid routed through its key
client in the region, Saudi Arabia. By 1975 the last group of
rebels had surrendered or crossed the border into Yemen. The
Western-directed order in this part of the Middle East was
preserved.

The same, elsewhere

At a conference of regional MI6 Directors in the mid-1960s,
Tim Milne, the Director for the Middle East, spoke of the
continuing British use of 'disruptive actions' such as bribes,
covert funding, buggings and telephone taps and the use of
'pencil bombs' in dirty tricks operations.[26]

These methods are part of the story of British support for
elites and violence against opponents threatening an
independent route, repeated throughout the postwar period in
the Middle East.

In Aden (later South Yemen) from 1964 to 1967, Britain
sought to counter a national liberation movement in favour of
continued rule by friendly despots; this time, however, British
troops eventually withdrew in failure. A UN call in 1963 for
Britain to withdraw from Aden and permit self-determination
was rejected. The SAS set up plain-clothes hit squads to make
arrests and engage in shoot-outs with political opponents.
Attacking the civilian population, RAF bombing destroyed
rebel villages and crops, causing tens of thousands of people to
flee.

An official British investigation in 1971 observed that the
British army had engaged in the torture of detainees, using

methods including 'wall-standing, hooding, noise, bread and water diet and deprivation of sleep'. These techniques, the investigation found:

> have played an important part in counter-insurgency operations in Palestine, Malaya, Kenya and Cyprus and more recently in the British Cameroons (1960–61), Brunei (1963), British Guiana (1964), Aden (1964–67), Borneo/Malaysia (1965–66), the Persian Gulf (1970–71) and in Northern Ireland (1971).

Another official investigation concluded that pierced ear-drums had been observed on detainees coming from an interrogation centre in Aden. The Red Cross and Amnesty International were refused permission to interview detainees in one notorious prison.[27]

Britain also pursued a covert war in North Yemen in the 1960s in which 200,000 people were killed. Colluding with Israel's Mossad and the Saudi regime, British Labour and Conservative governments secretly supplied arms and funding to royalist rebels fighting pro-Egyptian republican forces that had overthrown the pro-British Imam in a 1962 coup.

In fact, Britain conducted a dirty war, with MI6 working with tribesmen recruited locally to 'direct the planting of bombs' at Egyptian military outposts while garrison towns were 'shot up' and political figures murdered. The RAF also conducted some secret bombings against Egyptian targets. The British government decided there could be no official SAS involvement, but authorised it to organise a mercenary operation that eventually involved dozens of ex-SAS servicemen. MI6 provided intelligence and logistical support to the rebels and GCHQ pinpointed the locations of republican troops. While Whitehall denied official involvement, the secret funds provided to the operation had been earmarked to the overseas aid programme. The rebels, however, failed to dislodge the government and in 1970 a treaty was signed ending the war.[28]

Coups have been another way of installing favoured elites

and/or removing unfavoured ones. Alongside the British coup in Oman in 1970 went coups against rulers in the Gulf emirates of Sharjah in 1965 and Abu Dhabi in 1966. In the mid-1950s, Britain also planned the assassination of Nasser and the overthrow of the government in Syria. This followed a successful British-backed coup in Syria in 1949.

The invasion of Egypt in 1956 was nothing unusual; actually quite normal practice for British policy in the 1950s. Three years before, Britain had sent troops to overthrow the government of British Guiana and organised a coup to overthrow Musaddiq in Iran. In 1948 it had deployed troops in Malaya and in 1952 in Kenya to promote colonial and commercial interests and to conduct vicious wars.

The invasion of Egypt is rarely described as such. Commentators usually prefer the 'Suez fiasco' or 'Suez crisis', or variants. Much analysis has also dwelt on the illness of prime minister Anthony Eden as an explanation for Britain's behaviour – as if it were doing anything other than the standard practice. At the Cabinet meeting on 28 August 1956, military intervention was decided upon unanimously, the reservation being that Eden had to recognise that 'the possibilities of a peaceful settlement must be fully explored'.[29]

Egyptian president Nasser was an independent, popular nationalist who posed the threat of independent development, both for the people of Egypt – who had been long exploited by de facto colonial rule – and as a model in the wider Middle East. Britain publicly tried to portray Nasser as a stooge of Moscow, indulging in the usual pretext for intervention. But the Foreign Office understood in private that Nasser was 'avowedly anti-Communist' and was 'unfortunately . . . strongly neutralist'. It noted:

> He will not only seek to get help without strings from both the West and the Soviet bloc, but to the extent that he succeeds he will encourage other Arab countries to do the same . . . At the worst . . . our

traditional friends may start to wonder whether enmity or at least neutrality is not more profitable than friendship.

The problem was that Nasser 'was aiming at leadership of the Arab world', the Foreign Secretary stated a few months before the invasion.[30]

Britain feared that Nasser's heretical design in nationalising the Suez Canal company was 'using the revenues for her own internal purposes'. This is not what development as understood by Britain – then or now – should be about. Rather, Britain regarded the Suez Canal as 'an international asset' vital to 'the free world'; that is, it was ours to control.[31]

British planning to remove Nasser began well before the latter's decision to nationalise the Suez Canal company in July 1956. Various assassinations were planned, as noted in chapter 3. Eden was prepared to pay any price to remove Nasser (or the 'Muslim Mussolini', as he once called him). He told Foreign Office Minister Anthony Nutting: 'I don't give a damn if there's anarchy and chaos in Egypt' as a result.[32]

US opposition to the British invasion was decisive in causing its failure. British officials consistently tried to enlist US support; the MI6 director, George Young, in particular became frustrated at the US knocking down 'every proposal for bashing the Gyppos', as he put it.[33]

But US concerns were actually more ambivalent. Eisenhower later said that if Britain had 'done it quickly, we would have accepted it'. With military action under way, one State Department official told the CIA officer liaising with the British to:

> tell your friends to comply with the goddam ceasefire or go ahead with the goddam invasion. Either way, we'll back them up if they do it fast. What we can't stand is their goddam hesitation, waltzing while Hungary is burning.

This referred to the Soviet invasion of Hungary, which the Russians had launched at the same time. The US also appears to have been concerned with the timing of the invasion since it disrupted well-laid US and British plans for a coup in Syria at the same time.[34]

13

THE SINGLE-IDEOLOGY TOTALITARIAN STATE

Bugger the public's right to know. The game is the security of the state – not the public's right to know.

Bernard Ingham, Margaret Thatcher's
press spokesman

Many commentators refer to a 'consensus' on foreign policy between the major political parties, with few differences between Labour and the Conservatives. This is certainly true, indeed of the whole postwar period. But it has deepened under Blair to the point where there are barely any significant differences on any international issue. But the term 'consensus' doesn't capture the reality.

My view is that in its foreign policy Britain has become a Single-Ideology Totalitarian State. I am not exaggerating by using the word 'totalitarian'. But let me explain what I mean by 'single ideology' first.

The state we're really in

By 'single-ideology state', I mean that British foreign policy is shaped and managed by a domestic elite that shares the same basic viewpoint on all major aspects of foreign policy. This elite spans the influential figures in all the mainstream parties, the civil service and technocrats who implement the policy, and also senior academic and media figures who help shape public opinion. This elite promotes the basic pillars of Britain's role in the world, such as: strong general support (involving consistent apologia) for US foreign policy and maintaining a special relationship; maintaining a powerful interventionist military capability and using it; promotion of 'free trade' and worldwide economic 'liberalisation'; retention of nuclear weapons; promoting military industry and Britain's role as an arms exporter; and strong support for the traditional order in the Middle East, Gulf regimes and other key bilateral allies.

The only major foreign-related issues on which there is current disagreement within the elite are: first, the euro, together with the extent of Britain's integration into the EU; and second, war against Iraq. But the debate within the elite on launching a full-scale war against Iraq was more a disagreement over tactics on how to secure British goals in the Middle East, rather than over a fundamentally different British role in the region. On the 'pillars' of foreign policy, there are also debates and differences within the elite on tactics to promote them, but not on the fact that Britain should. These debates within the elite largely set the parameters of discussion in the mainstream political culture and the media, which I discuss further in chapters 18 and 19.

There have always been exceedingly few differences in foreign policy between Labour and the Conservatives in office. It is simply not true that Labour has pursued a distinct and progressive, 'internationalist' foreign policy, as many Labour supporters claim. As the chapters in this book show, it was the Attlee government that shamelessly drained poor colonies of scarce resources to aid Britain's postwar economic recovery and that began covert planning to oust the Musaddiq government in Iran. It was the Wilson government that began the removal of the population of Diego Garcia to make way for a US military base and that supported the Indonesian generals' campaign of slaughter in 1965. And it was the Callaghan government that supplied the Indonesian military with weapons to slaughter the people of East Timor in the late 1970s. The Blair administration is just the most recent in a series of horrible Labour governments.

Despite this terrible Labour record, there were, though, some differences with the Conservatives. The latter have traditionally resorted more to military interventions and covert operations. Labour's policy in opposition in the 1980s of unilateral nuclear disarmament was a break with the postwar 'consensus'; it was the Attlee government that began the British nuclear programme and the Wilson government that acquired from the US Polaris long-range nuclear weapons in the 1960s.

Under Blair, however, the differences have virtually completely disappeared. A secret Pentagon study leaked to the *Guardian* noted the US view that 'beyond Europe, there are few apparent differences between the stated foreign policy goals of Labour and its Conservative predecessor'.[1] The Blair government is pursuing only a few slightly less malign policies than the Conservatives would be likely to, most of which are marginal in the bigger picture. On the issues just mentioned, there is now no difference on nuclear weapons, while the Blair government is more militarily interventionist than any other postwar British government. Indeed – even though it is a contradiction to say it – so 'similar' has Labour become to the Conservatives that its policies are worse in some cases. I'll give two examples of this.

First, on Israel, Blair has in effect condoned Israeli violence in a way that has surpassed even the Thatcher government. Traditionally, the Foreign Office has been worried about adopting a too pro-Israel stance for fear of upsetting our Arab despots. Under Blair, Britain has more clearly adopted a pro-Israel line – refusing to seriously pressure Israel while offering effective apologies along with favoured trade relations – at a time when Israeli violence is worse than for the past two decades.

Second, on its plans for reshaping the global economy and supporting big business globally, Labour must have surpassed the wildest expectations of business. As shown in chapter 9, the Blair government has become a leading international advocate for deepening global trade, investment and services 'liberalisation', especially in the WTO. Indeed, the Department for International Development is arguably the world's strongest 'development' voice in favour of global liberalisation and its policies are largely indistinguishable from the Conservative opposition.

But it is unfair to single out New Labour for blame in promoting the global economic liberalisation agenda. Support for this project is shared across the political class, in all mainstream political parties and in most of the media and academia, with dissent only at the margins. There is massive evidence showing that pure trade 'liberalisation' deepens poverty and inequality in poor developing countries. Yet even when the government's (hard to miss) support for this agenda is noticed at all – which is rare – it remains politically incorrect to challenge the doctrine and often even to mention alternatives to liberalisation such as import protection, domestic subsidies and significant regulation of companies. This is a clear example of the British single-ideology state, which sets the interests of its elite so clearly against the interests of the majority of the people on the planet.

If this explains a little of what I mean by 'single ideology', what about 'totalitarian'? This refers to the ability of outsiders to *influence* the government's foreign policy. In fact, despite the democratic facade that exists, the formal processes for doing this are basically non-existent.

The main means by which elected MPs scrutinise government policy is the select committee system, consisting of all-party groups of MPs who conduct inquiries into selected government policies by questioning ministers and producing reports. But the committees related to foreign policy – foreign affairs, international development, trade and industry and defence – all suffer from the same defects: whole policies can go completely unscrutinised, while in those that are scrutinised critical lines of inquiry are regularly ignored, and questions usually fail to put ministers on the spot.

Select committee scrutiny of the government's policies towards the global economy and WTO, for example, is frankly laughable, with generally uncritical endorsement of policy and the barest of accountability required of government ministers. British government positions on many global economic policies are often not even discussed in parliament before the government promotes them at EU and other international meetings.

Under globalisation, 'national' policies can quickly have 'global' impact, and vice versa. Yet the public's ability to hold political leaders to account by scrutinising their policies in this new interdependence has not increased – rather, powers have become more centralised and accountability reduced. British leaders can be promoting an enormously negative global 'liberalisation' project, but no new formal democratic means have been established to even detect it, let alone stop it.

Select committees are more part of the patronage system, either acting as a parking place for loyal backbench MPs or as a launch pad for promotion for the up-and-coming. Perhaps most importantly of all, the government is only obliged to provide a written response to the committees' reports; there is no obligation to accept recommendations or change policy in any way. Thus committee reports operate within the elite consensus, but when they do make some awkward recommendations for government, they can simply be ignored, and invariably are.

So it is with parliament more generally, where backbenchers have no formal powers, and few informal ones, to press for changes in government policy. As Andrew Marr – currently the BBC's political editor – has written, backbenchers influencing the executive is so rare that 'it's more like children shouting at passing aircraft'. Indeed, parliamentary government – a virtual absolutism of landowners – preceded parliamentary democracy by 250 years. In many ways it is this absolutism, not the democracy, that remains the dominant influence in British politics.[2]

Many things have barely changed in 500 years. Consider the following description of parliament's role in foreign-policy making in Tudor times:

> Parliament was an institution which, usually but not always, enabled Tudor governments to pursue their own foreign policies more efficiently than would have been possible without it. Occasionally, it resisted or embarrassed governments as they pursued their chosen policies. Parliament was not, however, the soil in which wholly new policies grew to be an influence in the councils of state.[3]

When the group Charter 88 was set up in 1988 to campaign for transforming British democracy, it noted the 'parliamentary oligarchy' that had been created from the shift away from absolute monarchy in 1688. It said that the 'inbuilt powers of the 1688 settlement have enabled the government to discipline British society to its ends', to impose its values on the civil service, to menace the independence of broadcasting, to threaten freedom in universities and schools and to tolerate abuses committed in the name of national security. These showed 'how vulnerable Britain has always been to elective dictatorship' and 'authoritarian rule'.

Indeed, power has in many ways become more centralised over recent decades. In 1867, Walter Bagehot wrote that the Cabinet acted as a 'board of control . . . to rule the nation'. By 1964, Labour Cabinet Minister, Richard Crossman, could write that the post-war epoch had seen Cabinet government transformed into prime ministerial government, with huge power invested in 'one single man' whose powers have steadily increased. Policy decisions, Crossman stated forty years ago, are nearly always taken by one person after consulting 'with a handful of advisers he has picked for the occasion'.[4]

How true of today. Former Northern Ireland minister Mo Mowlam has said that 'Cabinet itself is dead, it doesn't have a function to play.' Her former boss 'makes decisions with a small coterie of people, advisers, just like the president of the United States'. Indeed, the prime minister today probably has fewer checks on his power than Charles I had.[5]

This huge centralisation of power in the prime minister was partly what Lord Hailsham was referring to in 1976 when he called Britain an 'elective dictatorship'. The prime minister can take Britain to war without even consulting parliament. The Falklands and Gulf wars, for example, were never put to a parliamentary vote; the bombing of Yugoslavia in 1999 was barely even debated in parliament before the campaign was launched. Neither do international treaties need to be confirmed by the House of Commons. The Attlee government's agreement to allow US military bases to be established in Britain was entirely secret. The Treaty of Accession to the EU was given under royal prerogative and when prime minister Heath signed it, the text had not even been published. The government could have signed the Maastricht treaty in 1993 in the same way, had it chosen.[6]

According to political analyst Keith Sutherland:

> The majority party in parliament and the executive are effectively one and the same – a clear travesty of the principle of the constitutional separation of powers. Given the power of the party whips, and the impotence of the Upper House, this means that the leader of the majority party has a five year electoral mandate for dictatorship.[7]

The Blair government has of course devolved some political authority from London by establishing a parliament for Scotland, an Assembly for Wales and a mayor for London – all important developments. But the centralisation of local government – a postwar trend – is continuing while reform of the

House of Lords has replaced one form of illegitimacy with another. The prime minister's opposition to a wholly elected second chamber in the Lords has led to the replacement of hereditary peers with appointees of the government, with only some elected members. Thus one undemocratic body was replaced by another.

Together with the prime minister, the centre of power in Britain is the 'permanent government' of the senior echelons of the civil service. Most important is the network of civil service committees, especially the committee of permanent secretaries, known in Whitehall as Cabinet (o). George Young, former deputy head of MI6, has said that 'the higher reaches of the civil service undoubtedly make most of the decisions for Ministers and put them in front of them and say "Minister, do you agree?"'[8]

The lack of real democracy in Britain is so obvious that it is often openly recognised across the political spectrum. Indeed, the totalitarian nature of British democracy is sufficiently complete that elites can recognise it as such without a fear of change.

Outside of parliament, there are only very limited ways to influence government policy, all of which are informal. Consultations with civil society groups on key government policy statements have been a feature of New Labour. As well as consulting on its major policy documents, the Department for International Development, for example, holds an annual series of 'development fora' around the country to elicit people's views on key issues. But my experience of this is that it really is window-dressing and a fig leaf. It is hard to spot any ways in which significant government policies have ever actually been influenced in any major (or even minor) way by these consultations. The process is more about securing public support and NGO acquiescence in government strategy while offering the pretence of influencing the process.

'Insider lobbying' by groups to persuade decision-makers to change foreign policies by reasoned arguments is generally unlikely to get you very far, in my experience. This route can only influence minor, incremental policy change on more technical issues. The bigger shifts in policy will not come from this route. My experience of running advocacy strategies in development NGOs is that only sustained public pressure makes major policy change possible. For example, the Jubilee 2000 debt coalition raised significant public awareness about the injustice of debt, pressing the British government to become one of the more progressive governments on debt relief for developing countries (although the amount of debt relief delivered so far remains well below the promises).

The popular international campaign to stop the OECD's proposed Multilateral Agreement on Investment – involving a variety of NGOs and civil society groups – helped to scupper the proposal. And the 'fifty years is enough' campaign against the World Bank in the US severely embarrassed the Bank and forced it to make some changes, albeit mainly cosmetic. There are limits, though, to possible success in this area. It is simply not possible, for example, to have a public campaign on everything. And elites usually find ways of deflecting public pressure before it threatens them.

Clearly, the British political system does offer benefits for many people outside the elite. It is not only the people at the very top of the tree who benefit, clearly many others do. But the severe hardships that large numbers of people face in Britain – like poverty, decline in many public services and job insecurity – all relate to an elitist political system which does not generally promote policies in the wider public interest.

For the subject of this book, the lack of democracy in foreign policy-making is extremely serious, with huge human conse-quences. It is no exaggeration to say that Britain has visited widespread destruction on many parts of the world, over-throwing popular governments, trampling over human rights, undermining democratic forces in favour of repressive elites while helping to impose economic strategies that further impoverish many of the world's poorest people. It gets away with this largely because of the *domestic* structures of power.

Foreign policy is made by a relatively small number of people who are protected from serious accountability, with no formal obligations even to consult outside a small circle, and still less inclined to depart from pursuing traditional priorities – and therefore virtually impossible to influence in any meaningful way. The 'mother of all parliaments' has in reality become the midwife of a generally unethical foreign policy. The disastrous nature of Britain's 'democracy' for foreign policy is surely one of the great untold stories of the modern political culture.

To me the most useful public campaign would not be on a single issue but one that united the public and civil society groups from various sectors in a revigorised campaign for real democracy in Britain. If that existed, we would end the totalitarian decision-making that is the hallmark of domestic and foreign policies, and which produces British policies so abusive of human rights, development and peace overseas. I return to this in chapter 23.

Democracy for the elites

In chapter 10, I looked at how independent development and democratic forces are generally seen as a threat to British foreign policy. At the root of this lies the same issue that underpins Britain's domestic political system – the elitist conception of democracy.

'Liberal democracy' in Britain has been shaped above all by elitist thinking, rooted in the great liberal philosophers and political thinkers since the seventeenth century. In all this variety of political thinking across the liberal spectrum, one thing stands out: a belief that a special cadre of people should govern, often combined with virtual contempt for the public. The roots of our current democracy lie not in conceptions of popular democracy where people are to play a central role in decision-making. Rather, they lie in subordinating the majority of people to dominant groups seeking to preserve their property rights and the freedom of the market.

The great seventeenth-century liberal philosopher John Locke rejected democracy and argued in favour of a 'legislative or supreme authority' that would rule with the consent of, and in the interests of, the community. The task of government was to preserve the right of property, Locke argued. His thinking has been interpreted by many as arguing against arbitrary monarchy in favour of upholding the interests of the propertied class.

In the eighteenth century, John Stuart Mill, usually regarded as the greatest British liberal thinker, believed that only through the influence of an enlightened minority could the public aspire to self-improvement. Although accepting universal suffrage, he rejected the view that everyone should have an equal say on policies, arguing that some should have 'a superiority of influence proportioned to his higher qualifications'. He viewed democracy as a 'tyranny of the majority' which would pursue ignorant policies. Mill warned of the 'opinion of masses of merely average men' becoming dominant. The counter to this should come from the 'more pronounced individuality of those who stand on the higher eminences of thought'.[9]

Another eighteenth-century political thinker, John Austin, a follower of Jeremy Bentham's utilitarian school, favoured the idea of government helping to make the poor into good citizens and opposed the political power of inherited wealth. He contrasted 'the multitude' with the 'enlightened opinion . . . of the higher and more cultivated classes'. The latter's task was to ensure the provision of education for working people in order to 'extirpate their prejudices and correct their moral sentiments'.[10]

The theme of the unfitness of the 'multitude' for the exercise of power which had been dominant in the seventeenth, eighteenth and nineteenth centuries, continued into the twentieth. This was also true of the early socialist Fabians, especially George Bernard Shaw, who argued that 'a country governed by its people is as impossible as a theatre managed by its audience'. Government was rather 'a fine art' requiring 'a mental comprehensiveness and an energy which only a small percentage of people possess in the degree necessary for leadership'.[11] Shaw's allusion is an apt one – people are to be passive spectators, watching their superiors govern 'for' them.

The British ruling class held out for an exceedingly long time in opposing the universal right to vote, believing that power should reside only in the propertied classes, or men of enlightenment. But these elitist beliefs continued well after conceding universal suffrage. In the 1930s, for example, Barbara Wootton, an economist involved in government wartime boards that managed various economic activities, believed that the electorate should not concern itself with policy but defer to people of superior quality to let them get on with the business of governing.

This echoed the view of Harold Laski, a leading socialist intellectual who became the chair of the Labour party and who believed that democracy should be 'an aristocracy by delegation'. The administration of a modern state was a 'technical matter' and 'those who can penetrate its secrets are relatively few in number'. What was required was 'a body of experts working to satisfy vast populations', and the latter were 'uninterested in the processes by which those results are obtained'.[12]

John Major rejected proposals for holding a referendum on the Maastricht treaty in 1993, saying that the issues were 'highly complex' and that the electorate might be swayed by 'irrelevant' distractions. He was simply echoing his predecessors among the elites – like former Labour minister Douglas Jay who said in 1939 that 'in the case of nutrition and health, just as in the case of education, the gentleman in Whitehall really does know better what is good for the people than the people know themselves'.[13]

These conceptions of elitism, though conceived in different ages, are firmly rooted in British political culture, indeed across the political spectrum. Contempt for the public has always had cross-party support in Britain.

At stake in these conceptions of elitism has of course been

the preservation of power and wealth. Before the First World War, the top 5 per cent of the population owned a massive 87 per cent of personal wealth. From this staggeringly unequal benchmark, income gaps have narrowed in the UK over recent decades. But in 1996, the top 1 per cent of the population still owned 20 per cent of all wealth. Over half the total wealth was owned by just 10 per cent of the population. And the wealthiest 50 per cent owned nearly everything – 93 per cent. The gap between the highest paid and the lowest paid workers is now greater than at any time since records began in 1886. There are good reasons why many wish to preserve an elitist political system.[14]

The public as a threat

Bernard Ingham, Margaret Thatcher's press spokesman, once told American journalists in an off-the-record briefing:

> There is no freedom of information in this country; there's no public right to know. There's a common-sense idea of how to run a country and Britain is full of commonsense people . . . Bugger the public's right to know. The game is the security of the state – not the public's right to know.[15]

His view was echoed by Britain's Adjutant General, Sir David Ramsbottom, who told *Guardian* readers in 1991 that the media too often tried to press the government to release information 'on the pretext that the public has a right to know'.[16]

British leaders tell us that the major threats to Britain's interests are terrorists, drug traffickers, those seeking to acquire weapons of mass destruction and 'rogue states'. But my view is that the major threat to elites is really genuine democracy abroad and at home. The fact is, the public is viewed as a threat.

In democracies, the public can vote governments in and out but in between elections it is kept far away from decision-making to allow elites to 'govern', as outlined in the previous section. In times of crisis like wars, however, public opinion can definitely influence the way elites prosecute their priorities, and can even stop them.

This danger has long been understood by elites. As prime minister David Lloyd George confided to the editor of the *Guardian* at the height of the First World War: 'If people knew the truth, the war would be stopped tomorrow. But they don't know and can't know.'[17]

The danger that the public might oppose the state's major policies was recognised by British planners in the 1950s. Then, the big strategy was to combat – often brutally – nationalist forces in the colonies. A problem was that planners understood that the public was on the wrong side: 'British public opinion is in the main largely in sympathy with nationalist trends in the colonies'.[18] It was partly for this reason that leaders needed to invoke other demons Britain was supposedly fighting, the 'Soviet threat' being the most common.

The same basic concern is in evidence when a former MI6 officer says that the purpose of MI6's psychological warfare section is 'massaging public opinion into accepting controversial foreign policy decisions'.[19]

A glimpse into the elite's contempt for the public's right to even know about decision-making, together with the totalitarian mindset of elites, was revealed in the Scott inquiry into arms to Iraq in 1993–94. This is an episode worth briefly reviewing since, as *Guardian* correspondent Richard Norton-Taylor's excellent book on the inquiry noted, it is 'a goldmine for students of the way we are governed'.[20]

The inquiry showed how government lawyers were prepared to conspire with civil servants to suppress embarrassing information about arms exports to Iraq and worked with witnesses to change their statements. The Cabinet Office delayed passing on documents to hinder the inquiry and gave it misleading figures on arms-related exports. It also fought to the end to try to persuade Lord Justice Richard Scott to suppress embarrassing information contained in thousands of documents not read out in public hearings.

One Treasury solicitor told the inquiry that it is 'damaging to the public interest to have any decision-making process exposed'. Another said that confidentiality was 'necessary for the proper administration of the public service' – meaning the public is to be kept out of 'proper' decision-making.

Scott asked Robin Butler, the cabinet secretary and head of the civil service, whether he thought that 'the convenience of secrecy' inhibited the government from giving information about what it is doing. Butler replied: 'You can call that a matter of convenience, if you like. I would call it a matter of good government.'

Thatcher's Foreign Secretary Geoffrey Howe told Scott that to lay 'our thought processes before you' would do so to 'a worldwide range of uncomprehending or malicious commentators'. When Scott asked him: 'You can, can you not, expose your hand to people of this country?', Howe replied: 'There are reasons for caution. Justice is exposed to emotional misunderstandings in this country.'

Six years before the inquiry, Scott had attacked the Thatcher government's attempt to ban the book *Spycatcher* by former MI5 officer, Peter Wright. Scott said that 'I found myself unable to escape the reflection that the absolute protection of the Security Service that Sir Robert Armstrong [then cabinet secretary] was contending for, could not be achieved this side of the Iron Curtain.'

The Scott inquiry also revealed how contemptuously elites viewed their accountability to parliament. For years, ministers had given misleading or plainly inaccurate replies to parliamentary questions on British policy on arms to Iraq. Civil servants then variously said:

- 'Truth is a very difficult concept' (Ian Macdonald, head of Defence Export Services Secretariat, when asked how parliamentary questions should be answered).

- 'I think the way in which questions are answered in parliament tends to be something of an art form rather than a means of communication' (Eric Beston, a senior DTI official).
- 'Questions should be answered so as to give the maximum degree of satisfaction possible to the questioner' (David Gore-Booth, former British ambassador to Saudi Arabia and then head of the Foreign Office's Middle East department).
- 'The secrecy culture of Whitehall is essentially a product of British parliamentary democracy; economy with the truth is the essence of a professional reply to a parliamentary question' (Sir Patrick Nairne, former Whitehall permanent secretary).

Norton-Taylor concluded that 'Whitehall will do its utmost to ensure that never again will a judge be given such freedom to conduct a public inquiry into the activities of government.'

This culture of elitism and the totalitarian realm of deceit, rooted in centuries of much political thought, remains safe in New Labour's hands, as currently shown in the extraordinary state propaganda operations on Iraq, outlined in chapter 1.

PART III

EXPOSING THE SECRET HISTORY

Sitting in the Public Record Office in London is a mountain of evidence on the reality of Britain's past role in the world. These official records, consisting mainly of correspondence between government departments and embassies, are declassified under the thirty-year 'rule', although there are plenty of 'exceptions' where files remain classified, naturally for reasons of 'national security'. These records not only often make worrying – sometimes, frightening – reading but they also show the vast gulf that generally exists between the reality of Britain's foreign policy, on the one hand, and conventional media and academic analyses, on the other.

The following four chapters – all documenting the formerly secret record – contain four common threads.

The first is how brutal in war, and abusive of human rights, British elites have been in the past, much more so than is usually presented. The recent onslaughts against Afghanistan and Iraq are merely the current form of terrifying traditional British practice.

Second, they show Britain's overwhelming need to keep economic resources in the correct hands – elites who give favourable treatment to Western business. This is a crucial part of the organisation of key countries, regions, and the global economy, to 'our' benefit – the roots of current globalisation.

Third, they show that the primary 'threat' to British elite interests throughout the postwar period was not so much communism or Soviet expansion – the official threats intended for public consumption – but indigenous nationalism arising from within those countries. These nationalist forces offered in many cases the prospect of real development for poverty-stricken populations. But they were crushed by Britain.

The fourth thread is that these nationalist forces were popular and, in the case of British Guiana, democratically elected. These stories further reveal the British elite's contempt for democratic, popular groups when they fail to promote British interests. My view is that, even though these stories come from the colonial era, their key themes are contemporary as we enter a US-led imperial order, and they throw light on understanding Britain's current role in the world.

14

OVERTHROWING THE GOVERNMENT OF IRAN

Our policy was to get rid of Mossadeq as soon as possible.

Sir Donald Logan, British Embassy, Iran

Past British policy towards Iran shows how foreign policy planners prefer repressive, elite government to popular government, if their interests are better served. It also shows how dangerous this policy has been for the people of Iran and many others. The roots of the Islamic revolution in Iran and the current 'anti-Westernism' of Iranian leaders owe much to British and US actions in the 1950s and since. If Iran is currently a 'rogue state' (that is, official enemy of the US) it was encouraged to become so partly by US and British policy. Iran's past could have been very different and its future brighter. These links, however, are rarely mentioned in the mainstream political culture.

In August 1953, a coup covertly organised by MI6 and the CIA overthrew Iran's popular, nationalist government under Mohamed Musaddiq and installed the Shah in power. The Shah subsequently used widespread repression and torture to institute a dictatorship that lasted until the 1979 Islamic revolution. The Shah's regime was given full political and economic backing by Britain and the US, including its most brutal component, the Savak secret police. The new Islamic leaders turned on the US and Britain, partly for their role in installing and propping up the previous regime for a quarter of a century.

The CIA is conventionally regarded as the prime mover behind the 1953 coup. Yet the declassified British files show not only that Britain was the major instigator but also that British resources contributed significantly to it. Churchill once told the CIA agent responsible for the operation that he 'would have loved nothing better than to have served under your command in this great venture'.[1]

Two first-hand accounts of the coup – by the MI6 and CIA agents responsible for it – are useful in reconstructing events.[2] Many of the secret British planning documents have been removed from public access and remain classified. Despite this, a fairly clear picture still emerges.

Prelude to covert action

In the early 1950s the Anglo-Iranian Oil Company (AIOC) – later renamed British Petroleum – which was managed from London and owned by the British government and British private citizens, controlled Iran's main source of income: oil. According to one British official, the AIOC 'has become in effect an imperium in imperio in Persia'. The AIOC was recognised as 'a great foreign organisation controlling Persia's economic life and destiny'.

Iranian nationalists objected to the fact that the AIOC's revenues from oil were greater than the Iranian government's, with profits amounting to £170 million in 1950 alone. The Iranian government was being paid royalties of between 10 and 12 per cent of the company's net proceeds, while the British government received as much as 30 per cent of these in taxes alone.[3]

The British Minister of Fuel and Power explained that Iranians 'are of course morally entitled to a royalty' for oil extraction but to say 'that morally they are entitled to 50%, or . . . even more of the profits of enterprises to which they have made no contribution whatever, is bunk, and ought to be shown to be bunk'.[4]

Britain's ambassador in Tehran commented:

> It is so important to prevent the Persians from destroying their main source of revenue . . . by trying to run it themselves . . . The need for Persia is not to run the oil industry for herself (which she cannot do) but to profit from the technical ability of the West.[5]

Iranians could also point to the AIOC's low wage rates and its effectively autonomous rule in the parts of the country where the oilfields lay. Shown the overcrowded housing of some of the AIOC workers, a British official commented, 'well, this is just the way all Iranians live'. The AIOC regarded Iranians as 'merely wogs'.[6]

Britain's priority was to support political 'stability' by aiding Iranian parliamentarians 'to preserve the existing social order from which they profit so greatly' – as did British oil interests. One difference with the National Front (led by Musaddiq) was that its party members were 'comparatively free from the taint of having amassed wealth and influence through the improper use of official positions', Britain's ambassador in Iran privately admitted. Musaddiq had the support of the nationalists against the rich and corrupt. As prime minister he managed to break the grip over Iranian affairs exercised by the large landowners, wealthy merchants, the army and the civil service. Despite British public propaganda, Musaddiq's government was generally democratic, popular, nationalist and anti-communist. British planners noted that, unfortunately, Musaddiq is 'regarded by many of the ignorant as a messiah'.[7]

But Musaddiq overstepped the mark, as far as Britain was concerned, in nationalising oil operations in May 1951. In the dispute that followed, Musaddiq offered to compensate the AIOC but Britain demanded either a new oil concession or a settlement that would include compensation for loss of future profits. 'In other words', according to Iran scholar Homa Katouzian, 'the Iranians would have had either to give up the spirit of the nationalisation or to compensate the AIOC not just for its investment but for all the oil which it would have produced in the next forty years'.[8]

Iran's nationalisation and offer of compensation were perfectly legitimate in international law, but this was irrelevant to British planners. Britain did 'not consider that a deal on acceptable terms can ever be made with' Musaddiq. Instead, the Foreign Office noted that 'there is hope of a change which would bring moderate elements into control'.[9]

The first step taken to remove the threat of independent development was to stop the production and export of oil, which deprived Iran of its main source of income until the 1953 coup. This was done in the knowledge that 'the effect might be to bankrupt Persia thus possibly leading to revolution'.[10] Other, mainly US, oil companies lent their support by refusing to handle Iranian oil, to prevent other oil-exporting countries from learning a 'bad' lesson from Iran's example.

The second step was to begin covert planning. The month following Iran's nationalisation of oil operations, the Attlee Labour government began plans to overthrow Musaddiq, despatching to Iran an Oxford lecturer provided with considerable sums of money.[11] 'It has been our objective for some time to get Sayyid Zia appointed Prime Minister', the Foreign Office noted in September 1951. Zia had 'no popular support' and his appointment 'was likely to provoke a strong public reaction', according to Iranian academic Fakhreddin Azimi. But to the Foreign Office Zia was 'the one man who would be able and anxious to get a reasonable oil settlement with us' and promote Iran's 'future stability'.[12]

A third option was direct military intervention, especially military occupation of the area around Abadan, the world's largest oil refinery and centre of AIOC's operations. According to the Foreign Secretary, this:

> would demonstrate once and for all to the Persians British determination not to allow the . . . AIOC to be evicted from Persia and might well result in the downfall of the Musaddiq regime and its replacement by more reasonable elements prepared to negotiate a settlement . . . It might be expected to produce a salutary effect throughout the Middle East and elsewhere, as evidence that United Kingdom interests could not be recklessly molested with impunity.[13]

Plans were laid for war against Iran. But in the end the option was viewed by the Foreign Office as 'quite impracticable' because it was believed that Iran would be able to resist the comparatively small number of troops that Britain could deploy. The US was also opposed to the British use of force, and President Truman sent a personal message to this effect to Attlee. Both the British Foreign Secretary and the Defence Minister favoured the use of military force to seize the oil installations. The option of military intervention was kept open until September 1951, when London finally decided to evacuate British personnel, and continue covert action, instead.[14]

After winning the general election the following month, Churchill berated his predecessors 'who had scuttled and run from Abadan when a splutter of musketry would have ended the matter'. 'If we had fired the volley you were responsible for at Ismaila at Abadan' Churchill explained to his Foreign Secretary, Anthony Eden, 'none of these difficulties . . . would have occurred'. (The reference was to the British action at Ismaila, Egypt in January 1952. After Egyptian rebels assaulted a British military base, British soldiers occupied the town, surrounded the police headquarters, and proceeded to engage in a turkey shoot, killing fifty people and wounding a hundred before the surrender.)

A few months into his term, however, Churchill noted that

'by sitting still on the safety valve and showing no weariness we are gradually getting them into submission'.[15]

Preference for a dictator

Britain's aim was to install 'a more reliable government', Foreign Secretary Anthony Eden explained. 'Our policy', a British official later recalled, 'was to get rid of Mossadeq as soon as possible'. An adviser at the British embassy, Colonel Wheeler, explained that 'a change of government could almost certainly be effected without difficulty or disturbance'. So by November, a Foreign Office official was able to report that the 'unofficial efforts to undermine Dr Musaddiq are making good progress'.[16]

After the failure of the oil negotiations, the main British negotiator advised the Shah that the 'only solution' was 'a strong government under martial law and the bad boys in prison for two years or so'. Britain's ambassador in Tehran agreed, noting that 'if only the Shah can be induced to take a strong line there is a good chance that Musaddiq may be got rid of'. The new government should then 'take drastic action against individual extremists'.

With 1952 came Britain's preference for 'a non-communist coup d'etat preferably in the name of the Shah'. It was clearly understood by the British embassy in Tehran that 'this would mean an authoritarian regime'.[17]

British planners had no illusions about the Shah. They noted that 'the chief complaint of his political critics [is] that he wishes to monopolise power for himself'. Neither did he 'sufficiently check the members of his family and their entourage from interference in politics and their profitable incursions into business'.[18]

As with the secret planning in Indonesia in 1965 (see chapter 20), Britain supported the establishment of a strong-arm dictatorship in the face of popular, nationalist alternatives. A coup could be successful, planners noted, 'provided always a strong man can be found equal to the task'. This 'strong man' would 'rule in the name of the Shah'. The files show that the ambassador in Tehran preferred 'a dictator', who 'would carry out the necessary administrative and economic reforms and settle the oil question on reasonable terms'.[19]

The Foreign Office stated who such a reasonable new strongman might be: General Zahidi, who was to become prime minister after the coup. Zahidi had spent much of the war in prison in Palestine after being arrested for pro-Nazi activities by the British authorities. He was known as being ruthless and manipulative and had twice been chief of police in Tehran. British officials now began to talk to him about providing £10–20 million to the Iranian treasury on his taking power.[20]

By March 1952, the British embassy was lamenting that the Iranian army was 'unlikely to take overt action against Musaddiq' but that its attitude might become 'more positive'. The Shah was also reported to be resisting British pressures to act but the British 'made it abundantly clear that we desire the fall of Musaddiq as soon as possible'.[21]

British embassy official Sam Falle met Zahidi on 6 August and recorded that the latter was prepared to take on the premiership. Falle suggested that Zahidi make this known to the US. The ambassador confirmed that Zahidi 'will make his own contacts with [the] American embassy and does not wish to appear to be our candidate'.[22]

In October 1952, the Iranian government closed down the British embassy, claiming – correctly – that certain intrigues were taking place there, and thus removing the cover for British covert activities. An MI6 and Foreign Office team met with the CIA in November and proposed the joint overthrow of the Iranian government based on Britain's well-laid plans. British agents in Iran had been provided with a radio transmitter with which to maintain contact with MI6, while the head of the MI6 operation put the CIA in touch with other useful allies in the country.

British pay-offs had already secured the cooperation of senior officers of the army and police, deputies and senators, mullahs, merchants, newspaper editors and elder statesmen, as well as mob leaders. 'These forces', explained the MI6 agent in charge of the British end of the operation, 'were to seize control of Tehran, preferably with the support of the Shah but if necessary without it, and to arrest Musaddiq and his ministers'.[23]

On 3 February 1953 a British delegation met the CIA director and the US Secretary of State while the head of the CIA's operation, Kermit Roosevelt, was despatched to Iran to investigate the situation. On 18 March 'the CIA was ready to discuss tactics in detail with us for the overthrow of Musaddiq' and it was formally agreed in April that General Zahidi was the acceptable candidate to replace him.[24]

By then, British and US agents were also involved in plans to kidnap key officials and political personalities. In one incident the Chief of Police was abducted, tortured and murdered.

The final go-ahead for the coup was given by the US in late June. Britain had by then already presented a 'complete plan' to the CIA. Churchill's authorisation soon followed and the date was set for mid-August. That month, Kermit Roosevelt met the Shah, the CIA director visited some members of the Shah's family in Switzerland, and a US army general arrived in Tehran to meet the Shan and General Zahidi.[25]

The signal for the coup scenario to begin had been arranged with the BBC; the latter agreed to begin its Persian language news broadcast not with the usual 'it is now midnight in London', but instead with 'it is now *exactly* midnight'. On hearing these broadcasts the Shah fled the country and signed two blank decrees to be filled in at the right time, one dismissing Musaddiq, the other appointing Zahidi as prime minister.[26]

Huge demonstrations took place in the streets of Tehran, funded by CIA and MI6 money; $1 million was in a safe in the US embassy and £1.5 million had been delivered by Britain to its agents in Iran, according to the MI6 officer responsible.

According to the then CIA agent Richard Cottam, 'that mob that came into north Tehran and was decisive in the overthrow was a mercenary mob. It had no ideology. That mob was paid for by American dollars and the amount of money that was used has to have been very large'.

One key aspect of the plot was to portray the demonstrating mobs as supporters of the Iranian Communist Party – Tudeh – to provide a suitable pretext for the coup and the Shah's taking control in the name of anti-communism. Agents working for the British posed as Tudeh supporters, engaging in activities such as throwing rocks at mosques and priests.[27]

Roosevelt, the head of the CIA operation, sent envoys to the commanders of some provincial armies, encouraging them to move on to Tehran. In the fighting in the capital, 300 people were killed before Musaddiq's supporters were defeated by the Shah's forces. A US general later testified that 'the guns they had in their hands, the trucks they rode in, the armoured cars that they drove through the streets, and the radio communications that permitted their control, were all furnished through the [US] military defence assistance program'.[28]

The British input, however, had also been significant. One agent of the British – Shahpour Reporter, who subsequently served as adviser to the Shah – was rewarded with a knighthood, before becoming a chief middleman for British arms sales to Iran, in particular for the manufacturers of Chieftain tanks and Rapier missiles. Two years after the coup, the head of the MI6 end of the operation became director of the Royal Institute of International Affairs, one of Britain's leading research institutes.[29]

As in every other British and US military intervention until the collapse of the USSR, the 'communist threat' scenario was deployed as the Official Story. Much subsequent academic work and media commentary plays to the same tune. The real threat of nationalism (and dirtier aims like protecting oil profits) was downplayed or removed from the picture presented to the public. In the words of a secret Foreign Office telegram to the embassy in Washington:

It is essential at all costs that His Majesty's Government should avoid getting into a position where they could be represented as a capitalist power attacking a Nationalist Persia.[30]

There are two variants to the Official Story. The first is that the coup was a response to an impending takeover by the Communist Party, Tudeh – which had close contacts with the Soviet Union – and therefore prevented the establishment of a Soviet-backed regime. The second is that Tudeh was in the ascendancy within Musaddiq's government. Both variants are plainly false.

In September 1952 the British ambassador recognised that the Tudeh 'have played a largely passive role, content to let matters take their course with only general encouragement from the sidelines . . . they have not been a major factor in the development of the Musaddiq brand of nationalism'. The US embassy stated three months before the coup that 'there was little evidence that in recent months the Tudeh had gained in popular strength, although its steady infiltration of the Iranian government and other institutions [had] continued'.[31]

As for Tudeh attempting a coup, a State Department intelligence report noted that an open Tudeh move for power 'would probably unite independents and non-communists of all political leanings and would result . . . in energetic efforts to destroy the Tudeh by force'. As Iranian scholar Fakhreddin Azimi has pointed out, the seizure of power by means of a coup was not part of Tudeh strategy, and it was also unlikely that the Russians would anyway have endorsed such a move.[32] The deliberate funding of demonstrators posing as Tudeh supporters also gives the game away as to how seriously the communist threat was actually feared.

In their secret planning, the British deliberately played up the communist threat scenario to the Americans to persuade them to help overthrow the government. One file notes that, in proposing the overthrow of Musaddiq to the Americans, 'we could say that, although we naturally wish to reach an oil settlement eventually, we appreciate that the first and most important objective is to prevent Persia going communist'. The MI6 agent believed 'the Americans would be more likely to work with us if they saw the problem as one of containing communism rather than restoring the position of the AIOC'.[33]

'I owe my throne to God, my people, my army – and to you', the Shah told the head of the CIA operation responsible for installing him; by 'you' he meant the US and Britain.

Now that a 'dictator' had been installed in line with Foreign Office wishes, stability could be restored, initially under the favoured candidate for prime minister, General Zahidi. An agreement the following year established a new oil consortium that controlled the production, pricing and export of Iranian oil. This provided Britain and the US with a 40 per cent interest each. Indeed, the 40 per cent figure for the US was the price Britain secretly (and grudgingly) agreed to pay the US in exchange for US help in overthrowing Musaddiq.[34] Britain's share was thus reduced from the complete control it had prior to Musaddiq; but it had prevented the danger that Iranians might use oil primarily to benefit themselves. The US gain of a significant stake in Iranian oil showed the new relative power of the partners in the special relationship.

British aid for repression

The Shah's regime progressed in accordance with British expectations. As a 'dictator' with huge personal power, the Shah proceeded to 'monopolise power for himself', allowed family representatives to plunder the national coffers, and ended representative government.

The Shah's regime killed around 10,000 people, about half of these during the revolution in 1978/9. In 1975, Amnesty International observed that Iran had the 'highest rate of death penalties in the world, no valid system of civilian courts and a history of torture which is beyond belief. No country in the world has a worse record in human rights than Iran.' Iran analyst Barry Rubin notes that 'prisoners were subjected to horrendous torture, equal to the worst ever devised', while 'the entire population was subjected to a constant, all-pervasive terror'. For the US the Shah was 'that rarest of leaders, an unconditional ally', in Henry Kissinger's words.[35]

The secret police responsible for many of these atrocities – SAVAK – had been created by the US and was later trained by Israel's Mossad. A former CIA analyst stated that the CIA instructed SAVAK in torture techniques, and it appears that Mossad did likewise. Former Deputy Director of MI6, George Young, described SAVAK as an 'allied and friendly' intelligence service, along with South Africa's BOSS; he wrote this in 1990, while South Africa was still under apartheid.[36]

According to Hassan Sana, a former coordinator of SAVAK, Britain also trained some of SAVAK's officers in Britain when it was set up in 1957. MI6 was in close touch with leading SAVAK officials and several of its policy recommendations were implemented. In exchange for providing information on Arab countries, Sana claimed, SAVAK was given a free hand in intelligence gathering against the Shah's political opponents in Britain. Most targets were students but also included Labour MPs campaigning against the brutality of the Shah's regime.[37]

Maurice Oldfield, then head of MI6, met the Shah regularly in the middle and late 1970s and 'had a close and intimate relationship with His Imperial Majesty', according to a former MI6 officer. Young even promised the Shah that, as long as he were head of MI6, Britain would not conduct any internal espionage against Iran or have any direct contact with military officers.[38]

The SAS, meanwhile, loaned soldiers to the Iranian military to help train the Shah's special forces for operations against Kurdish guerillas in northern Iran. Britain also built a GCHQ monitoring station on the Iran-Soviet border that the SAS protected.[39]

The Shah also understood the right economic priorities, with the fruits of political repression going primarily to a minority elite. Twenty years after the coup, the top 20 per cent of households accounted for nearly half of all consumption expenditure, whilst the bottom 40 per cent accounted for 15 per cent, and less than 12 per cent of total income. Those who suffered from the extreme concentration of wealth – such as poor immigrants and squatters in Tehran – were forced into a desperate contest for shelter and land.[40] The system that partly resulted from the considered actions and priorities of Anglo-American power sowed the seeds for the revolution that followed.

15

DETERRING DEVELOPMENT IN KENYA

Short rations, overwork, brutality, humiliating and disgusting treatment and flogging – all in violation of the United Nations Universal Declaration on Human Rights.

A former officer describing a British
detention camp, Kenya, 1954–55

Former members of the Mau Mau movement in Kenya are currently trying to sue the British government for human rights abuses committed by British forces who fought against them in the 1950s. They are calling for compensation:

on behalf of the 90,000 people imprisoned and tortured in detention camps, 10,000 people who had land confiscated and a further half a million who were forced into protected villages.[1]

If Britain is forced to reveal more evidence from the formerly secret files, as it was in the court case with the islanders of Diego Garcia (see chapter 22), a terrible chapter in British history will be revealed. For the declassified files I have seen already paint a frightening picture of terrible human rights atrocities by the colonial authorities, especially in the Nazi-style detention camps and 'protected villages' they established. All in all, around 150,000 Africans are thought to have died as a result of British policy.

These files also reveal that Britain used the war against Mau Mau as a cover for halting the rise of popular, nationalist forces that threatened control of its then colony. It was an early postwar example, therefore, of wiping out the threat of independent development. Indeed, the shape of poverty in Kenya today owes much to British policy during those dark days.

By contrast, much standard history has essentially exonerated the British role in Kenya, ascribing to planners the usual noble value of protecting freedom in a good versus evil battle.

Exploitation and racism: Background to the war

Britain declared a state of emergency in Kenya in 1952 and sent its military to quell a rebellion by the Mau Mau movement. This was comprised predominantly of Kikuyu, the largest Kenyan ethnic group, who were among the most exploited of the poor under colonial rule. The Attorney General in the Kenyan colonial government called Mau Mau 'a secret underground nationalistic organisation which is virulently anti-European'. A government-sponsored report on the origins of Mau Mau noted that it was 'the violent manifestation of a limited revolutionary movement' and that 'it was no sudden uprising' but the result of 'a long period of political unrest among the Kikuyu people of Kenya'.[2]

Mau Mau was the often violent, nationalist expression of revolt against British colonial repression. 'The causes of the revolt', David Maughan-Brown writes in an extensively documented study of Mau Mau, were 'socio-economic and political and amounted, to put it crudely, to the economic exploitation and administrative repression of the Kikuyu by the white settlers and the colonial state'. It was a militant response 'to years of frustration at the refusal of the colonial government to redress grievances over land or to listen to demands for constitutional reform'; and a 'peasants revolt triggered off by the declaration of the state of emergency and the eviction of the squatters from the farms on the White Highlands', the most arable land in Kenya. Mau Mau demands were for the return of the 'stolen' land and self-government.[3]

The planning files clearly recognise that Mau Mau received no material support from elsewhere, and was decidedly not communist. 'There is no evidence that communism or communist agents have had any direct or indirect part in the organisation or direction of the Mau Mau itself, or its activities', a Colonial Office report stated.[4]

The British were unfortunately unable to present the rebels as being part of the international communist conspiracy. They therefore presented them as straight out of the heart of darkness – as gangsters who indulged in cannibalism, witchcraft, devil worship and sexual orgies and who terrorised white settlers and mutilated women and children. This deceit conveniently masked the Mau Mau's true struggle as a political and economic one mainly over the possession of land.

Britain had established in Kenya a system of institutionalised racism and exploitation of the indigenous population. It was estimated that half of the urban workers in private industry and one quarter of those in public services received wages too low to provide for their basic needs. As late as 1960 – three years before independence – Africans, who made up 90 per cent of the workforce, accounted for only 45 per cent of the total wage bill. A crucial aspect of the colonial economy was the taxation system which increased poverty and dependence in the reserves allocated to Africans by a net drain of resources out of them.[5]

The Governor of Kenya explained the racist policy to the Colonial Secretary in 1955:

> Up to 1923, the policy of segregation as between Europeans and other immigrant races followed as a

measure of sanitation. The White Paper of 1923 recommended 'as a sanitation measure, [that] segregation of Europeans and Asiatics is not absolutely essential for the preservation of the health of community', but that for the present it was considered desirable to keep residential quarters of natives, so far as practicable, separate from those of immigrant races.

These 'residential quarters' for the 'natives' – that is, the population – were, the Governor explained, 'behind anything that I have seen elsewhere on the continent'.[6]

This was the situation at home for the nearly 100,000 Kenyan Africans who had fought on Britain's side in the Second World War. It was, the Governor explained, a result of Britain's 'determination to persevere in the task to which we have set our minds – to civilise a great mass of human beings who are in a very primitive moral and social state'. In reality, the ideology and institutions of the British settlers and colonial state in Kenya closely resembled the fascist movements of the years between the First and Second World Wars.[7]

Land ownership was the clearest example of inequity and exploitation. The white settlers, who comprised a minuscule 0.7 per cent of the population, owned 20 per cent of the best land in Kenya, the White Highlands. This meant that fewer than 30,000 whites owned more arable land than one million Kikuyu. The colony's function was to produce primary products for export and because settler agricultural production depended on the availability of labour, it was essential for a large portion of the African peasantry to be deprived of their own land and forced on to the labour market. By 1945 there were over 200,000 registered African squatters in the White Highlands, over half of whom were Kikuyu. Called '"resident native" labourers', they performed tasks as 'a cheap, malleable and readily accessible African labour force'.[8]

The major African nationalist political group opposed to British rule was the Kenya African Union (KAU), which noted:

The chief characteristic of all labour – skilled or not . . . is the low wages obtaining in Kenya . . . The greatest problem which requires urgent consideration is that of the old man and woman who cannot perform hard manual labour. The settlers simply turn them off their land – rightly according to law . . . The greater majority of the dying Africans and those suffering from malnutrition accrues as an upshot of the meagre allowances that our people earn. Due to this, ninety per cent of our people live in the most deplorable conditions ever afforded to a human being.

The KAU referred to the squatter system as a 'new slavery' and explained that 'modern serfdom has come into being as cheap labour can be found everywhere in the colony'.[9]

British officials thought about things rather differently. In a 1945 report the colonial government noted that:

The principal item in the natural resources of Kenya is the land, and in this term we include the colony's mineral resources. It seems to us that our major objective must clearly be the preservation and the wise use of this most important asset.

The Deputy Governor explained:

It is of greatest importance on all grounds of Imperial policy and for the future well being and prosperity of the native people that there should be a vigorous and well established British settlement in these highlands, for without it there is no hope of successfully over-coming the immense problems which confront us in this part of the world and of erecting here a permanent structure of enlightenment and civilisation.[10]

The following year, the Governor declared in an after-dinner speech that 'the greater part of the wealth of the country is at present in our hands . . . This land we have made is our land by right – by right of achievement'. He explained to the Africans that 'their Africa has gone for ever', since they were now living in 'a world which we have made, under the humanitarian impulses of the late nineteenth and the twentieth century'. The Governor added:

> We appear to Africans as being immensely wealthy and nearly all of them are in fact very poor . . . But these are social and economic differences and the problems of this country in that respect are social and economic and not political; nor are they to be solved by political devices.

Britain was in Kenya 'as of right, the product of historical events which reflect the greatest glory of our fathers and grandfathers'.[11]

In fact, Britain had engaged in mass slaughter to subjugate Kenya. Winston Churchill referred in 1908 to one expedition by stating that 'surely it cannot be necessary to go on killing these defenceless people on such an enormous scale'.[12] The governor was using a traditional pretext for pursuing terrible policies – 'humanitarian impulses' – a strategy now taken up by the missionaries of New Labour.

Curbing the threat of nationalism

Unfortunately for the champions of 'enlightenment and civilisation', Africans were indeed engaging in politics.

In standard history, the declaration of the state of emergency in October 1952 is viewed as a response to Mau Mau terrorism which was getting increasingly out of control, with Britain portrayed as a noble defender of human rights. In reality the declaration was more a cause of the war. Moreover, the declassified files show that the declaration was intended to stamp out popular, nationalist political forces demanding land reform and self-government – the threat of independent development.

In the year previous to October 1952, there had actually been fewer murders and serious injuries than in previous years. A few days before the declaration – on 15 October – the Governor cabled London saying that in the previous week 'there had been some falling off in crimes, both Mau Mau and otherwise'. Yet two days later he confirmed that the declaration would take effect from 20 October. The declaration itself prompted an increase in these crimes.[13]

The real problem for the colonial government was the increasing popularity of KAU leaders, especially Jomo Kenyatta, who were drawing ever larger numbers of people to their public meetings. Radical trade unionists were taking control of the country's unions as the KAU gradually extended its influence throughout the country. The Governor explained to London that the plans for declaring the emergency might appear 'excessive' but 'Kenyatta has succeeded in building up right under the nose of authority a powerful organisation affecting all sides of life among the Kikuyu'.[14]

Two months prior to the declaration, a colonial official noted that recent large KAU meetings had been coupled with a 'serious increase of Mau Mau activities [sic] . . . in each area where [Kenyatta] spoke'. One meeting had been 'attended by twenty to thirty thousand people, who were so excited and truculent that the preservation of law and order hung upon a thread'. 'We decided', the official noted, 'that we would be wrong to allow any further meetings of the KAU'.

Another official noted that at recent KAU meetings at which Kenyatta had been the key speaker, 'large crowds have attended and treated him and his utterances with enthusiastic respect'. Even worse was that the KAU and other groups were 'demanding . . . the "return" of the White Highlands to the Kikuyu and self-government on the Gold Coast model'.[15]

The answer, the Governor declared a few days before the declaration, was that 'we must remove Kenyatta and several of his henchmen during the next few weeks'. The Attorney-General explained that Kenyatta and his associates should not be released from prison at the end of the emergency but be 'kept in custody for a very substantial period of years'. He further noted that 'one of the principal reasons' for declaring a state of emergency 'would be to enable us to make detention orders against the leading African agitators'.

The state of emergency was declared and the authorities jailed dozens of KAU leaders and every branch chairman who was not already in jail.[16]

In seeking to justify the repression of the popular nationalists, British authorities needed to portray Kenyatta as the instigator of the Mau Mau movement. The only problem was that Kenyatta had consistently denounced it. At one meeting, the Attorney-General observed Kenyatta publicly condemning Mau Mau, while the 30,000 Kikuyu present at the meeting held up their hands to 'signify that they approved of his denunciation of Mau Mau'.[17]

At his subsequent trial, Kenyatta was sentenced to seven years' imprisonment as a result of what the defending counsel called 'the most childishly weak case made against any man in any important trial in the history of the British empire', one that was patently trumped up to dispose of the country's leading nationalist.[18]

Human rights, colonial style

With the political road to reform blocked by Britain, just grievances found their expression in increasing violence. The subsequent war resulted in atrocities being committed by both Mau Mau and government forces but with far greater brutality by the latter. The sheer number of deaths at the hands of the government forces shows that there was an extensive shoot-to-kill policy and that killings were conducted with impunity. Colonial government forces killed around 10,000 Africans. By contrast, the Mau Mau killed 590 members of the security forces, 1,819 Africans, and 32 European and 26 Asian civilians. More white settlers were killed in road accidents in Nairobi during the emergency than by Mau Mau.[19]

Some British army battalions kept scoreboards recording kills, and gave £5 rewards for the first sub-unit to kill an insurgent. One army captain was quoted as informing a sergeant-major that 'he could shoot anybody he liked provided they were black'. Frank Kitson, a senior army officer and 'counter-insurgency' expert who would later apply his skills to Northern Ireland, once commented: 'three Africans appeared walking down the track towards us: a perfect target. Unfortunately they were policemen.'[20]

A Channel 4 documentary made in 1999 – offering a rare glimpse by the media into the reality of the British war – referred to 'free fire zones' where:

> Any African could be shot on sight . . . Rewards were offered to the units that produced the largest number of Mau Mau corpses, the hands of which were chopped off to make fingerprinting easier. Settlements suspected of harbouring Mau Mau were burned and Mau Mau suspects were tortured for information.[21]

The British also resorted to dictatorial police measures: 153,000 arrests, for example, were made in the first fourteen months of the war. But it was the methods used by the police that were particularly vile. There was 'a constant stream of reports of brutalities by police, military and home guards', noted Canon Bewes, of the Church Missionary Society, following a visit. These brutalities included slicing off ears, boring holes in eardrums, flogging until death, pouring paraffin over suspects who were then set alight, and burning eardrums with lit cigarettes.

'Some of the people', Bewes noted, 'had been using castrating instruments and . . . in one instance two men had died under castration.' A metal castrating instrument 'had also been reported as being used to clamp on to the fingers of people who were unwilling to give information and . . . if the information was not given the tips of the fingers were cut off'. Bewes stated that there were also a number of cases of rape perpetrated by the army. A Kenyan police team sent to the neighbouring colony of Tanganyika to 'screen' Kikuyu there were found guilty by the Tanganyikan authorities of 'violence, in the form of whipping on the soles of the feet, burning with lighted cigarettes and tying leather thongs round the neck and dragging the victims along the ground'. Of the 170–200 interrogated, 'at least 32 were badly injured'.[22]

A former district officer recently admitted:

> There was outright abuse of power and some of the crimes committed were horrific. One day six Mau Mau suspects were brought into a police station in the neighbouring district to mine. The British police inspector in charge lined them up against a wall and shot them. There was no trial.

Asked whether he thought colonial forces had committed human rights violations, he replied: 'If throwing a phosphorous grenade into a thatched hut with a sleeping family inside isn't a human rights abuse then I don't know what is.'[23]

Between 1952 and 1956, 1,015 people were hanged, 297 for murder and 559 for unlawful possession of arms or administering the Mau Mau oath. As well as widespread beating and torture of suspects, defendants rarely had a chance to prepare their case and judges were racially biased in their evaluation of evidence. There were mass trials of up to fifty men with numbers around their necks; in most of these, groups of between ten and twenty men went to the gallows together. 'There was appalling abuse of human rights at all stages of the legal process,' notes David Anderson of the University of London. A mobile gallows was transported around the country dispensing 'justice' to Mau Mau suspects, while dead rebels, especially commanders, were often displayed at cross-roads and market places.[24]

The Governor of Kenya even proposed that the death penalty be applied to people who were merely helping the insurgents, whether directly or indirectly, and to those committing acts of sabotage. This was too much even for the Colonial Secretary, who noted that this definition would be so broad that the death penalty 'would be applicable to deliberate obstruction by motorist of baker's van delivering bread to military unit or to intentional puncturing of sanitary inspector's bicycle [sic]'.[25]

By the mid 1950s the scale of atrocities was so great that news stories by the foreign press based in Nairobi reached London. A parliamentary delegation visited Kenya in 1954 and found that 'brutality and malpractices by the police have occurred on a scale which constitutes a threat to public confidence in the forces of law and order'. The following year the Labour MP Barbara Castle visited Kenya to investigate government involvement in torture and killings and concluded that the entire system of justice in Kenya had a 'Nazi' attitude towards Africans:

> In the heart of the British empire there is a police state where the rule of law has broken down, where murders and torture of Africans go unpunished and where the authorities pledged to enforce justice regularly connive at its violation.[26]

The key aspects of British repression in Kenya were 'resettlement' operations that forced 90,000 Kikuyu into detention camps surrounded by barbed wire and troops, and the compulsory 'villageisation' of the Kikuyu reserves. The Kikuyus' livestock was confiscated and many were subjected to forced labour. 'Villageisation' meant the destruction of formerly scattered homesteads and the erection of houses in fortified camps to replace them. This meant a traumatic break from the traditional Kikuyu way of life. Even when not accompanied, as it often was, by 23-hour curfews, it resulted in widespread famine and death. In total, around 150,000 Africans lost their lives due to the war, most dying of disease and starvation in the 'protected villages'.[27]

Shortly after the 'emergency' was declared, the Governor issued an order allowing the government to detain whomever it liked in a concentration camp for an indefinite period. In these camps, the inmates were classified as 'blacks' if they were Mau Mau officials or supporters, 'greys' if they were suspected of being such with no evidence, and 'whites' if they had no Mau Mau connections (the latter were subsequently released). Diseases spread in the camps. The declassified files report on one camp having over 400 typhoid cases, with around ninety people dying as a result.[28]

The colonial government reported:

> The sudden confinement of thousands of Africans behind barb wire has set very considerable and difficult medical problems. This has been aggravated by the fact that of necessity there has been little distinction between the fit and the unfit when the question of detention is being considered. Consequently, infectious disease has been introduced into the camps from the start.[29]

Historian V. G. Kiernan comments that the camps 'were probably as bad as any similar Nazi or Japanese establishments'. Brutality by the warders was systematic. One former officer noted that 'Japanese methods of torture' were being practised by one camp commandant.[30]

A former officer in one of the detention camps in 1954–55 witnessed routine 'short rations, overwork, brutality, humiliating and disgusting treatment and flogging – all in violation of the United Nations Universal Declaration on Human Rights'. In one camp, he said:

> The detainees were being systematically ill-treated, underfed, overworked and flogged by the Security Officer . . . The women and children, in conditions of severe overcrowding, were sleeping on the bare stone or wooden floors as the Commandant had forbidden them to construct beds . . . The lavatories were merely large pits in the ground . . . with the excreta lapping over the top.

At another camp, where forced labour was practised, 'one European officer made the detainees work at pointless hard labour tasks twelve hours a day'. The commandant was seen 'punching and kicking detainees' and, on the orders of a European officer, warders were 'sent into one of the compounds ... with orders to "beat up" the detainees. This they proceeded to do with sticks, lumps of wood and whips. Several European officers ... joined in the beating'. The order had been given 'for no apparent reason'. 'Some African detainees had been knocked unconscious and nearly 100 were treated in hospital.'[31]

The killings of eleven men by warders at Hola concentration camp in March 1959 proved to be a turning point in British policy. John Cowan, the Senior Superintendent of Prisons in Kenya from 1957 to 1963, told the Channel 4 documentary noted above of British officers forcing a group of prisoners at Hola camp to obey work orders. He said the policy was that if they did not 'prove amenable to work' then 'they should be – in the phrase "manhandled" to the site of work, and forced to carry out the task'. On 3 March 1959, 85 prisoners were marched to a site and ordered to work. One of the prisoners, John Maina Kahihu, said:

> We refused to do this work. We were fighting for our freedom. We were not slaves. There were two hundred guards. One hundred and seventy stood around us with machine guns. Thirty guards were inside the trench with us. The white man in charge blew his whistle and the guards started beating us. They beat us from 8 am to 11.30. They were beating us like dogs. I was covered by other bodies – just my arms and legs were exposed. I was very lucky to survive. But the others were still being beaten. There was no escape for them.[32]

Alongside the eleven dead were sixty seriously injured. When reports of the killings reached Britain there was political uproar; within weeks London closed the Kenyan camps and released the detainees.

Government attitudes to forced labour in 1950s Kenya show British elites' basic contempt for international law, equally blatant today. In February 1953 the Kenyan colonial authorities cabled London saying they were on the verge of putting people 'compulsorily to work' in 'the areas being prepared for settlement by Kikuyu or other African tribes.' To do this, the Governor asked London whether there was any possibility 'of obtaining exemption' from the provisions of the UN's Forced Labour Convention of 1930. The Colonial Office debated the issue and recognised that implementing the proposal would be illegal. It was clearly noted that 'compulsory labour as proposed by Kenya would be a breach of the Forced Labour Convention' and 'there was no procedure for claiming exemption from its provisions'. But despite this, the minutes of one meeting note that 'if the measures could be introduced without publicity, or delayed until after the [UN] session, the UK delegation's task would be easier'. The Colonial Secretary then wrote to the Governor explaining that 'if . . . the proposal for compulsory employment is to be pursued it means facing up to the fact that we shall be breaking the Convention'. The Colonial Secretary declared:

> The only justification I can see for sustaining this breach
> would be (a) that we are dealing with very exceptional
> circumstances not contemplated by the Convention and
> (b) that we are not offending against the spirit of the
> Convention which was framed primarily to prevent the
> exploitation of labour . . . I should be grateful to know of
> any further considerations there may be to strengthen
> the case for compulsion.

The Governor replied that he had 're-examined the position' and was 'very anxious not to embarrass you. I now think that by a combination of economic inducements and use of sanctions under existing law . . . it may well be possible to attain our objective.'[33]

Dependent independence

Britain's main objectives in Kenya were achieved largely by a combination of straightforward violence and repression. But the transition to a friendly government at independence in 1963 could not have been achieved without substantial manoeuvring in the political and economic fields as well.

The cultivation of an African elite who would preserve British interests after independence was not an easy one, since Britain had imprisoned many of the most able political leaders in 1952. Two months after the declaration of the state of emergency, the Colonial Office suggested 'giving moderate and loyal Africans some positive part to play in the present crisis'. Of course, 'there can be no question, so long as the emergency lasts, of any constitutional change at the centre'; the declaration of the state of emergency had been intended precisely to prevent this.

The Colonial Office suggested establishing interracial advisory committees. 'We are not so naive as to think that advisory committees will bring much increase in wisdom to bear on immediate problems.' Their importance was that 'they can . . . play a useful part in associating with the process of government persons who would otherwise be condemned to more sterile and therefore frequently dangerous activities'. This was 'of particular value in Kenya at the present when there is really so little that you can do to give moderate Africans a sense of purpose'.[34]

Britain also engaged in various covert activities to ensure the dominance of 'moderate' policies following independence. It was behind the creation of the Kenyan African Democratic Union (KADU) party, set up to unite African moderates against the stronger and more popular Kenyan African National Union (KANU) – the successor to the KAU – under Kenyatta. KADU received covert funding from British business interests in Kenya and also from the colonial authorities in advance of the 1963 election. However, at the final Lancaster House conference before independence, the British government realised that unfortunately KANU would win the election and abandoned KADU. MI6 also recruited Bruce McKenzie, an influential white settler politician who had moved over from KADU to KANU. After independence McKenzie was appointed Minister for Agriculture, and also had responsibility for overseeing the defence treaty with Britain.[35]

In the economic sphere, it was land reform for the White Highlands that was the most significant scheme for preserving British interests. The purpose of the Swynnerton Plan of the mid 1950s was to enable richer Africans to acquire more land and poorer farmers less, which had the effect of creating a landed and a landless class, the latter growing to around 400,000 people.[36]

In the land transfer schemes of the years shortly before independence, new African 'settlers' were forced to pay for land that they regarded as theirs and which had been taken over by European settlers. The majority of landless people were unable to raise even the basic sums needed as a downpayment for the purchase of land, so that over half the land was transferred almost intact to wealthy Africans in partnerships or limited liability companies. Those who were able to buy land did so by indebting themselves to cover the high prices paid to the European settlers. This meant that many poor African peasants were paying back debts to the ex-colonisers for decades after independence to compensate the latter for the land they originally stole.[37]

The World Bank and Britain's Commonwealth Development Corporation (the then aid programme) provided financial aid for these schemes, which 'reflected the European and colonial hopes of using foreign investment to bolster a moderate nationalist state and to preserve European economic (and political) interests', according to Gary Wasserman in his analysis of land ownership in Kenya. The African middle classes who were rich enough to acquire land through land titles and loan repayments 'were expected to acquire a vested interest against any radical transformation of the society'. There was the obligation to repay the loans, to maintain an economy favourable to private investment, to limit nationalisations, and to maintain the chief export-earner – European dominated capital agriculture, and an economic structure congenial to it – hence to refuse to expropriate Europeans or place limits on land holdings. Overall, 'the decolonisation process aimed to preserve the colonial political economy and, beyond that, to integrate an indigenous elite into positions of authority where they could protect the important interests in the system'.[38]

Ongoing disenfranchisement of the poor was therefore assured after independence. Political power now rested in the hands of the previously unreliable Kenyatta, who as the first President after independence accepted the validity of the land transfers, one of the worst aspects of colonialism. Subsequent policy aimed to 'Africanise' the economy while accommodating the interests of the transnational corporations who held – and continue to hold – a significant stake in the country. In 1958, one third of privately owned assets in Kenya were owned by non-residents, mainly TNCs. By 1978, fifteen years after political independence, analysts Bethwell Ogot and Tiyambe Zeleza note that 'Kenya was still a dependent export economy, heavily penetrated by foreign capital from all the major capitalist countries, so that she was more firmly and broadly integrated into the world capitalist system than at independence'.[39]

A 1978 International Labour Organisation report highlighted the effects of the British plans that post-independence leaders essentially implemented. Those who benefited from the rapid economic growth since independence included the elites who replaced the British 'in the high level jobs', some African settlers who had bought land from European farmers, and employees in the modern, urban sectors who secured increases of between 6 and 8 per cent a year in their real incomes. However, 'the group of persons who have failed to derive much benefit from the growth generated since independence includes the great majority of small holders, employees in the rural sector, the urban working poor and the urban and rural unemployed'.[40]

By the mid 1970s, the richest 20 per cent of the population received 70 per cent of total income, while the majority of the population continued to suffer from grinding poverty. Today, Kenya's income and ownership distribution remain heavily skewed in favour of a minority elite. This situation owes much to British priorities in the dying days of formal colonialism. As a recent report on Kenya's land laws by the Nairobi-based Kenya Human Rights Commission notes: 'The failure to reconsider these unjust laws after independence has meant that our government has continued the treatment of poor Kenyans as second-class citizens while the ruling class of Kenyans and foreigners enjoy the fruits of independence.'[41]

16

MALAYA: WAR IN DEFENCE OF THE RUBBER INDUSTRY

The hard core of armed communists in this country are
fanatics and must be, and will be, exterminated.
> Sir Gerald Templer, High Commissioner
> in colonial Malaya

Between 1948 and 1960 the British military fought what is
conventionally called the 'emergency' or 'counter-insurgency'
campaign in Malaya, a British colony until independence in
1957. The declassified files reveal that Britain resorted to very
brutal measures in the war, including widespread aerial
bombing and the use of a forerunner to modern cluster bombs.
Britain also set up a grotesque 'resettlement' programme
similar to that in Kenya, that provided a model for the US's
horrific 'strategic hamlet' programmes in Vietnam. It also used
chemical agents from which the US may again have drawn
lessons in its use of agent orange.

Defending the right of exploitation

British planners' primary concern was to enable British
business to exploit Malayan economic resources. Malaya

possessed valuable minerals such as coal, bauxite, tungsten, gold, iron ore, manganese, and, above all, rubber and tin. A Colonial Office report from 1950 noted that Malaya's rubber and tin mining industries were the biggest dollar earners in the British Commonwealth. Rubber accounted for 75 per cent, and tin 12–15 per cent, of Malaya's income.[1]

As a result of colonialism, Malaya was effectively owned by European, primarily British, businesses, with British capital behind most Malayan enterprises. Most importantly, 70 per cent of the acreage of rubber estates was owned by European (primarily British) companies, compared to 29 per cent Asian ownership.[2]

Malaya was described by one Lord in 1952 as the 'greatest material prize in South-East Asia', mainly due to its rubber and tin. These resources were 'very fortunate' for Britain, another Lord declared, since 'they have very largely supported the standard of living of the people of this country and the sterling area ever since the war ended'. 'What we should do without Malaya, and its earnings in tin and rubber, I do not know.'[3]

The insurgency that arose in Malaya threatened control over this 'material prize'. The Colonial Secretary remarked in 1948 that 'it would gravely worsen the whole dollar balance of the Sterling Area if there were serious interference with Malayan exports'. One other member of the House of Lords explained that existing deposits of tin were being 'quickly used up' and, owing to rebel activity, 'no new areas are being prospected for future working'. The danger was that tin mining would cease in around ten years, he alleged. The situation with rubber was 'no less alarming', with the fall in output 'largely due to the direct and indirect effects of communist sabotage', as it was described.[4]

An influential big-business pressure group called Joint Malayan Interests was warning the Colonial Office of 'soft-hearted doctrinaires, with emphasis on early self-government' for the colony. It noted that the insurgency was causing economic losses through direct damage and interruption of work, loss of manpower and falling outputs. It implored the government that 'until the fight against banditry has been won there can be no question of any further moves towards self-government'.[5]

The British military was thus despatched in a classic imperial role – largely to protect commercial interests. 'In its narrower context', the Foreign Office observed in a secret file, the 'war against bandits is very much a war in defence of [the] rubber industry.'[6]

The roots of the war lay in the failure of the British colonial authorities to guarantee the rights of the Chinese in Malaya, who made up nearly 45 per cent of the population. Britain had traditionally promoted the rights of the Malay community over and above those of the Chinese. Proposals for a new political structure to create a racial equilibrium between the Chinese and Malay communities and remove the latter's ascendancy over the former, had been defeated by Malays and the ex-colonial Malayan lobby. By 1948 Britain was promoting a new federal constitution that would confirm Malay privileges and consign about 90 per cent of Chinese to non-citizenship. Under this scheme, the High Commissioner would preside over an undemocratic, centralised state where the members of the Executive Council and the Legislative Council were all chosen by him.

At the same time, a series of strikes and general labour unrest, aided by an increasingly powerful trade union movement, was threatening order in the colony. The colonial authorities sought to suppress this unrest, banning some trade unions, imprisoning some of their members and harassing the left-wing press.

Thus Britain used the emergency, declared in 1948, not just to defeat the armed insurgency, but also to crack down on workers' rights. 'The emergency regulations and the police action under them have undoubtedly reduced the amount of active resistance to wage reductions and entrenchments', the

Governor of Singapore – part of colonial Malaya – noted. In Singapore, the number of unions 'has decreased since the emergency started'. Colonial officials also observed that the curfews imposed by the authorities 'have tended to damp down the endeavours of keen trade unionists'. Six months into the emergency the Colonial Office noted that in Singapore 'during this period the colony has been almost entirely free from labour troubles'.[7]

Britain had therefore effectively blocked the political path to reform, as in Kenya. This meant that the Malayan Communist Party – which was to provide the backbone of the insurgency – either had to accept that its future political role would be very limited, or go to ground and press the British to leave. An insurgent movement was formed out of one that had been trained and armed by Britain to resist the Japanese occupation during the Second World War; the Malayan Chinese had offered the only active resistance to the Japanese invaders.

The insurgents were drawn almost entirely from disaffected Chinese and received considerable support from Chinese 'squatters', who numbered over half a million. In the words of the Foreign Office in 1952:

> The vast majority of the poorer Chinese were employed in the tin mines and on the rubber estates and they suffered most from the Japanese occupation of the country ... During the Japanese occupation, they were deprived both of their normal employment and of the opportunity to return to their homeland . . . Large numbers of Chinese were forced out of useful employment and had no alternative but to follow the example of other distressed Chinese, who in small numbers had been obliged to scratch for a living in the jungle clearings even before the war.[8]

These 'squatters' were now to be the chief object of Britain's draconian measures in the colony.

The reality of the war

To combat an insurgent force of around 3,000–6,000, British forces embarked on a brutal war which involved large-scale bombing, dictatorial police measures and the wholesale 'resettlement' of hundreds of thousands of people.

The High Commissioner in Malaya, Gerald Templer, declared that 'the hard core of armed communists in this country are fanatics and must be, and will be, exterminated'. During Templer's two years in office, 'two-thirds of the guerrillas were wiped out', writes Richard Clutterbuck, a former British official in Malaya, which was a testament to Templer's 'dynamism and leadership'.[9]

Britain conducted 4,500 airstrikes in the first five years of the Malayan war.[10] Robert Jackson writes in his uncritical account:

> During 1956, some 545,000 lb of bombs had been dropped on a supposed [guerilla] encampment . . . but a lack of accurate pinpoints had nullified the effect. The camp was again attacked at the beginning of May 1957 . . . [dropping] a total of 94,000 lb of bombs, but because of the inaccurate target information this weight of explosive was 250 yards off target. Then, on 15 May . . . 70,000 lb of bombs were dropped.

'The attack was entirely successful', Jackson declares, since 'four terrorists were killed'.

The author also notes that a 500 lb nose-fused bomb was employed from August 1948 and had a mean area of effectiveness of 15,000 square feet. 'Another very viable weapon' was the 500 lb fragmentation bomb, a forerunner of cluster bombs. 'Since a Sutherland could carry a load of 190, its effect on terrorist morale was considerable', Jackson states. 'Unfortunately, it was not used in great numbers, despite its excellent potential as a harassing weapon.' Perhaps equally unfortunate was the case of a Lincoln bomber, once 'dropping its bombs 600 yards short . . . killing twelve civilians and injuring twenty-six others'.[11] Just one of numerous examples of 'collateral damage' from the forgotten past.

Atrocities were committed on both sides and the insurgents often indulged in horrific attacks and murders. A young British officer commented that, in combating the insurgents: 'We were shooting people. We were killing them . . . This was raw savage success. It was butchery. It was horror.'[12]

Running totals of British kills were published and became a source of competition between army units. One British army conscript recalled that 'when we had an officer who did come out with us on patrol I realised that he was only interested in one thing: killing as many people as possible'. British forces booby-trapped jungle food stores and secretly supplied self-detonating grenades and bullets to the insurgents to kill the user instantly. SAS squadrons from the racist regime in Rhodesia also served alongside the British, at one point led by Peter Walls, who became head of the Rhodesian army after the unilateral declaration of independence.[13]

Brian Lapping observes in his study of the end of the British empire that there was 'some vicious conduct by the British forces, who routinely beat up Chinese squatters when they refused, or possibly were unable, to give information' about the insurgents. There were also cases of bodies of dead guerillas being exhibited in public. This was good practice, according to the *Scotsman* newspaper, since 'simple-minded peasants are told and come to believe that the communist leaders are invulnerable'.[14]

At Batang Kali in December 1948 the British army slaughtered twenty-four Chinese, before burning the village. The British government initially claimed that the villagers were guerillas, and then that they were trying to escape, neither of which was true. A Scotland Yard inquiry into the massacre was called off by the Heath government in 1970 and the full details have never been officially investigated.

Decapitation of insurgents was a little more unusual – intended as a way of identifying dead guerillas when it was not possible to bring their corpses in from the jungle. A photograph of a Marine Commando holding two insurgents' heads caused a public outcry in April 1952. The Colonial Office privately noted that 'there is no doubt that under international law a similar case in wartime would be a war crime'. (Britain always denied it was technically at 'war' in Malaya, hence the use of the term 'emergency'.)[15]

Dyak headhunters from Borneo worked alongside the British forces. High Commissioner Templer suggested that Dyaks should be used not only for tracking 'but in their traditional role as head-hunters'. Templer 'thinks it is essential that the practice [decapitation] should continue', although this would only be necessary 'in very rare cases', the Colonial Office observed. It also noted that, because of the recent outcry over this issue, 'it would be well to delay any public statement on this matter for some months'. The *Daily Telgraph* offered support, commenting that the Dyaks 'would be superb fighters in the Malayan jungle and it would be absurd if uninformed public opinion at home were to oppose their use'. The Colonial Office also warned that in addition to decapitation, 'other practices may have grown up particularly in units which employ Dyaks, which would provide ugly photographs'.[16]

Templer famously said in Malaya that 'the answer lies not in pouring more troops into the jungle, but in the hearts and minds of the people'. Despite this rhetoric, British policy succeeded because it was grossly repressive, and was really about establishing control over the Chinese population. The centrepiece of this was the 'Briggs Plan', begun in 1950 – a 'resettlement' programme involving the removal of over half a million Chinese squatters into hundreds of 'new villages'. The Colonial Office referred to the policy as 'a great piece of social development'.[17]

Lapping describes what the policy meant in reality:

> A community of squatters would be surrounded in their huts at dawn, when they were all asleep, forced into lorries and settled in a new village encircled by

barbed wire with searchlights round the periphery to prevent movement at night. Before the 'new villagers' were let out in the mornings to go to work in the paddy fields, soldiers or police searched them for rice, clothes, weapons or messages. Many complained both that the new villages lacked essential facilities and that they were no more than concentration camps.[18]

In Jackson's view, however, the new villages were 'protected by barbed wire'![19]

A further gain from 'resettlement' was a pool of cheap labour available for employers. Following the official framing, however, this was described by Clutterbuck as 'an unprecedented opportunity for work for the displaced squatters on the rubber estates'.[20]

A government newsletter said that an essential aspect of 'resettlement' was 'to educate [the Chinese] into accepting the control of government'[21] – control over them, that is, by the British and Malays. 'We still have a long way to go in conditioning the [Chinese]', the colonial government declared, 'to accept policies which can easily be twisted by the opposition to appear as acts of colonial oppression.' But the task was made easier since 'it must always be emphasised that the Chinese mind is schizophrenic and ever subject to the twin stimuli of racialism and self-interest'.[22]

A key British war measure was inflicting 'collective punishments' on villages where people were deemed to be aiding the insurgents. At Tanjong Malim in March 1952 Templer imposed a twenty-two-hour house curfew, banned everyone from leaving the village, closed the schools, stopped bus services and reduced the rice rations for 20,000 people. The latter measure prompted the London School of Hygiene and Tropical Medicine to write to the Colonial Office noting that the 'chronically undernourished Malayan' might not be able to survive as a result. 'This measure is bound to result in an increase, not only of sickness but also of deaths, particularly amongst the mothers and very young children.' Some people were fined for leaving their homes to use outside latrines.[23]

In another collective punishment – at Sengei Pelek the following month – measures included a house curfew, a reduction of 40 per cent in the rice ration and the construction of a chain-link fence 22 yards outside the existing barbed wire fence around the town. Officials explained that these measures were being imposed upon the 4,000 villagers 'for their continually supplying food' to the insurgents and 'because they did not give information to the authorities' – surely far worse crimes than decapitation.[24]

British detention laws resulted in 34,000 people being held for varying periods in the first eight years of the emergency. The Foreign Office explained that detention regulations covered people 'who are a menace to public security but who cannot, because of insufficient evidence, be brought to trial'. Around 15,000 people were deported. The laws that enabled the High Commissioner to do this to detainees extended 'to certain categories of dependants of the person concerned'. The High Commissioner's view was that 'the removal of all the detainees to China would contribute more than any other single factor to the disruption' of the insurgency.[25]

Jackson comments: 'Templer's methods were certainly unorthodox but there was no doubt that they produced results.' Richard Allen, in another study, agrees, noting that 'one obvious justification of the Templer methods and measures . . . is that the course he set was maintained after his departure and achieved in the end virtually complete success'.[26] The ends justify the means.

Many British policies in the Malayan war were copied with even more devastating effect by the US in Vietnam. 'Resettlement' became the 'strategic hamlet' programme. Chemical agents were used by the British in Malaya for similar purposes as agent orange in Vietnam. Britain had experimented with the use of chemicals as defoliants and crop destroyers from the early 1950s. From June to October 1952, for example, 1,250 acres of roadside vegetation at possible ambush points were sprayed with defoliant, described as a policy of 'national importance'. The chemicals giant ICA saw it, according to the Colonial Office, as 'a lucrative field for experiment'.[27] I could find nothing further on this programme in the declassified files.

The convenient pretext

As noted above, the war was essentially fought to defend commercial interests. It was not that British planners believed there was no 'communist' threat at all – they did. But the nature of this threat needs to be understood. Communism in Malaya – as elsewhere in the Third World during the cold war – primarily threatened British and Western control over economic resources. There was never any question of military intervention in Malaya by either the USSR or China, nor did they provide any material support to the insurgents: 'No operational links have been established as existing', the Colonial Office reported four years after the beginning of the war.

Rather, the British feared that the Chinese revolution of 1949 might be repeated in Malaya. And as the *Economist* described, the significance of this was that communists 'are moving towards an economy and a type of trade in which there will be no place for the foreign manufacturer, the foreign banker or the foreign trader' – not strictly true, but a view that conveys the threat that the wrong kind of development poses to the West's commercial interests.[28]

British policy – then and now – cannot be presented as being based on furthering such crude aims as business interests, whether rubber and tin in Malaya or oil in Iraq. So the official pretext became that of resisting communist expansion, a concept shorn of any commercial motives and simply understood as defending the 'free world' against nasty totalitarians. Academics and journalists have overwhelmingly fallen into line, with the result that the British public have been deprived of the realistic picture.

Let us take a couple of examples of how the required doctrine has been promoted. One of the most reputed academic analysts of early postwar British foreign policy, Ritchie Ovendale, asserts that Britain was 'fighting the communist terrorists to enable Malaya to become independent and help itself'. Motives of straightforward commercial exploitation do not figure at all in Ovendale's account. Later, he only quickly mentions that Britain is 'dependent on the area for rubber, tea and jute' and that 'the economic ties could not be severed without serious consequences'. Ovendale writes that Britain's long-term objective in Southeast Asia was 'to improve economic and social conditions' there. How this is compatible with Britain's siphoning off profits from Malayan rubber and tin exports at the expense of the poverty-stricken population is left unexplained. Overall, Ovendale contends, Britain's 'immediate intention' in the region was to 'prevent the spread of communism and to resist Russian expansion'.[29]

An equally disciplined approach is by Robert Jackson who, in a book-length study of the war, also makes no mention of Britain's exploitation of rubber and tin resources for British purposes. Again, Britain was simply resisting communist expansion. 'Even by April 1950, the extent of the communist threat to Malaya was not fully appreciated by the British government', Jackson comments. Things changed, he claims, with the election of Churchill as prime minister in 1951: 'Churchill's shrewd instinct grasped the fact that if Malaya fell under communist domination, the rest of Asia would quickly follow'. Note how this contention, often repeated in the declassified files, is presented as a 'fact'.[30]

Other aspects of the war are dealt with within the official framework. In 1952 a memorandum by the British Defence Secretary stipulated that, from now on, the insurgents – previously usually referred to as 'bandits' – would be officially known as 'communist terrorists' or CTs.[31] Subsequent scholarship concurred. Richard Allen, for example, contrasts the 'CTs . . . as they came to be known' with the Malay and

British security forces, the 'defenders of Malaya', in his term.

Former *Sunday Times* correspondent James Adams notes in his book that since Malaya was a British colony 'responsibility for the conduct of the war fell to the British government'.[32] Saying that Malaya – subjugated by Britain for its own economic ends – was a British 'responsibility' is perhaps like saying that the former East Germany was a Soviet 'responsibility'.

Britain achieved its main aims in Malaya: the insurgents were defeated and, with independence in 1957, British business interests were essentially preserved. Britain handed over formal power at independence to the traditional Malay rulers and fostered a political alliance between the United Malay National Organisation and the Chinese businessmen's Malayan Chinese Association.

At independence, 85 per cent of Malayan export earnings still derived from tin and rubber. Around 70 per cent of company profits were in foreign, mainly British, hands and were largely repatriated. Largely European-owned agency houses controlled 70 per cent of foreign trade and 75 per cent of plantations. Independence hardly changed the extent of foreign control over the economy until the 1960s and 1970s. Even by 1972, 80 per cent of mining, 62 per cent of manufacturing and 58 per cent of construction were foreign-owned, mainly by British companies.[33] The established order had been protected.

17

BRITISH GUIANA: OVERSTEPPING 'DECENT GOVERNMENT'

> To secure desired result some preparation of public opinion seems to be essential [*sic*].
>
> British delegation to the UN, 1953

Ever so occasionally, in the media, there are mentions of the small South American country of Guyana, formerly British Guiana, which gained its independence from Britain in 1966. Almost never mentioned, however, are the events of 1953. They have been excised from history.

When it comes to US interventions in Latin America, a clear pattern is visible: a popular government comes into power with an agenda of addressing poverty and inequality; these priorities threaten the control of resources by US businesses; the government is deemed an agent of international communism; and the US sends troops, or covertly engineers a change in government, to restore 'order' and 'security'. This was essentially the course of events in Guatemala (1954), Brazil (1964), the Dominican Republic (1965), Chile (1973) and Nicaragua (1980s).

But the precedent for this pattern in Latin America was not set by the US, but by Britain. The events of 1953 reveal much about British elites' concerns to order the world according to their commercial interests, and also about their understanding of 'democracy'.

The popular, nationalist threat

In April 1953, the People's Progressive Party (PPP) under Cheddi Jagan won eighteen out of the twenty-four seats in British Guiana's first elections under universal suffrage. But Jagan's programme of social and economic reforms was the wrong type of democracy for British planners – since it threatened control over the territory's resources by British and allied business interests. Britain sent a cruiser, two frigates and 700 troops to its colony, suspended the constitution and overthrew the democratically elected government 133 days after it had assumed office.

If Britain's key interests in Malaya were rubber and tin and in Kenya land, in British Guiana the key resources were sugar and, to a lesser extent, bauxite. Twenty-eight thousand people out of the country's total working population of 100,000 were employed in the sugar industry. About 20 per cent of the population lived on the sugar estates, more than half of them in estate-owned houses. Almost all the sugar cane was grown on seventeen large plantations owned by private companies. One of these – Booker Bros. McConnell – had a controlling interest in the majority of the plantations. The colony's bauxite exports accounted for one fifth of total world production; 90 per cent of the colony's output was in the hands of a single company, the Demerara Bauxite Company, a subsidiary of the Aluminum Company of Canada (ALC). Together, sugar and bauxite accounted for 90 per cent of the country's exports: the country was therefore effectively owned and controlled by Britain in alliance with two transnational companies.

In 1953, Britain had great future plans for the colony. It was seeking to massively increase the extraction of timber and, according to the Governor, a 'great development is also taking place in the gold mining industry and quite recently there has been an upsurge of interest in the search for strategic minerals'. However, to attract the foreign capital to develop these resources required 'that in the coming years conditions in British Guiana should continue to be such as will attract it – conditions political as well as otherwise . . . Nothing must be done which could sap confidence.'[1]

British Guiana's colonial function was to provide cheap raw materials to Britain and other rich nations. Its bauxite provided 85 per cent of the supply for the Canadian aluminium industry, contributing to the large profits (Canadian $29 million in 1951) made by ALC. In turn, Britain secured most of its aluminium supplies from Canada. According to ALC's 1952 company report, a substantial amount of its aluminium shipments were to the 'defence needs' of Britain and the US.[2]

A British government report of 1953 observed with some understatement that:

> The mining companies (mostly Demerara Bauxite Co.) have made profits of approximately £1m a year for the past four years and have distributed £600,000 a year in dividends . . . There may well, therefore, be scope for some increase in mining taxation in the territory.

The Colonial Office later noted that the sugar companies were open to criticism for being ' "big business", very efficiently run, but run for the sole benefit of their owners or shareholders'.[3]

The less fortunate in this state of affairs were those upon whose backs the system functioned. The people of British Guiana endured 'squalor and poverty' in a society with a 'long glaring contrast between rich and poor', the *Manchester Guardian* commented in 1953. An earlier official report described the population as living 'closely crowded in ranges on the verge of collapse, lacking every amenity and frequently almost surrounded by stagnant water'. By 1949 there were 'dilapidated and obsolete ranges, long condemned from all quarters'. These ranges were built by the sugar estates to house the indentured labourers.[4]

The Governor noted:

> The sugar estates are to a considerable extent the crux of the situation . . . It is there that the extremist is so well supported. It is so easy for him to point to the dreadful housing and social conditions which exist (and to ignore the improvements) and compare them with the comfortable quarters and the neat compounds and the recreational facilities of the staff who are predominantly European. It is also easy for him to allege unfair profits being transferred to absentee landlords and to blame, as is done, the British government for the conditions which exist.[5]

It was mainly because Jagan's PPP sought to improve the 'dreadful housing and social conditions' that it was elected to office. The British Commonwealth Relations Office stated that the PPP 'was in fact elected to power on a mildly socialist programme, the implementation of which would have been in general of great value to the territory'. The Colonial Secretary – a key figure in later ordering the overthrow of the government – noted a week after the PPP's electoral triumph that its programme was 'no more extreme' than that of the British Labour Party. 'It contains none of the usual communist aims and it advocates industrial development through the encouragement of foreign capital'.[6]

The Colonial Secretary then magnanimously suggested: 'We should . . . accept the verdict of the electorate'. But Britain would 'take action without delay if [PPP leaders] seek to use their position to further the communist cause', whether elected or not.[7]

In practice Jagan's and the PPP's plans went beyond the acceptable. They called for redistributing resources towards the welfare needs of the workforce, increasing minimum wage levels and health services and strengthening the position of the trade unions. They also urged curbing the exploitation and dominance of the sugar multinational, Bookers, and exposed the sugar companies' privileged position in terms of their access to public funds which bolstered the profits the industry generated and sent abroad. Jagan's worldview was also beyond the pale to the British, correctly noting, for example:

> Present British foreign policy has meant a crushing burden of rearmament and dependence on the dollar areas for food and raw materials, which can be paid for, not by the export of industrial goods to the dollar areas, but only by the continued exploitation of dollar earning raw material, food and mineral resources from Malaya, Africa, British Guiana and other parts of the Colonial Empire. All the so-called development plans for the colonial territories have been devised with this aim in view.[8]

In August 1953, the PPP ministers called for a strike by the sugar workers who were fighting for the Sugar Producers' Association to recognise their union. By 10 September, the Governor of British Guiana was noting that the sugar industry was 'at complete standstill'. Bookers stated that the strike meant 'a loss of profits' and that 'the present situation can only be dealt with effectively by the Colonial Office'. Indeed, 'unless something drastic is done, Bookers will cease to exist as a large firm in five years'.[9]

Although the sugar strike effectively ended, it left its mark and it was clear that the PPP retained the wrong priorities. All in all, the PPP had 'overstepped the limits of what we regard as decent government', one British MP later explained.[10]

On 9 October, the British Governor announced that the constitution was being suspended and the elected ministers were being removed from office. A few hundred British troops landed and three warships remained stationed off the Guianan coast. The Queen signed the order to suspend the constitution and overthrow the government.

British pretexts and reality

British concerns were clear. The Colonial Secretary noted on the day that intervention was decided upon that the PPP had 'completely destroyed the confidence of the business community and all moderate opinion'. Later, he said that Britain 'took action before that further deterioration showed itself in the action of the business community'. He also stated that 'a number of American or overseas firms . . . were already abandoning their projects in British Guiana' and that they 'were very apprehensive about the dangerous political climate'. The danger was that conditions were being created that were 'inimical to investment either domestic or overseas'. Thus the PPP were 'threatening the order of the Colony' and undermining 'its present economic stability'.[11]

In December 1953 the Colonial Secretary again warned of the threat of democracy, noting that if Britain had permitted new elections in British Guiana 'the same party would have been elected again'.[12]

Since overthrowing nationalist leaders who advocate improving the social conditions of the poor is not good public relations, a suitable pretext was necessary. So when the intervention was announced to the Guianan people on 9 October, the Governor stated that Britain was acting 'to prevent Communist subversion of the government'. The elected ministers and the PPP were:

> completely under the control of a communist clique . . .
> Their objective was to turn British Guiana into a totalitarian state subordinate to Moscow and a dangerous platform for extending communist influence in the Western hemisphere.[13]

This public stance was repeated by the man who had previously said in secret correspondence that the PPP programme was 'no more extreme' than his own party's. The Colonial Secretary told the House of Commons that it was all 'part of the deadly design to turn British Guiana into a totalitarian state dominated by communist ideas'. Britain was 'faced with part of the international communist conspiracy'.[14]

The declassified files further give this game away. Britain's delegation to the United Nations cabled the Colonial Secretary a week before the overthrow and stated:

> If our action can be presented as firm step taken to prevent attempt by communist elements to sabotage new and progressive constitution, it will be welcomed by American public and accepted by most United Nations opinion. If on the other hand it is allowed to appear as just another attempt by Britain to stifle a popular nationalist movement... effect can only be bad ... To secure desired result some preparation of public opinion seems to be essential [sic].[15]

The US supported the British attack on British Guiana, saying that it was 'gratified to note that the British government is taking firm action to meet the situation'. The British embassy in Washington declared that the State Department had 'worked in very well with us over this crisis . . . if the Jagans wished to come to this country in order to publicise their case they would not be allowed visas. This goes for any of their buddies too.'[16]

The opposition Labour Party supported the intervention. James Griffiths, the former Colonial Secretary, agreed in the House of Commons with the Governor's statement that the PPP leader's aim 'was to turn British Guiana into a totalitarian state subordinate to Moscow'. Labour leader Clement Attlee also agreed, only questioning whether the government had exhausted all the options before acting; thus Labour accepted Britain's right to overthrow democracy, only disputing its timing.

Griffiths also sympathised with his successor as Colonial Secretary, noting that 'the office is an interesting, exciting, hard and responsible one for we are dealing with 70 million people who are growing up. They are adolescents who are politically immature.'[17]

The subsequent British task was to ensure that business as usual would prevail under conditions of economic stability. The elected government was replaced by one nominated by the Governor, which contained many members who had been defeated candidates in the April elections. Two of the PPP leaders – Cheddi and Janet Jagan – were sentenced to six months' hard labour for violating restriction orders; other leaders were detained without trial for three-month periods.

In a House of Commons debate two weeks after the overthrow of democracy, the Colonial Secretary observed, presumably again with a straight face, that the British Government 'must steadily . . . seek to build up a political system in British Guiana which will give the inhabitants a chance of developing democratic institutions'. Britain would now foster 'some body representing Guianese opinion upon whose advice the Governor may rely' but 'upon whose advice he will not be bound to act in the interim period'.[18]

Eighteen months after the intervention the Governor commented that he needed 'one company of regular troops until representative government has been successfully restored'. The presence of British troops would provide 'a short term insurance against disorders' since 'while political activity is at an enforced standstill it would be rash to dispense with all troops'.[19]

It took until 1964 before Britain's conception of 'representative government' was restored. In the 1957 elections Britain attempted to rig a defeat for Jagan, who remained PPP leader, but unfortunately the wrong party won nine of the fourteen elected seats and Jagan became prime minister once more. Still under Jagan's leadership, the PPP also won the 1961 elections. Beginning the following year, however, the CIA, operating in the country with British permission, helped finance a destabilisation campaign against the Jagan government, which culminated in a general strike beginning in April 1963. CIA agents gave advice to local union leaders on how to organise and sustain the strike, and provided funds and food supplies to keep the strikers going. At least $1 million is thought to have been spent on toppling the democratically elected government.[20]

Former CIA agent Philip Agee wrote that the 1964 election victory of Jagan's opponent, Forbes Burnham, was 'largely due to CIA operations over the past five years to strengthen the anti-Jagan trade unions'.[21] In these elections, however, the PPP remained the largest party and won twenty-four out of fifty-three seats. But the constitution had been amended by Britain to a system of proportional representation, so that a rival coalition grouping under the more acceptable leadership of Forbes Burnham could take power.

Britain had refused to grant independence to British Guiana if Jagan's PPP were to gain power. With the PPP removed from office after the 1964 elections, British Guiana was finally granted independence in 1966. The sugar transnational Bookers was assured of 'a remarkable degree of control over the economy, both through its dominant position in the sugar industry and through its interests in fisheries, cattle, timber, insurance, advertising and retail commerce'.[22]

PART IV

THE MASS PRODUCTION OF IGNORANCE

Tony Blair famously told the Labour party conference in 2001: 'I tell you if Rwanda happened again today as it did in 1994, when a million people were slaughtered in cold blood, we would have a moral duty to act.'[1]

Several of the media reported this the following day. But what Blair and journalists failed to mention was that Britain *contributed* to the slaughter in 1994. As a permanent member of the UN Security Council, Britain not only eschewed its obligations in this role but deliberately obstructed the deployment of UN troops that could have prevented the genocide.

This story has been buried, with only a minuscule number of mentions in the mainstream media. It may as well never have happened. The public has little way of knowing about it and British political leaders have not been held to account. What kind of media and political culture is it that deems the government's contribution to the slaughter of a million people unworthy of mention?

But Rwanda is just one example. In chapter 20, I tell the story of how Britain helped the Indonesian army slaughter a million people in 1965. London's aid was direct and multi-faceted; revealed in declassified files now publicly available. But this story – which I broke in 1996 – has been consigned to the memory hole. There are only one or two mentions in the mainstream media. It didn't happen.

Horrible British foreign policies are routinely either ignored (virtually) completely in mainstream media and academia, or reported but given ideological treatment that conforms to elite priorities. In my view, there exists an ideological system that prevents the public seeing the reality of Britain's role in the world – another key aspect of the single-ideology totalitarian state. It is not a conspiracy; rather, it works by journalists and academics *internalising* values, accepted wisdom and styles of reporting. Neither is the system monolithic. There is some space for dissent and there are several outstanding, independent journalists in the mainstream. But major criticism of government policy and dissent is infrequent and tends to occur only at the margins and within narrow limits. It amounts to a *system*, because it works across the mainstream media (and academia) in very visible ways.

People are just not informed about this country's real role in the world. They are provided with systematically distorted views and information about the past and the present that makes it easier for elites to pursue policies in their interests and often against the public interest.

18

ETHICAL FOREIGN POLICIES AND OTHER MYTHS

Like the Winds of Change speech that told Britain empire was over, this one will stand as a moment British politics became vigorously, unashamedly, social democratic. The day it became missionary and almost Swedish in pursuit of universal justice.

The *Guardian*'s Polly Toynbee, on Tony Blair's speech to the Labour party conference, October 2001

Contributing to genocide in Rwanda

In the hundreds of media articles on the 1994 Rwanda genocide, there is barely a mention of Britain being a permanent member of the UN security council and in any way responsible for what happened. I recounted something of Britain's role in my previous book, *The Great Deception*, so I will not repeat everything here.[2] Since then, however, another book, by Linda Melvern, an investigative journalist, confirms the quite terrible British, and US, role.[3]

After the killings began in early April 1994, the UN security council, instead of beefing up its peace mission in the country and giving it a stronger mandate to intervene, decided to reduce the troop presence from 2,500 to 270. This decision sent a green light to those who had planned the genocide showing that the UN would not intervene. A small UN military force arrived merely to rescue expats, and then left. Belgium's senior army officer in the UN peace mission believed that if this force had not been pulled out, the killing could have been stopped. Canadian general Romeo Dallaire, who commanded the UN force in Rwanda, later said that this evacuation showed 'inexcusable apathy by the sovereign states that made up the UN, that is completely beyond comprehension and moral acceptability'.

It was Britain's ambassador to the UN, Sir David Hannay, who proposed that the UN pull out its force; the US agreed. According to Melvern, it was left to the Nigerian ambassador, Ibrahim Gambari, to point out that tens of thousands of civilians were dying at the time. Gambari also pleaded with the security council to reinforce the UN presence. But both the US and Britain objected, suggesting that only a token force should be left behind – this became the 270 personnel.

By chance the Rwandan government was sitting on the security council at the time, as one of the ten non-permanent members. So British and US indifference and their policy of reducing the UN force, as expressed in the security council, was reported back to those directing the genocide in Rwanda. Melvern notes that 'confident of no significant international opposition, it was decided to push ahead with further "pacification" in the south of the country'. This led to tens of thousands more murders.

General Dallaire, who had pleaded for reinforcements, complained that:

> My force was standing knee deep in mutilated bodies, surrounded by the guttural moans of dying people, looking into the eyes of dying children bleeding to death with their wounds burning in the sun and being invaded by maggots and flies. I found myself walking through

villages where the only sign of life was a goat, or a chicken, or a songbird, as all the people were dead, their bodies being eaten by voracious packs of wild dogs.

By May 1994, with certainly tens of thousands and perhaps hundreds of thousands already dead, there was another UN proposal – to despatch 5,500 troops to help stop the massacres. This deployment was delayed by pressure, mainly from the US ambassador, but with strong support from Britain. Dallaire believes that if these troops had been speedily deployed, tens of thousands more lives could have been saved. But the US and Britain argued that before these troops went in, there needed to be a ceasefire in Rwanda, a quite insane suggestion given that one side was massacring innocent civilians. The US also ensured that this plan was watered down so that troops would have no mandate for using force to end the massacres.

Britain and the US also refused to provide the military airlift capability for the African states who were offering troops for this force. The RAF, for example, had plenty of transport aircraft that could have been deployed. Eventually, with delays continuing and thousands being killed by the day, Britain offered a measly fifty trucks. Lynda Chalker, then minister for overseas development, visited Dallaire in Rwanda in July. He gave her his list of requirements at the same time as noting that 'I was up to my knees in bodies by then.' The fifty trucks had still not yet materialised. Later, on BBC2's *Newsnight*, Chalker blamed Dallaire's lack of resources on 'the UN' which 'ought to get its procurement right'.

Britain also went out of its way to ensure that the UN did not use the word 'genocide' to describe the slaughter. Accepting that genocide was occurring would have obliged states to 'prevent and punish' those guilty under the terms of the Geneva Convention. In late April 1994, Britain, along with the US and China, secured a security council resolution that rejected the use of the term 'genocide'. This resolution was drafted by the British.

The Czech republic's ambassador to the UN, Karel Kovanda, confronted the security council about the fact of genocide at this time. He said that talking about withdrawing peacekeepers and securing a ceasefire was 'rather like wanting Hitler to reach a ceasefire with the Jews'. There were objections to his comments, Kovanda said, and British and US diplomats quietly told him that on no account was he to use such inflammatory language outside the security council.

A July 1994 resolution spoke simply of 'possible acts of genocide' and other security council documents used similarly restrained language. A year after the slaughter, the British Foreign Office sent a letter to an international inquiry saying that it still did not accept the term genocide. It said that it saw a discussion about whether the massacres constituted genocide as 'sterile'.

Journalist Linda Melvern was told by UN Secretary General Boutros Boutros-Ghali that during the genocide he had had individual private meetings with the British and US ambassadors to the UN (the US ambassador was Madeleine Albright, who went on to become Clinton's Secretary of State). Boutros-Ghali urged both of them to help stop the killing but said their reaction was: 'Come on, Boutros, relax . . . Don't put us in a difficult position . . . the mood is not for intervention, you will obtain nothing . . . we will not move.'

Let me summarise the British government's contribution to the genocide in Rwanda. Britain used its diplomatic weight to reduce severely a UN force that, according to military officers on the ground, could have prevented the killings. It then helped ensure the delay of other plans for intervention, which sent a direct green light to the murderers in Rwanda to continue. Britain also refused to provide the capability for other states to intervene, while blaming the lack of such capability on the UN. Throughout, Britain helped ensure that the UN did not use the word 'genocide' so the UN would not act, using diplomatic pressure on others to ensure this did not happen. British officials went out of their way to promote these policies and rebuffed personal pleas to stop the killings from the UN Secretary General and the commander of the UN force.

All this information is publicly available. We do not need to look across the Atlantic to think of trials of those who have acquiesced in genocide. There is a long list of British policy-makers who are to some degree responsible – Prime Minister John Major, Foreign Secretary Douglas Hurd, Defence Secretary Malcolm Rifkind and Overseas Development Minister Lynda Chalker foremost among them. But these people are being protected by the silence of the media and academia as well as the extreme lack of accountability in the political system.

Linda Melvern notes that, especially in the early stages of the genocide, the press insisted on reporting events as 'chaos and anarchy', not a systematic campaign well planned in advance by Hutu extremists. In her view, 'the media's failure to report that genocide was taking place, and thereby generate public pressure for something to be done to stop it, contributed to international indifference and inaction, and possibly to the crime itself'.

There was only one press article I could find that went into any detail on Britain's role on the security council. It noted that Britain's ambassador at the UN was still dealing regularly with the ambassador of the government engaged in state-sponsored genocide.[4]

Neither did the mother of parliaments attempt to address the British role in genocide – either at the time, or since. A debate in the House of Commons did not take place until nearly two months after the slaughter began. According to Melvern, 'the Labour party waited until May before putting pressure on the government to act, and then only because Oxfam telephoned the office of David Clark, shadow secretary of state for defence'.

Ethical foreign policies

Even the government's contribution to something as massive as the slaughter of a million people can be buried across the entire mainstream political culture. With this background, the prospects for reporting accurately on the policies of New Labour were not great. But if anything, the media has sunk to new depths.

There was previously much comment in the media on the government's claim to be pursuing an 'ethical' dimension to foreign policy. But there was a usual pattern to this comment. The starting point was accepting that the government was serious about wanting to promote an 'ethical foreign policy'. In many articles this term was used without quotation marks, suggesting that it actually existed. Most articles then went on to say that in one or two 'hard cases' (for example, arms exports to Indonesia), the government was failing to live up to its rhetoric, with the conclusion that it was guilty of double standards. Another common conclusion was that promoting the 'ethical foreign policy' was not 'practical' given Britain's other policies, such as arms exports. Again, the commitment to promoting such a policy is not questioned, while one or two policies that might deviate from this lofty goal showed the 'exception' to the rule. There were some deviations from this pattern of reporting, but not many.

It is interesting that journalists often chose arms exports to Indonesia to show Britain's 'double standards'. Yet in policy towards Indonesia, Britain has been dogged in pursuing a single standard for thirty years – support to Jakarta during gross repression in Indonesia and mass murder in East Timor. Arms exports are just one facet of this basic support. However, even pointing out this example gives the impression of an unethical exception to an ethical rule, whereas Britain actually supports repressive regimes across the world as a matter of course, selling arms to them in the process, as noted in several other chapters in this book.

The reality is that Britain clearly has a generally unethical foreign policy, easily seen if we peer even slightly beneath the veil. The hard task is to spot the ethical bits. The idea that the government has been, or ever seriously intended to be, promoting an 'ethical foreign policy' is so laughable that it is seriously hard to address the point. But let us try to do so, nonetheless.

The 'ethical dimension' to foreign policy announced by New Labour was simply a government fabrication, surely plain for anyone to see. 'Anyone' that is, except virtually the entire mainstream media, who, although often criticising whether it was being fully implemented, both played along with the fabrication and also played it up, dubbing it the 'ethical foreign policy' (the government has never used this term; it was invented by the media). As a construct of New Labour's propagandists and the media, it provides an interesting example of how propaganda is manufactured in the British ideological system.

One only needed to read Foreign Secretary Robin Cook's speech in July 1997, a few weeks after the election victory, where he outlined this 'ethical dimension'. The speech is very low key in content. Of the 'twelve-point plan' of exceedingly minor changes, one way of promoting an 'ethical dimension' was, Cook said, to continue sanctions against Iraq! (One might think this point alone would have alerted journalists to how the government understood 'ethical'.) Other points included condemning gross human rights abusers (naming only Nigeria), refusing to supply military equipment to some regimes and reviewing the British military training policy.[5]

Cook's points were consistent with Labour's election manifesto, and mainly continued the policies of the Major government. In three years as shadow Foreign Secretary until the election victory, Cook gave no hint of wanting to pursue an 'ethical dimension' to foreign policy. When the time came, the government simply played to the public, trying to depict themselves as different from the Tories, and more moral. Labour propagandists deliberately blew up Cook's speech to emphasise a mythical radical break with the past.[6]

This invention was taken seriously throughout the media. The *Financial Times* referred to 'the new doctrine'. A leading liberal commentator, John Lloyd, said it was 'one of the boldest initiatives taken by a major state to shift foreign policy on to new tracks'.[7]

The government played along with the construct of an 'ethical foreign policy' for a while, since it allowed it to bask beneath a cloak of morality while promoting, with minor exceptions, the same policies as the previous government. But it soon became a political liability, with simply too many commentators pointing out 'exceptions' to where Britain departed from otherwise promoting democracy, human rights and peace on Earth ('double standards'). The totalitarian mind is apt not to tolerate any criticism at all; and even New Labour propagandists were not able to hide completely some of their unethical policies, even with a media willing to be generally deluded.

The 'ethical dimension' to foreign policy that was born in July 1997 died a death in September 2000, when the government abandoned it. This abandonment was extraordinary. The *Guardian* announced on 4 September 2000 that 'Labour's ethical foreign policy . . . is to be dropped for the next general election'. It said that the policy 'is said to have become a "millstone" around the neck of the foreign secretary'. A 32-page document of the party's national policy forum 'fails to mention the ethical foreign policy or ethical dimension'.[8]

From the perspective of the mainstream media, which had viewed the 'ethical foreign policy' as official policy, the government's abandonment of it should surely have been newsworthy. Considering that every Labour minister from Blair downwards over the past three years had claimed that Labour was promoting the highest moral principles across all its policies, now suddenly saying this was no longer on, was surely worthy of note. But not so. There was barely a murmur of discussion in the media. Under the media's previous framing, the government was saying that from now on, ethics did not matter. So what? Saddam Hussein's journalists would have been proud.

Labour's announcement is new in modern democracy. There is surely no other case of a government explicitly serving notice that it will *not* promote ethical policies. Even though the government has made this announcement, its propaganda continues and minister after minister continues to express commitment to the highest values, as normal. The media continues to take this seriously, and has not noticed that the game is over. The ideological system, at root, is really very crude.

The abandonment of the 'ethical dimension' may have pleased many in the media and political class who do not want Britain to promote this ethical nonsense anyway. For example, the editors of the *Independent on Sunday* noted shortly after Cook's original speech that it would be 'welcome' if British officials thought about the human rights consequences of their actions, 'but Foreign Secretaries need to take care'. 'An unstintingly ethical approach to foreign affairs would forbid trade with China and make negotiation with [Congo president] Laurent Kabila tricky; yet both are necessary, for the sake of British interests.'[9]

A more extreme view came from Bruce Anderson, writing in the *Spectator*, who noted that 'humanitarian considerations should not be a major priority' in guiding British policy towards Kosovo. The reason was that no national interests were at stake as they were in, say, 1939. 'We fought Hitler because he was a threat to Britain', Anderson notes; 'we did not declare war against Hitler because he was a bloodstained dictator'.[10]

Eradicating poverty (from the mind)

In previous chapters I have looked at the media's ideological treatment of British foreign policy in the bombing of Yugoslavia and Afghanistan, and in the Israel–Palestine conflict. Let us consider briefly some other cases of how the media is in effect keeping the public in the dark.

Global poverty has not been eradicated from the world, but it has been largely eradicated from public view. The Glasgow

University Media Group (GUMG) has recently conducted several analyses of media reporting on the developing world. It concludes that:

> Audiences are misinformed about the developing world because of the low level of explanations and context which is given in television reporting and because some explanations which are present are partial and informed by what might be termed 'post-colonial' beliefs.

In particular, little effort is made to explain the background to conflicts, with struggles often portrayed simply as the result of 'tribal passions'. Television audiences therefore 'have in general very little understanding of events in the developing world or of major international institutions or relationships', such as the World Bank and the IMF. Much reporting promotes the view of 'the innate faults of Africans'.

The GUMG's research with BBC journalists shows that explaining the link between those conflicts and Northern countries' policies can produce a distinct change in the understanding and attitudes of audiences.[11] This is precisely the point: people appear more interested in foreign news stories when there is a link with Britain. But even though there is a media incentive to provide this link, it still rarely happens.

The reality is that British governments bear significant responsibility for global poverty – not only as a former colonial power that shaped many of the current unjust structures, but in their championing of a world trade system and economic ideology that enriches the few and impoverishes many more; in exporting arms that contribute to repression and worsen conflict; in supporting repressive regimes; and in undermining many popular, democratic political forces that try to address poverty.

Yet I do not think I have ever seen a media article that mentions that Britain might in some way systematically contribute to poverty in the world. Is this not extraordinary? Britain's partial responsibility for maintaining and deepening poverty globally is unmentionable.

I believe it is especially extraordinary, since poverty is surely the dominating fact of our world. One half of our species – over two and a half billion people – lives on $2 a day; poverty by any measure. Yet the public in Northern countries is largely protected even from *seeing* this everyday poverty, let alone the idea that their government might bear any responsibility for it. In other words, the single most important issue in today's world is kept from proper public understanding.

Consider how many wildlife programmes there are set in Kenya. The BBC must have a special deal with British Airways to Nairobi. And we should all by now have expert knowledge of the mating habits of cheetahs. But television audiences will know nothing of human poverty in Kenya, even though many of the political and economic structures maintaining it were shaped by the British. And they must know almost nothing about the massive human rights atrocities committed by British forces in Kenya in the 1950s, for which Kenyans are currently seeking justice through the British courts (see chapter 15).

One area where Britain and other Northern countries are sometimes criticised in the media is in 'neglecting' or 'forgetting' Africa. There is some truth in this, especially concerning the reduction of aid and the marginalisation of Africa from international decision-making. But the sense, and often overt message, behind these articles is that Britain is not *engaged enough* in Africa, as though more of its policies are needed; if only we paid them more attention, they would be better off. The opposite is the case. The belief that greater Western engagement in Africa is a solution is a staggering conclusion to reach after hundreds of years of Western impoverishment of poor countries. How much faith can be left that Western countries will promote anything short of further misery in the areas of the world where they seriously engage?

Britain is in fact already heavily engaged in Africa; its economic interventionism has been stepped up under New Labour. It is a leading champion of rewriting the rules of the global economy to benefit transnational business and to lock in

African countries to promote further 'neo-liberal' economic strategies which have already had devastating consequences in poor countries. The basic problem is that Britain is too engaged in Africa – it would be more useful to remove the British boot from the poor countries' necks, and conduct a withdrawal.

In chapter 9, I outlined the government's pursuit of world-wide economic 'liberalisation', especially through the WTO. This is already having enormous impact, often increasing poverty and inequality, with matters likely to get worse. It is not difficult to detect this strategy of promoting a fundamental reshaping of the global economy; reading ministerial speeches is a good starting point. There is little that is covert about government policy; ministers are specifically saying what their intentions are.

Yet this story is simply not covered in the media. Rather, the line continues to be peddled that the government is committed to development, that Clare Short is a staunch defender of the poor and that the government has a jolly good record on debt relief and so on. With no effective scrutiny of government policy, the media is surely guilty here – as in the Rwanda genocide, according to Linda Melvern noted above – of helping to exacerbate human misery.

The one international trade policy that receives regular media coverage is the protectionist barriers raised by the EU to restrict poor countries' key exports from reaching EU markets. This happens to be the one major trade policy the British elite wants to change, since removing EU trade barriers will make it easier to force developing countries to remove theirs, thus securing Western access to their markets. There are other Northern trade policies that have far greater impact on the poor and that developing countries want to change – such as actually being able to protect and subsidise their infant industries. However, the British elite is completely opposed to these, and they are largely ignored in the media.

The only stories in the media that criticise reporting on the developing world are those saying that coverage is dramatically falling. This is true, but misses the more important point. Media coverage of the developing world is so distorted, and plays so much into the hands of elite priorities, that it may well be better to have less coverage.

Third World development issues provide a good example of how the media parrots the government's line and generally accepts its stated aims as true. A *Guardian* editorial in November 1997, for example, begins: 'The government's new white paper on international development was presented yesterday by Clare Short with genuine commitment to the world's poor.' It notes that the first section of the White Paper 'lays out the dimensions of the problem facing the world with unusual clarity: it could serve as a study text for anyone – from sixth former to journalist trying to understand what development is all about'.[12]

It is comforting to note that *Guardian* journalists might be understanding 'what development is all about' by reading the government's view. Strangely, that view does not include noting that the government is itself a major part of the problem. And how, exactly, is the *Guardian* convinced, as stated in its first line, that the government has a 'genuine commitment to the world's poor'? Simply because the government has said it?

Similarly, another article begins: 'Clare Short, the international development secretary, will announce plans today for a wide-ranging autumn white paper on managing globalisation as the centrepiece of a government strategy to ensure that the world's poor benefit from economic changes'. The article proceeds to offer nothing to counter this grand assertion. Instead, it quotes Short rubbishing protectionism and refers blandly to the government's desire for new 'rules on global investment'. Readers are given no sense that these new rules might just not quite work to the advantage of the poor.[13]

Reporting more generally sometimes reaches North Korean levels of wonderment at our leaders' commitment to high values. Consider the *Guardian*'s Polly Toynbee on Blair's speech at the October 2001 Labour party conference, outlining a vision of a 'world acting as a community'. The speech 'will stand', she wrote, 'as a moment British politics became vigorously, unashamedly, social democratic. The day it became missionary and almost Swedish in pursuit of universal justice'. Toynbee mentioned Blair's 'noble sentiments for a new world order', and that he declared 'war on poverty, tyranny and injustice while barely using the word "war" at all'. The article was entitled: 'He promised to take on the world. And I believed him'.[14]

Similarly, the *Guardian*'s Hugo Young has asserted that Blair's vision of intervention for humanitarian purposes extends to 'anywhere the world might be made a better place by the benign intervention of a good, stable, rich and militarily capable country like Britain'. Blair's is a 'vision of the moralist', according to Young, who then goes on to criticise the Blair commitment to such military humanitarianism as 'terrifyingly naive'.[15] Thus our leaders are viewed as benign and sincere in their commitment to the highest values; they just won't in practice be able to achieve these lofty goals. This ridiculous view is the usual framing of foreign policy throughout the British ideological system.

Another key elite strategy is to retain nuclear weapons. Media discussion on nuclear weapons tends to be confined to the 'costs' of Trident and debates on the number of warheads on each missile. Yet the real story is the government's viewing these weapons for war-fighting purposes, and using them to threaten other states, as discussed in chapter 3. These issues have been largely removed from the list of publicly acceptable thoughts. When Defence Secretary Geoff Hoon said that Britain would nuke non-nuclear states if we were attacked with non-conventional weapons, it raised only a murmur in the media and then was quietly forgotten. Why should our blowing a few nations to smithereens matter?

But with that outrage does the mainstream media condemn other states' attempts to acquire nuclear weapons! One *Financial Times* editorial begins: 'India's nuclear test yesterday is dangerous and foolish in equal proportion.' Countries should 'unite in deploring India's test in the strongest terms', while India should sign the test ban treaty and participate fully 'in efforts to combat proliferation'.[16] Only we, the guardians of 'world order' and defenders of civilisation, are accorded the right to possess the most devastating weapons, presumably since only we can then use them to carry out our noble mission.

The public could also be forgiven for not knowing that Britain is directly aiding repression in the Gulf, through consistent political support to favoured despots together with military training, arms and trade deals. There is virtual complete silence on the Gulf states' horrible human rights records, especially that of our key ally, Saudi Arabia. It is well-understood, following the *Death of a Princess* episode – when Saudi Arabia complained to the government about British television screening a documentary showing the execution of a Saudi princess – that the Saudis will not tolerate any criticism of their regime. The government obliges and the media, apparently, follows this, with a nod and wink. Virtually complete silence also surrounds Britain's close military, intelligence and trade relations with regimes in Bahrain, Oman and Kuwait, whose special relationships with London form a key pillar of this country's role in the world.

Across the board, the crimes of Britain's allies tend to be downplayed or buried, while those of its enemies are raised up, analysed in detail and condemned. The demonisation of Milosevic and Mugabe compares to coverage bordering on apologia for Putin and often Sharon. Iraq's persecution of the Kurds is far better known than our ally Turkey's, which has been far worse in recent years. One thing preventing public understanding of the world's human rights abuses is the fact that they are often committed by regimes allied to Britain – this means they are in effect regularly out of bounds to serious media enquiry.

When the human rights abuses – committed on such a scale as to amount to state terrorism – of allied states such as Russia,

Israel and Turkey are reported, the British role in condoning or effectively supporting them tends to be omitted or downplayed. The idea that British policy can be partly responsible for such atrocities occurring – through the diplomatic, economic and military support we provide to the perpetrators – is heretical in the mainstream. This is all the more remarkable during a supposed 'war against terrorism' where our leaders profess their commitment to ridding the world of this evil scourge. They could do this more easily by removing their support for the world's most significant sponsors of terrorism – state governments such as those just mentioned. It is surely not hard to spot this, but I have yet to see a mention anywhere in the mainstream that London just might have a role in terrorism other than one that is on the side of the angels.

Britain has been widely praised for supporting the establishment of an international criminal court (ICC) that came into being in July 2002 and that will prosecute future war criminals. The media, like the government, has regularly criticised the US' blatant obstruction of the ICC and its refusal to sign the treaty. But how else have the media dealt with the issue of war crimes?

In the huge coverage of the trial of Slobodan Milosevic in The Hague, I have seen no mention of the rather obvious parallel of also trying NATO leaders for war crimes. This is despite the various war crimes and violations of international humanitarian law committed in the attack on Yugoslavia's civilian infrastructure, as noted in chapter 6. Media coverage of these crimes was sparse and almost universally dismissive. Neither was there previously much coverage of war crimes committed in the 1991 Gulf war against Iraq. Nor have I seen coverage of the possible indictment of US and British leaders for crimes against humanity from continuing sanctions against Iraq (the idea is inconceivable).

War crimes and violations of international humanitarian law have become permanent features of the Anglo-American wars at the turn of the millennium. Yet each time they receive little or no attention, surely a staggering indictment of the mainstream media. Indeed, in the mainstream media it is basically an oxymoron to say that Britain can commit war crimes, such is the extent of our benevolence.

Despite the evidence presented in this chapter, it is still possible for the *New Statesman*'s political correspondent, Steve Richards, to write that 'in my view, it is a myth that the government enjoys a good press'. He notes the 'instinctive even-handedness' of those writing for the liberal press. This is even-handedness between the Tories and Labour – the media definition of 'objective', but that in reality means working within the consensus among the elite.[17]

19

THE MEDIA'S PROPAGANDA ROLE

The news is not a neutral and natural phenomenon; it
is rather the manufactured production of ideology.
Glasgow University Media Group

As several chapters in this book show, Britain's mainstream
media provide critical support for the elite's promotion of
foreign policy. This chapter looks at the functioning of the
media in a little more detail. Even though it is possible to
express almost any view somewhere in a very diverse variety of
media, there is a strong tendency to favour certain views over
others, and on most issues there is a consensus within the
mainstream. There is only a small space in the mainstream for
alternative views that fall outside this consensus. There are
certainly some outstanding journalists working in the
mainstream media, such as the *Independent*'s Robert Fisk, the
Guardian's Jonathan Steele and Richard Norton-Taylor and
independent journalists like John Pilger and George Monbiot
who get regularly published in the mainstream. But these are
exceptions; only a few journalists, in my view, are able to report
consistently independently and challenge the consensus view.

The political bias of the different media is not the issue; the mainstream media generally supports elite strategies across the political spectrum. I believe that mainstream academic study of foreign policy is even more disciplined than the mainstream media in its support of that policy. What exists overall is an ideological system working to support elite interests.

Edward Said's description of how the ideological system, and consensus, works in the US is relevant here:

> The simplest and, I think, the most accurate way of characterising it is to say that it sets limits and maintains pressures. It does not dictate content, and it does not mechanically reflect a certain class or economic group's interests. We must think of it as drawing invisible lines beyond which a reporter or commentator does not feel it necessary to go. Thus the notion that American military power might be used for malevolent purposes is relatively impossible within the consensus, just as the idea that America is a force for good in the world is routine and normal.[1]

We might say the same about Britain in the British media.

Several media analysts have long shown this ideological function. One leading academic, Brian McNair, of Stirling University, concludes in a major study:

> On the basis of the evidence gained by content analysts over a period of more than twenty years, we can state with some confidence that the news media of a particular society – press and broadcasting – tend to construct accounts of events which are structured and framed by the dominant values and interests of that society, and to marginalise (if not necessarily exclude) alternative accounts. In this sense, the evidence supports the materialist thesis that there is a link between the power structure of a society and its journalistic output; that journalism is part of a stratified social system; part of the apparatus by which that system is presented to its members in terms with which they can be

persuaded to live.[2]

The news produced by the media is partly determined by their economic structure. The most influential mainstream media outlets – the national newspapers and television – are mainly large corporations in the business of maximising profits. It is obvious that they will have a tendency to be less than challenging to business and the corporate system or have an institutional interest in promoting alternatives. Four corporations control 90 per cent of the British press; a handful control the commercial broadcasting organisations. How news is made, and what the news is, increasingly takes place within a fiercely competitive market. Stories have to attract audiences to sell to advertisers in competition with soap operas and game shows.[3]

The Royal Commission on the Press stated as far back as 1947–49 that the press was failing adequately to inform the public because it was a product of the market, noting that 'the failure of the press to keep pace with the requirements of society is attributable largely to the plain fact that an industry that lives by the sale of its products must give the public what the public will buy'.[4]

The *Guardian*'s Nick Davies has written that the demand for investigative journalism 'is being smothered by the creeping commercialism of our profession'. 'Marketing experts have rewritten news values so that it is now commonplace for news editors to demand a particular story in order to appeal to some new target group in the market place.'[5]

Elements of media distortion

Let us turn to some of the specific ways in which media reporting distorts the reality of Britain's role in the world. The major ways include:

- by not reporting some policies at all (that is, by setting the agenda of what is important and what is not)

- by framing discussion within narrow parameters
- by ignoring relevant history
- by parroting, and failing to counter, elite explanations.

One of the ways in which discussion is often framed is by giving equal balance to pro-government and (usually only mildly) critical of government views. The voices critical of government that appear in the media tend to be drawn from within the mainstream, such as opposition politicians and middle-of-the road NGOs and academics. Giving equal balance to such views implies both are equally valid and simply a question of 'perception', and provides the illusion of 'objectivity'. The reality is that, often, one of the views is straightforward government propaganda while the other is the most mild criticism possible.

The media also has an important function in labelling opponents and categorising behaviour as 'deviant', including by scapegoating vulnerable groups in society for social or political crises, like refugees and asylum seekers. A leading media analyst, James Curran, notes that 'the modern mass media in Britain now perform many of the integrative functions of the church in the middle ages'. The media and the Church engage in very similar ideological work, especially in stigmatising 'outsiders' – such as drug addicts and trade union militants – and in branding dissenters as virtual 'infidels'. The parallel is with the Church's medieval function of hunting down and parading witches in order to protect the established order. The mass media have assumed the role of the Church in interpreting and making sense of the world to the mass public, legitimising the current social system and order.[6]

A major role of the media is in deciding what is important (what gets covered) and what isn't (which is often buried completely). In the 'buried' camp can be 'big' stories like British complicity in slaughters in Rwanda and Indonesia. In the 'covered' camp can come many stories of political tittle-tattle like intra-party squabbles, not to mention pure irrelevancies

377

like Posh and Becks. The system works by marginalising unwanted views or facts, however 'big'. The only issue regularly addressed in some of the mainstream media highlighting that Britain might depart from pursuing otherwise ethical foreign policies relates to arms exports. Even here, reporting takes place within very narrow limits, as discussed in the previous chapter.

The mainstream media often give the appearance of making trouble for politicians, sometimes posing toughish questions and following up stories, but usually on only the minor issues, while ignoring bigger ones. Here, the media play the same game as the political elite – both helping to ensure that many real issues are avoided altogether.

Thus 'gaffes' by ministers can get endless coverage, whereas policies pursued by them often receive none. The media seemed to love reporting Clare Short's comments about the people of Montserrat asking for 'golden elephants' from the British government in aid following the volcanic eruption there. They have failed to show any vigour – at any time – in reporting Short's vision for the future of the global economy.

The *framing* of discussion on issues is critical in setting the boundaries of debate. The programme *Question Time* is a microcosm of how the media works here. Previously, the format was always four people answering questions from the audience – a representative of each of the three largest parties, plus one other, such as a businessman or academic. No seriously critical voices appeared. The format recently changed to five people, usually adding a 'non-political' person such as an entertainer. Again, rarely are critical voices invited. If they are, it is so rare that their views can end up sounding ridiculous in comparison with the 'normal' and 'balanced' views of the other panellists. It is acceptable for *Question Time* panellists to criticise *each other* from within the elite consensus but not for anyone to criticise *all* of them from outside that consensus.

Question Time highlights that a major aspect of the ideological system is restricting debate to the best way of *managing the existing system* and excluding – or marginalising –

the possibility of alternatives. For example, the choice for postwar economic policy has been presented as between Keynesianism and monetarism. In foreign policy, the choice has simply been presented as whether Labour or Conservative should manage the same set of policies within the single ideology, outlined in chapter 13. Major alternatives are rarely presented in the media, and thus become largely inconceivable.

John Birt, Director General of the BBC, has said:

> The BBC fosters a rumbustious, vigorous and informed democracy. We strain to ensure that all voices are heard, however uncomfortable, that they are given a fair hearing and are tested. In recent times we have seen the collapse of deference.[7]

If John Birt really believes this, then I apologise for saying that I think he needs serious medical attention. The evidence is overwhelming that BBC and commercial television news report on Britain's foreign policy in ways that resemble straightforward state propaganda organs. Although by no means directed by the state, their output might as well be; it is not even subtle. BBC, ITV and Channel 5 news simply report nothing seriously critical on British foreign policy; the exception is the odd report on Channel 4 news. Television news – the source of most people's information – provides the most extreme media distortion of all the examples covered in the previous chapter, playing an even greater ideological function than the press.

The role of TV news has been well analysed by the Glasgow University Media Group. Its conclusions have been that 'the news is not a neutral and natural phenomenon; it is rather the manufactured production of ideology'; and that television news is 'a sequence of socially manufactured messages which carry many of the culturally dominant assumptions of our society'. On issues where the state is very sensitive, such as Northern Ireland, it notes that 'the news can become almost one-dimensional – alternatives are reduced to fragments or disappear altogether'.[8] This is certainly true of coverage of Britain's role in the world, in my view.

The concept of 'basic benevolence'

The ideological system promotes one key concept that underpins everything else – the idea of Britain's *basic benevolence*. Mainstream reporting and analysis usually actively promotes, or at least does not challenge, the idea that Britain promotes high principles – democracy, peace, human rights and development – in its foreign policy. Criticism of foreign policies is certainly possible, and normal, but within narrow limits which show 'exceptions' to, or 'mistakes' in, promoting the rule of basic benevolence. Government statements on its always noble intentions are invariably taken seriously and rarely even challenged, let alone ridiculed. These assumptions and ways of reporting are very deep-rooted.

Thus *Guardian* editors can write of 'Britain's reputation as both a respecter and champion of human rights'. One of its regular columnists can write that 'the foreign policies of democratic states, beyond the basic requirement of ensuring physical security, are now based firmly on two pillars – trade advantage and human rights'. In their book on the New Labour government, two *Guardian* writers can refer to Blair as 'a high minded champion of human rights'. Similarly, an academic can write of 'Britain's commitment to third world development' – a fact, requiring no justification. The list could go on, and cover the entire mainstream.[9]

Indeed, it is *only* we who are benevolent. As the *New Statesman*'s John Lloyd has written: 'the defence of human rights – or more accurately, the aggressive promotion of human rights in an arena, such as Kosovo, where they are being brutalised – is a posture confined to the rich and secure world'.[10]

Beneath this overarching concept of basic benevolence stands a set of pillars – key strategies promoted by the elite that are assumed to contribute to Britain's benevolent role in the world and promotion of high principles. These strategies make up the single ideology on which there is consensus across the elite, as outlined in chapter 13 – such as strong support for the US, in the context of a special relationship, promotion of global economic 'liberalisation', support for key elites, and a strong military intervention capability. Reporting and analysis that fall outside this construct – and certainly that directly challenge it – will tend to get excluded.

The ideological system gears into particular action during war, providing justification for the government's resort to force and backing its (always noble) aims. In war, the public is in effect actively mobilised by the various components of the elite in support of state policy. Television news functions even more extremely ideologically at these times, in practice usually abandoning any pretence of objectivity and acting simply as the mouthpiece of the state, though trying to preserve a facade of independence. Only rarely is real dissent possible in such crises in mainstream newspapers and never on television.

Consider how the media supported the Blair government during 1999 in mobilising the nation to bomb Yugoslavia supposedly in defence of the highest humanitarian values. This was no easy task since it soon became clear to any independent onlooker that it was the NATO bombing that precipitated, rather than prevented, the humanitarian catastrophe. At the same time, as noted in chapter 7, our allies in Indonesia were engaged in atrocities in East Timor similar to those of Milosevic; while a few months later the same values were still relevant as Putin's Russia was committing crimes in Chechnya greater in scale than those of Milosevic in Kosovo. But in these cases the values that provided the pretext for bombing Yugoslavia needed to be buried. After a few obvious parallels were drawn between the situations in the media, the previous humanitarian pretexts used for Kosovo were indeed safely forgotten in these other conflicts.

Criticism in the mainstream of British wars tends to be

restricted to the tactics used to achieve the assumed noble aims, and whether the government has chosen the right strategy to discharge its high nobility or whether it will make 'mistakes'.

The debate in the mainstream on bombing Yugoslavia over Kosovo, did involve argument over whether it was a 'just war' or not; but both sides of this debate generally accepted that the government was seeking to achieve its stated humanitarian aims. That the government may have been acting out of other motives entirely was almost never questioned, despite the evidence.

The same goes for much media coverage of Iraq. Most reporting assumes that British aims are basically benevolent – the more regular criticism is whether government strategy is the right one to achieve noble objectives. This contrasts with reporting on US policy, where US aims of controlling Iraqi oil, or of installing an undemocratic, pro-US regime, are more openly discussed than British involvement in the same. This said, media reporting on Iraq in 2002/3 has involved many more dissenting views than was the case over the bombing of Yugoslavia. The reason is that there is no elite consensus on war with Iraq, which is rather being promoted by a small band of people around the prime minister. Many parts of the establishment are opposed to war (for tactical reasons to achieve British objectives, not for moral reasons, which are irrelevant to them). Therefore, the media framing can be much wider and include many more critical voices.

The *Guardian*'s coverage of the war in Afghanistan was a real exception to normal reporting, in that a series of comment pieces over several months put various critical perspectives and exposed much of the reality of the war and its motives. This unusual occurrence was due to one comment editor, Seumas Milne, who allowed a diversity of views – evidence in fact of how individuals can help change even well-established systems. This did not, however, stop some other reporters from toeing the state line in numerous cases elsewhere in the newspaper.

It is interesting to note that there is only one British military intervention over the past fifty years that has been severely criticised and government motives questioned in the mainstream – the invasion of Egypt in 1956 (usually called the 'Suez crisis' or 'fiasco' in the ideological system). Since there are many horrible British interventions worthy of attention and condemnation, with effects worse than in Egypt in 1956, why is this singled out for criticism? The reason is obvious – Britain lost. It therefore deserves a lot of soul-searching within the elite. Other interventions where we successfully blasted the nips deserve no such criticism, since we won, therefore what could possibly be the problem?

A leading US analyst of the media and foreign policy, Edward Herman, has said that 'it is the function of experts and the mainstream media to normalise the unthinkable for the general public'.[11] This role sanitises quite terrible policies and presents them as 'normal', current examples of which include hundreds of thousands of deaths in Iraq through sanctions, war crimes in Yugoslavia and mass civilian deaths in Afghanistan. When presented in the mainstream media, none of these outcomes tend to elicit the horror they deserve; all are normal.

The French philosopher Jean Guehenno has said that 'the worst betrayal of intelligence is finding justification for the world as it is'. But this is often the role played by experts, to explain the everyday as normal, justifiable, requiring little change, but rather 'stability' and few upsets to 'world order' unless controlled by us. In fact, the everyday is a horror for many people – the half of the planet that lives in absolute poverty, as well as the victims of torture and repression in the US and British-backed client states, for example.

Elites throughout history have presented their policies as in the natural order of things, which helps to obscure the pursuit of their own particular interests. An important aspect of the ideological system is rendering a single view dominant or 'natural', presenting current policies as inevitable, and undermining the possibility of alternatives. 'Globalisation' is presented by elites as such a natural phenomenon, and critics ridiculed as Luddites who cannot stop the inevitable march of history. These curiously Marxist, determinist views mask the elite's goal under globalisation of promoting total global economic 'liberalisation' – a far from inevitable outcome, but a strategy chosen by the liberalisation theologists of New Labour, and their allies among the transnational elite.

If the current horrible policies are 'normal', the alternatives are 'unthinkable'. Even to mention the indictment of Tony Blair for war crimes, to oppose British cooperation with the US because it is a consistent supporter of human rights abuses overseas, or even to end arms exports is 'unthinkable' in the mainstream and would invite ridicule.

Take the *Guardian*'s Ian Black, who writes that a key aim of the International Criminal Court is to avoid:

> politically motivated or frivolous investigations – what one expert calls the 'nutcase factor': for instance, of the possible pursuit of [Northern Ireland secretary] Mo Mowlam or Tony Blair for crimes against humanity.

Only 'nutcases' could possibly believe Our Leader could ever be guilty of crimes against humanity. (One such 'nutcase' is former US Attorney General, Ramsay Clark, who lodged a complaint against Britain in July 1999 for war crimes during its assault on Yugoslavia.)[12]

A customary way for the elite to deflect criticism is to term it a 'conspiracy theory', which is common across the ideological system. There is a good reason for it. British elites have built a fundamentally secretive political system for which they are minimally accountable to the public. As noted in chapter 13, they believe the public should have only a marginal say in this system outside elections, and – to judge from some of the views expressed in the Scott inquiry – neither do they think the public should even *know* what the decision-making processes are. Elites are especially keen to deflect criticism exposing *how the system works*, which is more threatening than criticising specific policies (which can be dismissed as 'exceptions'). The term 'conspiracy theory' is often deployed once criticism has moved beyond the specific and is closer to exposing how the system as a whole works.

My view is that 'ordinary people' – and I count myself as one of these – generally distrust their sources of information and know, ultimately, not to believe what they read or see. This is partly because ordinary people, in my view, have a much healthier scepticism of those in power than those closer to power or those aspiring to the political class. People have little stake in the elite and therefore have no reason to trust it. But I do not believe that people can be aware of the *extent* to which they are being misinformed. Foreign policy is different from domestic issues, where you only have to spend time in a hospital or have a child who goes to school, to know the state of public services. But with foreign policy people are overwhelmingly reliant on news rather than personal experience, which makes indoctrination much easier. Even if people have enough self-defence mechanisms to avoid being directly told what to think, it is very likely that the media tells them what to think *about*.

It is not that one cannot discover much about the reality of government policy. All the sources I have used in this book are public. But you have to make a real effort, and spend considerable time, which is simply not possible for most people. It involves proactively looking for alternative sources of information, usually a variety of different sources, to piece together an accurate picture, and then weighing these against mainstream sources.

It also involves what the great Kenyan novelist Ngugi Wa Thiongo has called 'decolonising the mind'. Ngugi was referring to Africans needing to free themselves from ideologies often subconsciously adopted under colonialism.[13] The British public needs, in my view, to do the same thing, and consciously unlearn most of what we have been informed about and 'educated' on regarding Britain's role in the world. This applies not only to the media, but to school and university too. Again, these are not easy tasks.

Overall, I believe that people are being indoctrinated into a picture of Britain's role in the world that supports elite priorities. This *is the mass production of ignorance*. It actively works against our interests, which is precisely why the ideological system is critical to the elite, who essentially see the public as a threat.

The basic fact is that anyone who wants to understand the reality of Britain's past and current foreign policies cannot do so by relying on the mainstream. As the chapters on Kenya, Malaya, British Guiana, Iran and others have shown, the reality of British policy is systematically suppressed; whole episodes in Britain's history have become severely ideologically treated. Interpretations of history that accord with the preferences of elites are the dominant ones. Given the extent of this ideological treatment of the past, what has happened is akin to the destruction of history. The task of any independent historian is to reconstruct real-life history, to rescue it from a self-serving web of deceit.

In the chapters that follow in this section I try to recover from the official memory hole the terrible reality of some other buried government policies, big polices which have been excised from history across the mainstream: such as complicity in the slaughter of a million people in Indonesia, and the removal of the entire population of Diego Garcia.

20

INDONESIA: COMPLICITY IN A MILLION DEATHS

I have never concealed from you my belief that a little
shooting in Indonesia would be an essential preliminary
to effective change.
> Britain's ambassador to Indonesia, letter to the
> Foreign Office, 1965

In July 1996, I published an article in the *Observer* revealing
British complicity in the slaughter of a million people in
Indonesia in 1965. The article was based on the release of
formerly secret files available at the Public Record Office. I only
just managed to persuade the editors to publish it after the
Guardian turned it down. Following the appearance of the
article, I did a couple of minor radio interviews. The story then
disappeared into oblivion, with only one or two subsequent
mentions in the mainstream media.

I happened to be watching the ITV lunchtime news on 1
January 1997, which carried a report on just-released secret
files from 1966. It mentioned two items: a row between prime
minister Harold Wilson and the governor of the Bank of
England over interest rates; and the world cup football match
between England and Argentina. Yet the 1996 files reveal

much about the British role in the 1965 slaughters – an everyday indication of media selection that keeps important issues from the public.

The history of British complicity in massive human rights abuses in Indonesia has been buried by the mainstream media and academia. When the Suharto regime fell in May 1998, barely any journalists mentioned that Britain had supported the brutally repressive regime for the past thirty years as well as its murderous accession to power after 1965. Britain supported Indonesia's invasion of East Timor in 1975 – killing 200,000 people, a third of the population – and proceeded to give effective support to Indonesia in its illegal occupation. This basic fact was not noticed by journalists in reporting East Timor's independence from Indonesia in May 2002. Neither did the mainstream media appear to notice Britain's culpability in the human rights abuses committed in East Timor around the historic election in 1999.

The case of Indonesia shows how repressive the political culture is of basic facts when they provide the wrong picture about the role of the state. Perhaps in a democracy the truth would have been reported about British complicity in the tragedies of the peasant families massacred in 1965, the Timorese villagers sliced up by Indonesian troops in 1975, and the families forced to flee Indonesian terror in 1999. Instead, the British role in these tragic plights has been met largely by silence.

'A necessary task'

The formerly secret British files, together with recently de-classified US files, reveal an astonishing story. Although the Foreign Office is keeping many of the files secret until 2007, a clear picture still emerges of British and US support for one of the postwar world's worst bloodbaths – what US officials at the time called a 'reign of terror' and British officials 'ruthless terror'.

In his 600-page long autobiography, Denis Healey, then Britain's Defence Minister, failed to mention at all Suharto's brutal seizure of power, let alone Britain's role. It is not hard to see why.[1]

The killings in Indonesia started when a group of army officers loyal to President Sukarno assassinated several generals on 30 September 1965. They believed the generals were about to stage a coup to overthrow Sukarno. The instability, however, provided other anti-Sukarno generals, led by General Suharto, with an excuse for the army to move against a powerful and popular political faction with mass support, the Indonesian Communist Party (PKI). It did so brutally: in a few months hundreds of thousands of PKI members and ordinary people were killed and the PKI destroyed. Suharto emerged as leader and instituted a brutal regime that lasted until 1998.

Close relations between the US and British embassies in Jakarta are indicated in the declassified files and point to a somewhat coordinated joint operation in 1965. These files show five ways in which the Labour government under Harold Wilson together with the Democratic government under Lyndon Johnson were complicit in this slaughter.

First, the British wanted the army to act and encouraged it. 'I have never concealed from you my belief that a little shooting in Indonesia would be an essential preliminary to effective change', the ambassador in Jakarta, Sir Andrew Gilchrist, informed the Foreign Office on 5 October.[2]

The following day the Foreign Office stated that 'the crucial question still remains whether the Generals will pluck up enough courage to take decisive action against the PKI'. Later it noted that 'we must surely prefer an Army to a Communist regime' and declared:

> It seems pretty clear that the Generals are going to need all the help they can get and accept without being tagged as hopelessly pro-Western, if they are going to be able to gain ascendancy over the Communists. In the short run, and while the present confusion continues, we can hardly go wrong by tacitly backing the Generals.

British policy was 'to encourage the emergence of a General's regime', one intelligence official later explained.[3]

US officials similarly expressed their hope of 'army at long last to act effectively against Communists' [sic]. 'We are, as always, sympathetic to army's desire to eliminate communist influence' and 'it is important to assure the army of our full support of its efforts to crush the PKI'.[4]

US and British officials had clear knowledge of the killings. US Ambassador Marshall Green noted three weeks after the attempted coup, and with the killings having begun, that: 'Army has . . . been working hard at destroying PKI and I, for one, have increasing respect for its determination and organisation in carrying out this crucial assignment'. Green noted in the same despatch the 'execution of PKI cadres', putting the figure at 'several hundred of them' in 'Djakarta area alone' [sic].[5]

On 1 November, Green informed the State Department of the army's 'moving relentlessly to exterminate the PKI as far as that is possible to do'. Three days later he noted that 'Embassy and USG [US government] generally sympathetic with and admiring of what army doing' [sic]. Four days after this the US embassy reported that the army 'has continued systematic drive to destroy PKI in northern Sumatra with wholesale killings reported'.[6]

A British official reported on 25 November that 'PKI men and women are being executed in very large numbers.' Some victims 'are given a knife and invited to kill themselves. Most refuse and are told to turn around and are shot in the back'. One executioner considered it 'his duty to exterminate what he called "less than animals"'.[7]

A British official wrote to the ambassador on 16 December, saying:

> You – like me – may have been somewhat surprised to see estimates by the American embassy that well over 100,000 people have been killed in the troubles since

1 October. I am, however, readier to accept such figures after [receiving] some horrifying details of the purges that have been taking place . . . The local army commander . . . has a list of PKI members in five categories. He has been given orders to kill those in the first three categories . . . A woman of 78 . . . was taken away one night by a village execution squad . . . Half a dozen heads were neatly arranged on the parapet of a small bridge.[8]

The US Consulate in Medan was reporting that 'much indiscriminate killing is taking place':

Something like a reign of terror against PKI is taking place. This terror is not discriminating very carefully between PKI leaders and ordinary PKI members with no ideological bond to the party.[9]

By mid-December the State Department noted approvingly that 'Indonesian military leaders' campaign to destroy PKI is moving fairly swiftly and smoothly.' By 14 February 1966 Ambassador Green could note that 'the PKI has been destroyed as an effective political force for some time to come' and that 'the Communists . . . have been decimated by wholesale massacre'.[10]

The British files show that by February 1966 the British ambassador was estimating 400,000 dead – but even this was described by the Swedish ambassador as a 'gross underestimate'. By March, one British official wondered 'how much of it [the PKI] is left, after six months of killing' and believed that over 200,000 had been killed in Sumatra alone – in a report called 'The liquidation of the Indonesian Communist Party in Sumatra'. By April, the US Embassy stated that 'we frankly do not know whether the real figure is closer to 100,000 or 1,000,000 but believe it wiser to err on the side of the lower estimates, especially when questioned by the press'.[11]

Summarising the events of 1965 the British Consul in

Medan said: 'Posing as saviours of the nation from a communist terror, [the army] unleashed a ruthless terror of their own, the scars of which will take many years to heal.' Another British memo referred to 'an operation carried out on a very large scale and often with appalling savagery'. Another simply referred to the 'bloodbath'.[12]

British and US officials totally supported these massacres, the files show. I could find no reference to any concern about the extent of killing at all – only constant encouragement for the army to continue. As the files above indicate, there is no question that British and US officials knew exactly what they were supporting.

One British official noted, referring to 10,005 people arrested by the army: 'I hope they do not throw the 10,005 into the sea . . ., otherwise it will cause quite a shipping hazard.'[13]

It was not only PKI activists who were the targets of this terror. As the British files show, many of the victims were the 'merest rank and file' of the PKI who were 'often no more than bewildered peasants who give the wrong answer on a dark night to bloodthirsty hooligans bent on violence', with the connivance of the army.[14]

Britain connived even more closely with those conducting the slaughter. By 1965, Britain had deployed tens of thousands of troops in Borneo, to defend its former colony of Malaya against Indonesian encroachments following territorial claims by Jakarta – known as the 'confrontation'. British planners secretly noted that they 'did not want to distract the Indonesian army by getting them engaged in fighting in Borneo and so discourage them from the attempts which they now seem to be making to deal with the PKI'.[15]

The US was worried that Britain might take advantage of the instability in Indonesia to launch an offensive from Singapore 'to stab the good generals in the back', as Ambassador Gilchrist described the US fear.[16]

So the British ambassador proposed reassuring those Indonesians who were ordering mass slaughter, saying that 'we should get word to the Generals that we shall not attack them whilst they are chasing the PKI'. The British intelligence officer in Singapore agreed, believing this 'might ensure that the army is not detracted [sic] from what we consider to be a necessary task'.[17]

In October the British passed to the Generals, through a US contact, 'a carefully phrased oral message about not biting the Generals in the back for the present'.[18]

The US files confirm that the message from the US, conveyed on 14 October, read:

> First, we wish to assure you that we have no intention of interfering Indonesian internal affairs directly or indirectly. Second, we have good reason to believe that none of our allies intend to initiate any offensive action against Indonesia [sic].[19]

The message was greatly welcomed by the Indonesian army: an aide to the Defence Minister noted that 'this was just what was needed by way of assurances that we (the army) weren't going to be hit from all angles as we moved to straighten things out here'.[20]

According to former BBC correspondent Roland Challis, the counsellor at the British Embassy, (now Sir) James Murray, was authorised to tell Suharto that in the event of Indonesian troops being transferred from the confrontation area to Java, British forces would not take military advantage. Indeed, in his book, Challis notes a report in an Indonesian newspaper in 1980 stating that Britain even helped an Indonesian colonel transport an infantry brigade on confrontation duty back to Jakarta. 'Flying the Panamanian flag, she sailed safely down the heavily patrolled Malacca Strait – escorted by two British warships', Challis notes.[21]

The third means of support was propaganda operations, mainly involving the distribution of anti-Sukarno messages and stories through the media. This was organised from Britain's MI6 intelligence base in Singapore known as Phoenix Park.

The head of these operations, Norman Reddaway, told Roland Challis to 'do anything you can think of to get rid of Sukarno'.[22]

On 5 October Reddaway reported to the Foreign Office in London that:

> We should not miss the present opportunity to use the situation to our advantage . . . I recommend that we should have no hesitation in doing what we can surreptitiously to blacken the PKI in the eyes of the army and the people of Indonesia.

The Foreign Office replied:

> We certainly do not exclude any unattributable propaganda or psywar [psychological warfare] activities which would contribute to weakening the PKI permanently. We therefore agree with the [above] recommendation . . . Suitable propaganda themes might be . . . Chinese interference in particular arms shipments; PKI subverting Indonesia as agents of foreign communists.

It continued:

> We want to act quickly while the Indonesians are still off balance but treatment will need to be subtle . . . Please let us know of any suggestions you may have on these lines where we could be helpful at this end.[23]

On 9 October the intelligence officer confirmed that 'we have made arrangements for distribution of certain unattributable material based on the general guidance' in the Foreign Office memo. This involved 'promoting and coordinating publicity' critical of the Sukarno government to 'news agencies, newspapers and radio'. 'The impact has been considerable', one file notes. British propaganda covered in various newspapers included fabrications of nest-eggs accumulated abroad by Sukarno's ministers and PKI preparations for a coup by carving up Jakarta into districts to engage in systematic slaughter (forerunners of current modern propaganda on Iraq).[24]

The fourth method of support was a 'hit list' of targets supplied by the US to the Indonesian army. As the journalist Kathy Kadane has revealed, as many as 5,000 names of provincial, city and other local PKI committee members and leaders of the mass organisations of the PKI, such as the national labour federation, women's and youth groups, were passed on to the Generals, many of whom were subsequently killed. 'It really was a big help to the army' noted Robert Martens, a former official in the US Embassy. 'They probably killed a lot of people and I probably have a lot of blood on my hands, but that's not all bad. There's a time when you have to strike hard at a decisive moment.'[25]

The recently declassified US files do not provide many more details about this hit list, although they do further confirm it. One list of names, for example, was passed to the Indonesians in December 1965 and 'is apparently being used by Indonesian security authorities who seem to lack even the simplest overt information on PKI leadership at the time'. Also, 'lists of other officials in the PKI affiliates, Partindo and Baperki, were also provided to GOI [Government of Indonesia] officials at their request'.[26]

The final means of support was provision of arms – although this remains the murkiest area to uncover. Past US support to the Indonesian military 'should have established clearly in minds Army leaders that US stands behind them if they should need help [sic]', the State Department noted. US strategy was to 'avoid overt involvement in the power struggle but . . . indicate, clearly but covertly, to key Army officers our desire to assist where we can.'[27]

The first US supplies to the Indonesian army were radios 'to help in internal security' and to aid the Generals 'in their task of overcoming the Communists', as British ambassador Gilchrist pointed out. 'I see no reason to object or complain', he added.[28]

The US historian Gabriel Kolko has shown that in early November 1965 the US received a request from the Generals to 'arm Moslem and nationalist youths . . . for use against the PKI'. The recently published files confirm this approach from the Indonesians. On 1 November Ambassador Green cabled Washington that:

> As to the provision of small arms I would be leery about telling army we are in position to provide same, although we should act, not close our minds to this possibility . . . We could explore availability of small arms stocks, preferable of non-US origin, which could be obtained without any overt US government involvement. We might also examine channels through which we could, if necessary, provide covert assistance to army for purchase of weapons.[29]

A CIA memo of 9 November stated that the US should avoid being 'too hesitant about the propriety of extending such assistance provided we can do so covertly, in a manner which will not embarrass them or embarrass our government'. It then noted that mechanisms exist or can be created to deliver 'any of the types of the materiel requested to date in reasonable quantities'. One line of text is then not declassified before the memo notes: 'The same can be said of purchasers and transfer agents for such items as small arms, medicine and other items requested.' The memo goes on to note that 'we do not propose that the Indonesian army be furnished such equipment at this time' [sic]. However, 'if the Army leaders justify their needs in detail . . . it is likely that at least will help ensure their success and provide the basis for future collaboration with the US'. 'The means for covert implementation' of the delivery of arms 'are within our capabilities'.[30]

In response to Indonesia's request for arms, Kolko has shown that the US promised to provide such covert aid, and dubbed the arms 'medicines'. They were approved in a meeting in Washington on 4 December. The declassified files state that 'the Army really needed the medicines' and that the US was keen to indicate 'approval in a practical way of the actions of the Indonesian army'. The extent of arms provided is not revealed in the files but the amount 'the medicines would cost was a mere pittance compared with the advantages that might accrue to the US as a result of "getting in on the ground floor"', one file reads.[31]

The British knew of these arms supplies and it is likely they also approved them. Britain was initially reluctant to see US arms go to the Generals for fear that they might be used by Indonesia in the 'confrontation'. The British files show that the US State Department had 'undertaken to consult with us before they do anything to support the Generals'. It is possible that the US reneged on this commitment; however, in earlier discussions about this possibility, a British official at the embassy in Washington noted that 'I do not think that is very likely'.[32]

The threat of independent development

The struggle between the army and the PKI was 'a struggle basically for the commanding heights of the Indonesian economy', British officials noted.[33] At stake was using the resources of Indonesia for the primary benefit of its people or for businesses, including Western companies.

British and US planners supported the slaughter to promote interests deemed more important than peoples' lives. London wanted to see a change in regime in Jakarta to bring an end to the 'confrontation' with Malaya. But commercial interests were just as important. Southeast Asia was 'a major producer of some essential commodities' such as rubber, copra and chromium ore; 'the defence of the sources of these products and their denial to a possible enemy are major interests to the Western powers', the Foreign Office noted. This was a fancy way of saying that the resources would continue to be exploited by Western business. Indonesia was also strategically located at a nexus of important trading routes.[34]

British Foreign Secretary Michael Stewart wrote in the middle of the slaughter:

> It is only the economic chaos of Indonesia which prevents that country from offering great potential opportunities to British exporters. If there is going to be a deal in Indonesia, as I hope one day there may be, I think we ought to take an active part and try to secure a slice of the cake ourselves.[35]

Similarly, one Foreign Office memo noted that Indonesia was in a 'state of economic chaos but is potentially rich . . . American exporters, like their British counterparts, presumably see in Indonesia a potentially rich market once the economy has been brought under control.'[36]

For the US, Under Secretary of State George Ball had noted that Indonesia 'may be more important to us than South V-N [Vietnam]', against which the US was at the same time massively stepping up its assault. 'At stake' in Indonesia, one US memo read, 'are 100 million people, vast potential resources and a strategically important chain of islands'.[37]

US priorities were similar in Vietnam and Indonesia: to prevent the consolidation of an independent nationalist regime that threatened Western interests and that could be a successful development model for others.

President Sukarno clearly had the wrong economic priorities. In 1964, British-owned commercial interests had been placed under Indonesian management and control. However, under the Suharto regime, the British Foreign Secretary told one Indonesian army general that 'we are . . . glad that your government has decided to hand back the control of British estates to their original owners'.

The US ambassador in Malaysia cabled Washington a year before the October 1965 events in Indonesia saying that 'our difficulties with Indonesia stem basically from deliberate, positive GOI [Government of Indonesia] strategy of seeking to push Britain and the US out of Southeast Asia'. George Ball noted in March 1965 that 'our relations with Indonesia are on the verge of falling apart'. 'Not only has the management of the American rubber plants been taken over, but there are dangers of an imminent seizure of the American oil companies'.[38]

According to a US report for President Johnson:

> The [Indonesian] government occupies a dominant position in basic industry, public utilities, internal transportation and communication . . . It is probable that private ownership will disappear and may be succeeded by some form of production-profit-sharing contract arrangements to be applied to all foreign investment.

Overall, 'the avowed Indonesian objective is "to stand on their own feet" in developing their economy, free from foreign, especially Western, influence.'[39]

This was a serious danger that needed to be removed. As noted elsewhere, Third World countries are to develop under overall Western control, not by or for themselves, a truism about US and British foreign policy revealed time and again in the declassified files.

It is customary in the propaganda system to excuse past horrible British and US policies by referring to the cold war. In Indonesia, the main threat was indigenous nationalism. The British feared 'the resurgence of Communist and radical nationalism'.[40] One US memo says of future PKI policy: 'It is likely that PKI foreign policy decisions, like those of Sukarno, would stress Indonesian national interests above those of Peking, Moscow or international communism in general.'

The real danger was that Indonesia would be too successful, a constant US fear well documented by Kolko and Noam Chomsky in policy towards numerous other countries. A Special National Intelligence Estimate of 1 September 1965 referred to the PKI's moving 'to energize and unite the Indonesian nation' and stated that '*if these efforts succeeded, Indonesia would provide a powerful example for the underdeveloped world and hence a credit to communism and a setback for Western prestige*.[41] One critical area was the landlessness of the poor peasants – the source of the grinding poverty of most Indonesians – and land reform more generally, the key political issue in rural areas and the smaller cities. The PKI was recognised by British and US officials as the champion of the landless and poor in Indonesia.

Britain was keen to establish good relations with Suharto, that were to remain for thirty years. A year after the beginning of the slaughter, the Foreign Office noted that 'it was very necessary to demonstrate to the Indonesians that we regarded our relations with them as rapidly returning to normal'. Britain was keen to establish 'normal trade' and provide aid, and to express its 'goodwill and confidence' in the new regime. British officials spoke to the new Foreign Minister, Adam Malik, of the 'new relationship which we hope will develop between our two countries'. A Foreign Office brief for the Cabinet said that Britain 'shall do all we can to restore good relations with Indonesia and help her resume her rightful place in the world community'.[42]

There is no mention in any of the files – that I could find – of the morality of engaging with the new regime. The slaughter was simply an irrelevance.

Michael Stewart recalled in his autobiography that he visited Indonesia a year after the killings and was able to 'reach a good understanding with the Foreign Minister, Adam Malik', a 'remarkable man' who was 'evidently resolved to keep his country at peace'. Suharto's regime is 'like Sukarno's, harsh and tyrannical; but it is not aggressive', Stewart stated. Malik later acted as a primary apologist for Indonesian atrocities in East Timor. In 1977, for example, he was reported as saying: '50,000 or 80,000 people might have been killed during the war in East Timor . . . It was war . . . Then what is the big fuss?'[43]

A combination of Western advice, aid and investment helped transform the Indonesian economy into one that, although retaining some nationalist orientation, provided substantial opportunities and profits for Western investors. President Suharto's increasingly corrupt authoritarian regime kept economic order. Japan and the United States, working through consortia and the multilateral banks, used aid as a lever to rewrite Indonesia's basic economic legislation to favour foreign investors. Western businesses moved in. By the mid 1970s, a British CBI report noted that Indonesia presented 'enormous potential for the foreign investor'. The press reported that the country enjoyed a 'favourable political climate' and the 'encouragement of foreign investment by the country's authorities'. RTZ, BP, British Gas and Britoil were some of the companies that took advantage.[45] One consequence was that landlessness increased as land ownership became more concentrated; the peasants were afraid to organise, and the prospects of fundamental economic changes to *primarily* benefit the poor were successfully eradicated even though poverty levels were reduced.[44]

With Suharto gone after May 1998, one British minister at least was able to talk frankly of the regime Britain had supported. It could now be admitted that under Suharto there was 'severe political repression', the 'concentration of economic and political power in a few, extremely corrupt hands', and the 'involvement of the security forces in every tier of social and political life', for example.[46] All these things had been miraculously discovered.

21

EAST TIMOR: SMOTHERING THE BIRTH OF A NATION

Readers should have a look at press cuttings for August 2001, when East Timor held its first elections, and for May 2002, when it achieved independence after a long, heroic struggle. They should look for any mentions of the reality that for the previous twenty-five years successive British governments had helped prevent the right of the East Timorese to self-determination – both by supporting the horrific 1975 invasion as well as generally helping to prop up the Suharto regime. There is barely mention of this fact in the entire mainstream media.

Interestingly, one mention I have found is from then Foreign Office minister Peter Hain, who told a parliamentary inquiry of the importance of 'giving the people of East Timor the right to determine their own destiny, which they were denied for over a quarter of a century, often with Western complicity *including British complicity*'.[1]

This is an important fact, an unusual admission, which has been buried in the propaganda system. Only a small number of critical journalists, such as John Pilger with his outstanding documentaries and writing, have revealed the reality of British policy towards East Timor, and have kept the story alive in the face of silence from the mainstream. Let us try to throw some further light on this policy here.

Another 200,000

The brief background to the invasion of East Timor is that the majority of Timorese had long sought independence while a small political faction backed by Jakarta was calling for integration into Indonesia. An armed conflict broke out between the pro-Jakarta UDT and the party of the left, Fretilin, in August 1975. This was essentially engineered by Indonesian generals to bring about the integration of East Timor – then a Portuguese colony – into Indonesia. The generals informed UDT leaders that Fretilin was secretly training a communist force and was about to launch a coup. This was a pure fabrication but UDT heeded it and attempted a coup. The coup failed and within weeks Fretilin forces overwhelmed the UDT.

The Indonesian regime under Suharto had constantly feared that an East Timor controlled by Fretilin, which commanded widespread popular support in the territory, would win international recognition. It subsequently invaded and proceeded to enact one of the most brutal invasions by any country in the postwar period.

The population was for years subjected to aerial bombing, campaigns of deliberate starvation and the wholesale destruction of villages. By 1985, up to half a million people had been killed or displaced. Disappearances, or deaths in custody, the killing of prisoners who surrendered after being promised amnesty, the torture and imprisonment of people suspected of being disloyal to the Suharto regime were all common. One East Timorese catholic priest stated that 'a barbarous genocide of innocent people goes on, apparently with complete peace of conscience'. East Timor was being 'wiped out by an invasion, a brutal conquest that produces heaps of dead, maimed and orphaned'. Bishop Carlos Belo, who later won the Nobel Prize, said: 'We are dying as a people and as a nation.'[2]

When filing their reports on East Timor's elections and independence, all journalists should have been aware of Britain's support for the invasion. The following secret document has been publicly available for some time and has been cited in various studies. It shows the British ambassador in Jakarta informing the Foreign Office in July 1975 that:

> The people of Portuguese Timor are in no condition to exercise the right to self-determination . . . The arguments in favour of its integration into Indonesia are all the stronger . . . Developments in Lisbon now seem to argue in favour of greater sympathy towards Indonesia should the Indonesian government feel forced to take strong action by the deteriorating situation in Portuguese Timor.

He continued:

> Certainly, as seen from here, it is in Britain's interest that Indonesia should absorb the territory as soon and as unobtrusively as possible, and that if it should come to the crunch and there is a row in the United Nations, we should keep our heads down and avoid taking sides against the Indonesian government.[3]

Other formerly secret documents from the mid 1960s show that British planners believed that East Timor was not 'sufficiently viable to have an independent existence'. The files that I have seen contain debates among planners on whether it would be in Britain's interest to offer aid to Portugal to defend East Timor in the event of an Indonesian attack; the conclusion was no. One file mentions that Britain would take recourse to the UN in the event of an Indonesian attack (which did not happen, as the cable cited above shows).[4]

In none of the files that I have seen are the wishes of the East Timorese mentioned; they simply figure nowhere in British planning.

US declassified files show that Washington gave Suharto the green light for the invasion. President Ford told Suharto in their meeting the day before the invasion that if Indonesia were to take action in East Timor 'we will understand and will not press you on the issue. We understand the problem and the intentions that you have.' Secretary of State Kissinger added: 'it is important that whatever you do succeeds quickly'. The invasion was delayed until President Ford had returned home.[5]

A few days after the beginning of the intervention the US ambassador to Indonesia noted that the US had 'not disapproved' of the invasion; within a month, a US State Department official stated: 'We are more or less condoning the incursion into East Timor' since 'we regard Indonesia as a friendly, non-aligned state – a nation we do a lot of business with'.[6]

Britain, along with the US, also helped prevent UN action against Indonesia consistent with the view outlined in the secret cable noted above. London abstained on the first UN resolution condemning the invasion, supported two others (though these were widely acknowledged to be weakly worded and watered down) and abstained on all subsequent ones. The US representative to the UN, Daniel Moynihan, explained that in steering the international community away from effective action against Indonesia:

> The United States wished things to turn out as they did and worked to bring this about. The Department of State desired that the United Nations prove utterly ineffective in whatever measures it undertook. This task was given to me and I carried it forward with no inconsiderable success.[7]

The US dramatically increased arms supplies to Jakarta following the invasion, providing counter-insurgency and transport aircraft as well as an array of rifles, mortars, machine guns and communications equipment. All these directly aided Indonesia in the conduct of the campaign.

Britain later followed suit. In 1978 the Callaghan government permitted the export to Indonesia of eight Hawk aircraft, Rolls Royce engines, spares and the training of pilots and engineers. In November 1978, by which time near-genocide had taken place in East Timor, Labour Foreign Secretary David Owen stated that 'we believe that such fighting as still continues is on a very small scale'.[8] Britain had refused to give assurances that the aircraft would not be used by Indonesia in a combat role.

Much evidence suggests that the Hawks significantly helped the Indonesian military's campaign. Konis Santana, the leader of East Timor's resistance army, claims that British aircraft killed hundreds of civilians in raids against villages supporting the resistance in the late 1970s and early 1980s. He believes that:

> The war in East Timor would have taken another course if the Indonesians had not received military support from abroad, including the Hawks that Great Britain offered during the crucial period after the invasion.

Santana said in an interview in 1997 that the Indonesian air force no longer used British jets on raiding missions, but for intimidation, because the 'Hawks killed so many people in bombing attacks in 1978 and 1979 that today, whenever people hear the noise of the Hawks flying, they are scared and the authorities know they will not dare leave their homes.'[9]

By the early 1990s, a spokesman for East Timor's independence movement termed Britain 'the single worst obstructionist of any industrialised country' concerning Indonesian violence in East Timor.[10] The reason was that until independence, British military, political, economic and diplomatic relations all gave effective support to the Suharto regime and, in effect, its brutal occupation of East Timor.

Britain became a major regular supplier of an array of military equipment to the Indonesian armed forces, a relationship that continues to thrive today. As now, some of these past deals were made at the same time as major human rights violations in Indonesia and in East Timor. In 1983–85, as contracts for the British export of an air defence system were being signed, up to 4,500 people were murdered by army death squads in Indonesia. On the same day in 1991 that a co-production agreement between British Aerospace and Indonesia for the Hawk fighter-trainer and a light attack fighter was reported, the US press reported up to 5,000 people had been killed in Aceh province over recent months. Most were killed by the Indonesian army in its attempts to brutally suppress the independence movement.[11]

British officials and arms salesmen could have had no doubt of the brutality of those they were supplying. The Indonesian military commander in Aceh province was quoted as saying in November 1990: 'I have told the community, if you find a terrorist, kill him. There's no need to investigate him ... If they don't do as you order them, shoot them on the spot, or butcher them.' Chief of the armed forces and later Indonesian Vice President, General Try Sutrisno, promised to 'wipe out all separatist elements' in East Timor.[12]

As a major arms supplier and trainer of the armed forces, Britain had consistently cordial personal dealings with those ordering the violence. British officials dealt with Benny Murdani, for example, who became Defence minister, and who had also ordered and commanded the invasion of East Timor. In 1983 he issued a message to then resistance leader Xanana Gusmao (who was elected as East Timor's president in 2001) saying: 'there is no country on the globe that can help you. Our own army is prepared to destroy you if you are not willing to cooperate with our republic', before declaring that he would show 'no mercy' to resistance forces in East Timor.

Close relations throughout the 1990s were undisturbed by the massacre in Dili, East Timor's capital, in November 1991, when Indonesian troops killed hundreds of people demonstrating against the occupation. Britain simply delayed announcing the sale of a navy support ship to Indonesia because of the international outcry over the massacre, and the sale went ahead the following month. Military relations continued as normal.

1999: A few thousand more

New Labour has also had its chance to help prevent major violence in East Timor. It failed, and remains complicit in further massive human rights atrocities, though you wouldn't know so from mainstream media coverage.

Indonesian president Habibie announced in January 1999 that a referendum would be allowed in East Timor, enabling the population to choose between autonomy within Indonesia or full independence. The Indonesian military then secretly proceeded to create and arm pro-Jakarta militia groups in East Timor to intimidate people through a terror campaign to vote against independence. Between 3,000 and 5,000 people were killed in the run-up to the vote, with widespread rape, torture and maiming. Despite this, 78 per cent voted in favour of independence on 30 August 1999. The response to this vote by the army and militia was to continue such a ruthless campaign that around 1,000 more were killed, thousands of others shot, stabbed or raped and 500,000 (more than half the entire population) forced to flee for their lives, mainly into Indonesian West Timor.

These expulsions were the result of 'a planned, systematic campaign coordinated by the Indonesian military', according to Human Rights Watch:

> The tiny half-island had become what one diplomat described as a 'living hell'. Army-backed militia members, armed with automatic weapons, launched a scorched earth policy, targeting independence supporters for death; looting and burning homes, clinics, churches and stores; and forcing hundreds of thousands of people from their homes.[13]

The Blair government has consistently claimed it did all it could to stop the violence. It also tries to take credit for helping to bring about the UN peace enforcement mission in East Timor that the Indonesian government eventually agreed to. Foreign Secretary Robin Cook claimed in 2000 that East Timor 'would not now be independent without the help of an international coalition of which Britain was a prominent member'.[14]

In fact, Britain did little to help stop the violence and de facto aided it.

In the run-up to the referendum the Blair government (and the US) was insisting that security in East Timor be provided by the Indonesian army, despite the widespread knowledge that the same army was creating the insecurity, by arming and directing the militias' terror campaign. According to Tapol, the Indonesian human rights campaign, 'the government's willingness to rely on Indonesian assurances regarding security was an appalling disregard for the human rights of the East Timorese people'. With security handed to the occupying power, the Indonesian army and militias were effectively given a blank cheque to promote violence and intimidation.

In July, on the day before the start of registration for the vote, a British-supplied Hawk aircraft made two low passes over Dili, the capital of East Timor. This was a clear act of intimidation by the Indonesian military ahead of the referendum. Yet, instead of acting immediately to halt deliveries of Hawks, the British government 'chose to seek yet more meaningless assurances from the Indonesian government', according to Tapol. 'It preferred to wait until East Timor was in ruins' before imposing an arms ban.[15]

In this pre-vote period of atrocities committed by Indonesian forces, Britain continued business, including military business, as normal. Hawk aircraft continued to be supplied: two in April, two in May and three in August. Three Hawk aircraft were in fact delivered to Indonesia on 23 September, during the post-vote terror. They were from a 1996 deal; the government argued that it was powerless to stop the delivery since the aircraft were already the legal property of Indonesia.[16]

Western intelligence agencies were surely aware that the Indonesian army and allied militias were planning a terror campaign if the East Timorese voted for independence. The military commander in Dili had already declared before the referendum that if the vote went the wrong way 'all will be destroyed'. The Australian press had reported the stockpiling of arms and warned of a takeover of the territory by the militias. When the terror began, Britain, along with the US, preferred ambiguous reactions that could easily have been identified in Jakarta as a de facto nod and a wink to continue.[17]

Indeed, it appears likely that the US had – once again regarding East Timor – given the Indonesian army a green light to violence. The chief of US military forces in the Pacific region, Admiral Dennis Blair, had been sent to meet Indonesian armed forces commander, General Wiranto, in April. Meeting two days after the massacre at Liquica, Admiral Blair, rather than telling Wiranto to close the militias down, offered him promises of new US military assistance. Wiranto and other officers were reportedly delighted by the meeting and, according to Allan Nairn, the American journalist who broke this story, 'they took this as a green light to proceed with the militia operation'.[18]

Once the terror resumed following the vote, Robin Cook urged that the deployment of the UN peace mission be delayed, on the absurd grounds that the army needed time to secure control over the militias (the same that it had created and armed).[19]

Britain announced the suspension of existing arms export licences to Indonesia only on 11 September; a full seven days after the post-vote terror had begun on 4 September, following the announcement of the result of the vote. In this period of gross atrocities, Britain failed to freeze arms sales immediately and impose economic sanctions, thus failing to use a significant lever at its disposal to help halt the atrocities. ('The international community's response to the crisis in East Timor was swift', the Department for International Development managed to say with a straight face in December.)[20]

The EU agreed to impose an arms ban for only four months from September, a sign of its lack of seriousness in pressing Jakarta. The ban was duly lifted in January 2000, leaving each member state to decide whether to resume arms sales. Naturally, Britain did so, resuming the delivery of supplies to the military that had just undertaken a 'planned, systematic campaign' of murder and violence. At the same time, the press reported a secret assessment by Australian defence intelligence stating that extending the arms embargo would help to prevent further repression by the Indonesian army.[21]

But the reality is even worse: in fact, Britain had never imposed an embargo at all – it got around it by extending the existing licences for arms exports by four months. This ensured that Indonesia was not deprived of any arms at all. This was the first time that an extension had been made to the validity of export licences in relation to an EU arms embargo.[22]

The government had also invited Indonesia, along with sixty other countries, to an arms exhibition in September. Baroness Symons, then Defence Procurement Minister, claimed that Indonesia had a right to look at the equipment on offer for reasons of 'self-defence' – an assertion not worth commenting on. Despite apparent Foreign Office pressure on the Ministry of Defence, the latter did not withdraw the invitation and it was left to the Indonesians to decline. An MoD spokesman said on 8 September: 'Certain things are obviously on their mind domestically and they are obviously busy with things in East Timor.'[23]

Human Rights Watch noted that the post-vote violence was 'predictable and preventable'. It had been warning for months of escalating Indonesian-organised human rights atrocities in East Timor – notably the massacre of dozens of people in a church compound in Liquica in April – and called on aid donors to make aid conditional on human rights improvements.[24]

These calls also went in vain, as Indonesia's leading partners continued to support the regime and failed to use a variety of levers available to them. This was at the same time as Blair, Clinton and others were supposedly anguishing over the highest moral principles in responding to human rights abuses by the Yugoslav regime in Kosovo. In fact, the 3,000–5,000 deaths in East Timor in the months before the referendum was twice as many as in Kosovo before NATO bombing began.

It was only when the Clinton administration eventually

publicly condemned Indonesian-backed violence and announced in early September that it was suspending arms supplies and training programmes with the Indonesian military, that the latter conducted a volte face and withdrew from East Timor. This showed the latent power available to Washington to stop atrocities, but which is rarely used, and which was only belatedly used by Britain.[25]

However, violence by militias created by one of Britain's favoured militaries continued in East Timor. In August 2000 Human Rights Watch noted that the militias 'have escalated operations in East Timor over the past month', killing two UN peacekeepers and 'terrorising the civilian population'. These raids, Human Rights Watch added, 'are taking place under the nose of elite Indonesian troops'. It called on the international community, and specifically Britain, to reimpose an arms ban – once again in vain.[26]

The effects of the violence of 1999 were still felt by tens of thousands of people in late 2002. These were the forgotten East Timorese who remained displaced in West Timor and other parts of Indonesia, who were still prevented by security and other concerns from making a free decision as to whether to return to East Timor or remain in Indonesia. They were still being terrorised by the same militias who had devastated East Timor since 1999.[27]

According to Human Rights Watch, the UN and its member states 'have a particular obligation to see that justice is done for the crimes committed in East Timor', not least because UN personnel were among the targets of the violence and UN personnel were witnesses to crimes.[28]

But neither Britain nor the US support a war crimes tribunal for the 1999 events in East Timor, despite it being proposed by the UN mission. Neither does London support the call made by East Timorese NGOs for an international tribunal to prosecute crimes against humanity following the 1975 invasion. There is also naturally no support from the British government for a war crimes tribunal for Suharto (and thus no media campaign for the same, unlike for Milosevic who is fair game). Perhaps it is feared that an investigation into Suharto would lead to various British connections.

The Blair government has, in all seriousness, repeatedly tried to take credit for East Timor's transition to independence. Only a willing media has allowed the grotesqueness of this propaganda to reach the public and failed to offer a truer picture.

The current plight of East Timorese, together with ongoing Indonesian atrocities in Aceh and West Papua provinces, show that there are still plenty of reasons for the British government to stop supplying arms, military training and other means of support to Indonesia. A Foreign Office minister referred retrospectively to the 1999 violence in East Timor as 'state-sponsored terrorism'.[29] That is, by a government Britain continues to regard as favoured ally, as we supposedly engage in a 'war against terrorism'.

22

DIEGO GARCIA: REMOVING PEOPLE FROM HISTORY

> The object of the exercise was to get some rocks which will remain ours.
>
> Foreign Office, 1966

A landmark day in the history of Britain's foreign policy was 3 November 2000. On that day a group of Chagossians defeated the Foreign Office at the high court in London and secured the right to return to some of their homeland islands.

The chances are, however, that many readers of this book will not have heard of the Chagossians, and the date will not appear significant. They could be forgiven for this, but the mainstream political culture cannot in my view be forgiven for the silence that has surrounded the story.

Beginning in 1968 the British government removed the entire population of 1,500 Illois people from the Chagos island group in the Indian Ocean. This strategy – plainly illegal under international law – was pursued as covertly as possible to ensure minimal international attention. It was then the subject of systematic lying by seven British governments over nearly four decades. The removal was undertaken to make way for a US military base on the largest island in the Chagos group –

Diego Garcia. Diego Garcia is now regularly used as a US nuclear base and as a launch pad for military intervention in the Middle East. At the same time, the Chagossians have suffered a nightmare at the hands of successive British governments.

In November 2000, the high court ruled that 'the wholesale removal' of the islanders by the British government was an 'abject legal failure'. It ruled that the Chagossians should be allowed to return to the outlying islands in the group, a major success after decades of struggle for redress against the British. But the ruling did not allow the islanders to return to Diego Garcia itself. The Chagossians are therefore continuing their struggle for justice. And the nightmare goes on because Whitehall is continuing to oppose the Chagossians in court and even in effect refusing to implement the high court's ruling by hindering their return.[1]

That the Chagossians and Diego Garcia are not household names in Britain is, to me, testimony to the servility to power of mainstream British political culture. One would expect this court case to be regarded as significant. Indeed, one might expect the tragedy of the islanders' treatment by successive governments to be rather well known; their plight has been desperate for nearly four decades. But not so: the small flurry of press articles around the court case has been followed by the same silence that largely prevailed for the previous decades. Watchers of television will have remained almost completely in the dark. And the current scandal blocking their return has gone largely unreported.

The now 4,000 islanders who want to return home have become Unpeople in British political culture, deserving of virtually no attention. Through all the US interventions in the Middle East that used Diego Garcia as a base for bombers, the media buried the story. Through all the parliamentary debates on Britain's 'overseas territories' (the Chagos islands are officially known as the British Indian Ocean Territory), the tragedy has only ever been raised by a couple of MPs like Tam Dalyell and Jeremy Corbyn. All the memoirs of policy-makers excised the story from history – Defence Secretary at the time, Denis Healey, for example, makes no mention at all of the depopulation of the Chagos islands in his 600-page autobiography.[2] Equally, in hardly a single academic book on British foreign policy in the past decades are the Chagos islands even mentioned: merely one example of the extent to which British academics work within a framework established by elite priorities.

Olivier Bancoult, the chair of the Chagos Refugees Group and leader of the Chagossians in exile, says that:

> We believe that if the British public had known of these unlawful deportations at the time, we would probably still be living on the islands now. There is a lesson for our community, that we must learn to stand on our own feet and insist that we are consulted during the process leading to our return. We must never again rely on governments to tell us what we should have or not have.[3]

The Chagossians' plight was almost completely buried until late into the 1990s when a British solicitor, Richard Gifford, was on holiday in Mauritius and happened to meet some of the Chagossian community in exile and learnt first hand of their ordeal. His findings in Mauritius so alarmed him that he came back to Britain determined to seek redress through the British legal system.

Removing birds and people

During the decolonisation process in the 1960s Britain created a new colony – the British Indian Ocean Territory (BIOT). This included the Chagos island group which was detached from Mauritius, and other islands detached from the Seychelles. Mauritius had been granted independence by Britain in 1965 on the barely concealed condition that London be allowed to buy the Chagos island group from it – Britain gave Mauritius £3 million.

'The object of the exercise was to get some rocks which will remain ours', the Permanent Under Secretary at the Foreign Office, its chief civil servant, said in a secret file of 1966. The Colonial Office similarly noted that the 'prime object of BIOT exercise was that the islands . . . hived off into the new territory should be under the greatest possible degree of UK control [sic]'.[4]

In December 1966 the Wilson government signed a military agreement with the US leasing the BIOT to it for military purposes for fifty years with the option of a further twenty years. Britain thus ignored UN Resolution 2066XX passed by the General Assembly in December 1965 which called on the UK 'to take no action which would dismember the territory of Mauritius and violate its territorial integrity'.

Higher matters were at stake: Diego Garcia was well situated as a military base. Britain allowed the US to build up Diego Garcia as a nuclear base and as the launch pad for intervention in the Middle East. Using Diego Garcia, B52 bombers recently struck in Afghanistan and attacked Iraq in the 1991 Gulf War. As I write this in mid-March 2003, B2 stealth bombers are taking off from Diego Garcia to bomb Iraq. Diego Garcia's role 'has become increasingly important over the last decade in supporting peace and stability in the region', a Foreign Office spokesman managed to say with a straight face in 1997.[5]

Olivier Bancoult told me, in an interview in London in October 2002, that 'our birthplace is being used to kill innocent people. We can't give any backing to what is happening on Diego Garcia, like B52s attacking Afghanistan'.[6]

To militarise Diego Garcia, Britain removed the 1,500 indigenous inhabitants of the Chagos islands – 'the compulsory and unlawful removal of a small and unique population, Citizens of the UK and Colonies, from islands that had formed their home, and also the home of the parents, grand-parents and very possibly earlier ancestors', as the Chagossians' defence lawyers put it. The islanders were to be 'evacuated as and when defence interests require this', against which there should be 'no insurmountable obstacle', the Foreign Office had noted.[7]

The Chagossians were removed from Diego Garcia by 1971 and from the outlying islands of Salomen and Peros Banhos by 1973. The secret files show that the US wanted Diego Garcia to be cleared 'to reduce to a minimum the possibilities of trouble between their forces and any "natives". This removal of the population 'was made virtually a condition of the agreement when we negotiated it in 1965', in the words of one British official. Foreign Office officials recognised that they were open to 'charges of dishonesty' and needed to 'minimise adverse reaction' to US plans to establish the base. In secret, they referred to plans to 'cook the books' and 'old fashioned concerns about 'whopping fibs'.[8]

The Chagossians were described by a Foreign Office official in a secret file: 'unfortunately along with birds go some few Tarzans or man Fridays whose origins are obscure'. Another official wrote, referring to a UN body on women's issues: 'There will be no indigenous population except seagulls who have not yet got a committee (the status of women committee does not cover the rights of birds)'. According to the Foreign Office, 'these people have little aptitude for anything other than growing coconuts'. The Governor of the Seychelles noted that it was 'important to remember what type of people' the islanders are: 'extremely unsophisticated, illiterate, untrainable and unsuitable for any work other than the simplest labour tasks of a copra plantation'.[9]

Contrary to the racist indifference of British planners, the Chagossians had constructed a well-functioning society on the islands by the mid 1960s. They earned their living by fishing and rearing their own vegetables and poultry. Copra industry had been developed. The society was matriarchal, with Illois women having the major say over the bringing up of the children. The main religion was Roman Catholic and by the First World War the Illois had developed a distinct culture and identity together with a specific variation of the Creole language. There was a small hospital and a school. Life on the Chagos islands was certainly hard, but also settled. By the

1960s the community was enjoying a period of prosperity with the copra industry thriving as never before. The islanders were also exporting guano, used for phosphate, and there was talk of developing the tourist industry.

Then British foreign policy intervened. One of the victims recalled:

> We were assembled in front of the manager's house and informed that we could no longer stay on the island because the Americans were coming for good. We didn't want to go. We were born here. So were our fathers and forefathers who were buried in that land.[10]

Britain expelled the islanders to Mauritius without any workable resettlement scheme, gave them a tiny amount of compensation and later offered more on condition that the islanders renounced their rights ever to return home. Most were given little time to pack their possessions and some were allowed to take with them only a minimum of personal belongings packed into a small crate.

The Chagossians were also deceived into believing what awaited them. Olivier Bancoult said that the islanders 'had been told they would have a house, a portion of land, animals and a sum of money, but when they arrived [in Mauritius] nothing had been done'. Britain also deliberately closed down the copra plantations to increase the pressure to leave. A Foreign Office note from 1972 states that 'when BIOT formed, decided as a matter of policy not to put any new investment into plantations' [sic], but to let them run down. And the colonial authorities even cut off food imports to the Chagos islands; it appears that after 1968 food ships did not sail to the islands.[11]

Not all the islanders were physically expelled. Some, after visiting Mauritius, were simply – and suddenly – told they were not allowed back, meaning they were stranded, turned into exiles overnight. Many of the islanders later testified to having been tricked into leaving Diego Garcia by being offered a free trip.

Most of the islanders ended up living in the slums of the

Mauritian capital, Port Louis, in gross poverty; many were housed in shacks, most of them lacked enough food, some died of starvation and disease, and many committed suicide. A report commissioned by the Mauritian government in the early 1980s found that only sixty-five of the ninety-four Illois householders were owners of land and houses; and 40 per cent of adults had no job. Today, most Chagossians continue to live in poverty, with unemployment especially high.[12]

British officials were completely aware of the poverty and hardships likely to be faced by those they had removed from their homeland. When some of the last Chagossians were removed in 1973 and arrived in Mauritius, the High Commission noted that they at first refused to disembark, having 'nowhere to go, no money, no employment'. Britain offered a minuscule £650,000 in compensation, which only arrived in 1978, too late to offset the hardship of the islanders. The Foreign Office stated in a secret file that 'we must be satisfied that we could not discharge our obligation . . . more cheaply'. As the Chagossians' defence lawyers argue, 'the UK government knew at the time that the sum given [in compensation] would in no way be adequate for resettlement'.[13]

Ever since their removal, the islanders have campaigned for proper compensation and for the right to return. In 1975, for example, they presented a petition to the British High Commission in Mauritius. It said:

> We, the inhabitants of the Chagos islands – Diego Garcia, Peros Banhos and Salomen – have been uprooted from these islands because the Mauritius government sold the islands to the British government to build a base. Our ancestors were slaves on those islands but we know that we are the heirs of those islands. Although we were poor we were not dying of hunger. We were living free . . . Here in Mauritius . . . we, being mini-slaves, don't get anybody to help us. We are at a loss not knowing what to do.[14]

The response of the British was to tell the islanders to address their petition to the Mauritian government. The British High Commission in Mauritius responded to a petition in 1974 saying that the 'High Commission cannot intervene between yourselves as Mauritians and government of Mauritius, who assumed responsibility for your resettlement.'[15] This, as the British government well knew, was a complete lie, as many of the Chagossians could claim nationality 'of the UK and the colonies' (see below). In 1981, a group of Chagossian women went on hunger strike for twenty-one days and several hundred women demonstrated in vain in front of the British High Commission in Mauritius.

The Whitehall conspiracy

British policy was: after removing the islanders from their home, to remove them from history, in the manner of Winston Smith.

In 1972 the US Defence Department could tell Congress that 'the islands are virtually uninhabited and the erection of the base would thus cause no indigenous political problems'. In December 1974 a joint UK–US memorandum in question-and-answer form asked 'Is there any native population on the islands?'; its reply was 'no'. A British Ministry of Defence spokesman denied this was a deliberate misrepresentation of the situation by saying 'there is nothing in our files about inhabitants or about an evacuation', thus confirming that the Chagossians were official Unpeople.[16]

Formerly secret planning documents revealed in the court case show the lengths to which Labour and Conservative governments have gone to conceal the truth. Whitehall officials' strategy is revealed to have been 'to present to the outside world a scenario in which there were no permanent inhabitants on the archipelago'. This was essential 'because to recognise that there are permanent inhabitants will imply that there is a population whose democratic rights will have to be safeguarded'.

One official noted that British strategy towards the Chagossians should be to 'grant as few rights with as little formality as possible'. In particular, Britain wanted to avoid fulfilling its obligations to the islanders under the UN charter.[17]

From 1965, memoranda issued by the Foreign Office and then Commonwealth Relations Office to British embassies around the world mentioned the need to avoid all reference to any 'permanent inhabitants'. Various memos noted that: 'best wicket . . . to bat on . . . that these people are Mauritians and Seychellois [sic]'; 'best to avoid all references to permanent inhabitants'; and need to 'present a reasonable argument based on the proposition that the inhabitants . . . are merely a floating population'. The Foreign Office legal adviser noted in 1968 that 'we are able to make up the rules as we go along and treat inhabitants of BIOT as not "belonging" to it in any sense'.[18]

Then Labour Foreign Secretary Michael Stewart wrote to prime minister Harold Wilson in a secret note in 1969 that 'we could continue to refer to the inhabitants generally as essentially migrant contract labourers and their families'. It would be helpful 'if we can present any move as a change of employment for contract workers . . . rather than as a population resettlement'. The purpose of the Foreign Secretary's memo was to secure Wilson's approval to clear the whole of the Chagos islands of their inhabitants. This the prime minister gave, five days later on 26 April. By the time of this formal decision, however, the removal had already effectively started – Britain had in 1968 started refusing to return Chagossians who were visiting Mauritius or the Seychelles.[19]

A Foreign Office memo of 1970 outlined the Whitehall conspiracy:

> We would not wish it to become general knowledge that some of the inhabitants have lived on Diego Garcia for at least two generations and could, therefore, be regarded as 'belongers'. We shall therefore advise ministers in handling supplementary questions about

whether Diego Garcia is inhabited to say there is only a small number of contract labourers from the Seychelles and Mauritius engaged in work on the copra plantations on the island. That is being economical with the truth.

It continued:

Should a member [of the House of Commons] ask about what should happen to these contract labourers in the event of a base being set up on the island, we hope that, for the present, this can be brushed aside as a hypothetical question at least until any decision to go ahead with the Diego Garcia facility becomes public.[20]

Detailed guidance notes were issued to Foreign Office and Ministry of Defence press officers telling them to mislead the media if asked.

The reality that was being concealed was clearly understood. A secret document signed by Michael Stewart in 1968, said: 'By any stretch of the English language, there was an indigenous population, and the Foreign Office knew it.' A Foreign Office minute from 1965 recognises policy as 'to certify [the Chagossians], more or less fraudulently, as belonging somewhere else'. Another Whitehall document was entitled: 'Maintaining the Fiction'. The Foreign Office legal adviser wrote in January 1970 that it was important 'to maintain the fiction that the inhabitants of Chagos are not a permanent or semi-permanent population'.[21]

Yet all subsequent ministers have peddled this lie in public, hitting on the formula to designate the Chagossians merely as 'former plantation workers', while knowing this was palpably untrue. For example, Margaret Thatcher told the House of Commons in 1990 that:

Those concerned worked on the former copra plantations in the Chagos archipelago. After the plantations closed between 1971 and 1973 they and their families were resettled in Mauritius and given considerable financial assistance. Their future now lies in Mauritius.[22]

Foreign Office minister William Waldegrave said in 1989 that he had recently met 'a delegation of former plantation workers from the Chagos Islands', before falsely asserting that they 'are increasingly integrated into the Mauritian community'. Aid minister Baroness Chalker also told the House that 'the former plantation workers (Illois) are now largely integrated into Mauritian and Seychellese society'.[23]

New Labour has maintained the fiction in the twenty-first century, continuing to peddle the official line in the court case that the islanders were 'contract labourers'. As I write this, the Foreign Office website contains a country profile of the British Indian Ocean Territory that states there are 'no indigenous inhabitants'.[24]

Another issue that the British government went to great lengths to conceal was the fact that many of the Chagossians were 'citizens of the UK and the colonies'. Britain preferred to designate them Mauritians so they could be dumped there and left to the Mauritian authorities to deal with. The Foreign Secretary warned in 1968 of the 'possibility . . . [that] some of them might one day claim a right to remain in the BIOT by virtue of their citizenship of the UK and the Colonies'. A Ministry of Defence note in the same year states that it was 'of cardinal importance that no American official . . . should inadvertently divulge' that the islanders have dual nationality.[25]

Britain's High Commission in Mauritius noted in January 1971, before a meeting with the Mauritian prime minister, that

> Naturally, I shall not suggest to him that some of these have also UK nationality . . . always possible that they may spot this point, in which case, presumably, we shall have to come clean [sic].

In 1971 the Foreign Office was saying that it was 'not at present HMG's policy to advise "contract workers" of their dual citizenship' nor to inform the Mauritian government, referring to 'this policy of concealment'.[26]

Ministers also lied in public about the British role in the removal of the Chagossians. For example, Foreign Office minister Richard Luce wrote to an MP in 1981, in response to a letter from one of his constituents, that the islanders had been 'given the choice of either returning [to Mauritius or the Seychelles] or going to plantations on other islands in BIOT' [sic]. According to this revised history, the 'majority chose to return to Mauritius and their employers . . . made the arrangements for them to be transferred'.[27]

Ministers in the 1960s also lied about the terms under which Britain offered the Diego Garcia base to the US. The US paid Britain £5 million for the island, an amount deducted from the price Britain paid the US for buying the Polaris nuclear weapon system. The US asked for this deal to be kept secret and prime minister Harold Wilson complied, lying in public. A Foreign Office memo to the US of 1967 said that 'ultimately, under extreme pressure, we should have to deny the existence of a US contribution in any form, and to advise ministers to do so in [parliament] if necessary'.

A Foreign Office memo of 1980 recommended to the then Foreign Secretary that 'no journalists should be allowed to visit Diego Garcia' and that visits by MPs be kept to a minimum to keep out those 'who deliberately stir up unwelcome questions'.[28]

The defence lawyers for the Chagossians, who unearthed the secret files, note that:

> Concealment is a theme which runs through the official documents, concealment of the existence of a permanent population, of BIOT itself, concealment of the status of the Chagossians, concealment of the full extent of the responsibility of the United Kingdom government . . ., concealment of the fact that many of the Chagossians were Citizens of the UK and Colonies . . . This concealment was compounded by a continuing

refusal to accept that those who were removed from the islands in 1971–73 had not exercised a voluntary decision to leave the islands.

Indeed, the lawyers argue, 'for practical purposes, it may well be that the deceit of the world at large, in particular the United Nations, was the critical part' of the government's policy.[29]

New Labour, old values

I met Olivier Bancoult and a group of Chagossians on their visit to London in October/November 2002 to give evidence to a further high court hearing. They are demanding fuller compensation and the right to return to Diego Garcia, both opposed by the government, which is continuing to challenge them in court. On this visit they were not meeting Foreign Office officials. Bancoult told me that:

> Every time we come to explain clearly about the Chagossians, they always give us hope without anything coming. The Foreign Office is not acting in good faith to get things moving in our favour. It seems they are not interested in us, maybe because we're black skinned and African origin. If you take the example of the Falklands, the problem was solved. If you take Montserrat, everything was solved. It is shameful that the UK is head of the Commonwealth.[30]

I found the group of Chagossians a very dignified yet sorry sight. Most were bewildered by what they were having to go through – come over to London from Mauritius to sit in court hearings every day to give evidence on why they should be allowed to return to their homeland, in proceedings conducted in a language almost none of them spoke, and with some of them frail and ill. Their stay was only possible due to the firm of lawyers and the Chagos Support Group in Britain, which is itself run on a shoestring budget, scraping together the minimum finance. The government gave not a penny. When I met them, the group of Chagossians were huddled in a small basement of a London hotel, whose owners were providing them with the favour of basic food during their stay. The indignity of it all at the hands of the British government is part of the scandal.

As Labour's Treasury spokesperson in 1981, Robin Cook protested about the use of Diego Garcia by US nuclear-armed bombers; but as Foreign Secretary he was reportedly 'evading the issue' when it was raised at the UN, and supported the government's court case against the islanders. Britain also continues to reject calls by the Mauritian government to return Diego Garcia to it, saying it will do so only when no longer 'needed for defence purposes'.[31]

In the process of drawing up the Overseas Territories Bill, the Blair government initially tried to deny the Chagossians the full British citizenship on offer to inhabitants of the other overseas territories, saying they were citizens of Mauritius – a long-standing deception that British governments knew to be false. Only grudgingly did the government concede full citizenship rights.[32]

It has to be said that the government position has been quite extraordinary. The Blair government is continuing to oppose the Chagossians' search for justice, as well as maintaining much of the apologias and deceit that has marked elite policy for the last four decades. It doesn't even believe it has anything officially to apologise for. Foreign Office minister John Battle told the House of Commons that the court case concerned only the settlement of the outer islands 'not the rights and wrongs of the way in which the Illois were removed'.[33]

Whitehall is distinctly unhappy about the ruling in the court case and is in effect doing what it can to block its implementation. The Chagossians' return 'is not a realistic prospect', Foreign Office minister Tony Lloyd told the House of Commons in 1998, before the high court ruling of November 2000. He added that 'successive British governments have given generous financial assistance to help with the resettlement of the Illois in Mauritius', referring presumably to the small pay-outs made in 1978 and 1982.[34]

A mere three months before the high court ruling in favour of the islanders' right to return to the outlying islands, Foreign Office minister Peter Hain said that:

> The outer islands of the territory have been uninhabited for 30 years so any resettlement would present serious problems both because of the practical feasibility and in relation to our treaty obligations.[35]

Similarly, a Foreign Office memorandum to the House of Commons stated that resettlement of the outlying islands would be 'impractical and inconsistent with the existing defence facilities'. 'Our position on the future of the territory will be determined by our strategic and other interests and our treaty commitments to the USA.' The memo said nothing about the government's obligations to the rights of the islanders – which is at least honest, since it is clear that neither Conservative nor Labour governments have ever cared a hoot about the islanders or any weird notion of human rights.[36]

A year after the court case victory the government was effectively defying the ruling of the court. The Foreign Office blocked the first planned visit by the islanders to their home for thirty years, saying 'the security situation precludes this'. It said that 'we continue to give your general request to facilitate a visit careful consideration, without any commitment to fund such a visit'. The islanders merely intended to stay one night aboard ship, on a reconnaissance visit.[37]

The Foreign Office has also dragged out the process of conducting a feasibility study on resettlement, and then concluded from it that resettlement on the islands is largely infeasible anyway, saying that long-term habitation on the islands would be precarious and the costs prohibitive. The Chagossians were allowed to take no part in this study. By contrast, a feasibility study conducted for the islanders shows that resettlement is feasible and that there would be adequate water, fish and other supplies, even with low levels of investment. This study states that 'it is fatuous to suggest that the islands cannot be resettled' and that the conclusion of the government's feasibility study is 'erroneous in every assertion'. It notes that the Chagos islands are indeed already successfully settled – by the US military.[38]

So-called 'yachties' appear to spend months living on the outlying islands. Meanwhile, millions of euros have been set aside by the EU in aid for overseas territories – ™ 2 million for the Pitcairn islands, for example, with a population of around four dozen. The British government has not asked the EU for anything to resettle the Chagossians.

The court case resulted in a compromise, securing the islanders' right to return to the outlying islands, but not Diego Garcia. The British government remains adamantly opposed to their return to Diego Garcia, referring to 'treaty obligations' to the US – that is, the deal illegally stitched up between the two. Access to Diego Garcia 'will continue to be controlled strictly and will be by permit only', the government says. Thus Labour will require the deported inhabitants to have a special permit to visit their territory. This is in contrast to the 1,500 civilian workers currently employed on Diego Garcia, mainly from Mauritius and the Philippines, who service the US base. The British and US navies conduct sea and air patrols to ensure no one gets too close to Diego Garcia.[39]

The US was also strongly opposed to any resettlement, even in the outlying islands, and exerted pressure on the British government to prevent this. The *Guardian* published a confidential letter from the State Department to the Foreign Office saying that such resettlement 'would significantly downgrade the strategic importance of a vital military asset unique in the region'. The US disclosed that it was seeking permission from Britain to expand its military base on Diego Garcia and to 'develop the island as a forward operating location for expeditionary air force operations – one of only four such locations worldwide'. This was a year before September 11th provided easy pretexts for such increased power projection. Following the court case, the US conceded that it could not prevent the islanders from returning to the outer islands but will not allow them on Diego Garcia.[40]

A comparison between Diego Garcia and the Falklands is perhaps obvious. As John Madeley commented in a 1982 report for the Minority Rights Group:

> Britain's treatment of the Illois people stands in eloquent and stark contrast with the way the people of the Falkland islands were treated in the Spring of 1982. The invasion of the Falklands was furiously resisted by British forces travelling 8,000 miles at a cost of over a thousand million pounds and many British and Argentinian lives. Diego Garcia was handed over without its inhabitants – far from being defended – even being consulted before being removed.[41]

The Falklands parallel is also apt since five days before Argentina invaded the islands in 1982 – and well over a decade after the first removals from Diego Garcia began – a 'final' deal was 'agreed' between Britain and the Chagossians for compensation of £4 million.

The Argentinian invasion provoked outrage in the media and political culture, including declarations on the importance of maintaining high principles, international law and the defence of the human rights of British subjects. The editors of The *Financial Times*, for example, noted that the invasion of the Falklands was 'an illegal and immoral means to make good territorial claims'. A solution to this particular action 'should not pass over the wishes of the Falkland Islanders who wish to preserve their traditions'. 'If such bare-faced attacks were allowed to achieve their ends', they said, 'then the consequences would be grave not just in one or two remaining British outposts, but for peace in many areas'.[42]

The *Daily Telegraph* editors noted that 'we are pledged to

consider the wishes of the Falklanders "paramount", as Mrs Thatcher repeated last night' (in an emergency debate in the House of Commons). They stated that 'principle dictates' that the US should support Britain over the Falklands since it cannot 'be indifferent to the imposition of foreign rule on people who have no desire for it'. Britain's decision to send a task force 'was taken quite simply because it was the only alternative to a humiliating betrayal of the Falkland Islands'. The invasion 'was clearly as illegal an act as can be imagined and has been so proclaimed by the United Nations Security Council'.

All these violations also apply to the Chagos islanders. Their removal violated articles 9 and 13 of the UN Declaration of Human Rights, which stated that 'no one should be subjected to arbitrary exile' and 'everybody has the right to return to his country', among others.

But a different set of principles applies to them than to the Falklanders. High principles are defended only where violations occur against us. They rarely apply (or are even mentioned in the ideological system) in cases where the British government commits them. The Chagos islanders continue to be, tragically, just one group of victims of the irrelevance of human rights to British elites – and of the deceit behind the high-minded rhetoric – as I have tried to show throughout this book.

23

THE CHALLENGES AHEAD

The history of British foreign policy is partly one of complicity in some of the world's worst horrors. If we were honest, we would see Britain's role in the world to a large extent as a story of crimes against humanity. Currently, contrary to the extraordinary rhetoric of New Labour leaders and other elites, policies are continuing on this traditional course, systematically making the world more abusive of human rights as well as more unequal and less secure.

This is reason alone for a complete change in direction. But British policies are not only exacerbating the misery of others; they are also dangerous to the British public. There are at least five 'boomerangs', or ways in which foreign policies will continue to rebound on us, unless there is a drastic change of course.

The first concerns weapons of mass destruction. The British government's threats to use nuclear weapons, its view that they are 'sub-strategic' and war-fighting, combined with its extraordinary new military interventionism, are sending a clear signal to others: any regime wanting to take on the West – or perhaps even any nation serious about pursuing an independent course of development – should now acquire nuclear weapons. If a country does not have these weapons, it may be threatened with destruction and pulverised, as in Afghanistan, Yugoslavia and Iraq. Nuclear weapons could be seen as protection against this new phase of Western threats and interventionism masquerading as the 'war against terrorism'. It is inconceivable that NATO would have bombed Yugoslavia if Belgrade had possessed functioning weapons of mass destruction. This lesson is surely being drawn by every repressive regime around the world, not to mention terrorist groups, and perhaps some more benign governments too. The de facto encouragement to possess weapons of mass destruction is surely an ominous development for the future.

Only an illusion of 'security' is being provided, as Britain, especially with the US, increases military spending, heightens 'power projection' capabilities, develops ever more sophisticated weapons and ensures Western conventional military dominance. Rather, these priorities breed increasing insecurity and further encourage others to acquire ever more devastating weapons. All this is good for the arms corporations that New Labour is so eager to appease, but bad for everyone else.

A second obvious boomerang is from Britain's arms exports. The world's second largest exporter is helping to heighten tensions and sow the seeds of more destructive conflict on all continents. Britain is basically prepared to arm anyone with anything, with only a few exceptions, which is what the arms export guidelines – very elastic anyway, and routinely broken – are really meant to enable. As chapter 8 has shown, Britain regularly arms both sides in conflicts, the world's poorest countries, human rights abusers and states engaged in wars against their own populations or occupying territory. The prospects for peace and development – urgent tasks in numerous places – are made much more grim by the most fundamental of Whitehall's policies.

Arms exports are so entrenched in the British elite mind that anyone suggesting a halt is treated as insane – a good example of how 'normal' British policies are so destructive, not only to others but also to us. Increasingly, under globalisation, conflicts elsewhere are not simply containable and the idea that we can just wall ourselves off from them no longer holds. Selling arms around the world not only enables aggressors to pursue war but it reinforces the military's role in politics, often undermining democracy, and diverts scarce resources away from development needs. Arms exports often breed further conflict and add to the inequalities that breed violence and a more unstable world. Britain's arms exports are political interventions, often propping up elites, aiding their repression and helping one side gain advantage over another – they are part of Britain's general foreign policy, as well as a profitable business of death. The only insanity is that they continue.

Third, the 'war against terrorism' risks rebounding on us in a number of ways. This new phase of Western military inter-vention may well be creating new enemies, a new generation of anti-Western sentiment, and perhaps even a new generation of terrorists willing to succeed that also part-created by Britain and the US in 1980s Afghanistan. The US/British strategy of massive military retaliation in Afghanistan appears – quite predictably – to have dispersed rather than destroyed Al Qaida. The conscious US strategy of depicting a manichean struggle of good versus evil has surely played right into Al Qaida's, and other fanatical groups', hands, in a way that Bin Laden could only have dreamed of. The US, in its reaction to September 11th, is easily seen as the monster that the terrorists wanted to portray it as to justify their attacks in the first place. They have now got their full-scale war, Bush and the US elite having no trouble in rising to the task, since it also works in their interests. People in the West are paying the price in terms of heightened insecurity, reduced civil liberties and a more 'conservative' domestic elite agenda, while almost anywhere in the world, it seems, can be the object of Anglo-American wrath.

Do we expect those on the receiving end of US/British strategy – Palestinians in the occupied territories, the parents of Iraqi children killed under sanctions or bombing, Afghan villagers bombed – to pursue peaceful cooperation with

Western states? Or to work patiently through international institutions to seek justice, when these same bodies are so obviously manipulated to promote Western policies? As Bush has tried to divide the world into those with us and those against us, the fact is that there are an awful lot of people against 'us', perhaps most people on the planet – justifiably so. And of course, *we* should be against 'us', as defined by Bush and Blair, if we are concerned to build a better future.

Fourth, supporting elites, especially repressive ones, has major costs. The new wave of domestic repression unleashed in many countries under the cover of 'anti-terrorism' is stifling dissent, including by more democratic voices, and often pushing people and groups to more extreme, intolerant 'solutions'. This is especially so with the repressive regimes in the Middle East supported by Britain. Rather than changing course post-September 11th, London and Washington have done the opposite, deepening their backing for repressive regimes and continuing to promote short-term 'stability'. The most remarkable thing about the world post-September 11th is how similar it looks to the one before; little has changed, traditional Western policies have simply been reinforced.

The primary costs are borne by the local populations, of course, who associate – correctly – Western policy with their repressers. By siding with these elites, Britain is helping these brutal regimes maintain power, which in turn fails to address the underlying political and economic issues that underpin poverty and mal-development in those countries. All this is surely providing a breeding ground for future conflict and insecurity.

Britain should be on the side of democratic forces in the Middle East and elsewhere, supporting ordinary peoples' struggles for justice and rights. This is surely a far better route to a more peaceful world of interdependence than one where Britain chooses to side with repressive rulers. But we should have no illusions that London's existing strategy has many benefits to British elites, who care little about high principles like justice and rights but mainly about securing profit and power in the world.

Fifth, Britain's global economic policies are helping to prevent development, increase inequality, and often deepen poverty. The strategy championed by British leaders to reshape the global economy – worldwide economic 'liberalisation' – is creating untold miseries for many while empowering the transnational corporations in whose interests the global economy is increasingly set to function. Western 'advice' in Africa and Eastern Europe over the past two decades – with London playing a leading role – has produced unprecedented increases in poverty in many countries. The most unequal world in human history is being created as a tiny transnational 'overclass' enriches itself further while parts of the world fester in deepening poverty. London's basic priorities are, again, adding to a more unstable and dangerous world.

All this shows that the real threats to us, the public, are our own leaders more than the official threats designated by them. Our major ally is really our major threat – the US is the world's leading outlaw state and through its new phase of military interventionism and strategy to reshape the global economy, it is creating even greater boomerangs for us than our own elites. Whitehall is complicit in this, failing to help rein in the US, instead generally supporting and empowering it. One of the greatest issues in world affairs is surely how to contain the US.

Clearly, in this situation, an awful lot of specific policies need to change. Many of the fundamentals of British foreign policy need to be reversed.

Instead of a special relationship with the US, Britain should withdraw its general backing for Washington and instead pursue a policy of strategic non-cooperation. This would involve challenging US policy towards the Middle East, for example, and developing alternatives with those working locally to pursue justice and rights. Instead of supporting elites in the Middle East and elsewhere, Britain should pursue a strategy of support for more liberal and democratic groups who offer development prospects for their populations.

Instead of promoting a one-size-fits-all straitjacket of global economic 'liberalisation', Britain should champion diverse economic policies suited to local situations. Instead of exporting arms, Britain should convert its military industry to primarily civilian use. It should immediately stop training the militaries of human rights abusers and abolish its nuclear weapons. Instead of reconfiguring its armed forces to offensive operations, it should spend a minimum on genuine defence and invest the savings, and much more, in well-managed multilateral aid programmes free from the influence of British and Western elites. Britain should also work to bring about democratic governance in international institutions, allowing fair representation for poor countries and enabling ordinary people's voices to be heard.

Overall, we must also set about disempowering Britain's role in the world rather than clinging to absurd notions of 'punching above our weight' and imperial concepts of maintaining Britain as a 'great power'.

The list could go on. It might seem like an idealistic wish-list at first sight. But the changes are really not that preposterous and I would venture to say that they are probably already in line with the beliefs of most people outside the elite – which is another reason why the public is viewed as such a threat.

These changes are obviously not going to happen without massive public pressure. The basic reason is that we are not concerned with changing democratic decision-making but with confronting a very well-entrenched, elitist, secretive and totalitarian domestic governance system that is really not responsive at all to any major, let alone popular, change. And the idea of foreign policy genuinely promoting humanitarian values and standards is altogether new to Britain – London has always promoted fundamentally immoral policies.

A popular people's movement has arisen in recent years, misnamed the 'anti-globalisation' movement, conducting demonstrations, rallies and teach-ins all over the world. Although comprising a variety of perspectives, campaigns and concerns, the movement is united first, in opposing the control of the planet by big business and second, in seeking a world where justice and rights are respected for all.

One thing that binds this movement together is people's sense in both North and South that they are the victims of the same policies under the transnational elite's project to promote worldwide economic 'liberalisation'. The exploitative and increasingly dominant role of transnational corporations in developing countries, due partly to the new global rules of the WTO, is mirrored in Britain. Increasing areas of our national life and public services are becoming simply instruments of someone's profit. Such power in the hands of democratically unaccountable private corporations is a massive attack on democracy and our ability to make economic decisions in our own interests.

In both the rich and poor worlds, privatisation programmes have created private monopolies and handed over key economic infrastructure to profit-seeking corporations with minimal regulation. Increasing international competition is creating a 'race to the bottom' in labour rights, resulting in straightforward exploitation for many and increasing stress at work and job insecurity for others. The under-funding of health and education is resulting in declining public services for many in both North and South. Overall, poverty is rising in many countries – notably where 'liberalisation' has gone deepest, including in Britain – while inequality is increasing almost everywhere.

People's common experiences in North and South are creating new forms of international solidarity. The huge anti-war protests all over the world in 2003 are further evidence of this, showing people's opposition to the lawless use of force by the world's powerful states, essentially in solidarity with the victims on the receiving end of our government's policites. I believe a positive agenda for this movement should be first to establish genuine democracy in the local institutions, clubs and societies in which people are already involved, and, crucially, to strive for the same in workplaces. Democratising decision-making in groups organised on less hierarchical, more egalitarian lines is already happening all over the world at local level, in associations and increasingly in larger communities, usually outside media scrutiny. The participatory decision-making processes of the city of Porto Allegre in Brazil, where citizens are able to debate and make local policies, is one example, but there are many more.

But the movement also needs to transform national governments and international institutions into genuine democracies. This is surely not an easy task.

As noted in chapter 13, I believe there needs to be a big new push by concerned people and organisations to democratise policy-making and the governance system in Britain. Bringing about a genuine popular democracy in Britain means discarding an entrenched elitism for a system where there are democratically accountable bodies, an end to secrecy and where people play a real role in decision-making through many more forms of direct democracy, instead of relying solely on an elected elite posing as 'representing people'. No fundamental improvement in foreign policy will take place unless policy-making is transformed from elitist, secretive and totalitarian to popular, open and democratic. Single-issue campaigns that focus not on transforming the system but on (usually minor) policy changes within it will only ever secure very limited gains while all coming up against the same big block – that the current system will always exclude the likelihood of policies being made in the maximum public interest. Surely the major lesson from the government's launching of the war against Iraq is that unless the formal decision-making processes are democratised, even massive public pressure can continue to be ignored.

Along with political democratisation needs to go economic democratisation. We need to reverse the deepening of global economic 'liberalisation' that empowers transnational corporations, that makes all countries promote a 'one-size-fits-all' strategy, and that requires an elitist political system to preside over it. Instead, we need to be promoting forms of local economic democracy in which private actors are subject to democratic control and economic policies are organised around local priorities. This means a re-localisation of decision-making so that policies are made closer to people and communities.

It also means abandoning notions of 'international competitiveness' as the solution to national regeneration. Rather, a good future depends on acting according to the reality of global interdependence and sustainable development, thus deepening a culture of 'global citizenship'. Economic and social policies need to be based on recognising that our future depends on cooperation within and between countries and, indeed, on promoting genuinely ethical foreign policies.

Much of history is about people's struggle for democracy in the face of elitism, and it is a long, hard one. But I think that establishing democracy in Britain, alongside deepening the sense of global interdependence among people, is the big challenge in transforming Britain's foreign policy. It is desperately needed to halt what is currently being done in our name and to reconfigure Britain's role in the world to at long last promote human values.

A CHRONOLOGY OF
MAJOR EVENTS
COVERED IN THIS BOOK

1947   Foreign Office describes **Middle East oil** in secret document as 'a vital prize for any power interested in world influence or domination'.

1948   Britain declares 'emergency' in **Malaya** and begins 12-year war to defeat rebels, who are mainly marginalised Chinese. Britain secretly describes war as 'in defence of [the] rubber industry' and engages in widespread bombing, draconian police measures and 'resettlement' of hundreds of thousands of people in fortified 'new villages'.

1951   June: Attlee government begins covert plan to overthrow **Iranian** prime minister Musaddiq following the latter's nationalisation of oil operations.

1952   October: Britain declares state of emergency in colony of **Kenya**. British forces conduct human rights atrocities, establish Nazi-style concentration camps and 'resettle' hundreds of thousands of people in 'protected villages'. Around 150,000 Africans die.

1953   August: Musaddiq government in **Iran** overthrown in MI6/CIA-organised coup. Shah installed in power as per London's and Washington's plans.

1953   October: Britain conducts military intervention in **British Guiana** to overthrow democratically elected government.

1954   July: US overthrows **Guatemalan** government of Jacobo Arbenz and US-backed junta seizes power. Britain aids US position at UN.

1956   October: Britain invades **Egypt** to remove nationalist president Nasser, eventually being forced to withdraw due to US and financial pressure. MI6 plans and carries out several assassination attempts against Nasser.

1957   July: Britain begins military intervention in **Oman** in support of extremely repressive regime against rebellion by Omani Liberation Army. SAS fights covert war and RAF conducts widespread bombing of villages and strongholds, defeating rebels by 1959.

1958   July: Britain conducts military intervention in **Jordan**, ostensibly to protect regime from alleged Egyptian-backed coup. Declassified documents suggest, however, that British planners fabricated the coup scenario to justify intervention.

1961   Death of **UN Secretary-General** Dag Hammarskjold in mysterious plane crash while trying to secure peace in Congo. Recent evidence has emerged of possible MI5 involvement.

1961   US begins major intervention in **Vietnam**. As US atrocities mount in the war that follows, Britain secretly provides US with military intelligence, arms and covert SAS deployments, along with diplomatic support.

1961   July: Britain conducts military intervention in **Kuwait**, ostensibly to defend the country from imminent Iraqi invasion. Declassified documents suggest, however, that British planners fabricated the threat to justify intervention.

1962   MI6 and SAS begin covert operation in **North Yemen** that eventually involves providing arms, funding and logistical support to royalist rebels in dirty war against pro-Egyptian republican forces. Around 200,000 die in the war.

1964   Britain begins second war in support of **Oman** regime, against the Popular Front for the Liberation of the Occupied Arabian Gulf, fought mainly covertly by the SAS. The 'Dhofar Rebellion' is defeated by 1975.

1965   October: Bloodbath in **Indonesia** begins as army moves against supporters of Indonesian Communist Party, reaching around a million deaths. Declassified documents show Britain aids the Indonesian army in conducting the slaughter through covert operations and secret messages of support.

1968   Britain begins illegal and secret removal of 1,500 population of **Chagos islands**, including Diego Garcia, following agreement to lease islands to US. Whitehall conspiracy begins, contending there are no indigenous inhabitants.

1970   July: British coup in **Oman** overthrows Sultan and installs his son. Sultan Qaboos remains in power today.

1975   December: Indonesia invades **East Timor**, leading to 200,000 deaths. In secret cable, British ambassador in Jakarta says Indonesia 'should absorb the territory as soon and as unobtrusively as possible' and that Britain 'should avoid taking sides against the Indonesian government'.

1980   MI6 begins largest postwar covert operation in **Afghanistan** to train mojahidin groups fighting the Soviet occupation.

1981   US begins covert intervention against **Nicaragua**, training contra rebels in sabotage and terrorist operations. Britain provides strong diplomatic support to US and nod and wink to 'security' company, KMS, to train and recruit contra guerillas and conduct gun-running operations.

1983   October: US invades **Grenada**. British government privately furious at US failure to consult in invasion of Commonwealth country, but publicly backs intervention.

1985   First contract with **Saudi Arabia** signed in massive Al Yamamah arms deal. With second deal in 1988, overall worth is around £50 billion.

1986   Spring: MI6 begins supplying **Afghan** mojahidin groups with 'Blowpipe' shoulder-launched missiles, some of which are used to shoot down passenger airliners.

1986   April: US conducts air raids on **Libya**. Britain allows US use of British air bases and provides strong public support.

1989   December: US invades **Panama**. Britain is only major state to unstintingly support US.

1991   January: US, Britain and coalition begin massive bombing campaign against **Iraq** to force withdrawal from Kuwait following its invasion the previous August.

1991   April: Britain and US establish 'no fly zones' in northern and southern **Iraq**. They begin covert, permanent war of bombing in the zones.

1991   November: Indonesian forces massacre hundreds of peaceful demonstrators in Dili, **East Timor**. Britain continues arms exports and business as usual.

1992   MI6 draws up plans to assassinate **Yugoslav** president Milosevic, according to an MI6 official. These plans are apparently not carried out.

1993   June: US conducts cruise missile attacks against **Iraq**. Britain provides political support.

1994   April: **Rwanda** genocide begins, quickly killing a million people. Britain effectively aids the slaughter by helping to reduce UN force that could have prevented the killings, in helping to delay other plans for intervention and in resisting use of the term 'genocide' which would have obligated the international community to act.

1996   MoD quietly sends first of several training teams to assist **Saudi Arabia** in 'internal security' as part of wider support to Saudi Arabian National Guard, the force that protects the ruling family.

1996   February: Assassination and coup attempt against **Libya**'s Colonel Qadafi with, according to former MI5 officer David Shayler, MI6 funds and backing.

1996   April: British-supplied Scorpion light tanks used in **Indonesia** to repress demonstrators. It is the first of eight known occasions in 1996–2000 that British armoured cars are used for internal repression. Blair government continues arms to Indonesia.

1996   September: US conducts cruise missile attacks against **Iraq**. Britain provides political support.

1997   February: Labour leader Tony Blair reassures BAE Systems, Britain's largest **arms** company, that 'winning exports is vital to the long term success of Britain's defence industry'.

1998   August: US launches cruise missile attacks against Al Qaida training camps in **Afghanistan** and a pharmaceutical factory in **Sudan**. Britain provides strong political support.

1998   December: US and Britain begin four-day heavy bombing campaign against **Iraq**, followed by weeks-long secret escalation of bombing in 'no fly zones'.

1999   March: Britain and NATO begin bombing campaign against Milosevic's Yugoslavia over **Kosovo**. The humanitarian catastrophe that Western leaders claim they are preventing is in reality precipitated by NATO bombing.

1999   April: Former members of **Kenyan** Mau Mau movement announce they are suing British government for human rights atrocities committed in 1950s.

1999   August/September: Around 5,000 are killed in **East Timor** and 500,000 forced to flee from Indonesian-backed terror around the vote for independence. Britain continues arms sales to Jakarta and finally agrees only to delay not stop them, while inviting Indonesia to an arms fair in Britain. Blair government tries to take credit for stopping Indonesian violence by helping to establish UN peace enforcement mission.

1999   October: **Chinese** premier Jiang Zemin visits Britain. Blair government refuses to raise human rights issues publicly, while police deny protesters the right to peaceful assembly and illegally seize Tibetan flags.

2000   January: **Chinese** defence minister, General Chi Haotian, who commanded the 1989 Tiananmen Square massacre, visits Britain to explore 'military cooperation', showing London's apparent defiance of EU arms embargo on China.

2000   February: As **Russian** forces ferociously bomb the Chechnyan capital, Grozny, reducing the city to rubble, Foreign Secretary Robin Cook says he 'understood' Russia's problems in Chechnya.

2000   July: British national Ian Henderson resigns as adviser to **Bahraini** government after career as head of repressive internal security service.

2000   November: High Court rules against government that **Chagos islanders** be allowed to return to some of their homeland islands, but not Diego Garcia.

2001   British **arms exports** reach £5 billion for 2001.

2001   February: US/British airstrikes against **Iraq** in response to alleged threats to aircraft in 'no fly zones'.

2001   August: US and Britain secretly step up bombing campaign in 'no fly zones' in **Iraq**.

2001   October: US and Britain begin massive bombing campaign against Al Qaida and Taliban regime in **Afghanistan** following terrorist attacks of September 11th. Civilian deaths in the war outnumber those killed on September 11th.

2001   November: At the **World Trade Organisation** summit in Qatar, Britain with EU allies tries to force 'new issues' on to the WTO's negotiating agenda in face of opposition from developing countries. The latter remain united and the decision is delayed for two years.

2002   Foreign Office website continues to lie that there are 'no indigenous inhabitants' of the **Chagos islands**, while Foreign Office continues in effect to block islanders' return.

2002   August: With full-scale war against **Iraq** appearing imminent, US and Britain secretly step up bombing campaign in 'no fly zones'.

2002   October: In midst of continuing **Russian** atrocities in Chechnya, Tony Blair says 'it is important to understand the Russian perspective'.

2003   March: After months of build-up, US and Britain launch war against **Iraq**, discarding the UN weapons inspection process and bypassing the UN Security Council.

NOTES

Foreword

1   In Lord Justice Scott's draft report of the Arms-to-Iraq inquiry (which
    was leaked and published), Scott accused William Waldegrave, then
    Foreign Office Minister, of writing letters in 'terms that were apt to
    mislead the readers as to the nature of the policy on export sales to
    Iraq . . . Mr Waldegrave was unquestionably in a position to know that
    this was so.' In the final version, *Inquiry into the Export of Defence
    Equipment and Dual-Use Goods to Iraq and Related Prosecutions*
    (HMSO, London, 1996), there is the following change: 'Mr
    Waldegrave was in a position to know that was so although I accept
    that he did not intend his letters to be misleading and did not so
    regard them.' Waldegrave and others had been allowed to read Scott's
    judgements on them and successfully demand amendments.

Introduction

1   Tony Blair, speech to Labour party conference, 3 October 2001, and
    'Doctrine of the international community', Chicago, 23 April 1999,
    www.pm.gov.uk
2   Peter Hain, 'We cannot be effete: it's time to fight', *Guardian*, 24
    September 2001; Clare Short, 'Poverty eradication and the role of
    business: New challenges, new partnerships', London, 20 April 1999,
    www.dfid.gov.uk

Part I Blair's outlaw state

1 Iraq: Ignoring people, maintaining order

1   Richard Norton-Taylor, 'Blair to order invasion force this month', *Guardian*, 8 October 2002; Evidence to House of Commons, Foreign Affairs Committee (FAC), 25 September 2002, para 22, www.publications.parliament.uk/pa/cm200102; Norton-Taylor, 'Troops decision up to PM, says Hoon', *Guardian*, 11 November 2002

2   Patrick Wintour, 'Blair will urge Bush to win backing for action', *Guardian*, 5 September 2002; Suzanne Goldenberg, 'US will attack without approval', *Guardian*, 11 November 2002

3   Anthony Nutting, *No end of a lesson: The story of Suez*, Constable, London, 1967, p. 58

4   Tony Blair, House of Commons, *Hansard*, 17 December 1998, Col. 1103

5   Simons, *The scourging of Iraq: Sanctions, law and natural justice*, Macmillan, London, 1998, p. 67; Anthony Arnove, 'Introduction', in Arnove (ed), *Iraq under siege: The deadly impact of sanctions and war*, Pluto, London, 2000, p. 16

6   Milan Rai, 'No justifications for war – no link to September 11th', 6 March 2002, www.zmag.org; Bruce Clark and Roula Khalaf, 'US in same old dilemma on how to deal with Iraq', *Financial Times*, 10 February 1998

7   Cited in Naseer Aruri, 'America's war against Iraq: 1990–1999', in Arnove (ed), p. 27

8   Simons, p. 106; Said Aburish, *Saddam Hussein: The politics of revenge*, Bloomsbury, London, 2000, p. 342

9   Mike O'Brien, 'Morality in asymmetric warfare and intervention operations', 19 September 2002, www.fco.gov.uk

10 Jack Straw, interview on Channel 4 news, 23 January 2003, www.fco.gov.uk; House of Commons, *Hansard*, 27 November 1998, Col. 440. Emphasis added; Jack Straw, 'Strategic priorities for British foreign policy', 6 January 2003, www.fco.gov.uk

11 Robert Cooper, 'In the name of the law', *New Statesman*, 9 September 2002

12 Simons, p. 12

13 Introductory paper on the Middle East by the UK, 1947, *Foreign Relations of the United States [FRUS]*, US Government Printing Office, Washington DC, 1947, Vol. V, p. 569; Selwyn Lloyd to US Secretary of State Dulles, 23 January 1956, *FRUS, 1955–57*, Vol. XIII, p. 323

14 Memorandum by the Acting Chief of the Petroleum Division, 1 June 1945, *FRUS*, 1945, Vol. VIII, p. 54; cited in A. J. Chien, 'Iraq: Is it about oil?', www.zmag.org

15 Cited in James Paul, 'Iraq: The struggle for oil', December 2002, www.globalpolicy.org

16 'US begins secret talks to secure Iraq's oilfields', *Guardian*, 23 January 2003

17 Miriam Pemberton, 'War in Iraq: The oil factor', *Foreign Policy in Focus*, Talking points, September 2002, www.fpif.org; cited in Paul

18 Anthony Sampson, 'Oilmen don't want another Suez', *Observer*, 22 December 2002

19 Jack Straw interview with *Persian Morning Daily*, 12 October 2002, www.netiran.com

20 'Iraq hits back with CIA offer', *Guardian*, 23 December 2002; 'Secrets of Saddam's hidden arsenal', *Guardian*, 5 September 2002

21 Richard Norton-Taylor, 'UK spies reject Al Qaida link', *Guardian*, 10 October 2002

22 Mike Berry, letter to the *Guardian*, 22 January 2003

23 Cited in Peter Oborne, 'The silence of the sheep', *Spectator*, 15 January 2000

24 House of Commons, Defence Committee, *Fourteenth report*, session 1999/2000, paras 254–7, 324, www.publications.parliament.uk/pa/cm199900

25 *Economist*, 6 October 2001

26 Mark Leonard, 'Diplomacy by other means', *Foreign Policy*, September/October 2002, www.foreignpolicy.com, Emphasis added

27 Fred Halliday, 'Manipulation and limits: Media coverage of the Gulf war, 1990–91', in Tim Allen and Jean Seaton (eds.), *The media of conflict: War reporting and representations of ethnic violence*, Zed, London, 1999, pp. 132–5; Dorril, *The silent conspiracy: Inside the intelligence services in the 1990s*, Mandarin, London, 1993, pp. 415–6

28 Ian Black, 'The propaganda war', *Guardian*, 14 November 1998; Ian Black and Richard Norton-Taylor, 'Propaganda drive against Iraq', *Guardian*, 25 March 1999

29 Ministry of Defence, 'The future strategic context for defence' www.mod.uk/issues/strategic_context

30 Julian Borger, 'Air strikes on Iraq rise sharply', *Guardian*, 7 September 2002; 'Blair says UK must pay US "blood price"', *Guardian*, 6 September 2002; Richard Norton-Taylor, 'Britain and US step up bombing in Iraq', *Guardian*, 4 December 2002

31 House of Commons, *Hansard*, 17 December 1998, Col. 652

32 Eric Herring, 'The no fly zones in Iraq: The myth of a humanitarian intervention', http/geocities.com; Richard Norton-Taylor, 'Bombing strikes stepped up in "secret war" against Iraq', *Guardian*, 8 June 2000

33 Sarah Graham-Brown, 'No fly zones: Rhetoric and real intentions', 20 February 2001, *Middle East report*, www.merip.org; Phyllis Bennis, Stephen Zunes and Martha Honey, 'US policy towards Iraq: Policy alternatives', June 2001, www.foreignpolicy-infocus.org

34 Graham-Brown, 'No fly zones'; Julian Borger, 'Allies taking aim at Iraqi regime', *Guardian*, 6 February 1999; Norton-Taylor, 'Bombing strikes'

35 Borger, 'Allies taking aim'

36 Julian Borger and Richard Norton-Taylor, 'Allies hit hard at Saddam's air defence sites', *Guardian*, 11 August 2001

37 House of Commons Defence Committee, *Thirteenth report*, session 1999/2000, 26 July 2000, www.publications.parliament.uk/pac/cm199900, minutes of evidence, 19 April 2000, para 21

38 'US military builds up huge attack force', *Guardian*, 13 September 2002

39 Bennis, Zunes and Honey; Voices in the wilderness, 'Myths and realities', Arnove (ed), p. 73; Graham-Brown, 'No fly zones'

40 House of Commons Defence Committee, *Thirteenth report*, para 31

41 Timothy Garden, 'This war can't be left to the politicians', *Guardian*, 20 August 2002

42 Voices in the Wilderness, 'Myths and realities' and George Capaccio, 'Sanctions: Killing a country and a people', in Arnove (ed), pp. 67, 141

43 Peter Pellett, 'Sanctions, food, nutrition and health in Iraq', in Arnove (ed), p. 161

44 Cited in letter from aid agencies including Human Rights Watch and Save the Children UK, 4 August 2000, in Human Rights Watch, 'Groups call on security council to address Iraq humanitarian crisis', 4 August 2000, www.hrw.org; cited in Pellett, p. 163

45 Cited in Eric Herring, 'Between Iraq and a hard place: A critique of the British government's case for UN economic sanctions', *Review of International Studies*, 2002, pp. 39–56; House of Commons, *Hansard*, 16 December 1998, Col. 532

46 Cited in Arnove, 'Introduction', p. 15

47 Cited in Felicity Arbuthnot, 'Iraq still on the rack', *Tribune*, 2 March 2000; David Edwards, 'Iraq in the gunsights', 28 February 2002, www.zmag.org; Robert Fisk, 'The hidden war', in Arnove (ed), p. 97

48 Hans von Sponeck and Denis Halliday, 'The hostage nation' *Guardian*, 29 November 2001

49 Cited in Herring, 'Between Iraq and a hard place', pp. 39–56; Simons p. xviii

50 Simons, p. xvii

51 Blair statement on Iraq to House of Commons, 17 December 1998 www.pm.gov.uk

52 Von Sponeck and Halliday, 'The hostage nation'

53 Reuters, 'Washington blocks $5bn supplies to Iraq', *Guardian*, 21 February 2002

54 Simons, pp. 119, 166; John Pilger, *New Statesman*, 3 May 1999; House of Commons, *Hansard*, 13 January 2000, Col. 220

55 Von Sponeck and Halliday, 'The hostage nation'

56 John Sweeney, *Trading with the enemy: Britain's arming of Iraq*, Pan London, 1993, p. 52

57 Richard Norton-Taylor, *Truth is a difficult concept: Inside the Scott enquiry*, Guardian Books, London, 1995, pp. 57, 204; Sweeney p. 29

58 See, for example, Richard Norton-Taylor, *Truth is a difficult concept* and Norton-Taylor, Mark Lloyd and Stephen Cook, *Knee deep in dishonour: The Scott report and its aftermath*, Victor Gollancz, London 1996

59 Norton-Taylor, *Truth is a difficult concept*, pp. 52–3

60 Norton-Taylor, *Knee deep*, p. 21; *Truth is a difficult concept*, p. 26

61 Sweeney, pp. 29, 95, 119; Norton-Taylor, *Truth is a difficult concept*, pp. 198–9

62 Sweeney, p. 140; Norton-Taylor, *Knee deep*, pp. 20, 81–2; *Truth is a difficult concept*, p. 49

63 Norton-Taylor, *Truth is a difficult concept*, pp. 49, 53, 55; Sweeney, p. 93

64 Sweeney, pp. 101–2

65 Cited in Norton-Taylor, *Truth is a difficult concept*, 1995, pp. 59–60

66 Sweeney, pp. 107–8; 'Anger over Straw's dossier on Iraqi human rights', *Guardian*, 3 December 2002; Nicholas Watt, 'Media and political salvo hits activists', *Guardian*, 3 December 2002

67 Sweeney, p. 95

68 Dorril, *The silent conspiracy*, p. 350

69 Neil Mackay and Felicity Arbuthnot, 'How did Iraq get its weapons? We sold them', *Sunday Herald*, www.sundayherald.com/27572

70 Richard Norton-Taylor, 'Don't trust Bush or Blair on Iraq', *Guardian* 21 August 2002

71 Prime minister's press conference, 4 September

72 House of Commons, *Hansard*, 9 February 1998, Col. 11

73 House of Commons, *Hansard*, 15 January 1998, Col. 272, and 27 April 1998, Col. 27

74 House of Commons, *Hansard*, 4 December 1997, Col. 340

75 HRW, 'Displaced and disregarded: Turkey's failing village return programme', October 2002, www.hrw.org

76 HRW, 'Human Rights Watch analysis of the 2001 regular report on Turkey', December 2001; HRW, *World report 2002*, 'Turkey'

77 HRW letter to the *Financial Times*, 15 October 2001; HRW, *World report 2002*, 'Turkey'; House of Commons, FAC, *Sixth report*, session 2001–02, 23 April 2002, para 35, www.publications.parliament.uk/pa/ cm200102

78 HRW, 'Hits and misses on Turkey's EU accession targets', 7 October 2002, www.hrw.org

79 Campaign Against the Arms Trade (CAAT) memorandum to the FAC, *Sixth report*, inquiry into UK relations with Turkey

80 FAC, *Sixth report*, para 42; House of Lords, *Hansard*, 11 June 1998, Col. WA101

81 MPA news service, 31 March 1997, www.geocities.com

82 HRW, 'Human Rights Watch analysis of the 2001 regular report on Turkey', December 2001

83 House of Commons, *Hansard*, 18 January 2000, Col. 667; John Battle, speech to the Turkish-British business council, Istanbul, 8 November 2000, www.fco.gov.uk

84 FAC, *Sixth report*, para 94

85 Letter from Dr Kamal Mirawdeli to Tony Blair, 6 December 1999, www.kurdishmedia.com

86 FAC, *Sixth report*, para 20

87 cited in Sheri Laizer, *Martyrs, traitors and patriots: Kurdistan after the Gulf war*, Zed, London, 1996, pp. 144–5

88 John Pilger, *New Statesman*, 19 March 2001

89 Defence Committee, *Thirteenth report*, minutes of evidence, 19 April 2000, paras 88–90

2 Afghanistan: The new Unpeople

1 HRW, 'Afghanistan: US bombs kill twenty-three civilians', 26 October 2001, www.hrw.org

2 George Monbiot, 'Gagging the sceptics', *Guardian*, 16 October 2001; 'We won't lose our nerve or falter, Blair tells doubters', *Guardian*, 31 October 2001

3   Jonathan Steele, 'Forgotten victims', *Guardian*, 20 May 2002; Marc Herold, 'Counting the dead', *Guardian*, 8 August 2002

4   Defence Committee, *Second report*, Session 2001–2, 12 December 2001, www.publications.parliament.uk/pa/cm200102, 'Summary'; Richard Norton-Taylor, 'A quarter of US bombs missed target in Afghan conflict', *Guardian*, 10 April 2002

5   Rory Carroll, 'Marines seize al-Qaida caves as Afghan violence escalates', *Guardian*, 9 April 2002

6   HRW, *World report 2002*, 'Afghanistan'; Jonathan Steele, 'Fighting the wrong war', *Guardian*, 11 December 2001

7   HRW, 'Afghanistan: New civilian deaths due to US bombing', 30 October 2001

8   'Restraint urged over prisoners', *Guardian*, 24 November 2001

9   Kathy Gannon, 'Kabul awakes to the aftermath of another night's heavy bombing', *Guardian*, 27 October 2001; HRW, *World report 2002*, 'Afghanistan'

10 Marc Herold, 'A dossier on civilian victims of United States' aerial bombing of Afghanistan: A comprehensive accounting', December 2001, www.medialens.org; Marc Herold, 'Who will count the dead?', in Roger Burbach and Ben Clarke (eds.), *September 11 and the US war: Beyond the curtain of smoke*, City Light Books, San Francisco, 2002, p. 119

11 '"Arab CNN" first berated, then bombed by US', 14 November 2001, www.zmag.org

12 HRW, 'Cluster bombs in Afghanistan', October 2001

13 Richard Norton-Taylor, 'Afghanistan littered with 14,000 unexploded bomblets, says UN', *Guardian*, 23 March 2002; Suzanne Goldenberg, 'Long after the air raids, bomblets bring more death', *Guardian*, 28 January 2002; Marc Herold, 'A dossier on civilian victims'

14 Rory McCarthy, 'Pashtuns suffer in brutal raids by rival ethnic groups', *Guardian*, 3 April 2002; HRW, 'Afghanistan: Return of the warlords', June 2002, www.hrw.org

15 'Media ignores the mass death of civilians in 'Afghanistan', 3 January 2002, www.medialens.org

16 Stephen Sackur, *BBC 10 o'clock news*, March 4, 2002; David Cromwell and David Edwards, 'Debate over Iraq', 11 March 2002, www.zmag.org

17 'Blair plays it cooler', *Guardian*, 31 October 2001

18 'Tony Blair's dilemma', *Guardian*, 5 November 2001

19 'The world at war', *Guardian*, 8 October 2001; Martin Woollacott, 'A military response is risky but necessary for America', *Guardian*, 21 September 2001

20 Ewen MacAskill, 'Legal warning on assault aims', *Guardian*, 4 October 2001; Michael White, 'Blair says Bush asked for cruise attacks', *Guardian*, 8 October 2001; Stephen Shalom and Michael Albert, '9/11 and Afghanistan', 9 October 2002, www.zmag.org

21 Paul Rogers, 'There was an alternative', *Red Pepper*, December 2001

22 'Blair's response to jitters', *Guardian*, 29 October 2001; 'Travelling hopefully', *Guardian*, 3 November 2001; 'Mindless and mistaken', *Guardian*, 11 January 2002

23 Cited in Noam Chomsky, 'The world after September 11th', 8 December 2001, www.medialens.org; RAWA, 'Let us struggle against war and fundamentalism', 22 March 2002, www.zmag.org

24 John Cooley, *Unholy wars: Afghanistan, America and international terrorism*, Pluto, London, 2001, pp. 90–1

25 William Blum, *Rogue state: A guide to the world's only superpower*, Zed, London, 2002, pp. 34–7

26 Cooley, *Unholy wars*, pp. 120, 226, 228; Luke Harding, 'Chasing monsters', *Guardian*, 24 November 2000

27 Cooley, *Unholy wars*, pp. 3, 146

28 Fred Halliday, *Two hours that shook the world: September 11, 2001*, Saqi Books, London, 2002, p. 38

29 Chomsky, *World orders, old and new*, Pluto, London, 1994, pp. 97–8

30 Cooley, *Unholy wars*, pp. 95–7, 81

31 Mark Urban, *UK eyes alpha: The inside story of British intelligence*, Faber & Faber, London, 1996, pp. 35–7; Dorril, *MI6*, p. 752

32 Otto Kreisher, 'US copters not as vulnerable as Soviet craft in Afghanistan', 20 October 2001, Copley news service, www.signonsandiego.com; John Fullerton, 'Afghan authorities hand in Stinger missiles to US', 4 February 2002. Reuters, www.in.news.yahoo.com

33 Cooley, *Unholy wars*, pp. 93, 95–7; Dorril, *MI6*, p. 752; Dorril, *The silent conspiracy*, pp. 391–2

34 Dorril, *MI6*, p. 772

35 Cooley, *Unholy wars*, p. 260

36 Tom Carew, *Jihad: The secret war in Afghanistan*, Mainstream, London, 2000, pp. 200–1

37 Blum, *Rogue state*, p. 224

38 Cooley, *Unholy wars*, p. 5

39 'We'll destroy them, says Bush', *Observer*, 16 September 2001; Richard Norton-Taylor, 'Strident about Trident', *Guardian*, 7 December 2001

40 Cited in Stephen Shalom and Michael Albert, '45 questions and answers', www.zmag.org

41 'US prepares for long war as Taliban close path to peace', *Guardian*, 20 September 2001

42 Rory McCarthy, 'New offer on Bin Laden', *Guardian*, 17 October 2001

43 Jonathan Steele, 'Afghanistan coup "being planned"', *Guardian*, 1 October 2001

44 Cited in Halliday, *Two hours that shook the world*, pp. 217–8

45 'Britons left in jail amid fears that Saudi Arabia could fall to al-Qaeda', *Observer*, 28 July 2002; David Leigh and Richard Norton-Taylor, 'House of Saud looks close to collapse', *Guardian*, 12 November 2001

46 See Terry Clancy, 'Empire in Central Asia', www.flag.blackened.net

47 George Monbiot, 'America's pipe dream', *Guardian*, 23 October 2001

48 Ben Aris and Ahmed Rashid, 'Control of Central Asia's oil is the real goal', *Daily Telegraph*, 25 October 2001

49 Memorandum by BP, March 1999, in House of Commons, FAC, *Sixth report*, Session 1998–99, 20 July 1999, www.publications. parliament.uk/pa/cm199899

50 Memorandum by Monument Oil and Gas, March 1999, in FAC, *Sixth report*

51 Speech to the Royal United Services Institute, London, 7 December 1999, www.fco.gov.uk

52 FAC, *Sixth report*, Session 1998–99, www.publications.parliament.uk/ pa.cm199899, para. 99

3 Explaining the 'war against terrorism'

1 Dorril, *MI6*, p. 799; Donald Rumsfeld, 'The gathering storm: The threat of global terror and Asia/Pacific security', 1 June 2002, transcript of speech at Nellis air force base, Nevada, 20 February 2002, www.defenselink.mil

2 George Bush, speech on the White House lawn, 11 March 2002, www.whitehouse.gov

3 Donald Rumsfeld, 'The gathering storm'; George Bush, address to the nation, 6 June 2002, www.whitehouse.org; Patrick Wintour and Jamie Wilson, 'Pledge by Blair on terror warnings', *Guardian*, 19 November 2002

4 Michael Parenti, 'Terrorism meets reactionism', in Burbach and Clarke (eds.), p. 71; cited in Edward Herman, 'Axis of evil – in Washington DC', 16 March 2002, www.zmag.org

5 Hugo Young, 'Americans want a war on Iraq and we can't stop them', *Guardian*, 27 November 2001; Colin Powell remarks with Indonesian Foreign Minister Hassan Wirajuda, 2 August 2002,

www.defenselink.org; 'Why Carter is smarter', *Guardian*, 15 May 2002; 'Spies in Iranian skies', *Guardian*, 14 June 2002

6   John Pilger, 'The colder war', *Mirror*, 29 January 2002

7   'Follies in the forum', *Guardian*, 29 May 2002

8   US president, *The national security strategy of the United States*, Washington DC, September 2002, preface; 'Stonewalling over Iraq "frenzy"', *Guardian*, 22 August 2002; David Teather, 'Dispersed al-Qaida poses even bigger threat, US says', *Guardian*, 17 June 2002

9   *The national security strategy of the United States*, pp. 13, 15

10 George Monbiot, 'America's imperial war', *Guardian*, 12 February 2002; Ewen MacAskill, 'From Suez to the Pacific: US expands its presence across the globe', *Guardian*, 8 March 2002

11 Edward Helmore, 'Anger grows as US bases spread', *Observer*, 20 January 2002

12 Brid Brennan, 'Another Afghanistan', *Red Pepper*, March 2002

13 Binaj Gurubacharya, 'Nepal army to recruit troops, buy equipment to fight Maoist rebels', Associated Press, 21 August 2002

14 Bridget Kendall, 'UK urges military aid for Nepal', BBC online, 19 June 2002

15 *National security strategy of the United States*, pp. 6, 23, 29–31; Donald Rumsfeld, speech at national defence university, Washington, 31 January 2002; Department of Defence, *Annual report to President and Congress 2002*, Washington DC, pp. 4, 19

16 *National security strategy of the United States*, pp. 6, 23, 29–31

17 Introduction, paras. 6, 87, in Strategic Defence Review, www.mod.uk/issues/sdr/intro.htm

18 Denis MacShane, speech to the Royal College of Defence Studies, 25 April 2002, www.fco.gov.uk

19 SDR paper, 'Future military capabilities', para. 26; SDR, para. 24; House of Commons, *Hansard*, 25 January 1999, Col. 13

20 SDR, para. 208

21 Defence Committee, *Eighth report*, Session 1997–98, 3 September 1998, www.publications.parliament.uk/pa/cm199798, para. 129; Denis MacShane, speech to the Royal College of Defence Studies, 25 April 2002, www.fco.gov.uk; Jack Straw, 'Failed and failing states', 6 September 2002, www.fco.gov.uk

22 SDR, para. 129; Defence Committee, *Second report*, session 2001–02, 12 December 2001, www.publications.parliament.uk/pa/cm200102, para. 100

23 Robert Cooper, 'The post-modern state', in Mark Leonard (ed.), *Reordering the world*, Foreign Policy Centre, London, 2002, pp. 16–18

24 'Profits of doom', *CAAT newsletter*, December 2001, www.caat.org.uk

25 Richard Norton-Taylor, 'Armed forces hail biggest cash boost since cold war', *Guardian*, 17 July 2002

26 'Outrage as Pentagon nuclear hitlist revealed', *Observer*, 10 March 2002

27 John Kampfner, 'Britain warns Saddam against retaliation', *Financial Times*, 18 February 1998

28 SDR, para. 63; Richard Norton-Taylor, 'Bush's nuke bandwagon', *Guardian*, 27 March 2002; ARROW briefing, 'Don't nuke Iraq', 22 June 2002, www.j-n-v.org/arrow

29 SDR, paras, 61, 19. Emphasis added

30 House of Commons, *Hansard*, 12 November 1998, Col. 281; Richard Norton-Taylor, '£2bn "mini-nukes" investment', *Guardian*, 18 June 2002; Response of the Foreign Secretary to FAC, Foreign policy aspects of the war against terrorism report, Cm 5589, August 2002, para (y)

31 House of Commons, *Hansard*, 16 July 1996, Col. 484

32 HRW, 'Anti-terror campaign cloaking human rights abuse', 16 January 2002

33 HRW, *World report 2002*, 'Introduction'

34 HRW, 'Dangerous dealings: Changes to US military assistance after September 11', February 2002

35 Amnesty International, 'Creating a shadow criminal justice system in the name of "fighting international terrorism"', 16 November 2001; HRW, *World report 2002*, 'Introduction'

36 HRW, *World report 2002*, 'Introduction'

37 Donald Rumsfeld, 'The gathering storm'

38 Defence Committee, *Second report*, Minutes of evidence, para. 88

39 Defence Committee, *Eighth report*, para. 103

40 Blum, *Rogue state*, p. xiv; 'Air attacks will be stepped up', *Guardian*, 13 April 1999

41 Defence Committee, *Second report*, para. 5

42 Noam Chomsky, 'Who are the global terrorists?', 19 May 2002, www.zmag.org

43 Jonathan Bloch and Patrick Fitzgerald, *British intelligence and covert action*, Junction, London, 1983, p. 160; Dorril, *MI6*, pp. 365, 555, 612

44 'Britain denies conspiracy to kill UN chief', *Guardian*, 20 August 1998

45 Dorril, *MI6*, pp. 610, 613–14, 639, 792

46 Tony Geraghty, *Who dares wins: The story of the SAS, 1950–1980*, Fontana, London, 1980, pp. 100–2; Dorril, *The silent conspiracy*, p. 78; Dorril, *MI6*, p. 696

47 Cited in Dorril, *The silent conspiracy*, p. 104; John Newsinger, *Dangerous men: The SAS and popular culture*, Pluto, London, 1997, pp. 61–2

48 Dorril, *MI6*, p. 793; Richard Norton-Taylor, 'Gagging orders issued in MI6 trial', *Guardian*, 7 October 2002

49 http/cryptome.org/shayler-gaddafi.htm

50 Ben Bradshaw, statement in the House of Commons, 4 March 2002, www.fco.gov.uk

51 Dorril, *The silent conspiracy*, p. 89

52 Amnesty International, press release, 4 May 2001; John Newsinger, in *Lobster*, no. 37, Summer 1999, p. 30; Niall Stange, 'Britain's tame death squads', *Guardian*, 26 June 2002

53 Amnesty International press release, 23 April 2002, http/web. amnesty.org

4 Big Brother, our favourite ally

1 A. Balfour to E. Bevin, 9 August 1945, *Documents on British foreign policy*, Series I, Volume III, HMSO, London, p. 17

2 See Richard Immerman, *The CIA in Guatemala: The foreign policy of intervention*, University of Texas Press, Austin, 1982, pp. 64–6, 82–3, 171–3

3 Memorandum by K. Pridham, 8 September 1954, PRO, FO 371/108945/AG 10345/6

4 Anthony Eden, *Full circle*, Cassell, London, 1960, p. 135

5 Bloch and Fitzgerald, pp. 44, 64; Dorril, *MI6*, pp. 715–20

6 House of Commons, *Hansard*, 3 March 1964, Col. 1128, 29 April 1963, Col. 702

7 House of Commons, *Hansard*, 14 March 1962, Col. 1318, 25 March 1965, Col. 735

8 House of Commons, *Hansard*, 17 April 1972, Col. 17, 25 April 1972, Col. 1274, 15 May 1972, Col. 20

9 Robert Stephens, 'Britain silent on bombing', *Observer*, 24 December 1972

10 House of Commons, *Hansard*, 16 January 1984, Col. 6, 24 April 1985, Col. 872

11 Dorril, *The silent conspiracy*, pp. 271–2; James Adams, *Secret armies: The full story of the SAS*, Pan, London, 1988, p. 361

12 Hugh O'Shaughnessy, 'Secret FO block on Nicaragua aid', *Observer*, 12 May 1985; House of Commons, *Hansard*, 26 February 1985, Col. 178

13 James Ferguson, James Painter and Jenny Pearce, 'Under attack: Central America and the Caribbean', in Latin America Bureau, *The Thatcher years: Britain and Latin America*, LAB, London, 1985, pp. 30–4; House of Commons, *Hansard*, 9 November 1984, Col. 326

14 Dianna Melrose, *The threat of a good example?*, Oxfam, Oxford, 1985, pp. 45–8

15 James Astill, 'Strike one', *Guardian*, 2 October 2001

16 House of Commons, *Hansard*, 19 October 1998, Col. 915; Richard Norton-Taylor, 'This is Britain's moment', *Guardian*, 13 September 2001; 'Clinton takes revenge', *Guardian*, 21 August 1998

17 House of Commons, *Hansard*, 4 February 1999, Col. 743; Foreign Office, *Human Rights: Annual report 2002*, chapter 3

18 Cited in Chomsky, *9/11*, Seven stories, New York, 2001, p. 48

19 Press conference, 25 July 2002, www.pm.gov.uk; Jack Straw evidence to FAC, 25 September 2002, www.publications.parliament.uk/pa/cm200102

20 Cited in 'America's newest ambassador to the rest of the world', *Guardian*, 6 October 2001

21 Patricia Hewitt, statement to the House of Commons, 6 March 2002, www.dti.gov.uk

22 'Targeting the terrorists', *Financial Times*, 21 August 1998

23 Polly Toynbee, 'Let's hope Gore wins', *Guardian*, 10 March 2000; Martin Walker, 'US tells Croatia it must leave Bosnia alone', *Guardian*, 25 October 1995

24 Martin Woollacott, 'Iraq cannot be left to its own dangerous devices', *Guardian*, 23 August 2002; Woollacott, 'Presidential hopefuls show interest in the world beyond', *Guardian*, 18 February 2000

25 Martin Woollacott, 'The policeman's lot', *Guardian*, 21 February 1998

26 'Reluctant cop', *Financial Times*, 13 January 1997

27 Geoffrey Wheatcroft, 'Send forth the best, ye breed', *New Statesman*, 5 July 1999

28 Cited in Blum, *Rogue state*, p. 1

5 Israel: Siding with the aggressor

1 Cited in HRW, 'Opportunism in the face of tragedy: Repression in the name of anti-terrorism', undated, 2002, www.hrw.org

2 Transcript of interview to BBC Radio 4, 2 April 2002, www.britemb.org.il

3 HRW, 'Jenin war crimes investigation needed', 3 May 2002

4 Ben Bradshaw, evidence to Foreign Affairs Committee (FAC), 23 April 2002, para. 209, www.publications.parliament.uk/pa/cm200102

5   Transcript of interview with Jack Straw, *Today programme*, Radio 4, 29 April 2002, www.fco.gov.uk

6   Ben Bradshaw, evidence to FAC, 23 April 2002, para. 239, 245, www.publications.parliament.uk/pa/cm200102

7   BBC2 *Newsnight*, 15 May 2002; Foreign Office memorandum, October 2000, in FAC, minutes of evidence, session 1999–2000, 25 October 2000, para. 8, www.publications.parliament.uk/pa/cm199900; Khader Shkirat, 'Conspiracy of silence', *Guardian*, 15 March 2002

8   Prime Minister's statement on the Middle East, 10 April 2002, www.pm.gov.uk

9   Nicholas Watt, 'Britain to push for "final" Middle East talks this year', *Guardian*, 2 October 2002

10   FAC, minutes of evidence, session 1999–2000, 25 October 2000, www.publications.parliament.uk/pa/cm199900, para. 22; Suzanne Goldenberg, 'Sharon tries to destroy all traces of Arafat rule', *Guardian*, 6 April 2002

11   'Fundraiser's role as envoy under attack', *Guardian*, 1 October 2001; 'Israel faces rage over "massacre"', *Guardian*, 17 April 2002

12   Ibid.; Ewen MacAskill, 'Show Israelis more sympathy, urges Straw', *Guardian*, 3 April 2002; Jack Straw, 'First steps to Middle East peace', www.fco.gov.uk

13   Israeli embassy press release, undated [November 2001], www.israel-embassy.org.uk

14   Ewen MacAskill, 'Arafat is a disaster; but to blame him alone is perverse', *Guardian*, 20 February 2002

15   Derek Fatchett, House of Commons, *Hansard*, 23 June 1998, Col. 957

16   'UK rift with Bush over Middle East', *Guardian*, 21 June 2002; Parliamentary question answered by Jack Straw, 25 June 2002, www.fco.gov.uk

17   'UK's forgotten arms exports to Israel', *CAAT newsletter*, June 2001, www.caat.org.uk; House of Commons, *Hansard*, 16 May 2002, Col. 779; Amnon Barzilai, 'UK tightening embargo on Israel', *Haaretz*, 22 August 2002

18   'The UK's role: A friend of Israel?', *CAAT newsletter*, November 2001

19   'Modified tanks are used in raids', *Guardian*, 13 March 2002; House of Commons, *Hansard*, 15 April 2002, Col. 723

20   Richard Norton-Taylor, 'UK equipment being used in Israeli attacks', *Guardian*, 29 May 2002; 'Straw provokes row over arms for Israel', *Guardian*, 9 July 2002; Richard Norton-Taylor, 'MPs question "nuclear upgrade" of Israel's Jaguar bomber', *Guardian*, 24 April 2002

21 Response of the Secretaries of State for Defence, Foreign Affairs and Trade and Industry, 'Strategic export controls: Annual report for 1999 and parliamentary prior scrutiny', Cm 5141, July 2001, para. f

22 British embassy, Tel Aviv, 'Britain-Israel relations', undated www.britemb.org.il

23 Patricia Hewitt, speech to the annual dinner of the British–Israel chamber of commerce, 16 January 2002, www.dti.gov.uk; DTI, Trade partners UK, 'Israel', www.tradepartners.go.uk

24 Philo, Bad news from Israel: media coverage of the Israeli/Palestinian conflict, May 2001, www.gla.ac.uk

25 Robert Fisk, 'When journalists refuse to tell the truth about Israel', Independent, 17 April 2001

26 Robert Fisk, 'The biased reporting that makes killing acceptable', Independent, 14 November 2000; 'When journalists forget that murder is murder', Independent, 18 August 2001. Emphasis added

27 'The unblessed peacemaker', Economist, 6 October 2001

6 Kosovo: Anti-humanitarian intervention

1 'Air attacks will be stepped up', Guardian, 13 April 1999

2 'It is simply the right thing to do', Guardian, 27 March 1999

3 FAC, Seventh report, session 1998/99, 20 July 1999, www publications. parliament.uk/pa/cm/199899, para. 287; John Pilger, 'Kosovo killing fields?', New Statesman, 15 November 1999

4 See Eric Canepa, 'Important internal documents from Germany's Foreign Office regarding pre-bombardment genocide in Kosovo', www.zmag.org; Edward Herman and David Peterson, 'Kosovo one year later: From Serb repression to NATO-sponsored ethnic cleansing', www.zmag.org; 'In the beginning was the big lie' www.iacenter.org/deichmann.htm

5 Response of the Foreign Secretary to FAC, Fourth report, Kosovo, Cm 4825, August 2000, para. 11; HRW, World Report 1999, 'Federal Republic of Yugoslavia', www.hrw.org.wr2k

6 Cited in Noam Chomsky, 'In retrospect', www.zmag.org

7 FAC, Fourth report, session 1999/2000, 23 May 2000, para. 89, www.publications.parliament.uk/pa/cm199900; Chomsky, The new military humanism: Lessons from Kosovo, Pluto, London, 1999, pp. 86–7

8 FAC, Fourth report, session 1999/2000, paras. 87–8

9 Defence Committee, Fourteenth report, session 1999/2000, 23 October 2000, para. 299, www.publications.parliament.uk/pa/cm199900

10 *Guardian*, 28 April 1999; 'NATO's tragic errors', *Observer*, 4 April 1999

11 Cited in FAC, *Seventh report*, session 1998/99, paras. 108, 110

12 Chomsky, *The new military humanism*, pp. 201–1

13 Evidence 14 April 1999, FAC, *Seventh report*, session 1998/99, paras. 107, 153

14 FAC, *Fourth report*, session 1999/2000, para. 101

15 Edward Herman, 'Body counts in imperial service', www.zmag.org

16 'No choice but to act, says Solana', *Guardian*, 24 March 1999; Richard Norton-Taylor, '"No plans for ground war"', *Guardian*, 24 March 1999

17 Richard Norton-Taylor, 'UK to send more troops', *Guardian*, 14 April 1999; Chomsky, *The new military humanism*, p. 36

18 Richard Norton-Taylor, 'Military chief's doubts', *Guardian*, 12 May 1999; Richard Norton-Taylor, 'Mystery Swede with Kremlin links who helped end war', *Guardian*, 9 March 2000

19 House of Commons, *Hansard*, 23 March 1999, Col. 161; FAC, *Seventh report*, session 1998/99, para. 344

20 Tony Blair, 'Doctrine of the international community', 23 April 1999, www.pm.gov.uk

21 Chomsky, *The new military humanism*, p. 135

22 FAC, *Fourth report*, session 1999/2000, para. 136

23 HRW, 'Civilian deaths in the NATO air campaign', February 2000, www.hrw.org

24 Amnesty International, 'NATO violations of the laws of war during Operation Allied Force must be investigated', 7 June 2000, http//web.amnesty.org

25 Cited in Leonard Sanford and Forrest Schmidt, 'Assassination attempts and other attacks on Yugoslav leaders', www.iacenter.org

26 Amnesty International, 'Amnesty International's initial comments on the review by the ICTFY of NATO's Operation Allied Force', 13 June 2000, http//web.amnesty.org; Richard Norton-Taylor, 'Allies count the cost of unity', *Guardian*, 13 March 2000

27 Michael Mandel and others, 'War crimes charges for the Hague tribunal against NATO leaders', www.flamemag.dircon.co.uk

28 See, for example, Edward Herman, 'The Milosevic trial: The final service of the Tribunal as a political and propaganda arm of NATO' and 'Propaganda system No. 1', www.zmag.org

29 Kenneth Roth, letter to the *Guardian*, 12 January 2000

30 'An appeal from various NGOs in Belgrade', Belgrade Centre for Human Rights, undated, www.zmag.org

31 HRW, 'Ticking time bombs', June 1999, www.hrw.org

32 HRW, 'Civilian deaths in the NATO air campaign', February 2000, www.hrw.org

33 In Defence Committee, *Fourteenth report*, session 1999/2000, paras. 134, 148; Peter Capella, 'NATO bombs "still killing" in Kosovo', *Guardian*, 6 September 2000

34 Chomsky, *The new military humanism*, p. 107; FAC, *Fourth report*, session 1999/2000, para. 63; FAIR, 'What reporters knew about Kosovo talks – but didn't tell', 2 June 1999, www.zmag.org

35 FAC, *Fourth report*, session 1999/2000, para. 66

36 Chomsky, *The new military humanism*, pp. 108–9

37 Ian Black, 'Russia gives peace plan its backing', *Guardian*, 15 April 1999

38 Chomsky, *The new military humanism*, p. 111

39 Ibid., pp. 114–15

40 Cited in Edward Herman, 'Propaganda system No. 1', www.zmag.org; HRW, 'Under orders', 2001, www.hrw.org/reports/2001

41 Philip Hammond, 'Third way war: New Labour, the British media and Kosovo', in Philip Hammond and Edward Herman (eds.), *Degraded capability: The media and the Kosovo crisis*, Pluto, London, 2000, pp. 127–8

42 Polly Toynbee, 'Winged victory', *Guardian*, 4 June 1999; Polly Toynbee, 'Left behind and left seething as a new way struggles to be born', *Guardian*, 12 April 1999

43 Jonathan Freedland, 'No way to spin a war', *Guardian*, 21 April 1999; John Lloyd, '"The liberation of Kosovo is as important, historically, as the fall of the Berlin Wall"', *New Statesman*, 5 July 1999

44 Hugo Young, 'Mr Blair, beware. Easter may yet rise upon your apocalypse', *Guardian*, 1 April 1999; Hugo Young, 'When "progressives" go to war, it has dangers. One is optimism', *Guardian*, 13 April 1999

45 'NATO's crimes', *Spectator*, 11 March 2000

46 *Guardian* editorial, 26 March 1999; 'No need for revision', *Guardian*, 20 March 2000

47 Ambassador Vershbow on NATO enlargement, 1 June 2000, www.uspolicy.be/archive/Europeandefense

48 Johannes Linn, World Bank, Address to the Joint EU presidency conference, 15 November 2000, http/1nweb18.worldbank.org

49 John Lloyd, '"The liberation of Kosovo is as important, historically, as the fall of the Berlin Wall"', *New Statesman*, 5 July 1999; Keith Vaz, speech to the 'South east Europe – Joining the European mainstream' conference, London, 7 July 2000, www.fco.gov.uk

50 John Pilger, 'Censorship by omission', in Hammond and Herman (eds.), p. 138; Chris Patten, 'EU strategy in the Balkans', 10 July 2001, http/europa.eu.int/comm; Ministry of Defence, 'Kosovo: Lessons from the crisis', undated, www.mod.uk/publications; Response of the Secretary of State for Foreign and Commonwealth Affairs, 'Government policy towards the Federal Republic of Yugoslavia and the wider region following the fall of Milosevic', Cm 5220, para. (oo)

51 Baroness Symons, 'A new partner for investment in Yugoslavia', London, 29 November 2001, www.fco.gov.uk. The actual text reads 'contribute', but this makes no sense and I am assuming that what is meant is 'continue'

52 Cited in John Pilger, '"Humanitarian intervention" is the latest brand name for imperialism', *New Statesman*, 28 June 1999

7 Chechnya: A chronicle of complicity

1 Cited in FAC, *First report*, session 1999/2000, 25 January 2000, www.publications.parliament.uk/pa/cm199900, para. 40

2 Chris Bird, 'Recak [sic] report finds Serbs guilty', *Guardian*, 18 March 1999; FAC, *Seventh report*, session 1998/99, 20 July 1999, para. 2 www.publications.parliament.uk/pa/cm199899

3 Cited in Edward Herman, 'The Milosevic trial: The final service of the tribunal as a political and propaganda arm of NATO'; David Edwards, 'How to fool the whole world', 10 May 2002, www.zmag.org

4 John Aglionby, 'Massacre that made Liquica a ghost town', *Guardian*, 9 April 1999

5 HRW, 'Indonesia: Justice for East Timor still elusive', 21 February 2002, www.hrw.org

6 HRW, 'Indonesia: Accountability for human rights violations in Aceh', March 2002

7 HRW, 'Burying the evidence: The botched investigation into a mass grave in Chechnya', May 2001

8 *Chechnya Weekly*, 6 September 2001, cited from Anna Politkovskaya, *A Dirty War*, Harvill Press, London, p. 158

9 Anatol Lieven, *Chechnya: Tombstone of Russian power*, Yale University Press, London, 1999, p. 3

10 HRW, *World Report 2001*, 'The Russian Federation'

11 Maggie O'Kane, 'Russians in Grozny bloodbath', *Guardian*, 16 December 1999

12 Martin Kettle, 'Pressure mounts on Russia to pull back from rebel city', *Guardian*, 5 November 1999

13 HRW letter to Tony Blair, 'Russia's president-elect Vladimir Putin's forthcoming visit to the UK', 12 April 2000

14 MoD, 'Strategic Defence Review', paper no 1, 'Defence diplomacy', para. b, undated www.mod.uk

15 House of Commons, *Hansard*, 17 January 2000, Col. 327; *Hansard*, 17 January, Col. 284

16 FCO Memorandum, 'The FCO's role in promoting British interests in and relations with Russia', 27 January 2000, in FAC, *Third report*, session 1999/00, www.publications.parliament.uk/pa/cm199900

17 Robin Cook, speech to the Royal Institute of International Affairs, 28 January 2000, www.fco.gov.uk

18 FAC, *Third report*, session 1999/00, para. 20

19 Patrick Cockburn, 'Cook tells Putin of his "concerns" about Chechnya', *Independent*, 24 February 2000; John Sweeney, 'Revealed: Russia's worst war crime in Chechnya', *Observer*, 5 March 2000

20 Amelia Gentleman, '80 civilians feared dead in Chechen massacre', *Guardian*, 23 February 2000

21 Keith Vaz, Speech on Caspian Sea region, 9 March 2000, www.fco.gov.uk

22 John Sweeney, 'Revealed: Russia's worst war crime in Chechnya', the *Observer*, 5 March 2000

23 Ian Traynor and Michael White, 'Blair courts outrage with Putin visit', *Guardian*, 11 March 2000

24 Giles Whitehall, 'Pragmatic Blair welcomes Putin on to the world stage', *The Times*, 10 March 2000

25 'Blair accused of endorsing brutal Putin at summit', *Observer*, 12 March 2000

26 'Blair to give Putin lesson in reform', *The Times*, 13 March 2000

27 House of Commons, *Hansard*, 21 March 2000, Cols. 478–9

28 Colin Brown, 'Putin to make UK his first official visit', *Independent*, 11 April 2000

29 HRW letter to Tony Blair, 12 April 2000

30 Prime Minister's internet broadcast, 13 April 2000, www.pm.gov.uk

31 HRW, 'Principal concerns of Human Rights Watch for the 58th Session of the United Nations Commission on Human Rights', undated

32 HRW, 'The "dirty war" in Chechnya', March 2001

33 *Chechnya Weekly*, 27 March 2001

34 Ian Black, 'Russian resolution', *Guardian*, 5 October 2001; Ian Black, 'Russia hints at rethink on NATO', *Guardian*, 4 October 2001; Ian Traynor, 'NATO pledge to reward Putin', *Guardian*, 24 November 2001; Ian Traynor, 'NATO ready to form an alliance with Russia', *Guardian*, 23 November 2001

35 *Chechnya Weekly*, 13 November 2001
36 Joint press conference, 5 October 2001, www.pm.gov.uk; Richard Norton-Taylor, 'Blair sees security role for Russia', *Guardian*, 17 November 2001
37 Joint press conference, 22 December 2001, www.pm.gov.uk
38 HRW, *World report 2002*, 'Russian Federation'
39 HRW, 'Opportunism in the face of tragedy: Repression in the name of anti-terrorism', 2002; *Chechnya Weekly*, 29 January 2002
40 HRW, 'Last seen . . . : Continued "disappearances" in Chechnya', April 2002; *Chechnya Weekly*, 26 March 2002
41 Ian Traynor, 'Russia and NATO reach historic deal', *Guardian*, 15 May 2002
42 *Chechnya Weekly*, 30 April 2002
43 *Chechnya Weekly*, 7 August 2002
44 Interview with BBC World Service, 9 October 2002, www.pm.gov.uk
45 HRW, Letter to Prime Minister Blair, 1 October 2002, www.hrw.org
46 Krystyna Kurczab-Redlich, 'Torture and rape stalk the streets of Chechnya', the *Observer*, 27 October 2002
47 *Chechnya Weekly*, 13 November 2001
48 *Chechnya Weekly*, 24 July 2002
49 *Chechnya Weekly*, 30 April 2002
50 *Chechnya Weekly*, 9 April 2002
51 Nafeez Ahmed, 'The smashing of Chechnya', 17 May 2001, Media monitors network
52 *Chechnya Weekly*, 11 March 2002
53 *Chechnya Weekly*, 1 July 2002
54 *Chechnya Weekly*, 9 January 2001
55 FAC, *Third report*, session 1999/00, para. 260
56 Ben Bradshaw, House of Commons, *Hansard*, 30 April 2002, Col. 656
57 Ewen MacAskill, 'The west does what it can. Not much', *Guardian*, 9 December 1999
58 Memorandum by the Foreign Office, 'The FCO's role in promoting British interest . . .'
59 FAC, *Third report*, session 1999/00, para. 109
60 MoD, 'Strategic Defence Review', paper no 1, 'Defence diplomacy', para. b, undated www.mod.uk
61 Robin Cook speech to the Royal Institute of International Affairs, 28 January 2000, www.fco.gov.uk
62 Patricia Hewitt, 'Russian economic forum', 18 April 2002, www.dti.gov.uk; Mike O'Brien, 'Russian business today', 28 October 2002, www.fco.gov.uk

63 Boris Kagarlitsky, *Russia under Yeltsin and Putin*, Pluto, London
    2002, pp. 3–6

8 *Labour's real policy on arms exports*

1   Cited in John Pilger, 'Moral policy won't stop British bullets', the
    Observer, 20 July 1997
2   CAAT, Submission to ECGD review, October 1999
3   'Arms to Africa', *CAAT newsletter*, December 2001
4   House of Commons, *Hansard*, 6 November 1997, Cols. 1486–7
5   House of Commons, *Hansard*, 8 July 1998, Col. 1091
6   Nicholas Gilby, 'Arms exports to Indonesia', October 1999,
    www.caat.org.uk
7   Richard Bingley, 'Publicly funded, privately run', *CAAT newsletter*,
    November 2001
8   Paul Dunne, 'The globalisation of arms production and trade:
    implications for the UK economy', CAAT inaugural annual lecture,
    November 1999
9   David Gow and David Fairhall, 'Britain tries to harness military R&D',
    Guardian, 6 March 1998
10 Dorril, *MI6*, p. 721
11 *CAAT newsletter*, November 2000; Richard Norton-Taylor, 'Labour arms
    shares listed', *Guardian*, 22 February 2000; Corporate Watch, *BAE
    Systems: A corporate profile*, June 2002, www.corporatewatch.org.uk
12 Ian Black and Richard Norton-Taylor, 'Britain hints at arms sale
    limits', *Guardian*, 24 May 1997
13 Statement by Foreign Secretary, 28 July 1997, in Select Committees
    on Defence, Foreign Affairs, International Development and Trade
    and Industry, *Third, Second, Third, Fourth report*, session 1999/2000,
    www.publications.parliament.uk/pa/cm199900
14 Neil Cooper, Memorandum to the House of Commons Defence
    Committee, August 1999, www.parliament.the-stationary-office.co.uk
15 'EU arms code', *Financial Times*, 17 February 1998
16 Cooper, Memorandum to the Defence Committee; Ian Black and
    Richard Norton-Taylor, 'Britain bans use and sale of mines',
    Guardian, 22 May 1997; George Parker, 'Cook orders scrapping of
    landmines', *Financial Times*, 22 May 1997
17 'Making a killing', *CAAT newsletter*, September 2001
18 Richard Norton-Taylor and William Raynor, 'Jailed "go-between" on
    UK-Iran arms deals is freed to keep MI6 secrets out of court',
    Guardian, 6 February 1999

19 'Making a killing'; John Pilger, 'Salesmen of death', 27 May 2002, www.medialens.org

20 Richard Norton-Taylor, 'British plane sales to India raise fears of nuclear use', *Guardian*, 23 April 2002

21 'Arms trade shorts', *CAAT newsletter*, January 2001; Pilger, 'Salesmen'

22 Richard Norton-Taylor and Ewen MacAskill, '£1bn arms push to India', *Guardian*, 12 January 2002

23 'Making a killing'

24 Statement by Foreign Secretary, 28 July 1997, in Select Committees on Defence, Foreign Affairs, International Development and Trade and Industry, *Third, Second, Third, Fourth report*, session 1999/2000

25 Responses of the Secretaries of State for Defence, Foreign Affairs and Trade and Industry, Session 1999–2000, December 2000, Cm. 4872, para. 8

26 Ewen MacAskill, 'Cabinet battle rages over sales of arms to Pakistan', *Guardian*, 12 January 2000

27 Ewen MacAskill, 'Britain lifts ban on Pakistan arms sales', *Guardian*, 6 July 2000

28 'Making a killing'; 'Arms to Africa', *CAAT newsletter*, December 2001

29 See Foreign Affairs Committee, *Seventh report*, Session 1999–2000, paras. 8–29, www.publications.parliament.uk/pa/cm199900

30 Amnesty International magazine, March/April 2000, www.amnesty.org.uk; FAC, *Seventh report*, Session 1999–2000, paras. 8–29, www.publications.parliament.uk/pa/cm199900

31 FAC, *Seventh report*, paras. 8–29, www.publications.parliament.uk/pa/cm199900

32 House of Commons, *Hansard*, 1 December 1998, Col. 160

33 CAAT, 'Basic methods, mass killing', *CAAT newsletter*, May 2001

34 CAAT, 'Labour's hypocrisy over small arms', 13 February 2001

35 CAAT memorandum to the FAC, January 1998, www.parliament.the-stationery-office.co.uk

36 Richard Lloyd Parry, 'British water cannons used on marchers', *Independent*, 23 May 1997

37 Letter from Tapol to Derek Fatchett, 24 February 1999, www.tapol.gn.apc.org

38 Nicholas Gilby, 'Labour, arms and Indonesia: Has anything changed?', July 2001, www.caat.org.uk

39 'Still accepting Indonesian assurances', *CAAT newsletter*, November 2000; House of Commons, *Hansard*, 13 May 1998, Col. 139

40 Amnesty International, 'Indonesia and East Timor: Arms and security transfers undermine human rights', 3 June 1997, http//web.amnesty.org; Nicholas Gilby, 'Arms exports to Indonesia'

41 Amnesty International, 'Making a killing', undated, www.amnesty.org.uk

42 Amnesty International memorandum to the Trade and Industry Committee, www.parliament.the-stationary-office.co.uk; Gilby, 'Arms exports to Indonesia'; Richard Lloyd Parry, 'Suharto's brutal protégé casts a show of fear over UN peacekeepers', *Independent*, 16 February 2000

43 Gilby, 'Arms exports to Indonesia'

44 Gilby, 'Labour, arms and Indonesia'

45 Gilby, 'Arms exports to Indonesia'

46 Tapol, 'Hawk aircraft terrorise Papua', 2 October 2000, http//tapol.gn.apc.org

47 HRW, *World report 2002*, 'Indonesia', www.hrw.org

48 Letter from Tapol to Ben Bradshaw, 26 June 2001, http/tapol.gn.apc.org

49 Gilby, 'Labour, arms and Indonesia'; John Aglionby, 'Indonesian army drives rich region into rebels' arms', *Guardian*, 11 March 2000

50 'Indonesian use of British jets "against civilians" investigated', *Guardian*, 3 July 2002

51 House of Commons, *Hansard*, 20 January 1999, Col. 504

52 Richard Lloyd Parry, 'Britain urged to halt Indonesia arms trade', *Independent*, 23 June 1997

53 Robin Oakley, 'China: arms trading under an embargo', October 2000, www.caat.org.uk

54 HRW, 'Principal concerns of Human Rights Watch for the 58th session of the United Nations Commission on Human Rights', 2002, www.hrw.org/unchr.58.htm; FAC, *First report*, session 1999/2000, para. 13, www.publications.parliament.uk/pa/cm199900

55 Oakley, 'China'

56 Trade Partners UK, www.tradepartners.gov.uk; Baroness Symons, 'Developing a closer relationship between China and the UK', 11 February 2002, www.fco.gov.uk

57 Reuter, 'Embargo-hit Pakistan buys British frigates', *Guardian*, 28 July 1993

58 Pilger, 'Salesmen'; 'Arms to Africa'

59 CAAT, 'New global US arms report released', undated; CAAT Africa briefing, February 2002

60 CAAT, 'British government sponsors African arms fair'

61 Derek Fatchett, House of Commons, *Hansard*, 1 June 1998, Cols. 151–2

62 EU Code of Conduct on arms exports, in Select Committee on Defence, Foreign Affairs, International Development and Trade and Industry, *Third, Second, Third, Fourth report*, session 1999/2000

63 See Curtis, *The great deception: Anglo-American power and world order*, Pluto, London, 1998, pp. 57–60

64 Memorandum by Tapol to the FAC, *Third report*, session 1993–94, 13 July 1994, p. 282

65 Select Committee on Defence, *Sixteenth special report*, annex, www.publications.parliament.uk/pa/cm199900

66 House of Commons, *Hansard*, 7 May 2002, Col. 42, and 10 June 1998, Col. 610

67 House of Commons, FAC, *First report*, session 1998/99, para. 46, www.publications.parliament.uk/pa/cm199899

Part II Elites and the global economy

9 *Trading off international development*

1 Speech by the Prime Minister, Cape Town, 8 January 1999, www.dfid.gov.uk

2 Speech by Gordon Brown, Speech to Federal Reserve Bank, New York, 16 November 2001, www.hmtreasury.gov.uk

3 Richard Norton-Taylor, 'Useless spies', *Guardian*, 23 March 2000

4 Patricia Hewitt, 'Free trade for a fair, prosperous world', Washington, 24 July 2001, www.dti.gov.uk

5 Baroness Symons, 'Meeting the challenges of the global market place', London, 13 February 2002, www.fco.gov.uk; 'Hewitt welcomes breakthrough for world trade landmark agreement at Doha summit', undated, www.dti.gov.uk

6 Margaret Beckett, 'Towards full market access', *Financial Times*, 10 July 1997

7 Tony Blair, speech at the World Economic Forum, Davos, 18 January 2000, www.pm.gov.uk

8 Cited in Graham Dunkley, *The free trade adventure: The WTO, the Uruguay Round and globalism*, Zed, London, 2000, p. 232

9 J. Michael Finger and Philip Schuler, 'Implementation of Uruguay Round commitments: The development challenge', World Bank, July 1999, mimeo; cited in Dunkley, p. 228

10 See Mark Curtis, *Trade for life: Making trade work for poor people*, Christian Aid, London, 2001, p. 90

11 John Keay, *The Honourable company: A history of the East India Company*, Harper Collins, London, 1991, p. 9–10

12 Clare Short, 'Poverty eradication and the role of business: New challenges, new partnerships', London, 20 April 1999, www.dfid.gov.uk

13 See, for example, Clare Short, speech to the National Association of Pensions Funds Investment Conference, 15 March 2000, www.dfid.gov.uk

14 Baroness Amos, 'International corporate social responsibility', 2 November 2000, www.dfid.gov.uk; George Foulkes, speech to the Commonwealth Business Forum, Johannesburg, 9 November 1999, www.dfid.gov.uk; Baroness Amos, 'New partnership for Africa's development: The challenges and opportunities', London, 28 January 2002

15 Clare Short, 'Advancing the world trade debate: Beyond Seattle', 30 May 2000; www.dfid.gov.uk

16 Cited in George Monbiot, *Captive state: The corporate takeover of Britain*, Pan, London, 2000, p. 344

17 Gordon Brown, Speech to the CBI, 10 November 1997; Brown, Speech to the CBI, 5 November 2001, www.hm-treasury.gov.uk; Tony Blair, Speech to the CBI, 17 May 2000, www.pm.gov.uk

18 Gordon Brown, Speech to the British-American Chamber of Commerce, 22 February 2000, www.hm-treasury.gov.uk; Tony Blair, Speech to the CBI, 17 May 2000, www.pm.gov.uk; Tony Blair, Speech to the Global Borrowers and Investors Forum, London, 22 June 2000, www.pm.gov.uk

19 Anthony Barnett, 'Big business profits from "giving" staff to Whitehall', *Observer*, 12 March 2000; Nick Cohen, 'Who audits the auditors?', *Observer*, 10 February 2002; House of Commons, *Hansard*, 24 July 1998, Cols., 143–4 and 9 December 1998, Cols. 223–4

20 Bloch and Fitzgerald, p. 305, Thomas Frank, *One market under God. Extreme capitalism, market populism and the end of economic democracy*, Vintage, London, 2002, p. 30

21 See Curtis, *Trade for life*, pp. 155–7

22 UN General Assembly, Intergovernmental preparatory committee for the third United Nations conference on the least developed countries, 'A compendium of the major constraints on development and desirable actions for the decade 2001–2010', A/CONF. 191/IPC/18, 26 January 2001

23 UN Subcommission on the Promotion and Protection of Human Rights, The realisation of economic social and cultural rights: Globalisation and its impact on the full enjoyment of human rights, *Preliminary report*, 52nd session, 15 June 2000, p.6

24 House of Commons, *Hansard*, 24 January 2000, Col. 73

25 South Commission cited in James Petras and Henry Veltmeyer, *Globalisation unmasked: Imperialism in the 21st century*, Madhyam Books, Delhi, 2001, p. 18; B. Milancovic, 'True world income distribution, 1988 and 1993', World Bank, Washington DC, 1999

26 Kate Watson-Smith, 'UK is now "worst place in Europe to be growing up"', *Independent*, 17 March 2000; Alexandra Frean, 'Britain heads EU for child poverty', *The Times*, 17 March 2000

27 Charlotte Denny, 'Legacy left Britain with worst deprivation in West', *Guardian*, 12 January 2000; 'UK condemned over poverty', www.bbc.co.uk, 13 June 2000; Larry Elliott, 'Britain's poor worse off than ever, says UN', *Guardian*, 9 September 1998

28 'Cold killed 20,000 elderly people last winter, says charity', *Guardian*, 28 December 2001. '20,000 may die from new flu', *Independent*, 9 January 2000

29 UNCTAD, *The least developed countries 2000 report*, internet edition, pp. 1, 110

30 Patricia Hewitt, 'Free and fair trade for peace and prosperity', London, 6 November 2001; 'Hewitt welcomes breakthrough for world trade landmark agreement at Doha summit', undated, www.dti.gov.uk

31 Government response to the Select Committee's report on the Globalisation White Paper, Appendix to the third special report, www.publications.parliament.uk/pa/com200001

32 George Foulkes, Speech to the OECD conference on the role of international investment in development, Paris, 20 September 1999, www.dfid.gov.uk; Baroness Symons, 'Trade and its role in sustainable development', 13 May 2002, www.dti.gov.uk

33 House of Commons, *Hansard*, 3 June 1998, Col. 234

34 House of Commons, *Hansard*, 17 November 1998, Col. 530

35 Select Committee on Trade and Industry, *Third report*, session 1998/99, para. 126, www.publications.parliament.uk/pa/cm 199998

36 Baroness Symons, 'Meeting the challenges of the global market place', London, 13 February 2002, www.fco.gov.uk

37 Baroness Symons, 'The contribution of services to the Doha development agenda', 24 April 2002, www.fco.gov.uk

38 'Towards GATS 2000', EU website at gats-info.eu.int; George Monbiot, 'Trade piracy unmasked', *Guardian*, 6 November 2001

39 Speech by DTI minister, not indicated whom, Unison seminar o
   GATS, 10 April 2001, www.dti.gov.uk. Emphasis added.

40 Christian Aid, *Master or servant? How global trade can work to th
   benefit of poor people*, London, 2001

41 Baroness Symons, 'The contribution of services . . .'

42 John Vereker, 'How we can help responsible business', London,
   December 1997, www.dfid.gov.uk

43 Clare Short, 'Future multilateral trade negotiations: A "developmer
   round"?', Geneva, 2 March 1999, www.dfid.gov.uk

44 Richard Caborn, Speech to the EABC, Washington, 7 March 200
   www.dti.gov.uk

45 DFID press releases, 17 December 1998 and 7 November 200
   www.dfid.gov.uk; Richard Caborn, Speech at UNCTAD X conferenc
   Bangkok, 13 February 2000, www.dti.gov.uk

46 Larry Elliott, '$100bn to win the peace', *Guardian*, 17 December 200

47 House of Commons, *Hansard*, 24 January 2000, Col. 47; Charlott
   Denny, 'Debt relief leaving the poor worse off', *Guardian*, 21 Augus
   2000

10 *The threat of democracy*

1 National advisory council on international monetary and financia
  problems, 'Investments in less developed areas', 12 December 195
  FRUS, 1955–1957, Vol. IX, p. 353; Memorandum by George Kenna
  to Secretary of State, 6 January 1950, *FRUS*, 1950, Col. I, p. 134

2 See Mark Curtis, *The ambiguities of power: British foreign policy sinc
  1945*, Zed, London, 1995, p. 13

3 E. Bevin to N. Ronald, 23 October 1948, *BDEE*, Ser. A, Vol. 2
  Part II, p. 271 Bevin cited in John Kent, 'Bevin's imperialism an
  the idea of Euro-Africa, 1945–49', in Michael Dockrill and Joh
  Young (eds.), *British foreign policy, 1945–56*, Macmillan, London
  1989,
  pp. 52–66

4 Kent, 'Bevin's imperialism', pp. 52–66

5 Oliver Lyttleton to R. Butler, 26 November 1951, *BDEE*, Ser. A, Vol. 3
  Part III, p. 303; Ernest Bevin to Clement Attlee, 4 October 1947
  BDEE, Ser. A, Vol. 2, Part II, pp. 53; Minute by Norman Brook, 1.
  January 1948, BDEE, Ser. A, Vol. 2, Part II, p. 257

6 See Curtis, *The ambiguities of power*, pp. 16–20

7 In W. Strang to T. Lloyd, 21 June 1952, *BDEE*, Ser. A, Vol. 3, Part I, pp
  13–19

8   See Chomsky, *World orders*, pp. 122–3

9   Paper by Richard Clarke, 11 May 1945, in Alec Cairncross (ed), *Anglo-American economic collaboration in war and peace, 1942–1949, by Sir Richard Clarke*, Clarendon, Oxford, 1982, pp. 109–11

10 Cited in Chomsky, *World orders*, pp. 75, 122–3

11 A. J. Morton, *A people's history of England*, Lawrence & Wishart, London, 1996, pp. 295–9

12 UNDP, *Human development report 1999*, New York/Geneva, 1999, p. 35; UNCTAD, *Trade and development report 1994*, UN, New York/Geneva, 1994, p. xii

13 Ajit Singh, 'How did East Asia grow so fast?: Slow progress towards analytical consensus', *UNCTAD bulletin*, May 1995, pp. 4–14

14 UNDP, *Human development report 1999*, pp. 6, 68–70

15 Morton, *A people's history*, p. 400

16 The following section on polyarchy is drawn from William Robinson, *Promoting polyarchy: Globalisation, US intervention and hegemony*, Cambridge University Press, 1996, passim

17 Peter Hain, speech in Cape Town, 3 February 2000, www.foc.gov.uk; Tony Lloyd, Speech to the British-African Business Association, 27 April 1999, www.foc.gov.uk

18 Robinson, *Promoting polyarchy*, p. 329

19 Cited in Patrick Bond, *Elite transition: From apartheid to neoliberalism in South Africa*, Pluto, London, 2000, p. 15, on which this section draws: see also pp. 16, 145, 148, 183–4

20 Tony Blair, speech in the South African parliament, 8 January 1999, www.fco.gov.uk

21 Hein Marais, *South Africa: Limits to change*, Zed, London, 1998, p. 157; Bond, pp. 78–81

22 Patricia Hewitt, speech to the 'Investing in South Africa' conference, London, 14 June 2001, www.dti.gov.uk

23 Trade Partners UK, 'South Africa', www.tradepartners.gov.uk

11 *Our allies, the Gulf elites*

1   Cited in W. Louis, *The British empire in the Middle East, 1945–1951: Arab nationalism, the United States and postwar imperialism*, Clarendon, Oxford, 1984, p. 121

2   Peter de la Billiere, *Storm Command: A personal account of the Gulf war*, Harper Collins, London, 1993, p. 116

3   Robert Fisk, 'So no one cay say "we didn't know"', *Middle East Report*, Fall 1998, www.merip.org/mer/mer208/fisk.htm

4   Cited in House of Commons, Defence Committee, *Thirteenth report*, Session 1999–2000, para. 7, www.publications.parliament. uk/pa cm1999900

5   *The great deception: Anglo-American power and world order*, Pluto London, 1998

6   See *The great deception*, pp. 126–7, for sources

7   Cited in Dorril, *MI6*, p. 675

8   Foreign Office memorandum, 'The Persian Gulf', undated (1957) PRO, FO 371/126915/EA 1051/1

9   Said Aburish, *A brutal friendship: The West and the Arab elite*, Indigo London, 1998, p. 65

10   State Department, Office of Near Eastern Affairs, 'Regional policy statement: Near East', 28 December 1950, *FRUS*, 1950, Vol. V, p. 274

11   Aburish, *A brutal friendship*, p. 58

12   HRW, 'Saudi Arabia', *World report 2002*, www.hrw.org/wr2k2 mena7.html; HRW, 'Human rights in Saudi Arabia: A deafening silence', December 2001, http/hrw.org.backgrounder/mena/saudi

13   Response of the Foreign Secretary to the House of Commons Foreign Affairs Committee report on the FCO's 1999 annual report on human rights, March 2000, Cm. 4687, para 12.

14   HRW, 'Saudi Arabia', *World report 2002*

15   House of Commons, FAC, *First report*, Session 1999–2000, paras. 15, 16, www.publications.parliament.uk/pa/ cm1999900

16   Peter Hain, speech to the Investing in Saudi Arabia conference, 20 June 2000, www.fco.gov.uk/news/speechtext

17   Interview with the Prime Minister in Riyadh, Saudi Arabia, November 2001, www.pm.gov.uk/news.asp; Ministry of Defence memorandum to House of Commons Defence Committee

18   HRW, 'Saudi Arabia: New evidence of torture', 5 February 2002, www.hrw.org/press/2002

19   Said Aburish, *The rise, corruption and coming fall of the House of Saud*, Bloomsbury, London, 1994, p. 110

20   Para. 65 and MoD memorandum to House of Commons Defence Committee, *Thirteenth report*

21   Office of the Programme Manager, Saudi Arabian National Guard modernisation programme, www.globalsecurity.org/military/agency dod/opm-sang.htm

22   Urban, *UK eyes alpha*, pp. 156–7

23   State Department memorandum, 'Specific current questions', undated (1947), *FRUS*, 1947, Vol. V, p. 553

24 Urban, *UK eyes alpha*, p. 236

25 CAAT, 'The Arabian connection: The UK arms trade to Saudi Arabia', undated, www.caat.org.uk/research

26 David Pallister, 'No sweeteners added', *Guardian*, 14 April 1998

27 House of Commons, *Hansard*, 3 February 1999, Col. 650; CAAT, 'The Arabian connection: The UK arms trade to Saudi Arabia', undated, www.caat.org.uk/research

28 See CAAT, 'The Arabian connection: The UK arms trade to Saudi Arabia', undated, www.caat.org.uk/ research

29 HRW, 'Routine abuse, routine denial', June 1997, www.hrw.org/reports/1997/bahrain

30 Kathy Evans, 'British backing for Bahrain', *Guardian*, 25 July 1997

31 House of Commons, *Hansard*, 26 January 1998, Col. 31

32 House of Commons, *Hansard*, 15 February 1999, Col. 585

33 Joe Stork, 'Bahraini regime stages confessions, rejects compromise', Middle East Report, 2000, www.merip.org/mer/mer2000.stork.htm

34 Parliamentary Human Rights Group, 'Speak together of freedom: The present struggle for democracy and human rights in Bahrain', March 1996, p. 8

35 Robin Allen, 'Bahrain economy suffers as Shia dissent simmers', *Financial Times*, 28 May 1998

36 Bahrain freedom movement, 'latest news', 29 June 2002, 18 July 2002, www.vob.org

37 Mike O'Brien, House of Commons, *Hansard*, 23 July 2002, Col. 836

38 House of Commons, *Hansard*, 25 June 1998, Col. 42; Ministry of Defence memorandum to House of Commons Defence Committee, *Thirteenth report*, and para 61

39 Baroness Symons, speech to the 'Doing business in Bahrain' seminar, London, 9 October 2001

40 *Economist*, 14 May 1966

41 HRW, 'Routine abuse, routine denial'

42 'Amnesty International welcomes investigation into Henderson's role in torture in Bahrain', 7 January 2000; Fran Abrams, 'Anti-torture groups object to visit by Bahrain's emir', *Independent*, 24 November 1999

43 Paul Lashmar, 'Britain fails to detain Bahrain's "torturer in chief"', *Independent*, 6 January 2000; Brian Whitaker, 'British "torture chief" quits', *Guardian*, 4 July 2000; Andrew Rowell, 'Butcher's holiday', *Big issue magazine*, 17 January 2000, www.vob.org

44 'Amnesty International welcomes investigation into Henderson's role in torture in Bahrain', 7 January 2000

45 Paul Lashmar, 'Alleged torturer facing police inquiry', *Independent*,
    January 2000

12 *The forgotten past in the Middle East*

1   Mustafa Alani, *Operation Vantage: British military intervention in
    Kuwait, 1961*, LAAM, Surbiton, 1990, pp. 72–3

2   Memorandum by the Lord Privy Seal, 2 October 1961, PRO, CAB 129
    C (61) 140

3   Cited in Noam Chomsky, *Deterring democracy*, Vintage, London
    1992, p. 184

4   Alani, *Operation Vantage*, pp. 54, 57–8, 199, 251

5   Memorandum by the Lord Privy Seal, 2 October 1961, PRO, CAB 129
    C (61) 49. Emphasis added

6   Foreign Office to Kuwait, 26 June 1961, PRO, FO 371/156845
    BK1083/3; Washington to Foreign Office, 27 June 1971, PRO, FO
    371/156845/BK1083/9; Dorril, *MI6*, p. 672

7   Basra to Foreign Office, 28 June 1961, PRO, FO 371/156873
    BK1193/9

8   Baghdad to Foreign Office, 28 June 1961, PRO, FO 371/156845
    BK1193/14

9   Foreign Office to Washington, 29 June 1961, PRO, FO 371/156874
    BK1193/16; Foreign Office to Kuwait, 29 June 1961, PRO, FO
    371/156874/BK 1193/24

10 Basra to Foreign Office, 29 June 1961, PRO, FO 371/156874
    BK1193/26. What the 'further' referred to is unclear: I could find no
    indications of any 'intended aggressive action' in the PRO files before
    this memo; Basra to Foreign Office, 1 July 1961, PRO, FO 371/156874
    BK1193/26

11 Alani, *Operation Vantage*, p. 103; Dorril, *MI6*, p. 673

12 Alani, *Operation Vantage*, pp. 108–9, 160–1

13 Foreign Office to Ankara, 29 June 1961, PRO, FO 371/156874
    BK1193/23; Foreign Office to Kuwait, 29 June 1961, PRO, FO
    371/156874/BK1193/24

14 Foreign Office to Washington, 29 June 1961, PRO, FO 371/156874
    BK1193/16; Foreign Office to Kuwait, 29 June 1961, PRO, FO
    371/156874/BK1193/24; Dorril, *MI6*, p. 673

15 Dorril, *MI6*, p. 674

16 Denis Healey, *Time of my life*, Penguin, Harmondsworth, 1989
    p. 279

17 Cited in Dorril, *MI6*, p. 673

18 John Townsend, *Oman: The making of a modern state*, Croom Helm, London, 1977, pp. 81–2

19 Bahrain to Foreign Office, 21 July 1957, PRO, FO 371/126876/EA 1015/59

20 Foreign Office memorandum, 29 October, 1957, PRO, FO 371/126890/EA 1015/440

21 Air Ministry memorandum, 13 January 1959, PRO, FO 371/140167/BA 1195/7; Newsinger, *Dangerous men*, pp. 18–19

22 John Wilkinson, *The imamate tradition of Oman*, CUP, Cambridge, 1987, p. 326

23 Townsend, *Oman*, p. 98; Fred Halliday, 'Britain and the hidden war', *Sunday Times*, 22 March 1970

24 Dorril, *MI6*, pp. 731–4; Bloch and Fitzgerald, pp. 136–8

25 Cited in Gulf Committee, 'Dhofar: Britain's colonial war in the Gulf', London, January 1972, p. 58

26 Dorril, *MI6*, p. 696

27 Fred Halliday, *Arabia without Sultans*, Penguin, Harmondsworth, 1974, pp. 205–6

28 See Dorril, *MI6*, pp. 677–98

29 Cited in Anthony Adamthwaite, 'Suez revisited', in Dockrill and Young (eds.), p. 240

30 Foreign Office brief, 11 January 1956, FO 371/118861/JE 1053/1; cited in Anthony Gorst and Lewis Johnman, *The Suez Crisis*, Routledge, London, 1997, p. 46

31 Cited in Gorst and Johnman, *The Suez Crisis*, p. 61

32 Dorril, *MI6*, p. 623; Anthony Nutting, *No end of a lesson: The Story of Suez*, Constable, London, 1967, pp. 34–5

33 Dorril, *MI6*, p. 627

34 Andrew, *For the President's eyes only*, p. 236; Chomsky, *World orders*, p. 201

13 The single-ideology totalitarian state

1 Richard Norton-Taylor and Rob Evans, 'US sees no change in British policies', *Guardian*, 19 November 1999

2 Andrew Marr, *Ruling Britannia: The failure and future of British democracy*, Penguin, Harmondsworth, 1996, pp. 109, 115

3 Philip Crowson, *Tudor foreign policy*, A and C Black, London, 1973, p. 36

4 Cited in Jack Lively and Adam Lively (eds.), *Democracy in Britain: A reader*, Blackwell, Oxford, 1994, pp. 33, 52, 56–7

5 Lucy Ward, '"President Blair" killed Cabinet, says Mowlam', *Guardian*, 17 November 2001; Keith Sutherland, 'Introduction: Bagehot revisited', in Sutherland (ed.), *The rape of the constitution?*, Imprint Academic, London, 2000, p. 2

6 Tony Benn, 'How democratic is Britain?', in Sutherland (ed.), p. 34

7 Sutherland, 'Introduction', p. 14

8 Cited in Benn, 'How democratic is Britain?', p. 46

9 Cited in Eccleshall (ed.), *British liberalism: Political thought from the 1640s to the 1980s*, Longman, London, 1986, pp. 33, 162, 165

10 Ibid., pp. 11, 33, 81–2, 145–7, 162, 165

11 Cited in Rodney Barker, *Political ideas in modern Britain: In and after the 20th century*, Routledge, London, 1997, p. 112

12 Ibid., pp. 146–7

13 Cited in Jonathan Freedland, 'Ten steps to the revolution', in Sutherland (ed.), p. 63

14 Eric Hobsbawm, *Industry and empire*, Penguin, Harmondsworth, 1990, p. 274; Alan Travis, 'How gap between rich and poor has grown', *Guardian*, 11 May 2000; Julian Le Grand, 'How to cage the fat cats', *New Statesman*, 26 July 1999

15 Cited in Edward Herman, *Beyond hypocrisy: Decoding the news in an age of propaganda*, South End Press, Boston, 1992, p. 17

16 David Ramsbottom, 'Front lines and deadlines', *Guardian*, 11 February 1991

17 Cited in John Pilger, 'Censorship by omission', in Hammond and Herman (eds), p. 132

18 W. Strang to T. Lloyd, 21 June 1952, *BDEE*, Ser. A, Vol. 3, Part I, pp. 13–19

19 Dorril, *MI6*, p. 766

20 Richard Norton-Taylor, *Truth is a difficult concept*, pp. 15, 23–6, 37, 86, 91, 96–7, 149, 177, 181, 209

Part III Exposing the secret history

14 Overthrowing the government of Iran

1 Cited in Kermit Roosevelt, *Countercoup: The struggle for the control of Iran*, McGraw Hill, London, 1979, p. 207

2 Roosevelt; C. M. Woodhouse, *Something ventured*, Granada, London, 1982.

3 D. Fergusson to R. Stokes, 3 October 1951, PRO, FO 371/919599; W. Roger Louis, *The British empire in the Middle East*, p. 682.

4   D. Fergusson to R. Stokes, 3 October 1951, PRO, FO 371/91599

5   F. Shepherd to O. Franks, 2 October 1951, PRO, FO 371/91464

6   Homa Katouzian, *Musaddiq and the struggle for power in Iran*, I. B.
     Tauris and Co, London, 1990, p. 139; Barry Rubin, *Paved with good
     intentions: The American experience and Iran*, Oxford University Press,
     Oxford, 1980, p. 67; cited in Dorril, *MI6*, p. 560

7   G. Middleton to A. Eden, 25 February 1952, PRO, FO 248/1531; F.
     Shepherd to H. Morrison, 15 March 1951, PRO, FO 371/91454; Louis,
     The British Empire, p. 653; Memoranda by S. Falle, 2 August 1952 and
     4 August 1952, PRO, FO 248/1531

8   Katouzian, p. 144

9   F. Shepherd to Foreign Office, 26 January 1952, PRO, FO 248/1531;
     Foreign Office memorandum, 'Persia: The State Department's
     views', 16 April 1952, PRO, FO 371/98688

10   Chiefs of Staff Committee, Confidential annex to COS (51), 16 May
     1951, PRO, FO 371/91460

11   E. Berthoud to R. Bowker, 15 June 1951, PRO, FO 371/91548;
     Fakhreddin Azimi, *Iran: The crisis of democracy, 1941–1953*, I. B.
     Tauris and Co, London, 1989; pp. 264–5

12   A. Eden, 'Persia: memorandum by the Secretary of State for Foreign
     Affairs', 5 August 1952, PRO, CAB 129/54/CP(52) 276; R. Bowker to
     Prime Minister, 2 September 1951, PRO, FO 371/91463; Azimi, p. 251;
     R. Bowker to Prime Minister, 2 September 1951, PRO, FO 371/91463

13   H. Morrison, 'Persia', 20 July 1951, PRO, CAB 129/46/CP(51) 212

14   Memorandum by G. Furlonge, 24 May 1951, PRO, FO 371/91460;
     Louis, p. 676

15   Brian Lapping, *End of Empire*, Paladin, London, p. 303; Prime
     Minister to Foreign Secretary, 17 June 1952, PRO, FO 371/98600

16   A. Eden, 'Persia', 5 August 1952, PRO, CAB 129/54/CP(52) 276;
     Lapping, p. 266; Azimi, *Iran*, p. 262; F. Shepherd to W. Strang, 11
     September 1951, PRO, FO 371/91463; Tehran to Foreign Office, 26
     September 1951, PRO, FO 371/91464; G. Wheeler to R. Bowker, 29
     October 1951, PRO, FO 371/91464; Memorandum to E. Berthoud, 2
     November 1951, PRO, FO 371/91609

17   Tehran to Foreign Office, 26 January 1952, PRO, FO 371/98684

18   F. Shepherd to H. Morrison, 21 May 1951, PRO, FO 371/91459

19   Foreign Office memorandum, 'Sir F. Shepherd's analysis of the
     Persian situation', 28 January 1952, PRO, FO 371/98684

20   Dorril, *MI6*, p. 575

21   G. Middleton to Foreign Office, 5 March 1992, PRO, FO 248/1531;
     Memorandum by Dr Zaehner, 17 May 1952, PO, FO 248/1531;

Memorandum by Pyman, 17 April 1952; PRO, FO 248/1531; Tehran to Foreign Office, 28 July 1952, CAB 129/54/CP(52)/275

22 G. Middleton to Foreign Office, 7 August 1952, PRO, FO 248/1531
23 Lapping, pp. 269–270; Rubin, *Paved with good intentions*, p. 77; Woodhouse, *Something ventured*, p. 118
24 Rubin, *Paved with good intentions*, p. 78; Woodhouse, p. 124
25 Katouzian, pp. 183–4; Azimi, p. 320; Roosevelt, pp. 1, 146–55; Lapping, p. 271
26 Dorril, *MI6*, p. 589
27 Blum, *The CIA: A forgotten history*, Zed, London, 1986, p. 72; Rubin, p. 82; Lapping, pp. 268–274; Azimi, p. 331
28 Katouzian, p. 190; Blum, p. 73
29 Sephehr Zabih, *The Mossadegh era: Roots of the Iranian revolution*, Lake View Press, Chicago, 1982, pp. 140–2, pp. 14–2; Woodhouse, p. 138
30 Foreign Office to Washington, 8 June 1951, PRO FO 371/91459
31 G. Middleton to A. Eden, 23 September 1952, PRO, FO 248/1531; US embassy Tehran despatch, 19 May 1953, PRO, FO 371/104566
32 Blum, *The CIA*, p. 70; Azimi, *Iran*, pp. 331–41
33 Memorandum by S. Falle, 4 August 1952, PRO, FO 248/1531
34 Dorril, *MI6*, p. 583
35 Blum, *The CIA*, p. 76; Rubin, pp. 177–8; Gabriel Kolko, *Confronting the Third World: United States foreign policy, 1945–1980*, Pantheon, New York, 1988, p. 265
36 Anthony Cavendish, *Inside intelligence*, Collins, London, 1990, p. viii
37 Bloch and Fitzgerald, pp. 44, 113
38 Cavendish, *Inside intelligence*, p. 141
39 Dorril, *MI6*, pp. 654, 744; Blum, *The CIA*, p. 76; Bloch and Fitzgerald, p. 44
40 Farhad Kazemi, *Poverty and revolution in Iran: The migrant poor, urban marginality and politics*, New York University Press, New York, 1980, pp. 51, 90

15 Deterring development in Kenya

1 David Gough, 'Mau Mau will sue Britain for human rights abuses', *Guardian*, 29 April 1999
2 J. Whyatt to P. Rogers, 2 September 1952, PRO CO 822/437; The Corfield report, 'Historical survey of the origins and growth of Mau Mau', PRO, CO, 822/1222

3   David Maughan-Brown, *Land, freedom and fiction: History and ideology in Kenya*, Zed, London, 1985, pp. 47, 49, 31

4   Intel no. 228, 17 October 1952, PRO, CO 822/462

5   Maughan-Brown, *Land, freedom and fiction*, pp. 29, 185; Arthur Hazlewood, *The economy of Kenya: The Kenyatta era*, Oxford University Press, Oxford, 1979, p. 7

6   E. Baring to Secretary of State for the Colonies, 21 November 1955, PRO, CO 822/937

7   Cited in the Corfield report, Ch. XVI, p. 1; Maughan-Brown, *Land, freedom and fiction*, pp. 93–7

8   Tabitha Tanogo, *Squatters and the roots of Mau Mau, 1905–63*, James Currey, London, 1987, pp. 150, 126; 2; Maughan-Brown, *Land, freedom and fiction*, pp. 24, 67

9   'A memorandum on the economic, political, educational and social aspects of the African in Kenya colony by the Kenya African Union', undated (1947), PRO, CO 533/534/11

10 Deputy Governor to Secretary of State for the Colonies, 19 March 1945, PRO, CO 533/534/11

11 Speech, 30 November 1946, PRO, CO 533/549/2

12 Cited in Lapping, p. 469

13 Maughan-Brown, p. 36; E. Baring to Secretary of State for the Colonies, 15 October 1952 and 17 October 1952, PRO, CO 822/444

14 E. Baring to Secretary of State for the Colonies, 9 October 1952, PRO, CO 822/444

15 Government of Kenya Secretariat to P. Rogers, 25 August 1952, PRO CO 822/435; H. Potter to P. Rogers, 17 August 1952, PRO, CO 822/436

16 E. Baring to Secretary of State for the Colonies, 10 October 1952, PRO, CO 822/443; J. Whyatt to K. Roberts-Wray, 19 October 1952 and 8 October 1952, PRO, CO 822/728

17 J. Whyatt to P. Rogers, 2 September 1952, PRO, CO 822/437

18 Lapping, p. 491

19 A. Clayton, *Counter-insurgency in Kenya, 1952–1960*, Transafrica, Nairobi, 1976, p. 54

20 Clayton, pp. 111, 38; Maughan-Brown, pp. 39–40

21 Cited in Barbara Slaughter, 'How Britain crushed the "Mau Mau rebellion"', 15 September 1999, www.wsws.org/articles/1999/sep99

22 Canon Bewes to N. Langford-Smith, 9 February 1953, PRO, CO 822/471; Maughan-Brown, pp. 40–1; Clayton, p. 44; Canon Bewes to Governor, 28 January 1953, PRO, CO 822/471; E. Twining to W. Gorell Barnes, 25 November 1953, PRO, CO 822/499

23 David Gough, 'Mau Mau will sue Britain for human rights abuses', *Guardian*, 29 April 1999

24 Stephen Cook, 'Whitehall put in the dock over Kenyan hangings', *Guardian*, 1 December 1999; Slaughter, 'How Britain crushed the "Mau Mau rebellion"'

25 Clayton, pp. 54, 14; E. Baring to Secretary of State for the Colonies, 20 April 1953, 13 October 1953 and 24 October 1953, PRO, CO 822/728/729

26 Cited in Jean Shaoul, 'Kenyan Mau Mau seek compensation from British government', 26 May 1999, www.wsws.org/articles/1999/may1999

27 Maughan-Brown, p. 38; Slaughter, 'How Britain crushed the "Mau Mau rebellion"'

28 E. Baring to Secretary of State for the Colonies, 16 October 1954, PRO, CO 822/801

29 'Health in detention camps', report by H. Stott, 23 September 1954, PRO, CO 822/801

30 V. G. Kiernan, *European empires from conquest to collapse, 1815–1960*, Fontana, London, 1982, p. 221; Kenneth Wanstall, 'I saw men tortured', *Reynolds News*, 13 January 1957

31 Philip Meldon, 'My two years in Kenya', undated [January 1957], PRO, CO 822/1237, affidavit of Victor Shuter, 10 January 1959, PRO, CO 822/1271; Eileen Fletcher, 'My comments on the government memorandum concerning my charges about Kenya', 8 January 1957, PRO, CO 822/1236

32 Cited in Slaughter, 'How Britain crushed the "Mau Mau rebellion"'

33 Deputy Governor to Secretary of State for the Colonies, 19 February 1953; E. Baring to Secretary of State for the Colonies, 28 September 1953 and 15 October 1953; Notes of a Colonial Office meeting, 28 September 1953; Secretary of State for the Colonies to E. Baring, 7 October 1953, PRO, CO 822/505

34 W. Gorell Barnes to E. Baring, 1 December 1952, PRO, CO 822/450

35 Bloch and Fitzgerald, pp. 143–55

36 Hazlewood, pp. 34, 10

37 Tanogo, p. 172; Bethwell Ogot and Tiyambe Zeleza, 'Kenya: The road to independence and after', in Prosser Gifford and W. Roger Louis, *Decolonisation and African independence: The transfer of power, 1960–1980*, Yale University Press, London, 1988, p. 413; Maughan-Brown, p. 188

38 Gary Wasserman, *Politics of decolonisation: Kenya, Europeans and the land issue 1960–1965*, CUP, Cambridge, 1976, pp. 172–4

39 Nicola Swainson, *The development of corporate capitalism in Kenya, 1918–1977*, University of California Press, Los Angeles, 1980, p. 130; Ogot and Zeleza, p. 426

40 'Employment, income distribution, poverty alleviation and basic needs in Kenya', Report of an ILO consulting mission, Cornell University, 1978, p. 96

41 Cited in Cathy Majtenyin, 'Landless: Beggars in their own house', *Africa News*, September 2001, www.peaceline.it/afrinews

16 Malaya: War in defence of the rubber industry

1 Colonial Office report, 28 March 1950, PRO, CO 717/196/52821/20; Lennox Mills, *Malaya: A political and economic appraisal*, University of Minnesota Press, Minneapolis, 1958, p. 206; 'Papers on the emergency in Malaya', January 1952, PRO, CO 1022/22/SEA 10/14/08

2 Colonial Office, 'Malaya: Brief for Minister of State', undated (1952), PRO, CO 1022/267/SEA 192/469/01; Mills, p. 206

3 House of Lords, *Hansard*, 27 February 1952, Col. 302

4 Ibid., Col. 346

5 Memo to the Colonial Office, 15 November 1951, PRO, CO 1022/39/SEA 10/93/01

6 Foreign Office to Washington, 26 October 1950, PRO, CO 717/203/52911

7 Untitled memo (1949), PRO, CO 717/163/52748; Governor of Singapore to Secretary of State for the Colonies, 23 March 1949, PRO, CO 717/163/52748; J. Higham to Sir Francis Gimson, 14 February 1949, PRO, CO 717/163/52748

8 'The squatter problem in Malaya', March 1952, PRO, CO 1022/29/SEA 10/72/01

9 Broadcast speech to Australia, 12 October 1952, PRO, CO, 1022/2/SEA 10/03; Richard Clutterbuck, *Conflict and violence in Singapore and Malaysia, 1945–1983*, Graham Brash, Singapore, 1985, p. 186

10 Kiernan, p. 212

11 Robert Jackson, *The Malayan emergency: The Commonwealth's war, 1948–1966*, Routledge, London, 1991, pp. 77, 82, 84

12 Ibid., p. 45

13 Cited in Charles Allen, *The savage wars of peace: Soldiers voices 1945–1989*, Futura, 1990, pp. 12, 21–2, 26; Geraghty, *Who dares wins*, pp. 28, 39

14 Lapping, p. 219; 'Bodies of dead rebels on public view', *Scotsman*, 2
    August 1952; see PRO, CO 1030/33/FED 12/568/01

15 T. Jerrom to J. Higham, 30 April 1952, PRO, CO 1022/45/SEA
    10/162/02

16 T. Jerrom to J. Higham, 19 May 1952, 6 May, 12 May 1952, PRO, CO
    1022/45/SEA/10/162/02; '500 sea Dyaks for Malaya', *Daily Telgraph*
    23 May 1952

17 Cited in Lapping, p. 224; Brief for Selwyn Lloyd, 21 April 1953, PRO
    CO 1022/2/SEA/10/03

18 Lapping, p. 223

19 Jackson, p. 20, emphasis added

20 Clutterbuck, p. 176

21 'Monthly review of Chinese affairs', December 1949, PRO, CO
    717/182/52928

22 J. Biddulph, 6 June 1951, PRO, CO 1022/148/SEA/75/167/01

23 Letter to Colonial Office, undated (1952), PRO, CO 1022/54/SEA
    10/409/01; 'Templer sends a letter to his people', *Observer*, 6 April
    1952

24 Selangor government press statement, 10 April 1952, PRO, CO
    1022/55/SEA 10/409/02

25 Foreign Office telegram, 22 March 1951, PRO, CO 1022/2/SEA
    10/03; Memo by the Secretary of State for the Colonies, CAB 21/1682,
    DO (50) 93, 15 November 1950

26 Jackson, p. 26; Allen, p. 101

27 H. Kearns and E. Woodford, 'The chemical control of roadside
    vegetation', 2 February 1953, PRO, CO 1022/26/SEA 10/45/01; A.
    Humphrey to J. Higham, 19 January 1953, PRO, CO 1022/26/SEA
    10/45/01

28 'A plan for rubber', *Economist*, 9 October 1954

29 Ritchie Ovendale, *The English-speaking alliance: Britain, the United
    States, the Dominions and the cold war, 1945–1951*, George Allen &
    Unwin, London, 1985, pp. 151–63

30 Jackson, pp. 19, 39

31 'Official designation of the communist forces', PRO, CO 1022/48,
    SEA 10/172/01

32 James Adams, *Secret armies: The full story of the SAS, Delta Force and
    Spetsnaz*, Pan, London, 1988

33 Chris Dixon, *Southeast Asia in the world economy*, Cambridge
    University Press, Cambridge, 1991, pp. 183, 186

7 British Guiana: Overstepping 'decent government'

1 Farewell address by Governor Sir Charles Campbell Woolley, PRO, CO 1031/287

2 ALC Ltd, 25th Annual Report, PRO, CO 1031/1103

3 'British Guiana: The economic consequences of the PPP', undated (1953), PRO, CO 1031/298; 'The economic production of sugar cane by individual farmers', 8 January 1954, PRO, CO 1031/1444

4 Cited in K. Martin to J. Campbell, 26 October 1953, PRO, CO 1031/6; Colonial Office, 'British Guiana: Housing', undated (1953), PRO, CO 1031/235

5 Note by the Governor, undated (September 1953), PRO, CO 1031/121

6 CRO to High Commissioners, 30 September 1953, PRO, PREM 11/827

7 O. Lyttleton to Prime Minister, 5 May 1953, PRO, PREM 11/827

8 Press statement, 1 November 1951, PRO, CO 1031/776

9 H. Seaford to J. Campbell, 8 September 1953, PRO, CO 1031/121

10 Nigel Nicholson, House of Commons, *Hansard*, 22 October 1953, Col. 2259

11 O. Lyttleton, 'Cabinet: British Guiana', 25 September 1953, PRO, PREM 11/827; House of Commons debates, 22 October 1953, Cols. 2179, 2166; 'British Guiana: The economic consequences of the PPP', undated (1953), PRO, CO 1031/298

12 House of Commons debates, 7 December 1953, cited in Thomas Spinner, *A political and social history of Guyana, 1945–1983*, Westview Press, London, 1984, p. 55

13 'Statement by Her Majesty's government', 9 October 1953, PRO, CO 1031/1003

14 House of Commons, *Hansard*, 22 October 1953, Col.s 2166, 2173

15 UK delegation to the UN to Secretary of State for the Colonies, 30 September 1953, PRO, PREM 11/827

16 State Department policy information, 'Situation in British Guiana (2)', 9 October 1953, PRO, CO 1031/1189; A. Campbell to J. Vernon, 16 October 1953, PRO, CO 1031/1189

17 House of Commons, *Hansard*, 22 October 1953, Cols. 2190–8

18 House of Commons, *Hansard*, 22 October 1953, Col. 2183

19 Governor to Secretary of State for the Colonies, 23 May 1955, PRO, CO 1031/1437; Officer Administering the Government of British Guiana to Secretary of State for the Colonies, 5 September 1955, PRO, CO 1031/1437

20 Spinner, pp. 91–101; Blum, *The CIA*, pp. 118–23

21   Philip Agee, *Inside the company: CIA diary*, London, 1975, p. 406

22   Latin American Bureau, *Guyana: Fraudulent revolution*, LAB, London, 1984, p. 47

Part IV The mass production of ignorance

1   Speech to Labour party conference, 3 October 2001, www.labour.org.uk

18 Ethical foreign policies and other myths

2   See my *The Great Deception*, pp. 208–13

3   See Linda Melvern, *A people betrayed: The role of the West in Rwanda's genocide*, Zed, London, 2000, pp. 138, 147–8, 153–4, 163, 174–5, 179–80, 228–32 for sources

4   James Bone and Catherine Bond, 'Rwanda minister snubbed at UN over massacre', *The Times*, 13 May 1994

5   Robin Cook, 'Human rights into a new century', speech at the Foreign Office, 17 July 1997, www.fco.gov.uk

6   Mark Wickham-Jones, 'Labour party politics and foreign policy', in Richard Little and Mark Wickham-Jones (eds.), *New Labour's foreign policy: A new moral crusade?*, Manchester University Press, Manchester 2000, pp. 93, 105

7   'Cook's Asian tour', *Financial Times*, 2 September 1997; John Lloyd, 'Mandarins, guns and morals', *New Statesman*, 25 October 1999

8   Vikram Dodd and Ewen MacAskill, 'Labour drops "ethical" tag', *Guardian*, 4 September 2000

9   'Foreign policy needs a portrait in reality', *Independent on Sunday*, 11 May 1997

10   Bruce Anderson, 'Mr Blair's misunderstanding of 1939 is making him botch 1999', *Spectator*, 17 April 1999

11   'Media coverage of the developing world: Audience understanding and interest', www.gla.ac.uk

12   'The cash is what counts', *Guardian*, 6 November 1997

13   Larry Elliott, 'Short's blueprint for poor', *Guardian*, 26 January 2000

14   Polly Toynbee, 'He promised to take on the world. And I believed him'. *Guardian*, 4 October 2001

15   Hugo Young, 'The terrifying naivety of Blair the great intervener', *Guardian*, 30 April 2002

16   'Nuclear fall-out', *Financial Times*, 12 May 1998

17 Steve Richards, 'The special advisers are here to stay', *New Statesman*, 17 January 2000

19 *The media's propaganda role*

1 Edward Said, *Covering Islam: How the media and the experts determine how we see the rest of the world*, Vintage, London 1997, pp. 54–5
2 Brian McNair, *News and journalism in the UK*, Routledge, London, 1999, p. 43
3 Allen and Seaton, p. 45
4 James Curran, 'Mass media and democracy revisited', in James Curran and Michael Gurevitch (eds.), *Mass media and society*, Arnold, London, 1995, p. 98
5 'Keeping a foot in the door', *Guardian*, 10 January 2000
6 James Curran, 'Communications, power and social order', in Michael Gurevitch et al (eds.), *Culture, society and the media*, Routledge, London, 1997, p. 227
7 John Birt, 'The prize and the price', *New Statesman* media lecture, London, 6 July 1999
8 Cited in McNair, p. 40; Greg Philo, *Seeing is believing: The influence of television*, Routledge, London, 1995, p. 170
9 'Rights and wrongs', *Guardian*, 6 March 2000; Martin Woollacott, 'The see-through reality of sanctions', *Guardian*, 31 August 1996; Polly Toynbee and David Walker, *Did things get better?: An audit of Labour's successes and failures*, Penguin, London, 2001, p. 122, Ralph Young, 'New Labour and international development', in David Coates and Peter Lawler (eds.), *New Labour in power*, Manchester University Press, Manchester, 2000, p. 254
10 John Lloyd, 'Europe grows after Kosovo', *New Statesman*, 7 June 1999
11 John Pilger, 'Censorship by omission', in Hammond and Herman (eds.), p. 136
12 Ian Black, 'Dictators in the dock', *Guardian*, 3 June 1998
13 Ngugi Wa Thiongo, *Decolonising the mind: The politics of language in African literature*, James Currey, London, 1997

20 *Indonesia: Complicity in a million deaths*

1 See Denis Healey, *The time of my life*, Penguin, Harmondsworth, 1990
2 A. Gilchrist to E. Peck, 5 October 1965, PRO, FO 371/180318, DH1015/187

3   Foreign Office to Embassy in Indonesia, 16 October 1965, PRO, FO
    371/18031/DH 1015/179; Memo by H. Stanley, 17 June 1966, PRO, IM
    1193/32/G
4   Embassy in Indonesia to State Department, 5 October 1965; State
    Department to Embassy in Indonesia, 13 October 1965; Memorandum
    from Assistant for Indonesia to Deputy Assistant Secretary of Defence,
    4 November 1964, *Foreign Relations of the United States, 1964–1968*,
    Vol. XXVI, USGPO, Washington, 2001, pp. 307, 320, 352 – hereafter
    FRUS
5   Embassy in Indonesia to State Department, 20 October 1965, *FRUS*,
    pp. 329–30
6   Embassy in Indonesia to State Department, 1, 4 and 8 November
    1965, *FRUS*, pp. 346, 355, 338
7   J. Murray to E. Peck, 25 November 1965, PRO, FO 371/180325/
    DH1015/327
8   Report by H. Windle, 16 December 1965, PRO, FO 371/180325/DH
    1015/335
9   Consulate in Medan to State Department, 16 November 1965, *FRUS*,
    p. 366
10 State Department to Embassy in Indonesia, 16 December 1965;
    Memorandum of conversation, 14 February 1965, *FRUS*, pp. 385,
    399–400
11 A. Gilchrist to Foreign Office, 21 February 1966, PRO, FO
    371/186028/DH 1015/62; J. Murray to A. De La Mare, 13 January
    1966, PRO, FO 371/186027/DH1015/20; Memo by J. Wright, 'The
    liquidation of the Indonesian communist party in Sumatra', 30
    March 1966, PRO, FO 371/186030/DH 1015/151; Embassy in
    Indonesia to State Department, 15 April 1966, *FRUS*, p. 339
12 J. Wright to J. Murray, 3 January 1966, PRO, FO 371/186027/DH
    1015/29; Memo by J. Cable, 7 January 1966, PRO, FO 371/186044/DH
    1051/2; Embassy brief, 30 June 1966, FO 371/186044/DH 1051/39
13 Report by Consul in Surabaya, 31 August 1966, PRO, FO
    371/186032/DH 1015/216
14 J. Wright to S. Cambridge, 30 October 1965, PRO, FO 371/180309/
    DH 1013/19
15 Foreign Office to Singapore, 6 October 1965, PRO, FO 371/180317/
    DH 1015/167
16 A. Gilchrist to Foreign Office, 11 October 1965, PRO, FO 371/180318/
    DH 1015/179
17 Singapore to Foreign Office, 8 October 1965, PRO, FO 371/180318/
    DH 1015/186

18 A. Gilchrist to Foreign Office, 9 October 1965, PRO, FO 371/180318/ DH 1015/186

19 See *FRUS*, p. 318

20 Embassy in Indonesia to State Department, 14 October 1965, *FRUS*, p. 321

21 Roland Challis, *Shadow of a revolution: Indonesia and the Generals*, Sutton Publishing, 2001, pp. 107, 113

22 Ibid., p. 95

23 Singapore to Foreign Office, 5 October 1965; Foreign Office to Singapore, 6 October 1965, PRO, FO 371/180317/DH 1015/167

24 Singapore to Foreign Office, 9 October 1965, FO 371/180318/DH 1015/167; A. Adams to J. Murray, 19 May 1966, PRO, FO 371/ 187587/IM 1193/29; Challis, pp. 102–3

25 See Kathy Kadane, *Inside Indonesia*, June 1990

26 See *FRUS*, p. 387

27 State Department to Embassy in Indonesia, 6 October 1965; Embassy in Indonesia to State Department, 5 October 1965, *FRUS*, pp. 309, 307

28 A. Gilchrist to Foreign Office, 14 November 1965, PRO, FO 371/181519/IM 1121/15

29 Embassy in Indonesia to State Department, 1 November 1965, *FRUS*, p. 346

30 CIA memorandum, 9 November 1965, *FRUS*, pp. 362–3

31 Memorandum by the Deputy Director for Coordination, Bureau of Intelligence and Research, 4 December 1965, *FRUS*, p. 382

32 M. Stewart to E. Peck, 28 October 1965, PRO, FO 371/181519/IM 1121/8

33 J. Wright to J. Murray, 3 January 1966, PRO, FO 371/186027/DH 1015/29

34 Foreign Office Research Department, 'United Kingdom interests, commitments and objectives in South East Asia', 13 August 1964, PRO, FO 371/185940/D 1691/1

35 M. Stewart to Prime Minister, 6 December 1965, PRO, FO 371/181477/IM 103145/19

36 A. De La Mare to Foreign Secretary, 12 August 1966, PRO, FO 371/186044/DH 1015/67

37 See *FRUS*, pp. 251, 253

38 Embassy in Malaysia to State Department, 17 December 1964; Memorandum by George Ball, 18 March 1965, *FRUS*, pp. 203, 252

39 'Indonesia-American relations', Report from Ambassador Ellsworth Bunker to President Johnson, undated (1965), *FRUS*, p. 257

40 Embassy brief, October 1966, PRO, FO 371/186044/DH 1051/67

41 Special National Intelligence Estimate, 1 September 1965, *FRUS*, p. 292

42 Memo by D. Marston, 2 November 1966, PRO, FO 371/186064/DH
1191/3; Foreign Office to Embassy in Indonesia, 19 April 1966, PRO,
FO 371/187572/IM 1051/39/G; Memo by J. Rob, undated (April 1966),
PRO, FO 371/187572/IM 1051/49/G; Memo by British embassy, 27
April 1966, PRO, FO 371/187573/IM 1051/71; Foreign Office brief for
Cabinet, 23 August 1966, PRO, FO 37/187574/IM 1051/117/G

43 Michael Stewart, *Life and Labour: An autobiography*, Sidgwick &
Jackson, London, 1980, p. 149; cited in Carmel Budiardjo and Liem
Soei Liong, *The war against East Timor*, Zed, London, 1984, p. 49

44 Kolko, *Confronting the Third World*, pp. 184–5

45 'Opportunities in Indonesia', *Daily Telegraph*, 21 July 1975; Peter Hill,
'CBI says UK neglects trade with Indonesia', *The Times*, 21 August 1975

46 John Battle, speech at the Royal United Services Institute, London, 22
November 2000, www.fco.gov.uk/news/speechtext

21 East Timor: Smothering the birth of a nation

1 Evidence to FAC, 23 November 1999, Q. 65, Foreign Affairs
Committee, *First Report*, Session 1999–2000

2 Jonathan Mirsky, 'War by famine kills 200,000', *Observer* foreign
news service, 20 November 1979; 'ET bishop reports persecution',
International Herald Tribune, 16 February 1990

3 Cited in G. Munster and J. Walsh, *Documents on Australian defence and
foreign policy, 1968–1975*, Hong Kong, 1980, pp. 192–3

4 Foreign Office memorandum, 'Portuguese Timor', 1 January 1965,
PRO, FO 371/180256/DE 1015/1; Embassy in Indonesia to Foreign
Office, 3 January 1962, PRO, FO 371/166422/DE 103162/1

5 'East Timor revisited', 6 December 2001, National Security Archive:
www.gwu.edu/nsarchiv

6 Munster and Walsh, pp. 199–200; Carmel Budiardjo, 'Indonesia:
Mass extermination and the consolidation of authoritarian power', in
Alexander George (ed.), *Western state terrorism*, Polity Press,
Cambridge, 1991, p. 200

7 Cited in Budiardjo, 'Indonesia', p. 203

8 Ibid., p. 205

9 Sue Lloyd-Roberts, 'British arms help Jakarta fight war against its own
people', *Independent*, 27 March 1997

10 John Gittings, 'East Timorese accuse Britain of blocking action on
Indonesia', *Guardian*, 17 June 1992

11 'In Sumatra uprising, army is said to execute hundreds', *International Herald Tribune*, 21 June 1991

12 Amnesty International newsletter, July 1993; *International Herald Tribune*, 10 December 1991

13 HRW, 'East Timorese still trapped in Indonesia', 15 December 1999, www.hrw.org

14 Speech to Chatham House, 28 January 2000, www.fco.gov.uk/news/speechtext

15 Tapol memorandum to FAC, 18 November 1999, www.tapol.gn.apc.org

16 Nicholas Gilby, 'Arms exports to Indonesia', CAAT, October 1999, www.caat.org.uk

17 Chomsky, *Rogue States*, Pluto, London, 2000, p. 58

18 Allan Nairn, 'US complicity in Timor', *Nation*, 27 September 1999

19 See Eric Herring, 'Wiping the state clean?', http//uk.geocities.com/dstokes14/Eric/stateclean.htm

20 DFID, Statement by the UK delegation, East Timor donor meeting, 17 December 1999, www.dfid.gov.uk

21 Richard Norton-Taylor, 'Lifting of arms ban angers campaigners', *Guardian*, 14 January 2000

22 Kim Howells, House of Commons, *Hansard*, 29 October 1999, Col. 1016; Defence, Foreign Affairs, International Development and Trade and Industry Committees, *Second, Third and Fourth Reports*, Session 1999–2000, para 29, www.publications.parliament.uk/pa/cm1999900

23 Nicholas Gilby, 'Arms exports to Indonesia'

24 HRW, 'Indonesian government must prevent East Timor bloodbath', 3 September 1999, www.hrw.org

25 Chomsky, *Rogue States*, p. 58

26 HRW, 'Ban arms sales to Indonesia unless Timor militias stopped', 17 August 2000, www.hrw.org

27 Amnesty International, 'Indonesia: The UN's highest human rights body fails victims in Indonesia and East Timor', 22 April 2002, http//web.amnesty.org

28 HRW, 'Unfinished business: Justice for East Timor', August 2000, www.hrw.org

29 John Battle, speech to the Royal United Services Institute, 22 November 2000, www.fco.gov.uk/news/speechtext

22 *Diego Garcia: Removing people from history*

1   Ewen MacAskill, 'Evicted islanders to go home', *Guardian*, 4 November 2000

2   Healey, *The time of my life*, Penguin, Harmondsworth, 1989

3   Letter to the *Guardian*, 10 November 2000

4   Foreign Office memorandum, 31 August 1966, in Chagos islands group litigation, Claimants chronology (hereafter Litigation chronology), p. 7; Colonial Office minute, 24 June 1968, Litigation chronology, p. 12

5   Ian Black, 'Colonial victims seek resettlement', *Guardian*, 16 October 1997

6   Personal interview, London, 30 October 2002

7   Chagos Islands group litigation, Claimants' skeleton argument (hereafter Skeleton argument), para 2.5

8   Richard Norton-Taylor, 'Dumped islanders seek to return home', *Guardian*, 18 July 2000; Foreign Office memorandum, 23 September 1964, in Litigation chronology, p. 2; Foreign Office minute, 18 March 1966, Litigation chronology, p. 7; Foreign Office minute, 8 February 1971, Litigation chronology, p. 33

9   Foreign Office to High Commission, Mauritius, 12 March 1971, Litigation chronology, p. 34; Governor, Seychelles to Foreign Office, 25 March 1971, Litigation chronology, p. 35

10 John Madeley, *Diego Garcia: A contrast to the Falklands*, Minority Rights Group, London, 1985, pp. 1–4, 5

11 Natasha Mann and Bonnie Malkin, 'Deserted islanders', *Guardian*, 6 July 2000; Foreign Office brief, 1 March 1972, Litigation chronology, p. 43

12 Madeley, *Diego Garcia*, pp. 3–8

13 High Commission, Mauritius to Administrator, BIOT, 11 May 1973, Litigation chronology, p. 46; Foreign Office to Treasury, 19 April 1972, Litigation chronology, p. 44; Skeleton argument, para. 6.30

14 Cited in Madeley, p. 6

15 High Commission to petitioners, 11 November 1974, Litigation chronology, p. 47

16 Martin Walker, 'Britain evicts for base aims', *Guardian*, 10 September 1975

17 Foreign Office memos, 1966, Skeleton argument, paras 2.8.4 and 2.8.5; Colonial Office memorandum, January 1966, Litigation chronology, p. 6

18 Foreign Office to UK Mission to the UN, 9 November 1965, Litigation chronology, p. 4; UK Mission to UN to Foreign Office, 9 November 1965, Litigation chronology, p. 5; Foreign Office legal adviser, 7 February 1969, Litigation chronology, p. 19; Note by Foreign Office legal adviser, 23 October 1968, Litigation chronology, p. 17

19 Michael Stewart to Harold Wilson, 21 April 1969, Litigation chronology, p. 21

20 Cited by Tam Dalyell MP, House of Commons, *Hansard*, 9 January 2001, Cols. 182–3

21 Ibid.; Foreign Office minute, 24 May 1965, Litigation chronology, p. 7; Foreign Office legal adviser, 16 January 1970, Litigation chronology, p. 25

22 House of Commons, *Hansard*, 9 July 1990, Col. 36

23 House of Commons, *Hansard*, 18 December 1989, Col. 47; 19 May 1992, Col. 28

24 Foreign Office, 'Country profiles', British Indian Ocean Territory, www.fco.gov.uk

25 Michael Stewart to Harold Wilson, 21 April 1969, Litigation chronology, p. 21; MoD to UK embassy, Washington, 13 June 1969, Litigation chronology, p. 23

26 High Commission, Mauritius to Foreign Office, 13 January 1971, Litigation chronology, p. 32; Foreign Office to High Commission, Mauritius, 12 March 1971, Litigation chronology, p. 34

27 Richard Luce letter, 2 February 1981, Litigation chronology, p. 53

28 Ewen MacAskill and Rob Evans, 'Thirty years of lies, deceit and trickery that robbed a people of their island home', *Guardian*, 4 November 2000

29 Skeleton argument, paras. 2.14, 9.21

30 Personal interview, London, 30 October 2002

31 Ian Black, 'Colonial victims seek resettlement', *Guardian*, 16 October 1997

32 House of Commons, *Hansard*, 22 June 1999, Col. 925

33 House of Commons, *Hansard*, 9 January 2001, Col. 191

34 House of Commons, *Hansard*, 24 February 1998, Col. 192

35 House of Commons, *Hansard*, 24 July 2000, Col. 423

36 Foreign Office memorandum on British Indian Ocean Territory, 31 July 2000, in House of Commons Foreign Affairs Committee, *First Special Report*, Session 2000/2001, Appendix 10

37 Ewen MacAskill, 'US base deals blow to displaced islanders', *Guardian*, 9 October 2001

38 Jonathan Jenness, 'Chagos islands resettlement: A review', 1
    September 2002, p. 67
39 House of Commons, *Hansard*, 13 November 2000, Col. 510W
40 Ewen MacAskill and Rob Evans, 'US blocks return home for exiled
    islanders', *Guardian*, 1 September 2000; Ewen MacAskill, 'Diego
    Garcia exiles to seek £4bn from US', *Guardian*, 13 December 2000
41 Madeley, p. 3
42 'Jingoism is not the way', *Financial Times*, 5 April 1982; 'After Lord
    Carington', *Financial Times*, 6 April 1982

INDEX